Charism and Mission Since Vatican II

Charism and Mission Since Vatican II

Superiors' General Letters to the Spiritan Congregation, 1968-2020

Edited by JAMES CHUKWUMA OKOYE

Foreword by STEPHEN B. BEVANS

CHARISM AND MISSION SINCE VATICAN II
Superiors' General Letters to the Spiritan Congregation, 1968–2020

Copyright © 2021 Center for Spiritan Studies. All rights reserved. Except for brief quotations in critical publications or reviews, no part of this book may be reproduced in any manner without prior written permission from the publisher. Write: Permissions, Wipf and Stock Publishers, 199 W. 8th Ave., Suite 3, Eugene, OR 97401.

Resource Publications
An Imprint of Wipf and Stock Publishers
199 W. 8th Ave., Suite 3
Eugene, OR 97401

www.wipfandstock.com

PAPERBACK ISBN: 978-1-6667-2804-0
HARDCOVER ISBN: 978-1-6667-2802-6
EBOOK ISBN: 978-1-6667-2803-3

NOVEMBER 1, 2021

IMPRIMI POTEST
Very Rev. Fr. John Fogarty, C.S.Sp.,
Superior General

Center for Spiritan Studies
Duquesne University, Pittsburgh
September 2021

Unless otherwise stated, biblical texts are cited according to the *New American Bible Revised Edition* (NABRE) 2010.

CONTENTS

Abbreviations | vii

Preface | ix

Foreword by STEPHEN B. BEVANS, S.V.D. | xv

✧

CHAPTER ONE
    Very Rev. Fr. JOSEPH LÉCUYER, C.S.Sp. | 1

CHAPTER TWO
    Very Rev. Fr. FRANS TIMMERMANS, C.S.Sp. | 65

CHAPTER THREE
    Very Rev. Fr. PIERRE HAAS, C.S.Sp. | 155

CHAPTER FOUR
    Very Rev. Fr. PIERRE SCHOUVER, C.S.Sp. | 187

CHAPTER FIVE
    Very Rev. Fr. JEAN-PAUL HOCH, C.S.Sp. | 269

CHAPTER SIX
    Very Rev. Fr. JOHN FOGARTY, C.S.Sp. | 309

✧

Bibliography | 363

ABBREVIATIONS

AG	Decree on the Missionary Activity of the Church, *Ad gentes*.
Bagamoyo	General Chapter 2012, Bagamoyo, Tanzania.
CDD	General Chapter 1968-69, *Directives and Decisions*. Rome, 1970.
Const	Constitutions.
Ecclesiae sanctae	Paul VI, Motu Proprio, Apostolic Letter Ecclesiae sanctae Implementing the following Decrees of Vatican Council II: Christus dominus, Decree on the Pastoral Office of Bishops in the Church; Presbyterorum ordinis, Decree on the Ministry and Life of Priests; Perfectae caritatis Decree on the Adaptation and Renewal of Religious Life; Ad Gentes divinitus Decree on the Missionary Activity of the Church.
EG	*Pope Francis, Postapostolic Exhortation Evangelii gaudium on the Proclamation of the Gospel in Today's World. 2013.*
EN	Paul VI, Apostolic Exhortation *Evangelium nuntiandi*. December 8, 1975.
ES	*Ecrits spituels du Vénérable Libermann*. Paris, Librairie Victor Lecoffre, 1891.
GA	*Guidelines for Animation*. General Chapter, 1974.
I/D	*Informations and Documentation*.
Itaici	General Chapter 1992, *Where is the Spirit Leading us?* Itaici, Brazil.
Laudato Si'	Pope Francis, Encyclical Letter *Laudato Si'* On Care For Our Common Home, May 2015.
Letters to Clergy and Religious	*The Spiritual Letters of the Venerable Francis Libermann*. Vol. 3: *Letters to Clergy and Religious*, vol. 1 (nos. 1-75). Pittsburgh: Duquesne University Press, 1963.
Letters to Sisters and Aspirants	Venerable Francis Libermann, C.S.Sp., *Spiritual Letters to Sisters and Aspirants*. Pittsburgh: Duquesne University Press, 1963.

LS	*Lettres spirituelles du Vénérable Libermann*. 2 vols + Supplément. Paris : Librairie Poussielgue Frères, 1874.
Maynooth	General Chapter 1998. *Launch out into the Deep*. Maynooth College, Dublin, Ireland.
Mémoire Spiritaine	*Mémoire spiritaine: histoire, mission, spiritualité*. Congrégation du Saint-Esprit.
NA	Declaration on the Relation of the Church to Non-Christian Religions, *Nostra aetate*.
NCR	National Catholic Reporter. Catholic Newspaper based in Kansas City, Missouri.
ND	*Notes et Documents Relatifs à la vie et à l'Oeuvre du Vénérable François Marie Paul Libermann*. 16 volumes. Paris, 1929-2015.
PC	Decree On the Adaptation and Renewal of Religious Life, *Perfectae caritatis*.
Provisional Rule	*Provisional Rule of Father Libermann. Text and Commentary*. Translated by Walter van de Putte, C.S.Sp. Pittsburgh: Center for Spiritan Studies, 2015.
Règlements	*Règlements*: Regulations of the Congregation of the Holy Ghost under the Invocation of the Immaculate Heart of Mary, 1949. Translation in Daly, *Spiritan Wellsprings*, 63-157.
RM	John Paul II, *Redemptoris missio*, On the Permanent Validity of the Church's missionary Mandate, 1990.
Spiritan Life	General Chapter 1980.
SRL	*Spiritan Rule of Life*, 1987.
Torre d'Aguilha	General Chapter 2004, *Faithful to the Gift entrusted to Us*. Torre d'Aguilha, Portugal.

PREFACE

WORLD AND CHURCH HAVE changed so much since the Second Vatican Council (1962–65). Each change spurred new embodiments of the Spiritan charism and ever new emphases in Spiritan spirituality and mission. The 122 letters of the post-Vatican II superiors general published here were responses in the Spirit to the "signs of the times."

The election of Father Lécuyer, following Msgr. Léfèbvre's difficult relationships with Rome and the Congregation itself, was the work of the Spirit. Father Lécuyer, an authority on the theology of the priesthood, contributed much to the Council's theology of collegiality. In that era of "calling everything in[to] question . . . discussions on the nature of the religious and missionary vocation, the violent controversies in the bosom of the church herself . . . " (Letter of April-June 1974), *sentire cum ecclesia* (thinking with the church), fidelity to authentic religious life, and internal unity in harmony became his watch-words. In this connection, he called attention to "the invaluable writings of Father Libermann" (Nov/Dec., 1970). What is proper to the Spiritan vocation was "the evangelization of non-Christians in those groups of humankind which are the poorest materially and spiritually" (Letter of February 25, 1969). As vocations dropped in Europe, he plotted withdrawals in certain places to enhance the Congregation's ability to respond according to its proper charism to the challenges of the hour. A forced withdrawal from Nigeria of over 300 Irish Spiritans at the end of the Nigerian Civil War created a crisis of replacement. It also fell to him to encourage and uplift confreres beginning to doubt their missionary vocation, now that the foundations of mission had shifted.

By 1974, the decentralization ushered in by the 1968 Chapter had eventuated in that diversity by which Provinces and units began to take on individual characteristics and identity. Vocations were dropping in the older churches, many confreres were leaving the Congregation (Letter of October 1974). Father Timmermans, confident that "God never closes a door without opening a window at the same time," led the quest for new faces of Spiritan mission, stressing the incarnation of the message in the various cultures and co-responsibility with missionaries of the Third World (November 1975). Reflection began on international teams and an apposite restructuring of the Congregation to enable greater mobility (May 1976). I/D (*Informations Documentation*) was founded as a communication channel of the Congregation. The Spiritan Studies Group, to promote greater knowledge of the Founders and the Spiritan charism, had its first meeting in Rome (January 1976). They began publishing their research in the series of *Spiritan Papers*. New administrative units called Foundations began to emerge in the young churches. With the 1980 Chapter, Spiritan mission embraced the language of Justice and Peace, Spiritan mission now being conceived no longer as necessarily from the First World to the Third World, but to and from the four winds. The needs of the increasing number of refugees sprang into view (Christmas 1981). Two Spiritans were beatified under this administration: Blessed Jacques Desiré Laval, C.S.Sp. (September 1978), and Blessed Daniel Brottier, C.S.Sp. (June 1984).

Fr. Pierre Haas received from the 1986 Chapter the mandate to develop the Chapter discussions and decisions into a Spiritan Rule of Life (1987). The task was also to manifest "the deep links between Libermann and Poullart des Places" and to "recognize a legitimate plurality in our commitments" (Christmas 1986). He promoted a face of mission endorsed by the 1980 Chapter by establishing an Office for Justice and Peace at the generalate. With the new Foundations developing, the Congregation was becoming very diverse in life and mission. Communion demanded curating diversity into unity, not uniformity. Such unity was found in Spiritan "apostolic life," with the three essential dimensions of "the proclamation of the Good News, the practice of the evangelical counsels, and a life in fraternal and praying community" (Pentecost 1988; cf. SRL, 3). Structures of solidarity and a certain re-centralization of aspects of the organization of the Congregation emerged. Diverse views of mission called for working tirelessly on the criteria for our choices (Pentecost 1990). At least two international meetings on Spiritan formation sought to identify the essentially Spiritan in the plethora of diverging approaches between the older Provinces and the new Foundations. At least one year of Overseas Experience became part of Spiritan formation. First appointments reverted to the superior general and his council; those appointed had to complete an initial term (unless agreement between the home and mission superiors was sanctioned by the general council).

Fr. Pierre Schouver was the first to address us as "Dear Brothers and Sisters" (December 1993) or "Dear Spiritan Brothers and Sisters" (Christmas 1995), thereby recognizing the developing Spiritan Lay Associates. Search began for different forms of association with lay people. The general council consciously adhered to the "see, judge, and act" legacy of the Itaici (Brazil) Chapter. Solidarity began to define Spiritan mission, solidarity among ourselves (financial and personnel-wise), solidarity with the poor and marginalized (Christmas 1995). The process began of the former Districts voluntarily merging with the new Foundations (Central Africa, East Africa). Besides geographical frontiers, new frontiers to be crossed included cultural and economic frontiers: slum-dwellers, street-children, drug addicts, victims of AIDS, abandoned rural peoples, the young who cannot find work (Pentecost 1996). For the first time, ecology figured among Spiritan horizons: "the earth which was created for us to live in, is being disfigured by the demands of production and the struggle for survival of the poorest" (ibid.). The mission to South-East Asia, called for by Itaici, opened, relying on a widening of our hearts, without reckoning "how many divisions we have" (Christmas 1996). Ministry to youth, whom Itaici referred to as a "new continent," received a great push. The Maynooth Chapter pushed for greater attention to and study of the Spiritan charism and history, especially in view of the coming 300 Years Anniversary.

The 2004 Chapter that elected Fr. Jean Paul Hoch limited the superior general's mandate to a single term, but of 8 years. Having worked in Taiwan, it was natural that he would promote mission to Asia. Commitments opened in Taiwan, Vietnam, and the Philippines; outreach was made to Bolivia and the Dominican Republic (Pentecost 2008). Emerging situations and needs were pointing to modifying the de-centralization ushered in by the 1968 Chapter. Increasing diversity within the Congregation could flow into unity through a shared common vision deriving from the Rule of Life and Spiritan spirituality based on it (Pentecost 2007). Processes were established for a central funding for new or fragile mission projects, and discussion began on centralizing the second cycle of formation (Christmas 2008). The more flexible approach to Spiritan mission in SRL - does not describe it in geographical terms, but in terms of a movement towards peoples, groups and individuals who have not yet heard the message of the Gospel (Pentecost 2007) - facilitated a continuing harmonization of the double charisms of Poullart des Places and Francis Libermann (Christmas 2007). The mission of Justice and Peace became that of Justice, Peace, and the Integrity of Creation (ibid.). Some circumscriptions, especially in Africa, began to stress education as a means of lifting up the poor. The return to our Spiritan sources, spearheaded by Torre d'Aguilha, was championed. One notes the establishment of the Center for Spiritan Studies at Duquesne University, Pittsburgh (2006) and similar centers in various circumscriptions, and the publication of *Spiritan Anthology*, 1 in 2011. Agglomerations of circumscriptions into Unions of Circumscriptions formed to respond to new challenges (Christmas 2008).

Fr. John Fogarty strove for "greater authenticity in our Spiritan life and mission . . . and a more inclusive Spiritan family" (Pentecost 2016). For this, he had the mandate of the Bagamoyo Chapter that called for an Animation Plan. The general council obliged with an eight-year Animation Plan in four phases: Spiritan identity and vocation, the Holy Spirit, community life, and mission (October 2, 2013). Under the auspices of the Center for Spiritan Studies, competitions were organized for all Spiritans in formation on each of these themes. The call of the hour was personal transformation, especially through prayer in the Holy Spirit, which is "at the very heart of our mission to serve the poor in the footsteps of our Founders" (Pentecost 2015). Intense focus on Spiritan spirituality and spreading it throughout the Congregation crystallized in suggestions for an Office of Spiritan Spirituality – to be suggested to the coming Chapter. A survey of all stages of Spiritan formation yielded data both for the Enlarged General Council and for a revision of the Guide for Spiritan Formation. Spiritans were invited to move away from a nationalistic understanding of Province, where there are those who belong and those who have come to help, to the concept of undifferentiated Spiritan presence and mission. A symbol of the new era: for the first time, the seven members of the general council are of different nationalities (Pentecost 2013). A Guide for Lay Spiritan Associates was produced, also a Guide for Financial Management (Pentecost 2016). A revised Directory for the Organization of the Congregation took account of recent developments, for example, the Unions of Circumscriptions. The finances of the Congregation received sustained review so "they continue to express our charism in the contemporary social and cultural reality" (Christmas 2015).

PREFACE

The Congregation owes a debt of gratitude to two confreres, John McFadden, C.S.Sp., and Philip Ng'oja, C.S.Sp., who painstakingly traced and assembled the letters in this collection.

Rereading these letters convinces one of the guidance of the Holy Spirit in the Congregation's efforts since Vatican II in re-appropriating its charism and mission. The struggles are there for all to see, but also, and above all, the graces. It is no exaggeration to say that these letters amply illustrate the context of Spiritan life in those years and are an apt commentary on both the *Spiritan Rule of Life* and the recent Chapters of the Congregation. They are also deep spiritual reading.

James Chukwuma Okoye, C.S.Sp.

Editor

Claude-François Poullart des Places

FOREWORD

IN A SEMINAL ARTICLE first published in 1988, eminent missiologist Robert J. Schreiter sketches out the history of twentieth century missionary thinking and practice in four periods.[1] The first period, which Schreiter names the "Period of Certainty," begins in 1919 with the publication of Pope Benedict XV's landmark encyclical *Maximum illud* and ends with the beginning of the Second Vatican Council in 1962. This was a period when the goal of mission, even if disputed by the Louvain and Münster schools of missiology, was clear: the expansion of the church and the salvation of souls. Vatican II marked a second period, a "Period of Ferment," in which ideas about mission that had been circulating beneath the surface as the colonial period came to an end found their way into the Council documents: the essential missionary nature of the church, the importance of culture in missionary work, and the possibility of salvation outside explicit faith in Christ and Baptism, the presence in non-Christian religions of reflections of rays "of that truth which enlightens all men and women."[2]

This period was earthshaking for many missionaries and missionary Congregations. It led to a "Period of Missionary Crisis" in which the very reason for mission was called into question, articulated strikingly by a book by the Lutheran mission scholar James Scherer entitled *Missionary Go Home*. This period—in some ways still with us—lasted from the end of the Council in 1965 until about 1975 when Schreiter says that the missionary movement was reborn with the 1974 Synod of Bishops on Evangelization, the publication of Paul VI's post-synodal Apostolic

---

1. Schreiter, "Changes in Roman Catholic Attitudes," 113-25. Roger Schroeder and I have quoted this article several times in our writings. See, for example, Bevans and Schroeder, *Constants in Context*, 244-55.

2. NA 2.

Exhortation *Evangelii nuntiandi*, and a significant meeting in 1980 sponsored by SEDOS, a Rome-based institute for the study of mission. The cause of this rebirth was a widening of the church's understanding of mission, away from *Ad Gentes*' more restricted description as "preaching the gospel and implanting the church among people who do not yet believe in Christ"[3] to a more complex action that includes inculturation, dialogue, and working for justice and reconciliation among peoples. Even though a central concern of John Paul II's 1990 encyclical *Redemptoris missio* was the importance of proclaiming Christ as humankind's universal savior, he spoke of mission in this more multivalent way. Such a rich concept of mission, while still emphasizing the importance of the missionary's invitation to faith in Christ, is also evident in Pope Francis's 2013 Apostolic Exhortation, *Evangelii gaudium*.

To Schreiter's four periods in the twentieth century, we might add a fifth—one that has emerged in our twenty-first century. We might call this the "Period of the World Church." What characterizes this period is the radical shift in the center of gravity of Christianity from the Global North to the Global South. It is on account of this shift that the traditional "mission-sending countries" have become themselves "mission countries," and that missionaries today—in all parts of the world—are overwhelmingly from the countries that had themselves been first evangelized in the last five hundred years, and especially in the nineteenth century. In addition, this new period has expanded the concern of mission to include the massive migrations of our time and the looming threat posed by climate change and global warming. Pope Francis, himself from the Global South, has emphasized these two additional concerns in his papal ministry.

When James Okoye invited me several months ago to write the Foreword to this fascinating collection of letters of Spiritan superiors general he indicated that "they give some idea of paths traced by missiology during the period." He was exactly right. The 122 letters in this volume offer a chronicle of missiological thinking through the turbulent time of crisis in the 1960s and early 1970s, and the gradual reclaiming of the Spiritans' essential charism of the evangelization of the poor, but in a very changed world and a very changed church.

In the wake of Vatican II, with confidence in the purpose of mission faltering, we read Fr. Joseph Lécuyer's strong defense of the missionary

---

3. AG 6.

vocation and the continuing importance of evangelization—despite his recognition of the need for Spiritans to relinquish many of their ministries because of lack of personnel. As the 1970s move toward a rethinking of mission, Fr. Frans Timmermans, who was elected general in 1974 just a month before the important Synod on Evangelization, begins to write about the importance of inculturation, the training of local leaders, and the importance of personal and corporate witness. In his long term as superior general, Fr. Timmermans presided over the dawning of a new missionary era. It is one, as his successor Fr. Pierre Haas notes, of continuing personnel decline, but one that opens the need for collaboration with the local church and with lay Christians. It is in this period that we begin to see a shift in the makeup of the Spiritan Congregation as more and more members come from the Global South. Fr. Haas was general when John Paul II's *Redemptoris missio* was published, and one of his letters offers an important reflection of the encyclical, emphasizing the importance of solidarity with the world's poor, and the growing importance of inculturation and interreligious dialogue.

In his Christmas 1993 letter, superior general Fr. Pierre Schouver, elected in 1992, wrote that "we are not living through tranquil times." This is a theme that runs through all the letters in one way or another, but Fr. Schouver's words capture the mood in a particularly understated but accurate way. At Pentecost, 1994, Fr. Schouver offers the Congregation a very comprehensive and accurate overview of the best of mission theology of the time. During his time of service as general, Fr. Schouver wrote eloquently about mission as presence, as living with and among the people. He also tackled difficult and concrete problems, like the struggles that young Spiritans were having on their first assignments.

As the Spiritans moved firmly into the twenty-first century under the leadership of Fr. Jean-Paul Hoch starting in 2004, the validity of seeing Europe as a proper mission field is acknowledged, as are the challenges of an increasingly intercultural Congregation. One of his letters also anchored the Congregation in a deep Trinitarian spirituality, animated by the Spirit.

At Pentecost, 2013, superior general John Fogarty, elected in 2012, offered some stunning statistics on the growing interculturality of the Spiritan community. Over half of the Congregation and an overwhelming number of students in formation were from Africa, a trend that is found in many, if not most, missionary Congregations today. A year later, Fr. Fogarty quoted a line from a talk by Pope Francis: *"do not be afraid of your fragility.*" "Fragile," he went on to say is a word that is commonplace in Spiritan vocabulary in these days—fragile circumscriptions, fragile communities, fragile confreres. But he noted as well that such fragility has been part and parcel of Spiritan history and spirituality, and that, indeed, "it is precisely the discovery of our fragility that enables us to see things in their proper perspective, that frees us from our compulsions and illusions." In several subsequent letters Fr. Fogarty challenged the community to embrace such fragility, weakness, simplicity, and poverty as a way of renewal as a missionary Congregation. Like much of missiological thinking and practice today, Fr. Fogarty's words are a call to a spirituality that is deeply contemplative.

So, indeed, these 122 letters from 1968 until 2020 "give some idea of paths traced by missiology during the period." These are letters from men of deep experience of frontline missionary work, broad theological and missiological knowledge and wisdom, and rooted in the charism, creativity, and faith of the Spiritan Founders, Claude-François Poullart des Places and Francis Libermann. In a very turbulent and difficult time, a time of relinquishment and one that calls for radical spiritual renewal, they steer their Congregation on a steady course, with firm grounding in Christian and Spiritan tradition, openness to what is happening on the ground and in the academy, and amazing resilience and creativity.

In one of his first letters to the Congregation, in 1986, superior general Fr. Haas quoted from the newly-approved *Spiritan Rule of Life*, developed after the renewal of religious life and missionary understanding of Vatican II. He writes that the role of the superior general is to confirm "his brothers in their Spiritan vocation in accordance with the spirit of the Founders and in the living tradition of the Institute," and to ensure "the unity of Spiritans between themselves and with the Church; he works for the common good and the vitality of the Congregation." This is precisely what these letters do. But they do much more. They offer an on-the-ground theology of mission that can both illumine and confirm missiological thinking today.

Stephen B. Bevans, S.V.D.

Professor Stephen B. Bevans is a priest in the missionary Congregation of the Society of the Divine Word (SVD). He is Louis J. Luzbetak, SVD Professor of Mission and Culture, Emeritus at Catholic Theological Union, Chicago. Among his books are *Models of Contextual Theology* (2002) and, with Roger P. Schroeder, *Constants in Context: A Theology of Mission for Today* (2004). A missionary to the Philippines from 1972 until 1981, he has taught and traveled all over the world. He is a member of the World Council of Churches' Commission on World Mission and Evangelism.

CHAPTER ONE

VERY REV. FR. JOSEPH LÉCUYER, C.S.Sp.

Superior General, 1968-74

VERY REV. FR. JOSEPH Lécuyer, C.S.Sp., from Brittany in northwestern France, followed two members of his family who were also Spiritans. He obtained doctorates in philosophy and theology from the Gregorian University in Rome and was ordained in 1936. During the second world war he taught theology in France. After the war he returned to Rome as director of the French Seminary until 1962. From 1962 to 1966 he was the Congregation's Procurator to the Holy See and in 1968 he was elected Superior General. He was a *peritus* at the Second Vatican Council and, after the Council, a consultant to the Sacred Congregations for Rites, the Doctrine of the Faith, and the Evangelization of Peoples. He was considered an authority on the theology of the priesthood and published several books on the subject. As superior general he guided the

Congregation through a difficult period and extended its work to several new territories: Ghana, Zambia, Malawi, Ethiopia, Papua New Guinea, and Australia. After 1974 he headed the Spiritan Studies Group and published a good deal of research on Frs. Poullart des Places and Libermann, and Blessed Laval. He died at Chevilly, France on 17th July 1983 at the age of seventy.

Rome, November 20, 1968

FROM THE NEW SUPERIOR GENERAL

My dear Confreres,

The Capitulants have just left Rome, eager to return to their Provinces and Districts, and your new superior general and those of the assistants who could remain here at present have come to the generalate at Monte Mario to assume the heavy duties entrusted to them by the chapter.

In spite of the many preoccupations that go with taking up my office and the changing of residence, I hasten to make contact with you all, and with each of you in particular for the first time. My thoughts embrace in one and the same solicitude those of you who carry on the work in the Provinces and those who devote themselves to the task of implanting the church in mission territories. In this first message to you, I should like to express the desire and will of your new superior general and his council to put themselves entirely at your service, to help you in turn to give yourselves wholly to the service of men and of Christ's Church wherever Our LORD has been pleased to call you. In our intention these are not empty words but a genuine pledge.

I take this opportunity also to express my own desire and that of the council to bring the generalate closer to you all. We wish to increase as much as possible our fraternal contacts with you in order to strengthen our unity and our family spirit. From you we expect the same eagerness to keep in touch with us, informing us of your joys and labors, conveying to us also, when the occasion calls for it, your fraternal criticism and your observations in order to help us to put ourselves more effectively at your service.

We are certainly not going to find miraculous solutions to the many complex problems that confront our Institute and our missionary apostolate, and we shall often have need of your indulgence and understanding. But we assure you that, following the directives of the Council, we shall make every effort to give a renewed image to our Congregation.

We shall endeavor above all, to help the Congregation and all its members to follow openly, unreservedly, and joyfully the path traced by the Council, to attune themselves to the church of today. Is not this will to "be with the church" one of the fundamental thoughts of our founders and one of the most cherished traditions of our history? This is the will that guided our work during the weeks we have just spent together at *Domus Mariae*.

It is along these lines that we have tried to clarify, first of all, our mission in today's church, to find our rightful place in it according to the teaching of our Founders and of the Council, and in keeping with the "signs of the times."

It is along these lines also that we have attempted to reflect together on our missionary apostolate. Finally, it is in this manner that we have reconsidered our community life, our consecrated life, and the evangelical counsels.

The documents drawn up by the General Chapter will be forwarded to you as soon as they are ready. These documents have not yet reached their final stage. Some are scarcely more than rough drafts prepared by the commissions. Others have been laboriously amended and corrected for many long weeks. They will be sent to you with an Introduction specifying exactly at what stage they have arrived.

But it is not enough to publish fine texts or new Constitutions in order to bring about our *aggiornamento*. Without a long period, not only of personal reflection but also of community discussion, all the work of the General Chapter runs the risk of remaining a dead letter, of not being incorporated into our lives. In the name of the General Chapter, therefore, we invite and exhort you all to profit by the period between the two sessions to organize this work of reflection. Your provincial and principal superiors and the delegates you have elected to represent you at the Chapter will certainly help and guide you in this work. Do not hesitate to give them your observations and suggestions. It is only with the participation of all of you that we shall be able to finalize the work we have undertaken.

All this immense work should help us to live in a greater and more effective apostolic charity. All this work of adaptation should give the whole Congregation a new impetus to that fervor and dynamism which animated our founders and our society at the beginning. May the Holy Spirit and our Blessed Lady come to our aid.

With this letter I am sending you the text of Pope Paul's Address to the capitulants during the audience of 11th November. Unfortunately, it was impossible to obtain an audience for ourselves alone. Two other religious Congregations were present with us. For this reason, the greater part of the Holy Father's Address dealt with the religious life in general. Let us accept with great respect and gratitude these words of the Pope who invites us to be faithful to the directives of the Council.

In conclusion, I ask your prayers for the General Council and myself, and once again I assure you all of my fraternal affection.

February 1969

INTRODUCTION

My dear Confreres,

Two months ago, the first session of our General Chapter ended; you have already received the first documents presented by the Inter-Session Commission. In the meantime, the capitulants have returned to their Provinces and Districts and have begun to make known their impressions, thereby stimulating reactions of one kind or another. The majority tell us of their enthusiasm, some of their misgivings, and others of their hesitation.

Echoes reach the generalate, where, as is fitting, we try to follow with interest all that is happening in the Congregation, the joys and sufferings of all, their anxieties, and hopes. We have replied to all who wrote to us, thanking them for telling us so frankly what they think.

It is natural that each capitulant has his own opinion about the first session of the Chapter: some would have desired more daring, more determination, and more confidence in setting about the renewal and adaptation to which the Council invites us. Others, more sensitive to the undoubted values of the past, would have preferred more caution, more slowness. The opinions that the capitulants express to their confreres about the Chapter necessarily arouse different, and sometimes, opposite reactions.

At the outset, let it be said that this is inevitable; if Chapters and Councils are useful, it is precisely because there can be a confrontation of different points of view. If everyone thought exactly alike on all points, such assemblies would be useless.

It is right then that there should be differences of opinion. But once the Chapter has decided in one way or another, it is right and necessary that this decision be accepted without reserve, without bitterness. Since it is a decision of the supreme authority in the Congregation (cf. Const, no. 74), there is no choice but to obey in a spirit of faith, for it is the will of God that is thus manifested.

Why should I not tell you that on certain points, I also would have preferred the Chapter to take a different line? But I would consider it disloyal to adopt a negative attitude on these points, or, above all, to belittle the Chapter systematically, or to create an atmosphere of suspicion by speaking of intrigue, subversive scheming etc. The Holy Spirit reveals his will to us by "the signs of the times"; Vatican II was one of these signs; for us, our General Chapter is another.

Doubtless, all was not perfect; none of us is. But grace works even through the imperfections of men. Let us have confidence in the LORD, in the church which encourages and controls our labors, in the Virgin Mary who will not abandon us in spite of our weakness and our faults. Besides, I must say in all sincerity that, in spite of certain defects, our Chapter was really wonderful. I certainly did not anticipate such an attitude of hard work, of, earnestness, of liturgical life, — and that on the part of everyone. If our debates were sometimes a bit lively, our discussions somewhat animated, that also was a sign of the keen interest which we all took in our work, and of the ardent wish for the good of the church and for better service on the part of our Institute.

Accordingly, in order that you all may be aware of what has been achieved, the general council thought it opportune to draw up an account of the first session. This is to respond to the lawful right of all members of the Congregation to be informed and to enable them to exercise more perfectly their duty of participating in the work of renewal required of us by Vatican II.

The work which this special number of the *General Bulletin* puts in your hands is entitled "An Outline of the General Chapter, 1968, First Session." The very title expresses its limitations.

It was, in fact, impossible to write a definitive history. Several of the documents produced are still in the course of elaboration and will be submitted to the capitulants during the second session. It also seemed preferable, for different reasons, to exclude practically all mention of names. The work of the Chapter is essentially a collective effort, a work, of research within the family, and the important thing was to show the different currents of opinion on the various questions and the stages in the development of the documents. I think that this has been successfully achieved.

Great freedom of speech was accorded to everyone. This permitted a healthy and fruitful confrontation of points of view and resulted in a wide consensus of opinion on the final decisions. This should favor the unity of our Institute in true diversity.

Our renewal has two great objectives: to give new impetus to the spiritual life of each member of the Congregation and to re-plan the missionary activity of its members according to the actual needs of the church today. With regard to the first objective, the research which resulted in the composition of the doctrinal texts was based on an intense work of return to our sources in the writings of our Venerable Father and a constant desire to start from the Word of God and incorporate conciliar teaching. In this, the Chapter was faithful to the directives of *Perfectae caritatis*, no. 2:

> The adaptation and renewal of the religious life includes both the constant return to the sources of all Christian life and to the original spirit of the Institutes and their adaptation to the changed conditions of our time.

In addition to these sources, account was taken of the concrete situations, as expressed in the pre-Capitular reports from Provinces and Districts.

Out of the work of this session, there has come a set of laws regulating the life of the Spiritan, aimed at renewal but within prudent limits. The tendency to give priority to life over law certainly predominated. Attention to the actual conditions of our missionary life has upset some regulations which were sources of tension, permitting an adjustment whereby members can express in their own way their self-donation to God. But rightful discipline, which is an indispensable element in all social life and a guarantee against waste of energy, has not been eliminated.

The light shed by the new definition of our specific end should, secondly, lead the Institute to a new missionary impulse in the service of the church. A clear study of our style of apostolate and of the historical evolution of some of our works, the frequent reminders of the present state of our recruiting — our average age continues to rise — as well as the urgent need to answer the call of those who are far from the Lord, should lead us to adopt certain courses of action; the criterion for these will be our will to be faithful to the daring of our Founders and to the magnificent drive of the great Spiritan pioneers in the evangelization of Africa.

These two great objectives were always before the minds of the capitulants. The texts which they produced, in their different stages, should from now on tend to rule the life of our Institute, which should profit by them in loyally trying them out. This is the responsibility, first and foremost, of individuals and communities — "it should be constantly kept in mind, therefore, that even the best adjustments made in accordance with the needs of our age will be ineffectual unless they are animated by a renewal of spirit. This must take precedence over even the active ministry" (PC, no. 2).

I pass on these pages to you and recommend you to read them. They have been written in understanding with the Inter-Session Commission; they can help you to understand better the work accomplished, and thus to give more enlightened assistance to the Chapter. They were drafted with the aid of the official minutes drawn up by the secretaries of the Chapter. I wish to thank the author who undertook this very heavy task for the service of all.

When these lines reach you, we shall already have celebrated the annual Feast of February 2nd. On this day, I shall be united more than ever with you all in thought and in prayer. May Father Libermann obtain for us that we be worthy of him and faithful to his spirit!

With renewed assurance of my fraternal affection and asking a remembrance in your prayers,

I remain,

Yours devotedly.

February 25, 1969

TO THE ORDINARIES AND SUPERIORS OF OUR MISSION DISTRICTS

Your Excellencies, Reverend Fathers,

The General Chapter of the Congregation, which has held its first session in 1968 and will hold its second session in 1969, has tried to analyze clearly the immense needs of those dioceses where the members of the Congregation are working. It has also tried to make an estimate of the personnel and the means at the disposal of the Congregation for the fulfilment of its obligations over the next six years. We are faced with the fact that in our Congregation, as elsewhere, there is a marked decline in vocations. In fact, it is estimated that the potential of young Fathers will be reduced to less than half during the period 1968-1974.

The General Chapter, in keeping with the teaching of Vatican II, has insisted strongly that the Congregation should be absolutely faithful to its proper vocation, namely, the evangelization of non-Christians in those groups of humankind which are the poorest materially and spiritually. Many capitulants are even of the opinion that the number of vocations to the Congregation will be in proportion to its fidelity to this specific end.

Taking all these factors into account, the general council has to work out a carefully studied plan for the posting of its members, the founding of new works, and the withdrawal from some existing works. I would not like to undertake this study without requesting the co-operation of the Bishops or without consulting the Principal Superiors who are in the best position to examine with the Bishops what steps should be taken.

From the outset, it must be stated that, because of our present commitments and the decline in vocations, it appears impossible for us to maintain all the works we staff at present and all the parishes for which we are responsible. If we take into account that the primary duty of the Congregation is the evangelization of non-Christians, that the Congregation cannot allow its members to wear themselves out prematurely through overwork, that the Chapter wishes all members to live some form of community life, we are forced to the conclusion that there must be a progressive withdrawal from certain works in order to engage in others that are more completely in conformity with the specific aim of the Congregation.

We should like to effect this Withdrawal in two Sectors:

1. In Africa, from the more advanced Christian communities. Although it is not our intention to leave the local church in difficulty, we take the liberty of asking Bishops to make a full study of the possibilities of recruiting vocations locally, and we ask all members of the Congregation to consider it a duty to collaborate wholeheartedly in this work, as recommended by our Venerable Father from the beginning.

2. In Europe and America, from certain works, so as to employ the greatest number possible in the work of first evangelization.

We respectfully suggest, therefore, that a thorough study be undertaken by mutual agreement in every diocese where the Congregation has placed members at the disposal of the Bishop. From your vantage point perhaps you could suggest some works we might relinquish and others we should adopt as corresponding better to our missionary aim.

To regulate future relations between the Bishops and the Congregation, it would be very useful to draw up contracts which would on the one hand guarantee the continuity of the missionary work, and on the other provide for the needs of the Congregation. These contracts would arrange for the appointment and employment of missionary personnel so as to ensure a definite number of missionaries for a definite period in a diocese. They would also stipulate the material conditions indispensable to the life of the missionary.

Your Excellencies, Reverend Fathers, more than ever the Congregation wishes to make an effective contribution to the missionary effort as it has been doing since 1842. But once the young churches are firmly established in a given place, our missionary work there has come to an end. In its General Chapter, the Congregation has reasserted its intention to collaborate according to its means in the missionary work which remains to be done among the two billion pagans in the world.

With respectful good wishes,

I remain yours devotedly in Christ.

PENTECOST 1969

My dear Confreres,

At the approach of the Feast of Pentecost, it gives me great pleasure to send my fraternal greetings to you all. May the Holy Spirit give each one of you, and the whole Congregation, the graces of which you stand in need. I am thinking, in particular, of the marvelous list of the "fruits of the Spirit" which St. Paul enumerates in his Letter to the Galatians: love, joy, peace, patience, kindness, generosity, faithfulness, gentleness, self-control (Gal 5:22-23). May every Spiritan receive these fruits in abundance in view of an ever more fruitful apostolate.

During these first six months in office, I have had the opportunity of coming into contact with a large number of you both directly, in the course of my visits and when missionaries were passing through Rome, and indirectly, by correspondence. I must say that, in general, these contacts have been for me a source of great joy and precious encouragement. In our Congregation, there is a wonderful store of generosity, enthusiasm and fervor, not only among those who for many years past have devoted themselves to the work of the missions, but also among the youth who are preparing themselves for this work or who have just begun their labors. The numerous reports we have received, following on the study of the documents of the first session of the General Chapter, are a sign of the vitality of our Institute and a pledge of future progress.

It is, therefore, above all, a message of confidence and hope that I send you in this Paschal Season — confidence and hope, in spite of all the difficulties and suffering you experience or anticipate, in spite of the falling-off in vocations, in spite of the crises which convulse many of the countries where we are working, in Africa and America. Our strength is in the risen and victorious LORD in whom we believe and whom we preach. This attitude of unshakeable faith in Christ and in his church is a fundamental obligation for us, the fundamental obligation of every apostle who "can do all things in him who strengthens him" (cf. Phil 4:13). The missionary is not ignorant either of his own weakness, or of the difficulties facing the Christian in the world, or of the magnitude of a task which always surpasses his strength, but he knows too that to him are addressed the words of Christ to his apostles: "In the world you will have trouble, but take courage, I have conquered the world" (John 16:33).

For some time now, there is apparent among various groups a certain hesitation or even doubt about the value and meaning of a missionary vocation, whether priestly or lay. These hesitations are understandable in the case of a person who considers the matter from any other standpoint than that of the faith. No sociological analysis, no philosophical considerations can give a solid motive for the missionary activity of the church or for the existence of a Congregation like ours, or for the vocation each of us has received. Neither St. Paul nor Father Libermann can be understood in terms of historical or psychological factors. Only the grace of Christ and faith in him can explain their dedicated work.

I invite you, therefore, to a deepening of this faith, by daily contemplation of the mysterious plan of God's love, by close union with the church and its leaders, by the practice of prayer. May Spiritans give to the world an ever-increasing witness of their faith under the action of the Spirit of God; it is thus we shall be strong, it is thus we shall be victorious. This is the grace which I ask for each one of you — from

Our Lady in this month of May, from the Spirit of God in these days of Pentecost.

September 10, 1969

AT THE CLOSING OF THE SECOND SESSION OF THE GENERAL CHAPTER

My dear Confreres,

At the conclusion of this General Chapter I wish, before all else, to thank the LORD for all he has given us during these long days that we have spent together: for the enlightenment received, for the work accomplished, for the brotherly atmosphere that was created and maintained amongst us. Yes, our gratitude must go to God for bringing our common efforts to a happy term, despite our imperfections, despite our often very different viewpoints. I am convinced that we can be happy about the work that has been accomplished. Sometimes, as the days went by, we had the impression that we were losing time, not reaching profound agreement. This has been surmounted, certainly, and I think that we can be satisfied that our Chapter has achieved something truly useful to the church and to our apostolic work.

I have spoken of the different viewpoints frequently expressed, sometimes quite vigorously. I told you at the beginning of this session that we must not be surprised by this variety of opinions. It is understandable that the different currents in the church at the present day should be mirrored in our Congregation which belongs to the whole church and consequently shares its life, its research, and its effort to adapt itself continually to the needs of men whom it has a mission to save.

In fact, it is this loyalty to the church to which I want to invite you in these final words. Loyalty to the church, such as it was intended by Christ to be, such as it exists in fact, with multiform features in the different local churches, yet with a profound unity, which no true Christian can think of ignoring. I must avow that I am surprised, in our day, by certain stands taken, by certain statements made, or rather by certain attitudes of mind, against which I would like you all to be vigilant. Some people speak about theological, pastoral, and moral questions as if the thinking of the church as a whole, of the hierarchy as a whole, and of the Pope, had no importance whatever. They approve of particular modes of action in the domain of pastoral work, of liturgical life, and of Christian morality as if the official teaching of the hierarchy, or even of the Council, need no longer be taken into consideration. They are much more impressed by some articles appearing in recent publications than by the entire traditional thought of the church. I must confess that I am sometimes astonished at the calm assurance with which they offer us what they call "modern" or "contemporary theology," when at best it is only a question of some obscure article in a so-called "avant-garde" publication. What complacent ignorance of so difficult and so demanding a science as theology!

I do not intend to belabor this point, but implore you, as St. Paul asked the Ephesians, not to be like children and not to allow yourselves to be "tossed by waves and swept along by every wind of teaching" (Eph 4.14), following ephemeral fashions or shallow slogans.

Without further delay, I wish here to thank all who wholeheartedly placed at the service of the Chapter their zeal and their knowledge, who tried to be makers of peace and mutual understanding, who refused to allow themselves to be narrowed by the famous dilemmas — youth or elders, conservatives or progressives, essentialists or existentialists, those who uphold the vertical or the horizontal, the particular or the universal church. These are false dilemmas: the church is one and complete including all these in her embrace.

I should like to thank all who worked in the secretariat, in the commissions, in the plenary sessions, the Moderators who were yesterday given a public acknowledgement of our appreciation, better, of our admiration; the secretaries who were so devoted, both those who worked here at the plenary sessions and those who accomplished their hidden task in the secretariat. All cannot be mentioned. I thank all, the typists, the translators — those we see there in their cabins — and all the other anonymous collaborators: the technicians too who saw to the proper functioning of the electrical apparatus, those who rendered us such pleasant service in the refectory and in general household chores. May the LORD reward all, including those whom I have perhaps omitted to mention specifically.

Our gratitude is extended to all for the work they have done, work in the service of the Congregation, but above all, work for the missions, since the Congregation itself serves those to whom we are sent.

Now we are about to depart, each one to his own field of work in America, Africa, Europe, wherever the LORD has placed us. Let each do his best to accomplish the will of God who called him. What else but this could I ask, that each in his own place, should accomplish the task which the LORD has confided to him, wholeheartedly, joyfully giving his whole life, as Christ gave his? But let us remember — only yesterday we voted it in one of the last documents — let us remember the words of Christ: "Without me you can do nothing," nothing, not even a first timid step towards our fellow men, not even the least effort for the development of the poorest, nothing without him. Father Libermann often recalled the need of a deep and steadfast supernatural life, a practical union in the midst of our apostolic activity with him who can do all things and who alone can do all things. Perhaps in our effort to bring about the necessary updating of our Institute, in our anxiety to discover the wisest and best adapted human methods to be employed in the contemporary world, we are sometimes tempted to forget that without Christ all these are nothing, and to substitute little by little our human wisdom for the wisdom of God.

Do not think that this is an absolute negation of all that is of profound value in the movement of secularization, for the benefits of this age and of this world are also from God. It is from him that our possession of them derives. If this temptation arises, let us be on our guard, for it would mean the ruin of our work, of all our endeavors and undertakings. I shall read for you two texts from Father Libermann on this subject. The first is from a letter to the Mother Superior of the Missionary Sisters of Castres, dated December 13, 1843:

> It is understood that we ought to work with all our strength at the work God is pleased to entrust to us, but we must avoid making it "our own work." We should make use of all the means He puts at our disposal to do the work as perfectly as possible for his glory, but all the time remaining at peace and not being excessively concerned about success. God has entrusted to us, but we must be on our guard against making them our own work. Let us employ all the means He puts at our disposal for the perfect accomplishment of what may be for his glory, but tranquilly, and unworried about success. It is for us to plant and water, but for him to give growth and harvest the fruits. Since the fruits belong to him, since the field is his, and since even the workers are his property, He is the Master who decides how to employ us and for what end. He is the Master who decides whether we are to be productive or sterile, whether we are to work or remain idle. Let us remain before him ready to be, in his hands, the kind of instruments he wishes us to be.[1]

---

1. *Letters to Sisters and Aspirants*, 112-115, here 113.

The second is from a letter lo Fr. Lossedat, à propos of the situation in Haiti, a difficult one even in 1844:

> Allow me to make a comparison to show you that you have done wrong in yielding to the temptation [of discouragement]. The farmer who cultivates his field during the winter does the hardest work of the year. He perspires and gets tired without seeing any fruit of his labors. The soil is black and rough and there is not one blade of green in sight. This is the situation in which you are at present. Have courage and patience ! God's hand will not be shortened in Haiti. All the considerations that trouble you are worthless. It is from the almighty power of God and your fidelity to grace that you must expect everything, and not from the political measures taken by the Government.[2]

It is then this union with Christ which should be the driving force of our apostolate and the source of our deepest union among ourselves, for it is God, the Spirit of God, who unites. Little will it avail us to remodel our structures and give them the most perfect forms from the point of view of modem science and human prudence. If wanting in this deep union in the Spirit of the LORD, we are not a family as we ought to be.

That is what I wished to say to you at the close of this Chapter. There are so many other things I could say to you! I shall confide them to the LORD for each one of you, for all whom I have come to know here in the Chapter and for all those whom you represent, the entire Congregation of the Holy Ghost, spread out over a large part of the world, which now seems so small when we look at it in photos coming to us from the moon. You represent the whole Congregation. It is this whole Congregation that I felt responsible for on the day that you elected me. It is the whole Congregation that I shall include in my prayer with you.

NOVEMBER 1969

My dear Confreres,

You have above Pope Paul VI's greetings to the missionaries on Mission Sunday, 19th October. I hope these words of the Holy Father will console and encourage all of you.

In these days in which we live, from all sides, in thousands of papers, reviews, books, it is the fashion to criticize the missionaries and the

---

2. *Letters to Clergy and Religious*, vol 3. Dec. 15, 1844, 315-317, here 316.

work they have done. Even theologians, alas! even Bishops have yielded to this fashion. Listening to them you would think that the missionaries were colonialists, had not the slightest understanding of the civilizations, cultures, and peoples whom they encountered that they imposed on Africa or Asia a Western style Church completely un-adapted to the mentality of the different peoples; sometimes even kept native Christian communities and their clergy in a state of inferiority or subjection, with a view to retaining power . . . One hears or reads all these accusations. I pass over them.

Another kind of criticism, which is more subtle though none less painful, is silence. People speak of the new churches, hail their youthful vitality, without making the slightest allusion to the missionaries who founded them, or worse, insinuating it is high time they should go.

I know that many of you are pained by all of this, as indeed I myself have been — profoundly. Yet I would not speak of it to you were it not that I consider this matter a great danger for the missionary work itself.

Consequently, it is not to underline the ingratitude or inexactness of these attitudes that I write to you; it is not in order to protest, in the name of so many missionaries, dead or living, who have given all, who have done their best — not without inevitable mistakes — and without whom we should not see the results we see today.

If I speak, it is first of all to put you on your guard against the temptation of doubting your missionary vocation, against discouragement in the face of the apparent uselessness of your efforts, in the face of misunderstanding, ingratitude, sometimes even contempt. But I also ask you not to allow yourselves to fall into the same excess, for even amongst the missionaries today one hears harsh criticism of past methods, the means employed by former missionaries. This does not mean that we should not acknowledge the deficiencies, even the errors; every human work has its defects and its limitations. It is easy with the passage of time and from a distance to criticize what pioneers have achieved with far less experience, much more restricted means, and a very imperfect knowledge of social conditions, mentalities, and customs. Will not our journeys to the moon, today, be considered in a hundred years' time as imprudent folly? Are we then never to risk anything for fear of making a mistake? It is the imperfect attempts of yesterday that make our clairvoyance today possible; it is the generosity, courage and enthusiasm of our elders which has prepared for us the new conditions in which it is possible for us to do as well as and, God willing, even better than they?

I want, especially, to draw your attention to the harm such generalized criticism can do to the radiation of the missionary spirit and to the awakening of new vocations. How can youth be attracted to a missionary Institute when everywhere they hear its past activity condemned, when they are told that it must be entirely reformed in its spirit and methods? Let us admit the shortcomings of the past and profit by them. But let us also recognize the authentic missionary spirit which we inherit, the magnificent testimony of generosity, intrepidity, faith, and charity given by so many missionaries, led by the Spirit of Christ. And let us be convinced that the Spirit of God is still at work.

Bagamayo Retreat, 1897

January 1970

WE ARE SERVANTS

My dear Confreres,

I am writing these lines on the day after the return of our Fathers who were jailed in Nigeria, eleven of whom came to the generalate. They speak of the country from which they have been expelled, but never without expressing the desire to return there, as soon as possible, to continue their missionary work. But will they be allowed to go back? We hope so, and we hope that it will be soon.

In this event, there is an important lesson for us all. The Congregation has labored in the District of Nigeria for close on a hundred years, with the tangible success of which all are aware. This work was, primarily, missionary work in the strictest sense of the term, introducing whole regions to Baptism and to the Church, founding a local clergy ready to take in hand the destiny of the young churches. In the field of development, too, the success has been extraordinary, especially the promotion of education and the establishment of schools.

Now, this has all been changed by the course of events, and the very existence of these churches seems to be in danger. Our missionaries found themselves obliged to adapt to an entirely new situation, to undertake an unprecedented task of providing aid and assistance, to organize a whole network for the distribution of food and medicine. This they did, without hesitation, to save their people from famine and death. They would have done the same for any other people, for any other tribe in a similar situation of extreme need.

Divergent judgments have been passed on this activity, and different views are still held. Now that the noise of battle has been finally (we hope) silenced, voices are heard which criticize severely what the missionaries have been doing during the war. This should not surprise us; indeed, it would be much more surprising if there were no criticism. But the interests of humans (no matter who they may be), must not be allowed to deform the truth: these Spiritans performed their duty as servants; they acted in complete understanding with their hierarchical superiors. Although the form of this service may be unprecedented, the spirit is the same — the spirit of the charity of Christ. They are ready now to resume ordinary mission work, like their confreres in other Provinces of Nigeria.

We are servants; our wish is to be the servants of the poorest. Let us always be available for the services that may be demanded of us.

MARCH/APRIL 1970

My dear Confreres,

In the latest issue of the Bulletin of the District of Yaoundé, I have read with great pleasure certain considerations which the principal superior proposed to the members of his district. It seems to me that they are worth bringing to the notice of all.

... The Chapter documents give us a rich insight into the evangelical counsels. Let us read these texts and let us meditate on them. Thus, we shall, perhaps, live out all the better our apostolic consecration, which, for us, includes these engagements.

Our Poverty. Sharing, detachment, community of goods, etc. The Chapter examined many synonyms in an effort to present our poverty more realistically and more positively. The problem is not to find words, which may console us and lull us to sleep, but to face facts. Let us leave the theoreticians, comfortably installed in their rooms, equipped with the most modern methods of communications and tele-communications, while they elaborate, for others, magnificent projects about poverty. For our part, let us rather live our poverty concretely and genuinely.

While it is true that some communities have a standard of living that calls, perhaps, for certain modifications, very many others, on the contrary, live rather austerely, and I do not think that it would be right for us, in the name of poverty, to endanger our health. We must strike a just balance, maintaining standards of cleanliness, repairing in good time our houses and our means of transport, not abusing them ... Trying to put all that into practice, is what is meant by being poor. We should also share what we have with those most in need: our old catechists, our incurably sick, our fervent old women, toothless maybe, but so joyful in their unshakeable faith. During Lent, many praiseworthy efforts have already been made along these lines. I think that all of us, in our group meetings, could reflect on the value of our witness in this matter.

Our Chastity or "voluntary celibacy for the kingdom of heaven." It is not a limit set to our love, but an extension of it, a greater liberty in order to be able to love better, making us all the more available for our apostolate ... Let us admit the fact: our training, at least in the words used, was perhaps tainted with a certain latent anti-feminism, capable, maybe, of causing certain complexes, which, in the circumstances, were baptized "means for safeguarding chastity." Without any thought of self, let us love generously every man, woman and child entrusted to our care.

I have already spoken to you about the Chapter Directive on the cloister. This new opening-up should not however make us neglect the rules of normal prudence. We are not made of plastic, and David has left us a number of psalms lamenting his imprudences.

If, for example, there should be exceptional occasions when the domestic service in our houses requires the presence of a woman or a girl in the evening, we should, in all simplicity, see to it that she is accompanied by a lady-friend. In this way, much useless and scandalous talk will be avoided. There is no need for puritanism, but there should be clear-sightedness supported by reasonable prudence.

Our Obedience. I do not think that any one of us has ever been called upon to act in the name of the vow, in the canonical sense as this is defined. But, on the other hand, it is the spirit of obedience that has made us what we are, that has placed us where we now find ourselves. Let us continue to practice this virtue. I will simply mention two areas where this virtue will help us to a greater apostolic efficiency.

a. In team-work (meetings of sectors, zones, regional communities, etc.). Let us have the humility to submit to the general desire, even if it does not correspond exactly with our own point of view. It is, of course, our duty, as long as the matter is under discussion, to speak firmly and with conviction but without passion. But once a line of conduct has emerged which is supported by the will of the majority, it becomes our duty to enter, with the utmost sincerity, into the spirit of what is being planned.

b. Within our diocese. It is the Bishop who is responsible for the apostolate, and it is our duty to obey him. Anything else would be wrong and mistaken. Our first duty is to collaborate with him.

These are the bright and the dark spots I wish to point out to you, so that all of us, each in his own place, may be better able to fulfil his task in the church, wherever the LORD has placed us.

I leave you these few thoughts to meditate on.

May the Risen Christ, grant that we all live more and more in the joy of Easter.

July/August 1970

DIALOGUE

My dear Confreres,

Among the problems considered most important today in all societies, and particularly in the church, is that of dialogue. You will recall the emphasis Pope Paul placed on this subject in the *Encyclical Ecclesiam suam*.³ My intention here is to speak of the place of dialogue in your day-to-day missionary activity.

Circumstances vary greatly from place to place and even in the same place many of you have witnessed a considerable evolution in the course of recent decades. Not so very long ago, a missionary coming from Europe or North America was considered — and for the most part, rightly so — as having a very special competence in all questions concerning the faith and Catholic practice in every sphere: family, social, professional, cultural. If one could speak of dialogue — since, according to *Gaudium et spes* it is essential to the mission of the church — this dialogue tended to be of a special kind, tainted with paternalism and condescension on the one side and by passive acceptance on the other. This, I hasten to say, was not confined to mission territories.

Yet on the missions, perhaps more than elsewhere, there has been a rapid evolution. The young local churches have produced lay people who are conscious of their responsibilities and determined to penetrate their whole life with the spirit of the gospel. It is impossible for the missionary, coming from overseas, to have a really thorough understanding of these lay people's lives; often he will notice only what is superficial. When it is a question of concrete problems concerning lay people, he has not got the right to take over from them, to settle the question by an appeal to authority, as if they were children and not adults. The missionary must collaborate with his lay Christians, but in the final analysis, it is up to them to work out solutions in the light of the faith — solutions which will not be simply transpositions of a European or Western mentality, but rather genuine "discoveries" resulting from the meeting of the gospel spirit with African or Asian or South American traditions and outlook.

This can happen only as a result of patient, confident dialogue in which the missionary will have at least as much to learn as to teach.

I should like to add that the missionaries must engage in dialogue with those lay people whether baptized or not who have come under the influence of non-Christian, or even anti-Christian, philosophies of life. More and more in our missions, there are to be found lay people, often very cultured, who have been influenced by Marxism, different forms of atheistic rationalism, scientism, etc It is important that there should be dialogue with these also, to the exclusion of all hostility and distrust. The missionary must acknowledge the competence of these lay people

---

3. Pope Paul VI, *Encyclical on the Church*. August 6, 1964.

in different spheres where we cannot claim to be specialists; above all, he must never question their good faith. We are sent out to all men to announce the message of salvation, but this is impossible unless we are ready to understand and speak the other person's language, that is to say, to engage in dialogue.

It does not suffice to learn an African language in order to understand and be understood by the Africans. We must love them, hear them, listen to them, as they speak to us today, with the ambitions and the hopes they have today, in today's language, which is not necessarily the language of their native village.

Do everything you can to ensure that each one can hear the gospel message "in his own tongue" as on the day of Pentecost!

September/October 1970

ABIDJAN: SOME REFLECTIONS

My dear Confreres,

As you already know, I was privileged to be present as a representative of the Union of Superiors General at the Symposium of African Episcopal Conferences (SECAM) held at Abidjan from August 17th to 23rd. You will find a report on this meeting in our Documentation Bulletin, as well as a summary of the address given in the name of the three Superiors General by Very Reverend Father Arrupe, S.J., President of the Union of Superiors General.

On another occasion, I shall have the opportunity to review the general conclusions of the Symposium. But now I should like to speak in particular of the impression made by this meeting of Bishops from the entire continent of Africa, who were, for the most part, Africans themselves. The work of the missionaries has not been in vain, even though, as in all human enterprises, it has been marred by unavoidable imperfections. It should be a source of great joy to us to see the African hierarchy take over responsibility for the apostolate on African soil. Father Libermann would have rejoiced had he been able to witness the development we see today.

For this very reason, our missionary role must be adapted to suit the new situation which will continue to evolve as time goes by. We must place ourselves, more and more at the service of the Bishops in charge of the young churches; we must cooperate with them in carrying out their missionary task. We must adapt ourselves increasingly to the necessary process of Africanization, for only Africans can build the new structures which will harmonize with local culture and evoke a new style of Christian life from the very depths of the African mentality. So, we must be willing to receive and learn from them — we who are accustomed to being in the position of the one who gives rather than receives!

We will collaborate wholeheartedly and completely with the Bishops in Africa and elsewhere, following the line traced by our specific vocation. We will work as a team with the clergy, religious, and laity of the local church. There should be no question of changing our mentality or culture, of losing our traditions or special vocation, just as we do not ask others to stop being themselves. On the contrary, each one should try to transmit whatever- is best, whatever is genuinely human and Christian, in his own personality and culture. In this way, the exchange of views and insight will be truly fruitful for all concerned. The Spirit of unity in the church has given us very varied gifts; unity is not the same as uniformity.

But the one thing the Bishops have a right to find in us is that we should be missionaries who serve the church to which we have been sent. Some may be ethnologists, some sociologists, some specialists in development, etc, sometimes highly qualified in their respective fields. But what is really expected of us is that we should be missionaries, ready to undertake the varying aspects of the apostolate which is never complete; and this means, oftentimes, that we must sacrifice our own choice. We will never be servants in the strict sense, if we fail to make this personal sacrifice.

November 11, 1970

A JOINT EXAMINATION OF CONSCIENCE

Dear Confreres,

Two years ago, the General Chapter asked me to accept the responsible post of Superior General. It is now time to look back, critically, at these two years, and I would like you to join me in an examination of conscience. Its scope will be as follows: how far have we responded to our common vocation which is to seek God's will in our lives.

The past two years have seen many changes in the Congregation. The majority of provincial and principal superiors are new; many Provinces and Districts have held or are preparing to hold their chapters. Spiritans have been forced to leave areas where they worked for many years. New missionary projects are being examined, and many Provinces are adopting or have already initiated new methods for training aspirants, and new forms of community life and common prayer are emerging.

In our Institute, as in other societies, the reaction to these changes varies according to persons and differences of mentality. Some feel that these changes have been too precipitate and that the real nature of the Congregation has been obscured. Others are impatient with gradual adaptation to the modern world. Some would tend to question everything; others are against any change at all. These tensions can easily lead to exasperation. Pressure groups are formed to overcome resistance that is deemed unjustified. Petitions are circulated and signatures collected; dialogue is abandoned in favor of the fait accompli. At the other extreme, sometimes, the individual cuts himself off from the group, gives up the common search, and refuses to accept any form of change.

But we are all jointly responsible, and the realization of this joint responsibility for our vocation and common task leads me to pose the following questions. I invite you to consider them and look for an answer, either individually or by means of a fraternal dialogue among yourselves or even with the General Council.

1. Renewal of our Way of Life

The first question I should like to put to you concerns the renewal of our Congregation. This renewal is called for by the church, and a re-reading of *Perfectae caritatis* or *Ecclesiae sanctae* should be enough to show that it is not a question of some superficial changes, but a call to re-examine our Rules, Constitutions and Customaries in the light of the Council documents and in relation to the world of today. The General Chapter began this task, and now we must put the directives and decisions into effect, each one doing his part at his own level of competence.

Have we all cooperated loyally with the Congregation as a whole in carrying out this task? At this stage we may note certain temptations which affect all of us to some extent: that of Pilate washing his hands (let them do what they want — it doesn't concern me!); that of the Pharisee judging the Publican (thank God for not being like those people!); that of the people invited to the banquet in the parable of that name (I have other things to do; count me out of that kind of drudgery); that of the Church of Laodicea (look at me, I'm rich and I need nothing, Rev 3:17); and there are many more.

Let us not delude ourselves; we are individually and jointly responsible for safeguarding our Spiritan heritage. Together we must search for God's intention regarding our Institute, and this common enquiry should be carried out prayerfully and thoughtfully, in fidelity to the church and attentiveness to the needs of humanity. I know that many have loyally accepted responsibility in this regard. But is this true of all? Is it not true to say that some are unsympathetic towards this common responsibility, either through fear of being disturbed in any way, or through a short-sighted involvement in their own province or work? Are not some prejudiced against the decisions of the General Chapter, as though nothing good could come from it? Some would seem to be so convinced of the truth of their own views or those of their own little group that they disregard everything else. I have no hesitation in stating that this is not in conformity with God's will. We cannot carry out our work except in communion with the entire church and with the Congregation as a whole.

2. A Return to the Sources

As I reminded the General Chapter on a previous occasion, Spiritan life does not need to be invented, as it were from thin air. We have a history which cannot be ignored or suppressed; we have a spirit which goes back to our Founders and has left its mark, over the years, on our way of life, prayer, and work.

I realize that during our history, also the letter of the law has often taken the place of the spirit; institutions and customs were sometimes given the primacy which rightfully belongs to interior dynamism. All human societies run this risk and we have not been spared.

At the other extreme however, do you think it would be wise to throw our entire past overboard, as if nothing remained valid today? I must confess that I am occasionally shocked at the complacent way in which certain confreres — not always young people — despise what was done before their time, claiming the backing of "new" theories, modern mentality, and the need for "being with it."

Each of us should ask himself the question: are we willing to find out and use the positive values of our Spiritan history, and especially the invaluable writings of Father Libermann? Have we attempted this task since the General Chapter ended? What can we do about it now?

3. Spirituality

Spiritan spirituality should be given a special place of honor in our heritage. Its general outline was traced during the time of Claude Poullart des Places; Father Libermann enriched it enormously, but we must remember that it evolved and deepened during the course of our history. I am convinced that our spirituality must be taken seriously, even though modern life demands that we separate the essential from the accidental. I am also convinced that in the eyes of the church we have the duty to guard and transmit this spiritual treasure, not only within but also outside our ranks.

We cannot, however, be genuine messengers of this spirituality unless we live it ourselves. And here, once more, I invite you to examine your conscience. As Vatican II stated, the renewal of our Spiritan life cannot be authentic without a deepening of our spiritual life. What have we done about this? When we say spiritual life, we mean, primarily, the exercise of the theological virtues, faith, hope, and charity. Unless our Spiritan apostolate and our attempts at renewal derive from this source, they will prove sterile:

> Faith is the essential element in any godly work. If one were to observe all the commandments of God, but do so without faith, they would be dead works. The spiritual worth of any activity derives from the inner spirit of those who carry it out. God sent his son in order that all our actions might be done in him and through faith. This comes about by the submission of all the powers of our souls to the graces he gives us under the influence of his Spirit. Every work done with such submission to our Lord, by the inspiration of his divine Spirit and under the influence of his grace, is a work of God, for it comes from God, who sent his son to share with us all that we have from God.[4]

These lines from Father Libermann's Commentary on *St. John's Gospel* (chap. VI) remind us of fundamental truths which give meaning to our lives. We are always in danger of succumbing to a form of naturalism which leads to undue reliance on human wisdom and neglect of the divine. Our brothers expect us to bring them the gift of God and not simply the results of human research. This we cannot do in an efficacious and convincing way, unless God has become the true center of our lives and interests. In other words, we must have a genuine spiritual life. This

---

4. *Commentary on John.* Part 2, 56.

is why I repeat my question: what effort have we made to improve the spiritual life in the Congregation?

This letter, long enough as it is, must end here, but I hope to continue it in the near future. I rely on all of you to help me promote and direct the renewal and adaptation of our Congregation. We will do it together, inspired by the church's teaching and by our spiritual tradition. This presupposes, firstly, a personal conversion at every stage of the process. May God give us the grace to do this!

Such is my prayer for you; I rely on your prayers in return, and thank you in anticipation.

January/February 1971

A JOINT EXAMINATION OF CONSCIENCE CONTINUED

My dear Confreres,

In my last message I invited you all to join me in an examination of conscience regarding what we have done since the General Chapter. Now Pope Paul VI, in a letter to the Bishops, dated December 8th, also invites them to join in an examination of their fidelity to the engagements they undertook at the council, especially their duty to proclaim divine truth in all its integrity and purity.

This invitation concerns us all, for all of us, under the Bishops' guidance, have to bring the message of Christ to the world without watering it down and without fear of criticism. Missionaries as we are, it is first of all for that purpose that we are sent: to proclaim the good news of salvation to the entire world, and not just any sort of message, product of human wisdom. But there is, nowadays, a tendency to construct a new Christianity based on psychological and sociological findings, unconnected with the two thousand year-old tradition of the faith. This true tradition reaches back to the apostles, while the new has been almost completely emptied of religious elements. Have we not perhaps been too indulgent with this trend at the risk of losing the substance of our role as missionaries and religious?

I put this question to you for we are all conscious of the need (commendable in itself) to speak to our brothers in a language acceptable to them. But it can happen that in adapting our mode of expression we are tempted to avoid the difficulties, to deform what is hard to accept. At ecumenical reunions in which I still have the pleasure to participate from time to time, several non-Catholic clergymen have complained to me about this tendency on the part of such and such a Catholic theologian: "He is no longer of interest to us," they say, "he does not tell us what the Catholic Church thinks, rather he gives us his own opinions, and that is not what we expect from him." And that goes as well for our dialogue with all men; what they expect from us is the message of Christ in all its integrity such as it is proclaimed by the church. Otherwise, what interest can we have for them? What have we to offer them that is any different from what others propose? What attraction can there be in the message and life of men who do not wish to say anything more than what the world says, and who do not wish their lives to be any different from those of other men, even unbelievers?

I should like you to join me in asking whether the danger feared by St. Paul is not already a reality, even in the Congregation: "For the time will come when people will no longer tolerate sound doctrine but, following their own desires and insatiable curiosity, will accumulate teachers and will stop listening to the truth (2 Tim 4:3). Indeed, one listens to a multitude of teachers, one devours the latest articles of theologians and experts in missiology, always provided they have something new to say, something slightly different to the official teaching of the church in one sense or another... On the other hand, they read in a superficial manner and with a mocking eye, the Council documents and papal or episcopal utterances. Do I exaggerate? I beg you to be honest. Is it honest to present an image of the mission, the priesthood, or the church as authentic, when it does not correspond to that which the hierarchy enjoins us to teach?

It is Christ whom we should preach to men, the Christ who should be mirrored in our lives. But as St. Paul says: "If we present Christ to them it must be the Son of God made man to save us and to make us share his life, and not an altogether human image however marvelous and attractive."[5] Let each of us then ask himself: Is it really Christ we are preaching; is he truly mirrored in our lives — the Christ, Son of God, Son of Mary, obedient to the Father, poor, chaste, entirely given to men, guided by the Holy Ghost, "Christ the power of God and the wisdom of God. For the foolishness of God is wiser than human wisdom, and the weakness of God is stronger than human strength" (1 Cor 1:24-25).

---

5. The quotation could not be verified [Ed.].

I write these lines, conscious of my duty towards you and towards all those who expect the Holy Ghost Fathers to be faithful missionaries of Christ and him crucified.

March/April 1971

POVERTY

My dear Confreres,

Continuing our previous examinations of conscience, I invite you today to reflect on our "poverty." Our General Chapter has given us some very simple and beautiful pages on this matter (nos. 87-111). Let us read them once more.

Are we truly poor? Are we poor before God, aware that everything comes to us from God, and that our whole missionary apostolate is grounded on the voluntary poverty of Christ and on his Cross?

Poor before men? I must honestly admit that many lamentable practices have come to my attention: the use of a "peculium," private bank accounts, money withheld from the community and used for personal satisfaction, as gifts to friends or family. Again, what is to be said about useless travelling, undertaken out of idle curiosity, without any apostolic motive to justify it, and under the pretext of gaining culture or joining in a pilgrimage? Could the poor among whom we live indulge in such travels? Do they own the latest photographic equipment or cameras, the most up-to-date transistors, etc.? Granted that occasionally such things may be justified as a means of furthering the apostolate, yet here again, let us be honest.

Then there is the question of gifts which one receives from parents or friends; too easily it is argued that one is entitled to keep them for one's own use, although they belong to the community by right.

Poverty suffers, too, when a person becomes so attached to "his" work, to "his" mission, to the buildings he constructed or the plantations he developed, that he refuses to make way for others. Thank God we can point to many instances in our history when missions and schools, the product of our own labor, have been handed over to the diocese, to the local clergy, or to other religious. This is a natural consequence of our missionary work, and if it is sometimes a heavy sacrifice for those who have labored in these works, it would be a cause of grave concern if we were to lose that special kind of generosity which goes hand-in-hand with detachment:

> The spirit of detachment and of total dedication to the apostolate will be clearly seen in the Congregation's willingness to leave works which it has sufficiently developed in favor of more neglected ones. (CDD, no. 106).

To develop the same idea, we have as a guideline this directive of the Vatican Council: "Provinces and houses of a religious community should share their resources with one another, those which are better supplied assisting those which suffer need." (PC, 13; cf. CDD, 109). It was to express this obligation in practical terms that the General Chapter (CDD, 317) revived a rule which appeared in our old constitutions (nos. 125 and 135), and which, in substance, goes back to Father Libermann (Rule of 1849, nos. 136-137): "The surplus funds of houses shall be sent to the provincial or district bursar, and those of Provinces and Districts to the general bursar."

Are we keeping this prescription? I ask superiors to examine themselves on this point. We receive here many requests, whether it be from impoverished works or from missions or Provinces not yet on their feet. How can we meet such needs if the Congregation as a whole is not contributing to the joint fund provided for by the General Chapter? We will be discussing this question at the next provincials' meeting; but each of you, in your own corner of the world, should give your attention to it by avoiding unnecessary expenses and by cooperating as best you can in establishing this reserve fund "for the most needy."

Much more could still be said but, on your side, make a beginning by reading over the documents of the General Chapter once more. Both in your private reading and by group discussion, search out ways of responding more effectively to the poverty God is asking of you.

Remember the laity, especially the poor, who are our judges and for whom we can so easily become a cause of scandal.

May/June 1971

OBEDIENCE

My dear Confreres,

We hear complaints everywhere, and not only in the religious life, that the sense of obedience has been lost. It is not possible in a few lines to treat the whole of this problem which has a special importance both for the religious and the missionary life. But I wish to invite you all once more to an examination of conscience, each one according to his own situation and bearing in mind the promises we made when entering the Congregation.

We have reason to be glad at the great insistence nowadays on respect for the individual; he is not to be treated as an impersonal entity or be moved about as one would a pawn on a chessboard. We recall the teaching of Vatican II, that superiors are there to serve their brothers and to exercise authority towards each one in a way which "manifests thereby the charity with which God loves them." (PC, 14).

It would be childish to ignore the facts and to claim that superiors always act in this manner. One can point to innumerable examples of that authoritarianism which is really a caricature of true authority, of arbitrary decisions, of refusal to take part in any kind of dialogue.

Such abuses have existed in the past and are still with us, but if they go a certain distance in explaining the crisis of authority, and consequently of obedience, can they be used to justify the kind of attitude which one meets within our own as well as in other Institutes? I will limit myself to a few examples.

Is it true obedience to present one's superiors each time with a "fait accompli" and hide behind the excuse that it adds to one's "experience" (it is the in-word nowadays)?

Is it true obedience to make use of a kind of blackmail and to threaten one's superiors with words such as these: "If you do not grant me this, or that permission or allow me to do this or that work, or transfer me elsewhere, I will leave the community or the province or the Congregation"?

Once this stage has been reached, of course, the individual concerned has already rejected obedience, since without any attempt at dialogue he is prepared to accept only one solution, that chosen by himself, and impose it on his superior and the other confreres. Bear in mind that it is not only the person of the superior that is being challenged here, but also the directives of the provincial or the General Chapters. In fact, we can say that these directives have been arbitrarily rejected even before they have come into being, since there is a refusal in advance to accept any decision which is contrary to a personal inclination. Even in our own Institute, cases are known of confreres turning down an offer to take part, either by consultation or by voting, in the election of a superior or in the discussions of a provincial chapter. In other words, they refuse to cooperate in the exercise of authority and also challenge every decision coming from it. One is tempted to speak ironically of the brand of "democracy" underlying all this.

I could mention too the existence of small groups which will accept only those decisions which are taken in common by all the members of the group. Even when living in a larger community, such people will not adapt to the common round of prayer and work.

Let my words be properly understood—this is not a one-way traffic only! There are those, it is true, who call in question anything which appears to them antiquated or out-of-fashion, but there are others who remain on the fringe of any community which is developing in a way which is unacceptable to them. This attitude of rebellion showed its head during Vatican II; it can be seen also in a general or provincial chapter, and whenever decisions are taken by a community acting as a group. To the extent that we refuse to let go any of our personal views, we put ourselves outside unity and true obedience.

At the same time, the superior is to seek after unanimity; too often he is conscious of being "pushed aside" and it is all the more distressing for him to the extent that he is aware of his own limitations. One can readily understand why so many confreres are unwilling to shoulder the burden of leadership!

However, every society requires authority, in whatever way it is exercised, and along with that an habitual willingness to submit to it for the common good. The submission of the man who has never understood that obedience is an expression of charity, to be offered in freedom and joy as a gift of love to his brothers, is not that of a child of God but a slave. He has no place in a society such as ours; he would only be a source of sorrow both for himself and for others.

The same could be said of a superior who, instead of serving others, allowed himself to be led by the tendency to dominate, to impose his preferences, and opinions. He is simply destroying what is human in an attempt to set up an artificial discipline created by himself, instead of joining with everyone in searching constantly and humbly for the will of God. Here again Christ has given us by word and action an incomparable example (cf. Luke 22:24-27). May his Spirit teach us to command and to obey!

July/August 1971

FATHER LIBERMANN AND OURSELVES

My dear Confreres,

By the time this message reaches you, I expect you will have already received and—hopefully—studied *Evangelica testificatio*, Paul VI's Exhortation which he addressed recently to men and women religious throughout the world. I do not intend examining it in detail nor summarizing it here. Obviously, we should study this document carefully; all the more so today when everybody claims the right to comment on subjects as complex as the priesthood and the religious life.

For my part, on reading this document I could not but think of Father Libermann, and once again, I was struck by the fact that, abstracting from out-dated expressions, his thought remains relevant to modern problems. Allow me to quote some paragraphs all of which were written at the beginning of his project on behalf of the African people. First comes a letter to M. Levavasseur (October 28, 1839; the very day he decided to devote his life to the new work) in which he provides an outline of the future Constitutions:

> I should like to have something established that is solid, fervent and apostolic; all this or nothing ! But "all" will be much, and weak souls will not wish to give or do so much. This ought to be a source of joy for us, for a congregation that is wholly apostolic should not have weaklings. We ought to have nothing but fervent and generous members who give themselves entirely and are ready to undertake and suffer all things for the greater glory of our most adorable Master ... Encourage them and tell them to make themselves ready before God to undertake anything, to suffer death—even the death of the cross. It is only at this price that we share in the spirit and the apostolic glory of Jesus Christ, the Sovereign LORD and the great Model of apostles[6] (ND, I, 661).

He returns to these ideas later on in a letter to M. Tisserant (November 27, 1839; ND, I, 648-649). But I should like to draw attention to

---

6. *Letters to Clergy and Religious* (nos. 185-274), 11.

one letter in particular, an exceptional one, written to M. Louis, Superior General of the Eudists, on December 15, 1839. Here we find Libermann, at that time only in minor orders, giving advice on how to solve the difficulties facing this Congregation. The letter contains a complete program for a special Chapter: all the members should be gathered including the novices and even those who seriously intend entering their ranks. The purpose of this assembly is to examine "the difficulties which can arise from the practice of certain points in the Constitutions and the customs of the Congregation. Besides the points which you present to the assembly, each one should be free to make his suggestions; I believe this will prove a powerful means of binding the hesitant definitively to the Congregation . . . " And the letter continues on this note (ND, I, 575).

For spiritual directors I also recommend the letter written on the same day to M. Féret. This contains eight pages on the discernment of vocations, and the missionary vocation in particular. M. Féret in point of fact was opposed to the missionary vocation of M. de la Bruniére (LS, II, 310-318). The latter did become a missionary eventually, but in the Paris Foreign Mission Society; his departure did not cause M. Libermann to lose heart, and some days later he wrote as follows to M. Levavasseur in Rome (June 12, 1840: ND, II, 83-84):

> Do not worry about the difficulties that were mentioned by the Superior of the Holy Ghost Fathers and will probably be mentioned also by others. It even astonished me that that word "difficulties" is constantly brought up. Is there any work of God that is not accomplished in the midst of difficulties? Have we not been aware at all times that we would meet with obstacles? We certainly have, and the obstacles will be considerable. If we were able to foresee them, we would study them and devise good means for over- coming them; but if this is impossible and we cannot choose such means, let us remain quiet. In any case, we should put our trust in God. When the time comes, we shall do what we can to bear the pains, afflictions and contradictions, and avoid as much as possible or overcome the difficulties that will stand in our way. Above all, let us put our entire confidence in Jesus and Mary alone; they will be our only resource, our only support on this earth . . . Be in peace and do not worry about anything. Be full of confidence in our Lord and His most Holy Mother. Union and charity are precious treasures, and I firmly hope that the divine Master will grant them to all of us. We should not be astonished if the enemy does his best to sow trouble among us; but let us be courageous, practice patience,

and refuse to attach exaggerated importance to such things. You know how great is the happiness that results from peace, charity, and union among you; and you strongly and earnestly desire and pursue them.[7]

These then are the principal elements of a supernatural optimism which is still valid today. Some will say, perhaps, that one should be realistic, that principles are not enough. Here is an extract from a letter of the same period (July 5, 1840) which I propose as a subject for meditation for all, but especially for any superior who may tend to act in the manner indicated here (ND, I, 571):

> There is another defect in his way of looking at things. He sees only the principles involved, he holds these principles strongly and wants to reduce everything to them. At the same time, prudent action in difficult situations requires more than a consideration of the relevant principles. One should examine carefully the situation in which the problem arises, the men involved and the circumstances which form the background. Our examination should aim at applying the principles while at the same time, modifying, explaining and adapting them to the actual situation as regards individuals and circumstances. He who is unable to make allowance for circumstances when prudence demands it, will never be able to direct a work, and cannot be considered a perfect priest, even though he be capable of working miracles.[8]

Without faith and prayer constantly exercised, without consideration for others and forgetfulness of self, without confidence in Christ and his church, how difficult it is to attain and preserve a state of equilibrium which is at the same time, supernatural and natural. This is my heartfelt wish for all of you.

---

7. *Letters to Clergy and Religious* (nos. 185-274), 14-16.
8. To M. Gaudaire, priest, superior of Maison Saint-Sauveur, Redon.

Ubangui 1928. Fr. Adrian Leperdriel teaching

September/October 1971

WHEN PROPHETS DISAGREE

My dear Confreres,

It is true that all the members of the people of God share in the spirit of prophecy, and Vatican II has happily recalled the texts of the New Testament which proclaim this common dignity of Christians (Acts 2:17-21 which recalls the prophecy of Joel 3:1-5; Rev 19:10). Thus, there exist today also, and there will always exist in the church, interventions of the Spirit of God which disconcert by their novelty because they do not fit into any of the existing categories. There will always be a flowering of extraordinary initiatives which manifest the action of him who, like the wind, "breathes where he will"; "you can hear the sound it makes, but you do not know where it comes from or where it goes" (John 3:8). It is true that the hierarchy cannot claim a kind of monopoly of the spirit of prophecy; very often authentic prophets have not only anticipated the initiative of their hierarchical superiors, but they even had to wait and suffer for a long time in patience before the authenticity of their prophetic mission was recognized. It would be puerile to be surprised at this tension between the two poles which a Protestant theologian has called "the institution" and "the event," since, although nobody has the right "to despise the gifts of prophecy," it will always be necessary to check on them so as to retain what is good (cf. 1 Thess 5:20-22).

In fact, there is no guarantee that every initiative which calls itself prophetic is truly inspired by the Spirit of God. Do we not know from our own experience how great the tendency is to present our own personal ideas as those of God? And it is quite obvious today that tendencies presented to us as prophetic are very different from, even opposed, to one another. When the "prophets" fail to agree, it is then most of all that we must apply what Christian tradition calls the "discernment of spirits." Whether it is a question of voluntary celibacy for the kingdom of heaven, or marriage, or the liturgy, or the priestly ministry, the most diverse points of view claim a hearing, and the more they conflict with the official teaching of the church, the more they claim to be prophetic. St. Paul himself already came up against such claims apparently, if we admit the full force of the expression which concludes the chapter affirming the excellence of voluntary celibacy: "And I think that I too have the Spirit of God" (I Cor 7:40).

There are criteria for the discernment of spirits, and I would like simply to invite you to reflect on them. There is the one which St. John gives in his First Epistle: fidelity to the apostolic teaching (1 John 4:1-6). There are also the principles which St. Paul recalls for the community of Corinth (1 Cor 12:14): the subordination of all the charisms to charity, to the common utility, to mutual edification, finally, order and peace in the acceptance of the apostolic tradition and authority (cf. 1 Cor 14:35-40). There is also the enumeration of the fruits of the flesh and the fruits of the Spirit in chapter 5 of the Epistle to the Galatians (5:19-24). In my opinion, there is no better commentary on this latter text than the teaching of the Venerable Libermann. It is well known how often he returns to this theme—the signs which enable us to recognize the action of the Spirit of God, whether it is a question of spiritual direction or of apostolic activity. The terms gentleness, kindness, patience, humility, peace, etc, are liberally sprinkled all over his letters and recall insistently the list of the fruits of the Spirit given by St. Paul: "love, joy, peace, patience, kindness, generosity, faithfulness, gentleness, self-control" (Gal. 5:22-23). I am sure he would say to us today what he taught throughout his life: the Spirit of God does not act in contention, in natural impulsiveness, in impatience, dissension, quarrels, but, as the Shepherd of Hermas says: "The prophet who has the Spirit which comes from on high is kind, calm, moderate . . . and he makes himself the inferior of all" (Mand. XI, 8).

This is not to preach conformism, still less blindness. But what I have said calls for constant attention to others (all the others), continual detachment from oneself, and a distrust of one's own judgment. Father Le Meste has recently written an article on the sense of humor of Father Libermann: we also should be attentive not to be too absolute in our preferences and our ideas, not to sacralize them as if they must necessarily come from God directly. It is the whole church which has received the spirit of prophecy: may we receive it in abundance, in the church which is qualified to discern it.

November/December 1971

AFTER THE SYNOD

My dear Confreres,

It is now a fortnight since the end of the 1971 Synod and it is right that we, Spiritans, try to learn some lessons from it. Next month, all the superiors general are invited to a three-day meeting to reflect on this event and to seek in common what it is that, through the Synod, God is asking their religious institutes to realize both within themselves and in the world. You will be given an account of this meeting but for the moment, I simply wish to share with you some of my impressions.

Much has been said about this Synod and about the part played in it by the superiors general. I was asked to act as spokesman for the latter in the discussion on the priesthood, and in the newspapers of certain countries in particular, I was personally criticized as if the views I expressed were simply my own. However, it is not my intention to discuss this aspect of recent events nor the atmosphere which the press tried to create, or even sometimes disturb.

The first aspect I wish to underline is precisely the diversity of the currents of thought which became apparent in the course of these five weeks. There is nothing strange about that; what use would a Synod be if all thought the same way? Very often the impatience shown, the protestations expressed, are due simply to the spontaneous tendency we all have to want other people to think as we do. We are all inclined to transpose to the whole church the problems and the mentality which we think we find in our own diocese or our country and we find it hard to accept that others are, or wish to be, different. Once again, this very point illustrates an aspect of the church which is very important from the missionary point of view. The church should find a form adapted to each people, and this involves necessarily a certain diversity, a certain multiformity even in church institutions, and in concrete forms of the pastoral ministry. The very history of this Synod, and also the texts which were adopted—though possibly too timidly here in the opinion of some—have drawn attention to this need.

The conclusions concerning the priesthood are important for us as they stand, and it is useless for us to speculate on what they might have been. First of all, it must be admitted that a sincere effort was made to identify the difficulties of the priestly ministry today, difficulties which are the real cause of much trouble and also of the losses which sadden us all. We should also receive with joy the renewed affirmation of the value and the importance of the priesthood. There is really nothing new in this and what is contained in these pages is found already, often better expressed, in the texts of Vatican II. At the same time, this renewed proclamation of the faith of the Bishops is in itself an encouragement and a source of peace. The section on "Evangelization and the Sacraments" does not pretend to solve all the problems which arise in the apostolate today, but it marks an attempt to strike a balance and indicates a certain line of research which we would be wrong to neglect in spite of all the agitation which the question of celibacy aroused in the press. Although some would have welcomed a greater opening on the question of ordaining married men, we must surely be impressed by the strong reassertion of the value of celibacy freely chosen for the sake of the kingdom.

This is a wonderful encouragement especially for us, religious, to sound the depths of the real significance of our consecrated celibacy. Obviously, it is not easy to demonstrate by logical argument the value of celibacy which involves a choice in the existential order, a choice which supposes that one has experienced the compelling demand of love. If this love is not carefully sustained and deepened, celibacy ceases to have any meaning. Because of the choice we have made as religious, independently of the reception of the priesthood, we have a special responsibility to illustrate the meaning of celibacy by our lives.

With regard to the document on Justice in the World, I am convinced that it marks a big step forward. There is strong and explicit denunciation of injustices, not only in individuals but in present structures and contemporary institutions, denunciation of the dangers with which the whole of humanity is faced, of the arms race and its disastrous consequences, of the concentration of riches, of power, of decision-making in the hands of a small minority, and so on.

Equally striking is the assertion of the right to human development, without which new forms of colonialism are inevitable. Clear reference is made to the problems of immigrants, of oppressed minorities, of racial and ethnic discriminations, of torture—in particular, for political reasons—and to other areas of injustice.

It would be puerile to expect that the Synod could find immediate and definitive solutions for all that. Still, having recalled the saving mission of Christ and of the church, it outlines certain basic requisites which are essential. First of all, there is the obvious need for the church to give an example of justice in its own internal relations. Many of the points mentioned here are new, and all of us, each in his own place, will have to examine himself honestly on these matters. Similarly, all of us, each in his own place, must try to promote a real education in, and to, justice as an integral part of our apostolic and missionary work.

I think I have said enough to invite you all to enter into the spirit of the Synod. The documents which have been published—exactly as they are, or perhaps with slight modification—certainly reflect the thinking of a large part, if not the majority, of the bishops of the world, of their clergy, and of their faithful. Whatever be our own personal preferences, we cannot remain indifferent to this challenge addressed to us, because, in this too, it is God who is speaking to us.

May/June 1972

COMMUNITY LIFE

My dear Confreres,

I have just come back from a seminar organized by the International Union of Superiors General on the subject of "Community Life in Religious Institutes Yesterday and Today." More than fifty superiors general, with ten representatives of National Religious Conferences and approximately ten experts, all gave their attention to this question during the three days discussion based on a questionnaire which had been sent to all religious institutes.

A report was drawn up of the findings of the questionnaire but as this is to be published by one of the better-known religious reviews, I do not need to deal here with all the various aspects of the problem. We all know, however—and my own contacts with the Provinces and Districts confirm this—that in our Congregation too there is a real problem concerning community life. Not all set the same value on the more recent developments in this domain.

I, personally, am convinced that, if the documents of the General Chapter of 1968-69 were read and thoroughly studied by everyone, many useless conflicts and upsets would have been avoided. Not so long ago, I met some confreres who had never even seen a copy of the Chapter Directives and Decisions! It is the fault of superiors at all levels if this necessary study of CDD has been neglected and no time should be lost in remedying the situation where necessary.

The changes which have come about, not only in our own Congregation, but among all religious societies, can be summed up as follows: there has been an evolution from a community of observance to a community of brotherhood. The accent is now put on the person, on the respect due to him as such, on personal relationships, on the co-responsibility of the members of the community and on fraternal charity, lived as perfectly as possible, so that the love which unites us in Christ becomes more and more apparent within the community and then radiates out from it.

In such a community, the superior is less an administrator than a co-ordinator, less an enforcer of the law and more the "animator" of his community, at the service of all, so that each one may actively participate in discerning God's will and faithfully accomplishing it. Nos. 122-124 of our last chapter, based on the gospel and on Father Libermann, express this point very well.

The superiors general at the Villa Cavalletti meeting all insisted on the importance of community prayer. Rather than refer you once again to our last chapter, I quote here from the replies to the questionnaire already mentioned: "In this new-style community life, prayer can more easily be experienced as a very special expression of our fraternal union, which is deepened and developed by this effort in common. In their common prayer, the members of the community place themselves in the presence of God, our Father, pledging themselves once again to live as his children and as brothers in Christ. In fraternal concelebration—the central meeting-point of the community, and a source of renewal and vitality—the confreres unite in making Christ present in their community by an ever more real and total fraternal union in his name. All those who have spoken about prayer emphasize the importance of an ever-fuller participation in the celebration of the Eucharist; the reform of the liturgy has served to make the life of prayer more liturgical, more significant and more attractive."

In comparison with some communities where common prayer has almost no place any longer, I have noticed with joy that many of our missionary communities, even some of the very small ones, are making a great effort to promote a more real and authentic life of prayer. Although, on the one hand, the times set for community prayer have in some instances become less frequent, it has happened, on the other hand, that common prayer is now all the more fervent and more and more congenial. Again, what has happened in other institutes is true of ours too:

> Many communities try to organize themselves in such a way as to maintain both a personal and community rhythm of prayer. It is noticeable too, that the results depend very much on the people involved and that—once a certain reserve, which is rather a form of human respect, has been overcome—communities, under the leadership of a member who has strong convictions, have succeeded in giving an example of a radiating life of prayer in which the Sisters of the mission and even the faithful, are sometimes invited to take part. Prayer, within the framework of brotherly participation, is still in its early stages: there should be no pressure on this point but already many confreres who thought that this form of prayer was not for them, have experienced what it can do and what meaning it can have in their community.[9]

These last remarks are directed at certain forms of community prayer: reading of the gospel together, reflection in common on a text for meditation, etc I know that, in our own Congregation too, some confreres have been amazed at what this can contribute to our community life.

I would like to conclude with a quotation from the Epistle to the Hebrews, which has always impressed me very much; it applies to the entire Christian community, but even more so to religious communities: "we must consider how to rouse one another to love and good works. We should not stay away from our assembly, as is the custom of some, but encourage one another . . . " (Heb 10:24-25).

---

9. I could not trace this reference [Ed.].

July/August 1972

OUR SPIRITUALITY

My dear Confreres,

During recent weeks, I have had the opportunity, in reflexion and prayer, to think about the Congregation of which we all form part, and for which, together, we all share responsibility. I have re-read a number of the works of Father Libermann, and certain sections of the history of the Congregation. In a few lines, I would now like to give you the results of this reflexion, this prayer, this study.

Like all religious Congregations, we are passing through a period of serious difficulties, whether it be concerning recruitment, the perseverance of our members in their vocation, the common life, or the very concept of the mission. It would be childish to deny that such difficulties exist.

In every Province, there are confreres who claim to have discovered the profound causes of this crisis, and to know the remedy to apply. Unfortunately, the diagnosis differs completely from one Province to another, even from one community to another. Suggestions in plenty, often diametrically opposed, have been propounded:—the return purely and simply to our way of life before Vatican II; or, on the contrary, out of so-called fidelity to Vatican II, the complete overthrow of all that goes by the name of structures—common life, poverty, obedience, celibacy, etc. I need not delay on all the varieties that may be found between these two extremes.

In spite of the efforts made by our General Chapter, many confreres still find it quasi-impossible to combine the apostolic or missionary life with the religious life. There is a tendency to oppose the two, or else, under the pretext of reconciling them, to suppress all that is not immediately and concretely apostolic. For some, a genuine Spiritan must be engaged exclusively in "first evangelization"; for others, his unique role is to form "basic communities"; others again, see only "development" as important. The list could be prolonged.

In the face of all that I see and hear, there is one question which I cannot avoid, and which I submit to you now: Are we still conscious of having a Spiritan spirituality of our own? Even the word 'spirituality' will shock some and cause others to smile. Nevertheless, let me ask you this question: Can we offer those who enter our Congregation something that is proper to us, over and above the missionary ideal that is common to every missionary Institute, or the more general idea of a fraternal community of Christians directed to a common purpose? In this body, which all together we constitute, is there a common soul which determines its personality, its unity, its unique character, and distinguishes it from all the others? If not, how can we hope to attract vocations? Nobody is attracted by an unspecified being; nobody can love a body without a soul.

I would like to be more specific. We bear in our official title itself the name of the Holy Spirit and the invocation of the Immaculate Heart of Mary. Has this any meaning for us still? Has this any influence on our conduct, on our manner of living, of praying, of preaching the gospel? More particularly, does this have any place in the training we propose to those who wish to join us? At the present time, when the presence of the Holy Spirit in the church is more and more occupying the attention of all the Christian faiths, what are we Spiritans doing, to bring it to the attention of all?

With regard to the Immaculate Heart of Mary, I realize that many of you have some difficulty, but no one should be too hasty in rejecting a spiritual experience which has been a source of light and joy for many in our Institute and elsewhere. Recently, the Jesuits solemnly renewed at Rome their consecration to the Sacred Heart of Jesus, which occupies a central place in their spirituality. Perhaps it would be well for us too, to deepen all that is authentic in our traditional devotion to the Holy Heart of Mary, though perhaps in a new form and with new formulas.

Then there is our whole history, the treasures of dedication spent on our works since the first foundation of the seminary of the Holy Spirit up to the time of Libermann and more especially since his time right up to the present day. Have we the right to ignore all that, to live and act as if we were without roots, without a past? A living body, no matter what its age, cannot develop without taking account of the years that have passed, which have left their mark on it, and which inevitably influence its future growth. I was very pleased to note among the novices of the United States, a real thirst to know the past history of the Congregation; and I also know that the group now finishing the novitiate in France has studied this history with the greatest interest. Personally, I regret very much that Father Koren's book, published in English at Pittsburgh, has not been translated into the other languages and brought up to date since 1958.

All religious spiritualties are nourished by their past, and it would be a terrible impoverishment for the church if all this were lost. A spirituality is simply a special way of contemplating and living the whole mystery of Christ, which no speculative treatise could ever fully express in words. The very diversity of these spiritualties is itself a sign of inexhaustible riches. We have a Spiritan spirituality and we have not the right to ignore it. The two volumes of Father Blanchard on Libermann would themselves suffice to prove that there are in our inheritance riches which have a value for the whole church. These riches have been confided to us. Let us not leave them in neglect and oblivion.

September/October 1972

ABOUT FATHER LAVAL

My dear Confreres,

In the July-August issue of the *General Bulletin* there appeared a translation of the Decree proclaiming the heroic nature of the virtues of Father Jacques-Desiré Laval, our first missionary in Mauritius. In the same Bulletin, I asked you to be faithful to our Spiritan spirituality, to advert to it, and to live by it more and more. In fact, Father Laval is one of the most extraordinary witnesses to this spirit, and I was deeply moved, on re-reading recently his biography, most especially by the wonderful letters which he wrote from Mauritius. I do not know what it is we should most admire—his courage, his spirit of faith, his life of prayer, his indefatigable zeal.

It so happened that this week, from the 16th to the 19th October, I was privileged to be present at a meeting of all the National Conferences of Major Superiors with the Sacred Congregation of Religious in Rome. There was much talk about present-day problems in the religious life, of which two were singled out for special attention—firstly, the life of prayer, and secondly, unity in religious communities. While reflecting on all I heard, I could not help thinking of Father Laval, of his absolute confidence in prayer, and of his love for community life of which he was deprived for so long. In the light of all this, I feel that I must recommend once more to all our confreres these two indispensable features of our apostolic and religious life, namely, prayer and unity in charity.

In these two matters, there has been, amongst us too, much neglect and much confusion, especially in these latter years. There can be no remedy until we are convinced of our own insufficiency. It is only when one is conscious of being poor that one can really pray; it is only with the heart of a poor man that one can love others, accept that they are different, and really listen to them in a spirit of genuine exchange without which there cannot be a true community. Our differences of opinion degenerate into quarrels when we are certain in advance that we have the whole truth, that we are right on every point, that is to say, when we are conscious of being "rich"—rich in our certitude, in our virtue, in our rights—and that we have nothing to learn from others.

Here again let Father Laval be our model. Re-read, for example, his two letters of the 6th and 7th September 1859, respectively, which show a wonderful spirit of poverty.

Through his prayer may it be granted to us that we be poor!

November 29, 1972

SALVATION TODAY

My dear Confreres,

An international meeting organized by the commission, "Mission and Evangelization," of the World Council of Churches will be held at Bangkok from the 29th of December 1972 to the 12th of January 1973 on the theme: "Salvation Today."

A missionary Congregation like ours cannot remain indifferent to such a subject, and the Congress of Bangkok can be for us an occasion to examine ourselves on the way we envisage and carry out this task. Salvation is at the very heart of the Christian message; what we have to announce to the world, is, first and foremost, that Jesus Christ is the Savior and "there is no salvation through anyone else" (Acts 4:12).

However, Christians are not the only ones to speak of salvation, to search for and to promise salvation. In this universal aspiration, which characterizes all places and all times, St. Irenaeus saw the mark of the invisible action of the Word of God, present in all cultures and in the whole evolution of human history, directing this latter towards the "liberation" operated in and by Christ. At this point, many questions of a missionary nature present themselves and we cannot simply ignore them: how should we dialogue with persons, who, though belonging to a different faith or a different culture, are also in quest of salvation; how can we express our message of salvation in terms that are relevant to their search? What is the quality of the witness which we give? . . . and so on. Although it is not possible here to deal with all the theoretical questions concerning salvation, I would like to invite you here and now to question yourselves on certain points which have a direct bearing on our position as religious and as missionaries.

First of all, does our whole way of life reflect the conviction that we are "saved," and that we have a message of salvation to bring to all men? Do our communities always breathe a spirit of hope? Does it not too often happen, on the contrary, that the prevailing atmosphere is one of discontent and discouragement? True, we cannot just close our eyes and refuse to see all that in the church and in the world today seems to jeopardize all hope of salvation—disputes, divisions, conflicts of interests, wars, more and more injustice in the way the goods of this world are distributed among men, etc. Indeed, in the face of all this, it is not surprising that so many people are tempted to renounce all hope. Yet, is it not an essential dimension of the Christian life to be "hoping against hope" (Rom 4:18), against all the appearances of defeat that recur with monotonous regularity. I am writing these lines in the liturgical season of Advent. It is my prayer that our Spiritan communities allow themselves to be impregnated by this attitude of certainty, awaiting serenely but also renewing our own efforts. However absurd it may seem, we know that our salvation will come, that in fact, it has already come.

We mean, however, a special kind of salvation, a special kind of liberation. It is salvation in him whom we call Our Savior, Our Lord Jesus Christ. Here again, we should examine ourselves on the witness we give. Is it really from Jesus Christ that we expect our salvation? Is it really he — sought and encountered in prayer, in listening to his word, in his church, in our fraternal contacts with others, in docility to his Spirit — is it really he who is the center of our hope? Do we sometimes give the impression that we count more on our efficiency, on our talents, on our access to sources of information, on our administrative planning, on the updating of our techniques? The opposition, even bitter sometimes, which exists between the so-called "conservatives" and "progressives" can be very illuminating. The one party puts its hope in the laws, the regulations, the customs of the past; the other rejects these "structures" as obstacles to development, to personal salvation, and so wants to replace them with new methods or techniques of dialogue, of consensus, of sharing, etc. Very often, we have good reason to ask, where does Jesus Christ come in? When St. Paul fights against the slavery of the Law, it is not in order to substitute new techniques for it. Over against the Law, he puts Jesus Christ and the liberation he brings — Jesus Christ and his Spirit by which we cry "Abba, Father." It is a terrible illusion to think that we can "renew" religious life without a renewal of our spiritual life, of our life in Christ and by Christ. If Christ is not found in our communities, why should we be surprised if some leave us in order to seek their salvation elsewhere?

Jesus Christ is our Savior, but he is a crucified Savior. Too often, we are afraid of words like "mortification" and "renouncement," as if we were "ashamed of the gospel" (Rom 1:16), as if we wished to abolish "the scandal of the cross" (Gal 5:11). How is it possible to understand obedience, poverty, chastity, and see in these a means of a fruitful apostolate, if one forgets that salvation comes to us by the Cross, and that the Passion leads to the Resurrection? Where do we stand on this point? Is it possible for each of us to say with St. Paul, "I have been crucified with Christ" (Gal 2:19)? No doubt, I will be told that in our age of "secularization," the world is not going to accept such a message. Yet, already at the time of the First Letter to the Corinthians, the Apostles preached "Christ crucified . . . foolishness to the Gentiles" (I Cor 1:23); but it is precisely "the foolishness of the proclamation" that God used "to save those who have faith" (I Cor 1: 21).

Is it not true we have too often yielded to the illusion of wishing to conform our style of religious life completely to that of the world? What then becomes of the "sign" we should be for others, the living preaching which our communities should give of the absolute demands of the Christian life?

These are some of the questions that occur to me as I take part in the preparations for this meeting in Bangkok. I am passing them on to you, asking you to put these questions to yourself.

In conclusion, I transcribe the following lines which Father Libermann wrote in January 1844 to the community of Cape Palmas:

> Keep in mind that the Sovereign Master lived a life of sorrow and that he underwent inexpressible pain for the salvation of the world. You are disciples of Jesus Christ! Don't seek to receive better treatment than your master. Never entertain fears because of the difficulties you encounter. It is not in your own name that you went to the missions nor is it you who will accomplish the work. The Master sent you and you are not alone; if you are faithful, he is always at your side. Hence, do not be fearful or weak in faith. An apostle of Jesus Christ must never be downcast in the presence of obstacles.[10]

---

10. *Letters to Clergy and Religious*, vol. 1, 241-242.

January-March 1973

MISSIONARY ZEAL

My dear Confreres,

My personal contacts with Spiritans everywhere, and especially in what are called mission countries, are enough to convince me of the missionary zeal of a great number of our confreres. Indeed, it is a great joy and encouragement for a superior general to witness such exemplary dedication in the case of the majority. However, I would like here to draw attention to two dangers which are by no means imaginary, two temptations to which some confreres seem inclined to yield.

On the one hand, in the case of some, there is the danger of a diminution of missionary zeal, perhaps even of its complete loss. This can be occasioned by one or other of a number of factors—the new difficulties which are being encountered in many countries; disappointments in one's apostolate; the questioning of the whole idea of mission and missionary work in various publications of unequal value; a lack of confidence and faith, perhaps, in the age-old mission of the church; or simply the very natural and understandable desire to find a quiet comfortable spot and settle down there—a desire, however, that is obviously quite incompatible with the missionary spirit. Nobody could deny that this has been known to happen in our Congregation, and that it is happening to some right now. Nor is it to be wondered at that many of us have felt this temptation. Yet, over against this, we must put the death-bed injunction of Father Libermann: " . . . to be fervent, fervent, always fervent."

It is to Father Libermann, again that I turn to describe the second temptation—that of imaginary zeal. In his Glossary on the Rule, he writes:

> There is rather a common illusion about the true nature of zeal. It consists in representing a zealous man as one who is always on the go, always on the move, always sensitively effervescent, always beside himself. This is the idea many have of St. Francis Xavier, but they are mistaken. For, although he had a heart that was burning with zeal, he also must have had a heart that was very calm. He spent long hours in mental prayer in which he united himself with his God. The soul of a missionary is sometimes portrayed as a boat forging ahead and whose sails are the spirit of the missionary, in which the holy Spirit is blowing. But this is not a right way of representing things.
>
> The sails are the will. With respect to the spirit of the missionary, he needs the grace of a pilot to direct his march. True

zeal consists in an ardent and pure charity, and therefore it is not in the imagination that we must seek it. The thing that distinguishes true zeal from a zeal which is merely the product of imagination is that true zeal is accompanied by calmness, gentleness, humility, and constancy amidst difficulties. Imaginary zeal, on the contrary, brings trouble to the soul and inspires sentiments of greatness and vanity. It makes missionaries compare themselves to the greatest apostolic men, and inspires great imaginary projects. Such men build castles in Spain and seek to attract the esteem of others. They like to talk about themselves. They also yield to bitterness. They sometimes are loud in their exclamations, attacking those whom they consider to be the causes of evil. They become discouraged when things are not successful according to their imaginary plans.

True zeal is peaceful, but it makes missionaries pray for souls which live in sin; it makes them offer themselves to God for them, so as to bear the pains resulting from those crimes. The other kind of zeal is not a sanctifying zeal.

While the truly zealous missionary is always more and more united with God and acts more and more for God, the other (who has imaginary zeal) goes farther and farther away from God because he is occupied only with phantasms of his imagination; he loses peace and has no more liking for mental prayer.[11]

I have quoted at length from this very special page of the Provisional Rule because it seems to me to be even more relevant than ever. Has there ever before been such an abundance of this imaginary zeal as in those who compare themselves to the most holy of apostolic men, and who propose new infallible methods of apostolate? They speak continually of themselves, and condemn bitterly all other methods, trusting more in their own "discoveries" than in the power of God and the wisdom of the church. On reading certain writings —sometimes produced by Spiritans—one gets the impression that the authors are the only ones gifted with clear-sightedness, and with wisdom. Their confidence affords no one else any merit—neither the Pope, the Bishops, nor their followers. All these are considered completely out-of-date people who are paralyzed by structures, cluttered up with traditions—the blind leading the blind, even egoists clinging desperately to their jobs.

---

11. *Provisional Rule*, 253-254.

Is it possible to describe true apostolic zeal? On this point, Father Blanchard has collected some marvelous texts by our Venerable Father.[12] As I cannot possibly recapture these sentiments fully here, I will just mention certain expressions which struck me forcibly: zeal is "the movement of the charity of Our LORD in us, a movement which leads us towards souls"; " . . . pure zeal is an effect of grace. It is a movement of God, therefore its action should conform to the activity of God." It can therefore be concluded that if "the exercise of our zeal causes us to be troubled, to be agitated, then it is obvious that nature is at work, this zeal is not the pure zeal of Our LORD, for where the LORD is present, peace is found." In the case of true zeal, one is at peace, both during and after the action. "False zeal leads to agitation at the time the work is being done and after its completion." "This is the test of true zeal, whether or not the soul is peaceful"; "wherever there is activism, tension or obstinacy, then it is the human spirit at work, and there is evil."

I cannot speak to you otherwise than did Father Libermann, if I am true to my mission. I pray that your zeal may be that of Our LORD acting in you, as it acts through the Spirit in the "completely apostolic" Heart of Mary!

April-June 1973

THE MESSAGE OF EASTER

My dear Confreres,

How could I speak to you at this time of Easter of anything else than Christ Risen? This year I had the joy of spending Holy Week and Easter among our confreres in Nigeria, and I could see for myself that the gladness of Christ is present and living in the new Christian churches to whose development Spiritans have contributed in no small way. I shared the joy of the people in the ordination to the priesthood of twelve young Nigerian Spiritans. Yes, Christ has risen and works in his church, spreading across the world his message of victory and happiness.

We are the witnesses of his message and as Spiritans our lives have no meaning without him. Already in the past I have often emphasized that our communities should manifest our Easter joy—that each of us

---

12. Blanchard, *Libermann*, vol. 1, 350-353, 351; 382-383.

should be a bearer and messenger of this joy to others. This is possible only on certain conditions.

We cannot be messengers of Easter if we do not believe in the church and its teaching, if we question even the most solemn affirmations of the ages-old faith of the church. On what will our joy be based if we undermine its foundations? A recent unanimous declaration of the International Theological Commission warns us against a false pluralism which can destroy the unity of faith and communion with the universal church past and present. How could we find joy in our Christian vocation—religious and missionary—if we are no longer certain of the resurrection of Christ, of the value of the religious life, of the meaning of church ministry, and of the priesthood? Recently some young Spiritans complained to me that their professors of theology gave them no clear teaching about their way of life. How can they feel at ease in their vocation if those who guide them do not know where they are going? "If the blind lead the blind . . . " In fact, however, all share this responsibility. I recently received an official request for laicization from one of our confreres who left the Congregation some time ago. As the first cause for leaving, his letter mentioned the infractions of the vow of poverty he had seen when he was a young bursar in one of our communities: priests keeping for their own use money received for ministry, old age, or war pensions, gifts from their families, etc. How can I show my joy in Christ Risen if I have recourse to such subterfuges to gain small unauthorized pleasures?

The same holds true as regards our bearing witness in obedience to the church. How many religious have confided to me their suffering—silent suffering since one is so quickly labelled a conservative or a progressive — because of the liberties taken with the liturgy? People come to participate in the Eucharist of the church and they are subjected to the innovations of Father So-and-So. Objectively, is it not the same state of mind that leads some to maintain the mass of St. Pius V and others to invent their liturgy? It is a question of personal preference which comes first. Do I, then, find it more joyful to celebrate the resurrection of Christ separate from his church, than in union with his church in the simplicity due to Christ (cf. 2 Cor 11:3)? And if I am in a position of authority, can I ask others to obey if I myself give public example of disobedience?

Speaking to superiors general on 25 May, Pope Paul VI reminded them that religious are among the principal agents in the efforts for renewal and conversion which the whole church is invited to make on the occasion of the next Jubilee. He underlined as special points for action: community prayer and private prayer, self-denial, a life of brotherly affection. And he added: "It is above all the example of a life characterized by spiritual joy and the unswerving will to serve God and men which today will still draw others to the religious life."

Have we within us this joy—the joy of Easter inseparable from the Cross, the joy of the suffering servant?

July-September 1973

BACK TO OUR ORIGINS

My dear Confreres,

I have just returned from what was unfortunately only a very short visit to Madagascar, Reunion, and Mauritius. As is always the case, I found there were some difficulties and some suffering, but I am glad to be able to say that the vast majority of confreres with whom I came in contact fully believe in their Spiritan and missionary vocation and are happy to devote themselves entirely to it.

For the first time, I had the opportunity of praying at the tomb of Father Laval in Mauritius and of seeing for myself the wonderful influence which his memory continues to exercise on the people of the Island: Christians, Muslims, and Hindus, are all united in their veneration of this man of God.

The evocation of Father Laval leads me once more to invite you to a new examination of conscience, or, perhaps I should say, to review your whole way of life. Are we as Spiritans sufficiently aware of our origins, of our continuity with a past from which we have received a particular inspiration and tradition of spirituality? Are we not tempted, at the present day especially, to try to reconstitute as it were, our Congregation, without sufficient reference to our past, our roots? Does it not happen frequently that Spiritans know little about the life and writings of Father Poullart des Places, Father Libermann, Father Laval, or at least that they have stopped reading their works? Two correspondents gave the following answer to a recent questionnaire sent by *Spiritus* (a mission journal) to our French-speaking confreres: "We would like to make a general comment on the questionnaire. We are amazed at the absence of any mention of Jesus Christ; there is no reference anywhere to the gospel, to the faith, or to the church." To this list I would add: "nor to Father Libermann, Father

Laval, etc. . . . ." Should we be consoled by the fact that non-Spiritans do not share our neglect? The most important work yet published on Father Libermann is by Father Blanchard, who is not a member of the Congregation. In the series of lectures organized by the French Studies Center in Rome for the year 1973-1974, Archbishop Jacques Martin will give a talk on the day-to-day life of Father Libermann on the occasion of his visit to Rome. A nun from the Philippines is at present preparing a thesis for the Regina Mundi Institute on the psychological evolution of Father Libermann. A Dutch priest, Father J. Kirkels, O.M.I., studying in Strasbourg, has submitted a thesis in Religious Science on the subject, "Project for Missionary Methodology in the 19th century, according to the Letters of Father Libermann to the Cardinal Prefect of Propaganda Fide."[13]

At the same time, I would like to mention some recent works by Spiritans which would seem to show that interest in our past is not yet completely spent. In German, I have just read Father Joseph Theodor Rath's *Geschichte der Kongregation vom Heiligen Geist*,[14] the first volume of which was published in 1972. I found I had a lot to learn from this book. Father J. Fitzsimmons has recently published a life of Father Laval in English.[15] Father Joseph Michel is also preparing a biography on Father Laval.[16] Those who already know the impressive *Claude François Poullart des Places*[17] by the same author will be glad to hear that this new work of his is to be published shortly. Lastly, I am very pleased to learn that the Editions S.O.S. in Paris are at present publishing a work by Most Rev. Jean Gay on Father Libermann, the title of which will be, *The Ways of Peace*.[18]

All this gives me great pleasure. However much one may prune or graft a tree, one cannot cut away all its roots or discount its previous growth. The same is true of the church itself, though too many tend to forget this. Congregations like ours are no different either. None of us should lose sight of this.

So, once more, no doubt, many will think that I am merely defending conservatism or even immobility. Must I also add, as I have so often done before, that a living organism must also adapt to its environment,

---

13. Kirkels later published a digest: Hollande, "*Méthodologie missionnaire de Libermann*."

14. Rath, *Geschichte*.

15. Fitzsimmons, *Father Laval*.

16. Michel, *Le Père Jacques Laval*.

17. *Claude-François Poullart des Places*, 2020.

18. Gay, *François Libermann*, 1974.

climate, everything which comes to it from outside, including pollution? At the risk of seeming to advocate "centralism," for which one of our provincials was recently criticized, I must say that this readiness to adapt constitutes in fact the deepest kind of fidelity—fidelity to the spirit of our Founders, fidelity to the Holy Spirit who has guided the church through the ages. Such fidelity, while always seeking to adapt to ever changing needs, is ever true to itself. It is with this fidelity that "we all attain to the unity of faith and knowledge of the Son of God, to mature manhood, to the extent of the full stature of Christ." (Eph 4:13). In the church — "all together"—the Congregation has its place and its role to fulfill, remaining faithful to what it is and what it has been since the time of its Founders, ready to listen to the Spirit whose name it bears and who is ever guiding the church, the one true church of Christ.

October-December 1973

ON THE HOLY YEAR

My dear Confreres,

Pope Paul has announced that there is to be a Holy Year which will be celebrated in all the dioceses of the world before reaching its climax in Rome itself in 1975. I do not intend to explain here the history of this practice which is, in any case, obscure, though it is linked up with the prophecies of the Old Testament (Lev 25; Isa 49:8ff. and 61:1-3) to which Jesus himself referred in the course of his public life (Luke 4:16-21).

In your various dioceses, the Bishops will no doubt have already made certain decisions concerning the celebration of the Holy Year. The first thing I would like to ask of you is to identify yourself with this effort which the whole church has been invited to make, and in so far as you can, to take an active part in the celebrations, in accordance with the directives of your bishops.

I would, however, like to go further. The Pope has on several occasions expressed clearly the significance he wishes this year to have, and it concerns us in particular, in our role as religious and missionaries, since it involves "a complete re-examination of our attitude towards two basic realities: the religion which we profess and the world in which we live" (Audience of 16th May, 1973).

We must first make this examination of conscience within the Spiritan communities themselves. Eight years after the close of Vatican

Council II, we must ask ourselves to what extent we have been faithful to its teaching or made a real effort to put into effect its guidelines and directives. We must ask ourselves in particular whether we have made a genuine effort to respond to the call made to us by the Council for reconciliation, peace, and justice, as this has been an essential aspect of the Jubilee Year ever since the time of the Old Testament. Even among us Spiritans, so much still needs to be done in this direction! I have often emphasized that we must learn how to accept one another in mutual love, such as we are, with our differences, our personal ways, and our preferences which sometimes conflict. How can we, in a divided world, be a sign of the unity, desired by Jesus Christ if we cannot succeed among ourselves in reconciling our differences of opinion and our disagreements on even minor points of detail? "But if you go on biting and devouring one another, beware that you are not consumed by one another" (Gal 5:15). On 15 April 1846, Father Libermann wrote to Father Lossedat:

> When you see that your confreres don't share your views, even when it is evident that they are not choosing the better course, it is preferable not to cling too much to your own ideas and not to contradict them. Allow everyone to follow his own ideas and accomplish the good in his own way and encourage them in doing so. This method will make them yield the maximum they can produce. They would have accomplished more if they had had other ideas but that can't be helped. They don't have those ideas. If you try to force them to adopt your own ideas, in general much less good will be accomplished. They will be upset and might even become discouraged. It is difficult to realize the importance of tolerance. We can't expect men to have identical views. When we are intolerant we arrest the good, we are always in trouble, we deprive ourselves of the necessary rest, discourage others and often discourage ourselves.[19]

It is my prayer that justice, peace, and reconciliation, the keywords of the Holy Year, should become a living reality in our whole Congregation, in each of our Provinces, in our missions, in our communities. Moreover, since this year involves an effort on the part of the whole church, these words must also find expression in our attitude towards all those who work with us among God's people. Too often, even among ourselves, there is an attitude of distrust, of criticism, if not of systematic opposition, to directives coming from the Catholic Church and to its

---

19. *Letters to Clergy and Religious*, III, 325.

official policy. It is so easy to condemn the defects of Christians, priests, Bishops, the Roman Curia, and the Pope. It is so easy to criticize when one does not oneself have to take decisions involving others who are in difficulty and looking for guidance. It is so tempting to take one's place in the small group of the "pure," of the "enlightened," and to look down from on high on the general mass of those who are simply trying as best they can to follow those whose responsibility it is to guide them! It is true that the Council and the Pope have called for dialogue at all levels, but abuse is not dialogue. I would like very much to see in all that Catholics, including Spiritans, write or say about their church, the same attitude of respect and mutual esteem which I have so often admired in our meetings with our Protestant brethren. I had the pleasure once again of witnessing such an attitude last week and I thank God for it.

Reconciliation, peace, justice among all: during this year of reflection and prayer, we must try more than ever to be the instruments of the mission of universal love which the LORD has entrusted to us. There is still so much injustice, so much misunderstanding in the world, so many people, often very near to us, who suffer from isolation and solitude. There are people near to us, perhaps even in our own house, who are only waiting for a gesture, a smile, a word of recognition and friendship from us. There are people like this all over the world whom Christ came to save and not one of them should be a matter of indifference to us. Our very distress at being unable to reach all, the terrible feeling of helplessness, should at least keep us constantly aware of the need to do whatever we can, to take all this misery into our hearts and into our prayers, and to work so that our Congregation may become an instrument ever more adapted to serving the poorest and most abandoned.

I now wish you a Happy New Year and a good Holy Year. Listen to the voice of the Pope inviting you to take part in it—that too is a "sign of the times.

January-March 1974

THE SYNOD AND THE GENERAL CHAPTER

My dear Confreres,

I have just returned from a long journey which took me to France, Ireland (for the provincial chapter) and Brazil (a seven weeks' visit to the five Spiritan Districts). The next issue of the C.S.Sp. Newsletter will contain a brief account of this visit.

On my return to Rome, I found awaiting me important preparatory documents for the forthcoming Synod which, as you know, will have for its theme Evangelization in the World of Today. You also know that the superiors general have elected me to be one of their representatives of the Synod, and that this choice has been sanctioned by the Pope. I am fully aware of the responsibility which has been entrusted to me, and I also think that preparation for this Synod concerns our whole Congregation in that its theme is so directly related to our Spiritan vocation. This is why I have chosen to deal with the subject here.

The theme of the forthcoming Synod is very wide. Evangelization involves, in the first place, those who have never been "evangelized." Our last General Chapter declared that "the Congregation shall give priority to the preaching of the gospel to those peoples or groups who have not yet heard it" (CDD, 5). This statement is very significant, much more so than one would think on a first reading. One of our Brazilian confreres told me recently that the large majority of his compatriots have never been "evangelized," even though almost all of them are baptized; and I think that the same could be said for virtually the whole of South America. This means that to the three billion people who, according to a general estimation, are still completely ignorant of the gospel message, must be added the many others who, though calling themselves Christians, have in fact as their sole link with the church a few external rites or customs which have merely been added on to other customs and rites which are often quite incompatible with the gospel teaching. Also to be taken into consideration are the numerous pagans who live in our traditionally Christian countries.

Yet, in spite of all this, some hold that the days of the mission are over, or else, see the mission task as merely one of social transformation. This, while no doubt necessary, cannot be identified with the integral gospel message which it is the church's mission to preach. On the other hand, it is true that in our missionary work today, problems appear in a different form than in the past. Among these problems are: the need for dialogue with the non-Christian religions; the need for the young churches to find their own identity and thus to break free from a certain number of external restrictions; the incompatibility of many social, economic, and political structures with the concept of justice as put forward by the gospel, etc... The missionary has to continually re-examine, with both courage and clear-sightedness, questions such as the relevance of his presence in a country other than his own; the means of integrating the message of Christ, without in any way distorting it, into a culture different from his own, the value of many customs inherited from the past which have lost their meaning in a rapidly developing world. The *aggiornamento* called for by the Second Vatican Council makes particularly serious, and often painful, demands on the missionary in his work.

These demands call once more for the self-denial which Father Libermann continually asked of his missionaries, i.e., the forsaking of our habits of thought and action, our comforts, our superiority complex, and our ever-recurring selfishness. Such self-denial enables the missionary to remain completely open to the call of the Holy Spirit working within the church and throughout the whole world. He is thus ready to forsake all like the apostles (Matt 19:27), to follow in the footsteps of Christ. This self-denial needs to be continually renewed, because it is not just once that one forsakes "house or wife or brothers or parents or children for the sake of the kingdom of God" (Luke 18:29). Throughout a whole life of poverty, celibacy, and obedience one must always be ready to go wherever God wishes, and bring the Good News of the kingdom of God.

Wherever God wishes, in the way that God wishes . . . It is the aim of the Synod to seek out the will of God and to try to interpret the signs of this will as shown in the world and the church. We should all join in this effort and ask ourselves how best we should approach evangelization in the present day. We should find out where are the poorest and most abandoned whom it is our vocation to assist. We must face these questions in view of our forthcoming General Chapter, and I shall be expected to give the Congregation's answers to the Synod of Bishops. I appeal to you therefore to give serious thought to these problems, and to play your part in the common research which the church has asked us to undertake. By preparing for the General Chapter you are also preparing for the Synod.

Above all, you must seek to hear the voice of God through prayer. On this point, I cannot do better than to repeat the constant teaching of Christ and St. Paul which we are so inclined to forget today: "we ought to pray continually" (Luke 18:1); "pray that (we) may not enter into temptation" (Luke 22:40); be "persevering in prayer" (Rom 12:12); "pray at all times" (Eph 6:18; 1 Thess 1:2); "pray everywhere" (1 Tim 2:8); "pray for one another" (Jas 5:16). How can we claim to spread the gospel, in which the mystery of prayer occupies such an important place if we do not bear witness to prayer in our lives? How can we teach others how to pray if we ourselves do not pray? It is my prayer, that on the occasion of our General Chapter, the Holy Spirit may come "to the aid of our weakness, for we do not know to pray as we ought, but the Spirit itself intercedes with inexpressible groanings. And the one who searches hearts knows what is the intention of the Spirit . . . " (Rom 8:26-27).

April-June 1974

ON THE EVE OF THE GENERAL CHAPTER

My dear Confreres,

This is the last General Bulletin you will receive before the opening of our General Chapter, so, too, it is the last opportunity for me to address myself to you as I have done so often previously in the Bulletin.

As I reflect over the six years that have just passed, I shall try to convey to you a few of my general impressions, as simply and fraternally as possible.

In the very first place I would like to say "Thank you." Thank you to God, thank you to everyone. It was only with the greatest apprehension that I accepted the post of Superior General in October 1968. Those who were present at the first session of the last Chapter will recall the particular difficulties involved in taking on the succession at such a crucial time, the controversial atmosphere, the deep diversity of varying and sometimes opposed currents of thought, which simply reflected a corresponding diversity throughout the whole Congregation. Furthermore, I was ill-prepared for the responsibility to which I was called, having no experience either of being a superior or of being on the missions. However, I considered it my duty to bow to the will of the Chapter, and I have endeavoured to serve the Congregation as best I could, relying on the Holy Spirit and the Virgin Mary. Everything has not been easy, and I recall many visits I have begun in deep distress and again others from which I have returned in grave anxiety. Confreres have sometimes complained about the shortness of my stay in their mission or territory, but I myself, I believe, was the first to suffer because of the impossibility of speaking personally to every individual, of listening to you at length, of bringing to each one, as I should have wished, the support and the joy of feeling understood and loved. Despite all this—leaving other things out of account—it is gratitude that is foremost in my mind. God has preserved me in joy, in confidence, and in peace. In very great numbers you have welcomed me in a way that has touched me profoundly; you have supported me and helped me; you have forgiven me my lack of knowledge and my mistakes. For this I would like to thank you very sincerely.

My second sentiment is one of confidence. It is impossible to ignore the sources of deep preoccupation that exist for us, as for all Congregations—numerous departures, among them some particularly sad ones; the uncertainty and disarray of quite a few in face of changes; the attitude of calling everything in question; the discussions on the nature of the religious and missionary vocation; the violent controversies in the bosom of the church herself; and then the impatience of others with the slowness of an evolution that they consider urgent and indispensable and that they wish to be much more deep and radical; the decrease in vocations and the impression that the way we live the religious and missionary life no longer attracts the young, etc. Despite all this I want to go on record as saying that I am full of confidence. Our Congregation is still very much alive, and I must bear witness that I have come across wonderful evidence of its vitality, of the generosity that animates the majority of its members, of their wish to be faithful to the ideal that inspired them to enter, their loyalty to the spirit that animated our Founders and so many more missionaries ever since. I believe in the future of the Congregation with the same assurance as I believe that many Spiritans want to be docile to the Holy Spirit who raised up in the church an Institute whose task remains important in our days in the service of the poorest and most abandoned. Doubtless, there are some adaptations we must make, faults to correct, structures to improve. The whole church invites us to this through the voice of her pastors, in Vatican II and since the end of the Council. I am convinced that we will be able to do all this, in the patience of faith. My conviction is not based on our cleverness or on our knowledge or on our sources of information, but on the certitude that there are still today in the Congregation precious stores of authentic spiritual life, of docility to the Spirit of God, of "fervor, charity, sacrifice," and that this will not remain without fruit.

This leads me to express a third sentiment that I have felt during these years of superior-ship: admiration at the generosity of so many Spiritans and at the spirit that animates them. Judging by the replies to the "Discussion Papers" sent out by the general council, it would seem that a good number call in doubt the existence of a special spirit of the Congregation, or at least they think it is impossible to describe or to define it. This is partly true; one cannot define, strictly, a mentality, a spirit;

just try to say in precise terms what the "French spirit" or the "English spirit" is and no Frenchman, Englishman will recognize himself in your definition. All the same, there exists a reality that one cannot deny, but that one experiences; that one tastes in the deepest levels of one's own self, that one recognizes spontaneously all the better and all the more deeply as one is more familiar with it and above all if one shares it. There is a spirit of the Congregation. It is more or less perceptible in our different communities and it may well be that it is, alas, hardly there at all in some of them. I have, for my part, very often experienced it with a great joy, this feeling of being in my own home, amongst my family, in my own surroundings, in a private world to which I belong and which I share: with those who are living in this community. In this feeling of belonging and of holding in common there are, obviously, many superficial and exterior elements. It may be remembrances or shared acquaintances, it used to be similarity in dress, in daily schedules, in common exercises, in prayers; and all this has its value as so many signs of deeper unity.

The Venerable Libermann, in the last two years of his life, tried on two occasions to describe what for him the spirit of the Congregation was. This we know from the notes taken by Father Lannurien in the course of the retreats preached at Notre Dame du Gard in August of 1850 and 1851.

> We have a special grace for the aim and the end of the Congregation; to this special grace there should correspond a certain uniformity in each one's dispositions and in the means of arriving at our common aim: this is what should be understood by the spirit of the Congregation (ND, XIII, 679).

This first text merely speaks of the aim and the end of the Congregation, the special grace involved, a certain uniformity in (interior) dispositions and in the means of arriving at this common end. There is also another text carefully preserved for us by Father Lannurien:

> The spirit of the Congregation consists in the simple and practical application of the precepts of evangelical perfection to our inner life, so that these become, by the guidance of God's grace, the foundation and the principle of our conduct in the religious and apostolic life to which God has dedicated us (ND, XIII, 684).

Emphasis is placed on the inner life "by the simple and practical application of the precepts of evangelical perfection," and yet this effort in our inner life is destined to become "the foundation and the principle of our conduct in the religious and apostolic life." Here then is something to startle those who rigorously insist that in our Spiritan life there exist two distinct aims, personal sanctity and the apostolate. I do not believe that these lines favor their thesis. Then Father Lannurien's notes go on:

> The Superior made a comment on each of his words; he delayed specially at the explanation of the word, simple, saying that simplicity should constitute our special spirit, that we should practice obedience, poverty, etc., with simplicity. He went on to emphasize that to practice the evangelical virtues with simplicity is to practice them to perfection, because it is to practice them in truth; it is to practice them just as they are conceived in the mind of Our LORD Jesus Christ (ND, XIII, 684).

Simplicity: this is the rejection of all that is complex, unusual, affected, showy, excessive—no spectacular poverty, no overdone or "victimized" obedience, no stupefying mortification. Above all it involves the sincere acceptance, without shirking, of all the demands of the imitation of Christ who was poor, obedient, chaste, and crucified, without noisy demonstrations or pointless dramatics, for the service of those who are the most disinherited.

All of this I have found in the case of many Spiritans, among those who are little talked about, but are ready to accept all, to go anywhere they are sent, to live the life of the poorest people, to devote themselves to the humblest tasks, and who never see in this anything extraordinary or abnormal, but on the contrary consider it perfectly normal; their lives, radiate joy and peace without their having specially tried to achieve this. I am not able, unfortunately, to say the same about all Spiritans. Yet there are men such as I have described, more of them than perhaps is thought. The spirit of the Congregation lives on; it must not be allowed to die.

CHAPTER TWO

VERY REV. FR. FRANS TIMMERMANS, C.S.Sp.

Superior General, 1974-86

VERY REV. FR. FRANS Timmermans, C.S.Sp., from the Netherlands, was professed on 8th September 1954 and ordained priest in 1959. He studied at the Ecole des Missionnaires d'Action Catholique et d'Action Sociale, Catholic University, Lille, France, 1960—1961. He was missionary at Mobaye, diocese of Bangassou, R.C.A. (1961-68) and Principal Superior of the Spiritans in R.C.A. (1968-74). He became superior general of the Congregation at the age of 39 on the 6th of September 1974 during the General Chapter held in Chevilly. President of SEDOS (a center for missionary documentation and study) in his first term, he was granted an honorary doctorate by Duquesne University in 1975. He was superior general for two terms, being re-elected for a further six years at the General Chapter of 1980. During his term of office the first computers were introduced into the generalate and during his second mandate, the first African confrere (Fr. Vincent Ezeonyia, C.S.Sp., later Bishop Ezeonyia) became a member of the general council. He spent one year studying at the University of Nijmegen, 1986-1987, before taking up a post in Harare as the Pastoral Co-Ordinator for Refugees, working for the Bishop's Conference of Southern Africa (IMBISA). Returning to the Netherlands he was on the Provincial Team, 1991-1993. From 1993-2001, he was the National Co-Ordinator for the Pontifical Mission Societies, then, 2002-2007, member of a Spiritan international team responsible for a group of intercultural parishes in Rotterdam. From 2007 he has been in retirement in the community of Gennep.

October 1974

TO ALL CONFRERES: TIMMERMANS

Dear Confreres,

I am pleased to have this first opportunity of making contact with you, particularly since the General Chapter wished the Superior General to be a unifying link between Spiritans. Many of you have taken the trouble to write to me personally. For this I thank you most sincerely. This token of your sympathy and confidence gives me courage, as also do the signs of attachment to our Spiritan family which are always more in evidence on occasions like this. I was struck by the missionary "bite" expressed in several letters and which was also a feature of the Chapter. Many thanks to everyone, including those who, without saying anything about it, quietly remembered the new team in their prayers.

I now find myself at the beginning of my mandate after having spent thirteen years in the Central African Republic. These were rich and full years for me. I shall miss being part of a young church that is still finding its way as I shall miss too the company of those among whom I lived. The same is true of all the new Assistants. You will appreciate that it is not without some apprehension that I approach my new task, and I have not yet gauged to what extent or in what ways I can be of real service to all. However, I would like this to be a service without limitations, assumed by the whole Council collegially. In this same issue, you will find a short article which gives some indications about the activities of the general council.

The Present Situation

When beginning something new, it is a good idea to take stock of the situation. What is the position of the Congregation now? What does it mean to us? What approach should we adopt at this new stage?

During the past six years, a rapid evolution has taken place in various sectors of the Congregation. The decentralization decided upon by the 1968 Chapter has had the effect of bringing into much greater evidence the individual characteristics and identity of each province. This evolution often took very different forms in the various Provinces. Within the

Provinces themselves even, different trends developed; a great diversity in life style, projects, options came to light, sometimes even at the cost of conflict.

There have been different reactions to this situation. Some feel that the Congregation risks losing the credibility of its "*cor unum et anima una.*" Others hold the opposite view that such diversity is itself a great richness which should not be lost at any price; they would like to combine the positive values of a large, international, diversified, missionary religious family with a genuine unity based on a common inspiration and common project. If there are some for whom the Congregation as a whole no longer acts as a source of inspiration, it is perhaps because for them this dynamic synthesis has not been sufficiently worked out in their Spiritan community.

Signs of Hope

Without in any way playing down existing difficulties, it may be said that one of the most important discoveries of this Chapter was the fact of a new unity observed as operating in practice. Diversity, which has greatly increased since 1968, is in many ways an illustration of the wealth of expression which can come from a common inspiration.

This common inspiration exists. It is expressed in the common end: the missions, the tasks for which the church has difficulty in getting workers. It is also exemplified in a certain attitude of simplicity and brotherliness, a type of apostolic commitment; things which are difficult to define but the constants of which are to be found scattered all over the Congregation. There is also a common source of spiritual inspiration which comes to us from our Founders and from the history of our Congregation.

It has been made clear that this diversity does not mean that each circumscription becomes a "water-tight compartment." On the whole, there has been more exchange and even mutual aid between the Provinces and Districts than ever before. This is a sphere where much can be done to reinforce our unity—reflection and analysis concerning what we have in common; exchange at all levels; active solidarity; greater coordination of efforts. You will find guidelines for all this in the capitular documents.

The Missions

On the level of the missions, research is going on everywhere and it converges on the same basic points. In general, Spiritans are aware of the transformations and profound changes which are taking place in the missionary sphere and have readily adapted to the new situation. Worth noting here are the efforts being made by the African Spiritans to discover a new African style of Spiritan missionary vocation. One of the participants at their Pan-African meeting spoke to us about it at the Chapter. Worthy of mention also is the extraordinary vitality of the young Province of Nigeria.

However, in many respects, the present evolution has also created new difficulties for the missionaries who find themselves faced with major problems which often have a serious effect on individuals or groups. They have a right to expect that the Congregation, while not of course solving their problems, should help them to open up the horizons again. More so than in the past, many expect that it should act as a support and a source of inspiration.

Religious Inspiration

The Chapter clearly expressed the importance it attaches to the fact that we are a religious family. A search for spiritual renewal is going on under many headings, and the numerous examples of an authentic religious life are so many signs of vitality. In certain Provinces and Districts, one can see in this field a real breath of new life.

Yet it is clear that in our sources of inspiration, in our way of looking at the church and in the way in which we live our faith, the differences go deep down. It is in this area, as in the outward forms of our religious-missionary life, that unity is certainly hardest to define.

The Chapter proved to us that it is possible for us to accept and love one another in spite of our differences, and to have great respect for each other. This is the line which our search for unity should take, but it does not mean that we just live side by side, leaving each other alone, putting up with the ways of others. In a community, there should be continual exchange between the members. While the theologies may be different, there is only one Gospel, and it is in connection with this that the confreres should be a support and a source of inspiration for one another.

One cannot expect a Chapter to solve everything. It is not a magic wand which can make all problems disappear. It is no longer possible for a Chapter to give precise and detailed directives regarding spirituality or organization of community life, nor to dictate what should be done. Where missionary research is concerned—and this is equally true of community life and personal relationships—there must be joint effort on the spot to find out what should be done. Those who wish to achieve this must be able to see each other, as they are, reflect together, evaluate together, as a group, the quality of our missionary integration, and the evangelical value of our life and prayer. This is being done already in many places and is proving satisfactory.

This spiritual and missionary renewal must be given its full importance. Why distrust systematically the new forms of prayer and sharing? We should not be afraid of new experiments as long as they do not cause divisions among people. So many people today are urging us to live the Gospel and its requirements in a more radical way and to open towards the future!

Prospects for the Future

The present state of affairs in our Congregation, as in so many others, is characterized by a number of elements which raise questions for the future—the ageing of our personnel, a decrease in the number of young people who join us and, at the same time, the departure of those who no longer feel able to share our life and work.

To live in hope means, first of all, not to close one's eyes to reality, but yet to face the future without losing heart. We must ask ourselves what are the causes behind this reality and see what can be done. Living in hope also means being responsive to all the signs of vitality which are in evidence.

In many Provinces, young people continue to join us, bringing with them their idealism, a new way of looking at things and new projects. It is important that we should have something to offer them, and that particularly where missionary research is concerned, we should keep our minds open and avoid any tendency to turn in on ourselves. If the missions present problems today, I think this is true mainly of a certain form of mission. So, even if in one particular country, a certain form of missionary presence comes to an end, this does not mean that the mission as such is finished. There are still so many fields open for evangelization! In addition, there are so many other missionary tasks to be carried out! How then can we integrate these old and new forms of mission into our program in such a way that they will set a challenge to the new generation? The encouragement of missionary vocations remains an important priority.

It should be added that the vitality of a province ought not be gauged exclusively according to the number of new admissions. Several Provinces, though they have no great increase in numbers, yet manage to courageously maintain a strong missionary drive. They contribute their share to the vitality of the Institute and this proved to be very considerable at the Chapter.

The research being carried out by the African Spiritans and by the young Provinces of Africa and Latin America is moreover a promise of a new missionary dimension, i.e., co-operation between churches, and the undertaking of first evangelization on the spot!

There are many other reasons why we can continue to hope: growing collaboration and cooperation between missionary Institutes, the internationalization of missionary teams which causes barriers to fall and frees new energies, the opening out of our communities and their wish to integrate into their environment. It is also heartening to note that other forms of missionary service are coming into being within the church to compensate for the fact that the missionary Institutes no longer have the same power to attract as before.

So, at the beginning of this new stage, we can look to the future with confidence and tackle it with courage.

A Tribute to the Outgoing General Council

I do not wish to end without expressing in the name of all our very sincere thanks to Father Lécuyer and all the members of the previous council. Much has been achieved during these past six years. 1968 was a new departure on new lines which have changed the life of the Congregation. The outgoing team competently and generously put itself at the service of all to help us adapt to this new situation. Many will remember with gratitude the help given to individuals and groups, through correspondence, or visits, and the support given at the right moment. Now that we are here in Rome, we are in an even better position to appreciate the work they have done at the cost of great personal sacrifice. They were not an anonymous team: they succeeded in giving a personal touch to their dealings with the Congregation. They deserve all our thanks for what they achieved during this difficult period. Let us wish them success in their new field of work!

November 1975

SIGNS OF A LIVING CONGREGATION

Dear Confreres,

This first mailing from our new *Information Service* provides the generalate team with the opportunity to furnish you with "an account of our stewardship"—a balance sheet, if you will, of our first year of service to the Congregation and to all its members. I wish that it were possible to give you, in a single letter, a bird's-eye view of the Congregation—its vitality, the quality of its services, the major problems which face us and the ways in which we are trying to face them, and finally, our progress in implementing the directives of the General Chapter. To attempt all this in a letter of reasonable length, though, would demand so much simplification that the result would have very little real meaning.

My report then of the balance sheet which we have tried to draw up in the general council will limit itself to a few points which seem to me to be of prime importance. Thus, I offer you here the fruit of our common thinking and discussion. I would like at the same time to acquaint you with the ways in which we hope to coordinate at our level, as far as it is possible, the common efforts of all.

Problems there are indeed, we find them everywhere. Here though I would rather discuss the experiences and the undertakings which highlight the signs of real vitality that are evident in our Provinces and Districts; signs which we saw in our visits and heard from many who have visited the generalate during the past year.

New Missionary Orientations

Even though we hear much talk and even see signs of the "crisis of the missionaries," I firmly believe that the great majority of our missionaries are happy in their work. Happiness is a relative thing though, so lest it be misunderstood, let me point out that I use the term here principally to indicate that they believe in their work, that they are confident that there is a future for that part of the vineyard where they are working, and that they have been able to maintain an open mind which allows them to be receptive to new realities.

First of all, it is evident that missionary priorities are becoming clearer: the incarnation of the message in the various cultures, living Christian communities, the formation of community leaders, vocations, the apostolate of youth, etc. Merely to list these priorities however does not guarantee their realization. It does seem clear though that wherever there are well-organized efforts in the local church, there is a rebirth of hope. Of all the priorities, the efforts to form Christian communities of more human and natural dimensions seem to be the most successful. The very work of organizing programs to train catechists and committed lay people is a source of growth and development for the missionary as well.

We are happy to note, too, the growing interest in renewal and continuing formation. On our part we want to do whatever we can to encourage it. In several Districts teams for continuing formation are already doing excellent work. With the help of the Provinces, we are trying to offer even greater collaboration in these efforts.

We are happy too to see the efforts being made to improve the quality of community life and the role being played by regional communities. While there are some places where the generation gap is painfully evident, there is much evidence also of mutual confidence. Younger confreres are finding inspiration from the experience of their elders who, by the same token, are accepting new experiences. Many are convinced of the need to deepen our missionary spirituality, so that prayer and the search for God may be an illuminating experience in our communities and the insecurity and uncertainty of these times may give new meaning to religious poverty.

We wish that these often-isolated efforts could be made better known and shared, not only in District and area meetings, but throughout the entire Congregation as well.

Missionary Animation

In several of our Provinces, missionary animation is the subject of much study and research so that a real connection might be made between our commitments and the new situation in the missions, on the one hand, and the consciousness and sensibilities of today's Christians on the other. They have not hesitated to assign young and capable missionaries to this work. As a result, communities are springing up which are becoming real centers of influence and are eliciting a quite positive response among the young. In other places, this missionary animation is taking place in a setting of broad collaboration between missionary Institutes, under the direction of the Bishop and within an inter-diocesan network. In these efforts the mass media and documentary studies drawn up with the collaboration of experts and discussion groups are being profitably employed.

Interesting initiatives are being taken to collaborate with organizations of lay missionaries which involve participation in their formation and even going with them, in fact as well as in spirit, to the countries to which they have been assigned.

All of these efforts take on forms that are as varied as they are interesting. More and more animation is tending to become a give-and-take process for mutual enrichment, breaking down prejudice and opening up new frontiers between peoples and between Christian communities.

I would like to underline here the importance we attach to the witness given by those missionary communities which serve as meeting places and centers of personal contact. Even the best of national and regional organizations cannot get along without them. The written and the spoken word, if it is to be effective, must come alive in the everyday lives of deeply committed people and communities.

To take missionaries who are working in our mission Districts to place them in works of animation must not be considered as a lack of fidelity to our missionary commitments. We must take into account the fact that the mentality of Christians in Europe and in America has evolved a great deal. No longer can we be excused from a serious study of the efforts of the various persons and groups engaged in helping the so-called Third World or of the expressions of spiritual renewal which we encounter.

We cannot give in to the fatalism that says "this sort of thing no longer catches on." It is equally wrong, though, to content ourselves with improvisations.

Spiritual Renewal

From many directions we hear news of Spiritan groups who are engaged in a deep spiritual renewal. Sometimes it is under the influence of the so-called charismatic groups, sometimes it takes the more classic form of contemplation or discernment of spirits, but always responding to a more and more clearly defined need for true spirituality. An excellent development indeed, but one which draws attention to a real problem. Many are complaining that there is a lack of spirituality within the Congregation, that the characteristics of a real religious community are not very much in evidence. There is a desire, on the one hand, to see the community as a place wherein we live out together that relationship with the living Christ which gives meaning to our vocation—what are we except in relation to Christ? On the other hand, however, one searches for a particular inspiration and missionary outlook, for the spiritual legacy of the Founder, and for the living tradition of the Institute. I/D (*Information and Documentation*) proposes to acquaint us with these experiences in renewal. The directives of the last General Chapter too can help us in responding to these needs. I wonder though if they have really been studied well or if there has been sufficient community discussion about them.

In response to the wish of the Chapter, a group of Spiritans from different Provinces is going to begin a study of the life and writings of Father Libermann. They will begin with themes based on the point of view of contemporary man, thus enabling the Congregation to draw, from its origins, inspiration for the present. The results of their studies, it is hoped, will be, published as a series of Libermann Papers.[1]

Spiritan Vocations

The problem of vocations is a real one and one with many ramifications. It is manifestly false, though, to conclude that Spiritan vocations are a thing of the past. While the situation varies a great deal from one country to another, it is encouraging to see Provinces which are multiplying their efforts and initiatives to awaken missionary vocations, doing it with great flexibility and often with positive results. (I hope that I/D will take up this interesting subject.)

Our young Spiritan Foundations in Africa are a source of great hope for the missionary future of the local churches and for the Congregation too. However, the falling off in the number of vocations must surely give us food for thought. If we cannot expect ever to see again large numbers of aspirants, as in the past, perhaps we should see in this a sign of Providence.

What we must maintain is that there will always be, in every section of the church, a number of persons who commit themselves for life to

---

1. They eventually appeared as a series of *Spiritan Papers* [Ed.]

the service of the church's world-wide mission. Admitting that we can no longer propose to our candidates that they remain for life in the service of a particular mission, we must at the same time search for ways to clarify and to define the meaning of mission today. In the past, we know that mission meant to go for good to a mission country. Perhaps that is why certain missionaries who cannot return to that particular country find it so very difficult to become missionaries somewhere else, even in Europe or America. The last Chapter stated clearly that we cannot think of mission in purely geographic terms. Some apparently have concluded from this that now, whatever one does, falls somehow under the specific purpose of the Congregation. This is certainly not true and I hope to treat of this at length in a subsequent letter.

The idea of mission which we propose must, above all, focus on a universal service, transcending the boundaries of local church or nation. It is concerned with mutual assistance and exchange among Christian communities anywhere in the world. It involves bringing the Good News to those who have not yet heard it, true, but now in company with missionaries from the churches of the Third World. It is the recognition of the responsibility of the Christians of the First World for the true liberation of all men. It is a mission of many dimensions and one that will demand great mobility. We must prepare people to work in the Third World for as long as they are needed, and then be ready to be called somewhere else. And in all, and over all, there must be our own Spiritan charism for "work among the poorest, among those for whom the Church has difficulty in finding ministers."

Is there any place in an aging Congregation for young members? I think that we must begin to study how, within the Congregation, we can foster a climate favorable to their growth. Our younger men have much to contribute to such a study and we are presently exploring ways and means to make possible an international meeting of our younger confreres. Perhaps they will be pleasantly surprised to find that they are more numerous than they thought as they meet together to share their experiences and their hopes for the good of everyone. Such a meeting would be a kind of "Spiritan Congress" of the type already held by several of the Provinces. It should be obvious though that all of this will have little real effect unless there is a constant effort at personal conversion to a true missionary spirituality, and unless there is, on the part of all, a real openness and a willingness to listen. Nor should we ever forget that the Congregation's constant concern must extend to all its members. I am afraid that it can be said, regretfully, that there are ways in which our older confreres are being neglected. Our responsibility towards them is definitely not fulfilled merely by taking care of their physical needs.

A Final Word

These then are some of the items on our balance sheet which I think merit our attention and our study. I present them to you, regretting that the limitations of space make it necessary to pass over other signs of our vitality. May our common consideration of all of them though, help us to face the future with great hope in our hearts.

In Ireland, last Summer I heard a proverb which we could all do well to remember in these troubled days: "God never closes a door without opening a window at the same time!"

I pray that all of you will be successful and happy in your work.

DECEMBER 5, 1975

Dear Confreres,

As Christmas and the New Year approach, the generalate team and I offer you our sincere and brotherly good wishes. At this season our thoughts go out to all our Spiritan brothers at work in so many places in our "common project" of service to the gospel and especially of service to the poorest of God's people. At this time too, it is a pleasure to recall my meeting with so many of you, not only while on visitation, but also here at the generalate. I look forward too, to meeting all of you eventually.

At this Christmas of 1975 and during the year to come, I would like to speak with you of something that is close to my heart, our spiritual renewal.

During our general council meetings in October, we reflected deeply on the life style of the members of the Congregation, on their expectations and on their needs. It was during the retreat though, with which we concluded our meetings, that the prime importance of spiritual renewal was brought home to us. Reflecting together on the action of the Holy Spirit in the mission of the church and in our missionary community and rereading the writings of Father Libermann, we rediscovered, as it were, what was said in the Chapter of 1974: that spiritual renewal must be the first and most important priority not only for us as an animation team, but also for the entire Congregation.

Our conclusions were confirmed by a recent event. At the September Symposium of the Bishops of Africa and Madagascar (SECAM), in which I participated, over and over again, the Bishops stressed the importance of living witness in preaching the gospel. "The Church," they said, "cannot become an instrument of salvation for the world, except insofar as she herself is caught up in the life-giving Spirit of Jesus, converted from evil and led to the doing of God's will." They asked moreover, that religious communities working in Africa be, above all else, communities, who in their love for their people and their solidarity with them, give witness to their faith and to their hope.

Certainly, we are, first and foremost, a community alive with faith in Jesus Christ and his universal mission. This is our basic conviction, antecedent to all our pondering on our mission, and stronger than all the uncertainties of the present moment! When all our missionary methods have been tried, when the future of our work seems uncertain, we are forced to admit that we are, in the final assessment, witnesses to Jesus Christ, living at the heart of the mystery of his death and resurrection.

I would like here to recall some of the aspects of this spiritual renewal of which we see so many signs today in the Congregation.

1) Evangelization and the Action of the Holy Spirit

We speak here of the belief, and I would even say, of the experience, that the Holy Spirit is at the heart of our mission and the source of all our missionary commitments. In trying to better define our own spiritual identity, we are touching on a point that concerns us particularly, for our very name, "Spiritans" invites us to define ourselves primarily in our relation to the action of the Holy Spirit.

It should be particularly appealing to us that the church in our day is becoming increasingly more conscious of the presence and the action of the Spirit within her, calling forth a deep and profound renewal. It was impressive to see the African Bishops dedicating a whole day of the symposium to reflecting on the action of the Holy Spirit in evangelization.

For us, this openness to the Spirit is beautifully set forth in the life of Father Libermann and in his writings. His writings on the New Testament can really help us to better see how the Holy Spirit is at the heart of our life since he is at the heart of our mission, the same Spirit who inspired, directed, and pushed forward the missionary community of the Acts of the Apostles.

This quite naturally leads us to an identification with the poorest, to a willingness to listen to the men and women who speak to us since it is the Spirit who is speaking in them, as little by little, we learn to let ourselves be challenged by their lives. There are unexplored riches here, I think, for our Congregation; riches which could be a truly unifying element in our spirituality, sealed, inspired, and made bold by the Spirit.

2) The Missionary Community

It has been of great interest to me to note how many confreres spoke to me this year of the importance they attach to the community, which according to our Spiritan tradition, is the center of our missionary life. We are not missionaries as individuals but rather missionary communities.

The renewal of community life must be a constant concern of all our Provinces and Districts. We well know the obstacles that we will encounter, but we still feel that on-going spiritual and missionary renewal must take place here. For it is only where there is true brotherhood and mutual support that prayer, reflection, and common endeavor are possible. Only there can we form a true judgment on the missionary value of our work. All of this, taken together, constitutes the common witness to our beliefs that is required of us.

Brothers, insofar as we are concerned, we of the generalate team propose to place this spiritual renewal at the heart of our lives and at the core of the service asked of us by the Chapter. We propose this to you as well, so that all of us, together, may better serve the gospel, and the demands of the times in which we live.

Let us pray for each other. Finally, to all, a Merry Christmas and a good New Year.

January 1976

TOWARDS REDISCOVERING LIBERMANN

Dear Confreres,

With the approach of February 2, this issue of I/D is intended as an invitation to all of us to ask ourselves what place Father Libermann really occupies in our Spiritan family and to what extent he is or can be a source of inspiration for us, as Spiritans, in 1976.

I can only imagine your reactions to the issue of I/D. Some with no particular emotion, will simply recognize a situation of fact, with which they are already familiar. Others, especially those who in their life and work have discovered Libermann as "an artisan of spiritual renewal at the heart of the mission of the church" will be shocked or deeply disappointed to learn how little attention is paid to our Founder in large areas of the Congregation. Some will be surprised that this issue ends with a rather general question, and may well ask if the generalate team itself might not be too embarrassed to reply to the question proposed in our original inquiry.

By no means is this issue of I/D meant to be the end of the matter. On the contrary, it is a first step, inviting all of us to give careful consideration to the question, "What does Libermann mean to us today"? So that we may begin with the realities of the actual situation and not indulge in any wishful thinking, we have published a summary of the replies we received to our questionnaire. Like all summaries, it is necessarily incomplete, since we have not included evidence available from other sources. We still believe though that what we publish here is probably a fairly representative cross-section of opinion throughout the Congregation. It certainly invites us to consider the matter further and might even shock us into action. Basing ourselves on this summary, we have formulated the questions which you will find in "Our Comments."

However, I would like to think that we can take a still further step. For myself, I must say that I was deeply disturbed on reading the present report. Its implications must be faced up to, by me personally, and by the whole Congregation. How can we allow such fantastic riches, which we need so badly, to remain "buried in a napkin"?

You may well ask what use this treasure can be to us? Our missionary witness cannot derive its vitality from ideas alone, but needs to find inspiration in lived experiences. Furthermore, we are living today in an evolving situation, which is at once enriching and disconcerting. If we are to maintain a real liberty of spirit and fidelity to the basic values of our personal and community life, we need a center, a focus of unity in our life. Dispersion leads to dissolution, especially when it is a question of our inner selves. Certainly, the gospel contains all that is essential. We can be helped though to better live out the gospel in our own lives, when we see it reflected in the hearts and lives of other men.

Fortunately, such models are not lacking today. If in our search for a more authentic faith, we compare ourselves to other Congregations, and allow ourselves to be challenged by their resemblance to us, this is a good thing. The exclusiveness, which many fear when we speak of "Spiritan Spirituality" is not at all what we have in mind, even if it were remotely possible.

On the other hand, it would be wrong to adopt the principle that it would be better to dispense with someone who had inspired many generations of Spiritans, and who along with others, was at the origin of a missionary movement which marked a whole epoch. Obviously, Libermann cannot have the same impact on us that he had on the first generation of Spiritans. It has been said that "his role as founder belongs to his own particular historical period." But, is there nothing more to be said? Can we cut ourselves off from our roots, from a whole living tradition, as we set out forging our future?

I have spoken of "hidden riches" and indeed, it may well be that the teachings and writings of Father Libermann are to a large extent inaccessible to many. However, what is important is not a theoretical synthesis, but the basic intuition which he sought to express, his manner of living, the spiritual and missionary adventure which he shared with his brethren, the gospel written in his heart and in his life.

Someone remarked to me one day, "Why be so concerned with difficulties of language and expression? When we see how those first Spiritans lived, there is certainly something which makes us dream, which makes us dare—a radical and total generosity based entirely on faith and the gift of self to others, to the poorest. Do we still have this same generosity today"? It is this "something" that we speak of when we speak of rediscovering Libermann.

Even though many barriers remain, it is true that it is quite possible to be a real disciple of Libermann without knowing a lot of details about him; if there are "anonymous Christians," so there are surely many "anonymous Spiritans"! To become a more explicit one, though, can only be beneficial, but because of the obstacles, we need help in this effort. While this issue is being printed, the Spiritan Studies Group was holding its first meeting at Clivo di Cinna. We have great hopes that they will be able to help bring us into contact with Father Libermann and his experiences in the spiritual and missionary fields and to relate this to our contemporary background.

It is my sincere wish that every Spiritan will be willing to take the necessary efforts to share in this discovery.

February 1976

OUR MISSIONARY IDENTITY

Dear Confreres,

This issue of I/D proposes, as a new theme for your reflection, "Our Missionary Priorities and Commitments," a theme chosen as part of our common effort to promote a better understanding of the meaning of mission today. Such an understanding, we feel, is necessary not only in view of a better missionary service but also so that through this service we might know who we are and what is demanded of us because we are missionaries.

As in previous issues, we are concerned, not with presenting great theories, but rather with summarizing for you what our confreres have been trying to discover and to live in many parts of the world. We have given you clippings, as it were, from the very complex, total picture of the Spiritan missionary presence. In this way, we hope to seek, together with you, the roads over which, by many different experiences, we must travel toward renewal, and the recovery of our identity.

Presenting such clippings, though, always involves the risk of a simplification which could betray the reality, since the reader cannot reconstruct the background which forms the context of the experience, the complete ensemble of people and things, the moments of crisis, or experiences which are still in progress. Then too, an approach like this might seem too optimistic, lacking as it does a larger frame of reference in which we can also see, as one confrere writes, "the limitations and the setbacks, the moments of desperation, which risk destroying the credibility of these testimonies as a real point of reference for us."

Believe me, we are quite conscious of this risk. We too hear of "the limitations and the setbacks and the desperate situations." We meet them face to face on our visitations and in our correspondence too and, sooner or later, the question always comes up, "who are we as missionaries; what is our mission today"? Anxieties and uncertainties like these cannot be satisfied with easy answers.

What answers are we able to give? There is certainly an abundance of literature today, analyzing the contemporary mission situation, its causes, its concerns, the anxieties it engenders, and the new methods in which it proposes. I/D has no intention of substituting for these; studies like these are necessary to properly orient our thinking and our dialogue. It seems to us that the answer to our missionary identity is to be found elsewhere.

The elements of a response are to be found in the Provinces and Districts, in the situations and the experiences which can inspire others and help them to discover their own direction.

Through our many and varied contacts and because of our more universal view of things, we are able from our vantage point to see where these discoveries are taking place and in what ways these signs of life help us better to understand the meaning of mission today.

When a person has been doing the same thing for many years, or when he comes up against a completely frustrating situation, he is sometimes tempted to identify mission with the situation in which he finds himself. We often lack, in the apostolate, the broadness of vision which allows us to see these things in relation to the total picture. We feel that it is the task for l/D to bring together the elements necessary to broaden our view; to give opportunity for the voices of many lands to be heard, voices which in their words of encouragement can open new perspectives. Thus, mission takes on a community dimension which transcends the boundaries of the region of the diocese where we are working; and to belong to a missionary Congregation, perhaps, little by little, can take on a deeper signification.

We make no pretence here of giving a final answer; we are searching for it with you. What we are doing is gathering and presenting testimonies which in themselves are elements of the answer.

We are aware too that a simple presentation like this is not enough. All our considerations should lead to a plan of action which would favor a way out of our frustrations and allow us to hear more clearly the new calls to mission which today are everywhere apparent.

We hope to speak of this at greater length in subsequent issues of I/D and to try our best to bring it to realization by the efforts of our generalate team. We believe in our mission because so many of our confreres on the missions, in the midst of the struggle, and despite the difficulties of each day, believe in it. How we wish that this faith would be shared by all.

March 1976

MISSIONARY MOBILITY

Dear Confreres,

It seems that today, the quality we need most, and which we so often lack in missionary Institutes, is mobility. We need that mobility which enables us to take a new approach to our situation, mobility in the sense of being able to "fold our tents," to take up new duties when the call comes to go further, mobility which resists the temptation to "throw in the towel" and declare that we're completely defeated.

Happily, there are many examples of that mobility. Our older men, for instance, who gladly decide to take updating courses are a case in point. Then too, there are the places where the regrouping of missions, because of lack of personnel, suddenly transformed settled parish priests into members of mobile apostolic teams, responsible for the animation of several communities in charge of laymen. We could speak, too, of those, who even beyond middle age, in answer to some new appeal, have left to others the task of completing works they have begun, to go somewhere else, to learn a new language and to take up work in an entirely different environment. There are communities too in the Provinces which are experimenting with new types of missionary presence, often in common with other Congregations. All these are signs of the new mobility.

We could easily cite contrary examples as well, signs of dull, depressing, and suffocating attitudes. How many there are who complain that their every enthusiasm is blocked and restrained?

Certainly, we must recall the flexibility of the first Spiritans. True, they saw more clearly where they were going, the meaning of their mission was clearly defined, even if it was unconsciously marred by some ideas that were not entirely evangelic. In addition, they were encouraged by universal approval of a Christendom which understood and supported them, nor were they plagued by the questions and doubts of today. They had a missionary mystique though, which although different perhaps from ours, still has a great exemplary value.

No one wishes to minimize the limitations under which we labor. Limitations imposed by age, aptitudes, formation, and by the very complexity of our situation. Nor would anyone dare to cast a stone at the disillusioned and discouraged missionary, since no one really knows what he has been through. Often he has received scarcely any help at all. Well may we ask, just how much of a source of inspiration the Congregation was for him.

We simply cannot give up though, faced as we are with accomplished facts. The mission is there. The appeals are there in all their number and variety. We simply must recapture our missionary mobility.

How do we go about it? There are no formulas or ready-made answers. The causes of our lack of mobility, though, point out the direction in which we may find an answer. They seem to suggest three questions.

First there is the question, which, recurring constantly as it does, seems to be central: *which mission?* Or, if we push it to the heart of the matter, the question becomes, *which church?* Have we completely understood, I wonder, that to be missionaries today, we cannot bypass Vatican II?

Following this and closely related to it is the question: *what of the people who received us; what of the deep and irreversible changes which are shaking the countries where we work*, changes through which we are living at the cost of severe trials and setbacks?

These are not easy questions, nor can they resolve themselves in a single day. We are not alone in facing them though, nor are we without resources, although we are often badly equipped. Updating courses and continuing formation are not miracle remedies, but they can be a great help.

And finally, along the same lines, we can ask ourselves, *in the name of what faith, what internal dynamism?* The answer perhaps depends on the image of the church which we have conceived for ourselves. It is our vocation to witness in our poverty, both as believers and sinners, to the hope that is in us. "Our strength," a missionary wrote me recently, "is in the humble power of Christ crucified, Christ the servant, exposed defenseless to be received or rejected by men." That is not a theoretical answer. It is one that comes from the experience of a renewed faith, a faith both personal and communitarian.

Summing it all up then, it is to persons and to communities that we must all look for an answer to these questions. The large community of the Congregation cannot do it in your place. But it can, and ought to be the center where all our efforts are united, the center where calls for help as well as the signs and the experiences which mark the way are received and passed on. Despite the difficulty, this is an eminently worthwhile task to undertake together.

April 10, 1976

I/D INFORMATION-DOCUMENTATION.
SPECIAL EDITION: ANGOLA

My Brothers,

A few days ago, we received a telegram, fifteen days late, stating simply: "Father Martinho Thijssen and Brother Afonso Rodriguez killed in Caconda." The details came later; they were shot down, murdered. I knew these men personally, and as I remembered their faces, all the terrible horrors of this senseless war, supposed to be finished, came home to me. Today the Congregation mourns their deaths. The deaths of these men witness not only to their faithfulness, but also to the faithfulness of so many of our missionaries who stayed with their people in times of danger.

Every week Father Thijssen used to write to me from Tsumbe in Namibia giving me every bit of news he could get about the missions. I met him in Caconda this time last year, he was well over sixty, a nervous and fearful little man. When the war progressed, tension and insecurity increased in that isolated corner of the bush, and he crossed the border into Namibia, where he worked for more than four months in the refugee camps there; he served too as a liaison between his Province and the confreres inside Angola. Now and then he would cross over the border for a short visit. Quite recently he returned to stay permanently in Caconda, despite his 69 years.

Brother Alphonse Rodriguez stayed in Caconda with some Sisters throughout the war. He considered it his duty to stay, so he stayed. He was a solid, conscientious man, 62 years old, and he had worked in Angola since 1938, as had Father Thijssen. He found great satisfaction in preaching and teaching catechism. When the tragedy struck, there were again three confreres in the mission; Father Marquez de Sousa had arrived only six days before, and he escaped death by a miracle.

Are these just two more deaths among the thousands who have already died in this war? People often feel that the deaths that happen just before the end of a war are the most tragic of all; they are the deaths that show how stupid all the others were. One feels like saying that history is written with the blood of victims and that it is a history which makes no sense at all.

Only the Paschal Mystery can make sense out of war. The cross on which the Innocent One died to make life triumph stands at the center of human history and gives it meaning. It is in the paschal mystery which we are about to celebrate again that the sad history of war and death is reversed and redeemed, that war, these deaths, this loss of liberty are the price humanity pays for its progress. Let us hope that the deaths of our two confreres, of the two diocesan priests, and of so many Angolan Christians will be the harbingers of an Easter which will be God's answer to the people of Angola. Already that Easter is manifesting itself in a faith which is stronger than the test to which it was put and in the life of a people lifting itself up and beginning to live again.

These deaths should remind us that we must ourselves enter into the death and resurrection of the LORD, that the deepest meaning of our missionary work is to bear witness to the paschal mystery.

In closing, may I take this sad occasion to renew my appeal to all the members of the Congregation and to their sense of common responsibility. The Church of Angola is lifting itself up from the ground. A new Angolan episcopate has defined the pastoral priorities and the lines of action for the future. One of the great needs is that a more diversified and more international group of missionaries come to work in Angola. Let us hope that we can find volunteers in our own Congregation, who after the necessary training, will be able to take their place with the small group of confreres now working in Angola.

The Tragedy at Caconda

Extracts from a letter to Father Timmermans from Father Serafin Lourenco, principal superior of Lubango (formerly Sa da Bandeira).

> On March 9, I brought young Father de Sousa to his new appointment at the mission of Caconda to help Father Thijssen and Brother Afonso. Caconda, with three Spiritans, would be the best-staffed mission in the district. Most of the other missions have only one Father, who is usually an old man. But the happiness of Caconda was not to last long. On March 17, Father de Sousa came to tell me the terrible news. A bandit, dressed in military uniform, came to the mission on March 16. He spoke Portuguese but not Umbudu and said that he had spent 15 years in Cuba. He said that he wanted the mission to take care of a little boy and a girl. He visited the convent first and discussed the little girl. Then he went to the mission and mentioned the boy. He spoke to Father Thijssen first and then to Father Sousa.

But the orphanage was the responsibility of Brother Alfonso so he was called also.

The four of them were talking on the veranda when suddenly the man's eyes blazed in fury. Father de Sousa thinks he might have been a drug-addict. He screamed, "you Fathers are all thieves," and fired several rounds from his gun. Father Thijssen fell and then Brother Alfonso. Father Thijssen was still alive and cried to the man, "stop that, my brother." "So you are still alive, are you," he replied, and fired another round, killing Father Thijssen. He then sprayed the place until his gun was empty. Father de Sousa was lying beside the dying Brother Alfonso listening to his groans. When the man was gone, Father de Sousa ran down to the convent and went with a nursing sister and some people to report the matter to the Cubans in Caconda. They came in force and searched the area. It is strange that they did not find him because he had been seen on his way to the mission and also on his way back, carrying rosaries, money, and other things he had stolen. "The thieves are dead, so God is dead!" he was shouting.

I would have liked to transfer Father de Sousa, but since that would leave this important mission without a priest, he decided to stay at risk to his life, for the murderer was still at large in the area. The Christians agreed to guard the house to protect the Father and the Sisters.

We have shared the joys and the sorrows of the people of this area for over a hundred years now. The Congregation should not abandon this country after a war in which so many people have died, just at the moment of its independence. Father Thijssen was Dutch, Brother Afonso, Portuguese, representatives of the two countries who have contributed most missionaries to Angola. By killing them, the bandit apparently hoped to kill God too. But God is not dead, and from their death, as from the deaths of so many Angolans, united with the death of Christ on the cross, will be born the new Angola.

President Agostinho Neto and the Bishops of Angola

Some days before the murder of the two Spiritans, on March 9, 1976, the Bishops of Angola were received, at the close of their annual meeting, by the President of Angola, Agostinho Neto. The President said:

> This meeting is a happy one for me, for the members of my government, and for the militants of the MPLA. It confirms what

we have already noted during our visits in the Provinces that the church representatives have effectively assisted us in gaining our basic objective, independence.

I do not have to repeat here what we know already—that the members of the church have played their part in the fight for the freedom of our country.

There are among you some church representatives who for a long time were unable to live in Angola. They had to live abroad, in prison or in forced residence in other regions, only because they had taken part in the struggle for independence.

It seems to me that beginning from this group, the main body of the church is on the way to renewing itself. The church has taken a new direction and is becoming more Angolan. This is not because the people who represent the church today have black faces, but because those who represent it today are more rooted in Angola than those who have left the country and because they want to take part in the marvellous changes which are going on around us.

At this moment, I think that we can be absolutely sure that the Catholic Church will continue to help in the reconstruction of our country. We are still at war, for our enemies have not yet finished their destructive work. Our country needs the help of everybody. I have great hope that your Excellencies will make the greatest possible contribution to help us through the difficulties we are experiencing at present.

I thank your Excellencies for your visit which comes at the end of your important meeting during which you have without doubt taken important decisions for the church and for our people of Angola, decisions which we trust will be put into practice in the near future.

Other News from Angola

During their meeting, which began on March 9, the Episcopal Conference of Angola decided that the return of the missionaries and the arrival of new personnel should be arranged between the people concerned and the Bishop, with the principal superior as intermediary.

The President of the Republic has promised that entry-visa applications will be dealt with as soon as possible under the circumstances.

With the victory of the MPLA, the period of the open war is over. However, according to the statements of the leaders of Unita and FNLA, guerrilla war will continue in the bush.

Little by little, things are getting back to normal. The postal services and the telephone systems are working again and business is beginning to pick up. However, the effects of the war on the political, social, and economic life of the country will be felt for a long time to come. Food, medicine, and fuel are still in short supply. Transport is difficult, and there is still an air of insecurity which will take time to heal.

The past months have been very difficult for the missionaries, as for all the people of Angola. Everyone has lived, in various degrees, though anxiety and uncertainty. Four priests are dead and some have been beaten. Everywhere houses have been pillaged or destroyed, including some of the mission houses and churches. However, it must be said that these attacks were isolated incidents and that the responsible authorities came to the rescue if they heard of the matter in time. In general, the mission and the missionaries were held in respect and the local people were friendly and cooperative.

Luanda has already lost its war-time appearance. Radio-Ecclesia, unlike the other radio stations, has not been nationalized and is doing good work. Huambo, formerly Nova Lisboa, fell to the MPLA without a fight on February 8. Communications with other regions and with outside world are still difficult because of extensive war damage. Planning groups have arrived from Luanda and are studying reconstruction. The seminaries are closed but our novitiate is still open. It is hoped that this month (April) will see the reopening of schools and seminaries.

The Bishop of Bie (Silvan Porto) says that he has only 12 priests (4 diocesan, 6 Spiritans, 2 Redemptorists) but that missionary work there continued quite normally.

Baptism, Pont-Sondé, PANO

April/May 1976

INTERNATIONAL TEAMS

Dear Confreres,

Since, the last General Chapter, there has been much talk in the Congregation about "international teams" as a new form of missionary effort better responding to contemporary demands. Actually, the Chapter instructed the general council to proceed with the establishment of such teams in collaboration with the Provinces and Districts (GA, 27). Several appeals to this effect have appeared in I/D, and we have already begun work with the Provinces on the subject. However, I feel that what we are talking about isn't at all clear to everyone, why we need these international teams and what forms we intend for them to take.

As a consequence of the former practice of confiding specific territories to specific Institutes, missionary personnel tended to be organized in large national groups, all of the same Congregation. This was certainly the case with us with our large English, French, or Portuguese speaking Districts. For some time now, though, missionaries have felt that a greater diversity in Institutes as well as in languages would be a more eloquent witness to the Catholicism of our mission and an evangelistic approach consonant with the desires of churches who welcomed us (GA, 17).

Then too, these large Districts, firmly attached as they are to the Provinces which supply them with personnel, risk the danger of forming "mini-Congregations." It is always to the mother-Province that the Districts turn for personnel and financial aid. Nor can we forget the admirable sense of responsibility that the Provinces have always shown toward their own Districts.

For years now, this system has necessarily divided us, above all, into linguistic zones. The different groups have developed missionary styles very often quite diverse. And now with the new emphasis on exchange and dialogue affecting the entire field of mission, we too feel the necessity of a wider exchange. "We must all intensify collaboration at all levels, favor the exchange of personnel, give information, and communicate experiences." (GA, 28).

Besides, the Provinces today are finding themselves increasingly without the means necessary to assure effective stewardship of their Districts (for example, the case of Portugal in respect to Angola).

It is well to remark here, however, that for some time now a certain internationalization has been taking place by the fact of the presence in some Districts of small Spiritan groups from Provinces other than the original mother-Province. Several Districts are already quite diversified in the composition of their personnel.

Beside the problem of blocs, there is an additional problem as well. New needs are becoming apparent and translating themselves into new appeals, often quite varied, but most often concerning commitment to a new mode of missionary endeavor. More often than not, these appeals are addressed to the generalate rather than to the Provinces, because the Provinces by and large do not have the means to assume such projects by themselves. On the other hand, we are experiencing the fact that many in the Congregation are sensitive to these new demands.

A good number of confreres are turning to us to seek opportunities for a type of missionary commitment which their own Province cannot offer. This is often the case, for example, in a District when the development of the local church has progressed to the point where strictly missionary work has come to an end and a progressive disengagement is beginning.

Viewing the extent of the works which we have developed, and bearing in mind the decrease of missionary personnel, we sense the necessity of better discerning the real needs, and establishing definite missionary priorities. More and more it is becoming demanded, that this be done at the level of the entire Congregation and in concert with other Institutes. We must speak now of "personnel policy" at the level of the general council rather than at the level of the Provinces.

This is the background against which we must project the whole idea of international teams. It is a certain shifting of a responsibility that was almost exclusively that of Provinces toward "their" Districts toward a responsibility shared by all the Provinces and coordinated by the generalate; a collaboration which will take the form of mutual sharing in personnel and in many other spheres as well.

"Internationalization" thus viewed is a practical consequence of the development of mission. Even beyond that, though, we may justly say that in this "internationality" we shall make ourselves a much clearer sign of what mission is all about—bringing together, reconciling in Christ, breaking down walls. If in our missionary teams we could reconcile what is so often in conflict and opposition at the level of relations between nations—men of many different nations, from all parts of the world, East, West, North and South—what a sign we could be of the kingdom of God.

Here, then, are the steps we plan to take. We will begin with small teams of volunteers, assembled in response to a specific request for a well-defined task. These could be small teams of a like language and culture or teams which will be truly international in their make-up. It will be necessary to organize these teams carefully so as to guarantee a real collaboration and sharing. Once formed, a team will then prepare together for its task.

As we see it, there will be teams which will undertake long term projects, and also teams for projects of a very temporary nature. The great need of reorientation in our Districts goes far beyond our possibilities of assigning personnel permanently. It would be quite possible though to choose some of our many confreres with particular skills, who would agree to go together to this or that District for a few months, to offer their services there, without at the same time giving up their actual assignments.

In talking to our young people in formation during my travels, I realize that many of them are completely in accord with this idea of a more international concept of our missionary work. Such a course of action though, will have great consequences for formation; the element of internationality will have to occupy a much greater place than heretofore. During formation, candidates will have to familiarize themselves with other cultures and languages. They will have to know each other better to understand each other more. How this can be accomplished is an excellent subject for study for those in charge of formation and by our candidates themselves.

All of this is not easy. As of now, we certainly have not received many answers to our requests. I can understand this, nor do I underestimate the difficulty of leaving a familiar environment to undertake a new work filled with so many unknown factors. But I am certain too, that now, as in the past, no new challenge offered to us will ever be unaccepted.

June 1976

THE ENLARGED GENERAL COUNCIL

Extract from an Interview with Father Gagnon,
Provincial of Canada

Father Gagnon. Father General, we have had the experience of the enlarged general council. We appreciated it greatly and most of the confreres have said so. Could you tell us what your general impressions are?

Father General. As you say, the enlarged general council was a very rich experience. The first thing we all were aware of, and about which everybody has spoken, was the way we lived together in true fraternity. Somebody said to me at the end of the meeting: "once again we have not tried to make a definition of our Spiritan identity—what holds us together as a family—but we experienced it in real life. We felt very deeply that we are all engaged in the same work, the same mission."

Then too, I think that the enlarged council was a step ahead, carrying forward what was done at the 1974 Chapter. I am truly convinced that we have come a long way in the past two years. What was made very clear was passing beyond the frontiers of the Provinces. We did not see the least tendency to want to be on the defensive against other Provinces, but rather a willingness to be open, a desire to learn, to receive, to pool our strengths. In this way, the enlarged council was truly an international meeting. The concern about being international was evident in all the participants. Now we have unity in diversity as our ideal. Diversity exists, and we regard it as a richness. We no longer feel we have to defend it. Now we have to live more intensely its value and its distinctiveness.

I was also impressed during this meeting by the dynamic view of the mission. From the very beginning the question was asked, "What is the mission today? How can we remain faithful to it? It wasn't so much a theoretical study, we did not do much missiology, but we are trying to distinguish priorities. We said, "As we look at the mission to which we are committed today, what are the most important factors in it? It's there that we must devote ourselves by preference. What things are the most urgent? Where are the most pressing appeals"? Truly, I found on all sides a will to respond to such appeals. It was especially clear to me the final day, Saturday, at the eleventh hour, when the general council outlined some new appeals, i.e., Paraguay, Angola, and Pakistan.

I have already stressed the willingness to collaborate. For us on the general council, this meeting was a strengthening and an encouragement.

When we came here at the beginning of our mandate, we felt isolated. We said to one another that we were all united here together on the holy mountain, away from the places where we had been truly committed. We wondered, "What are we to do here? How can we keep in contact with the mission where we used to live? Shall we not be separated from our brethren"? We also recalled how little interest we had in the generalate when we were at the grass roots level. The generalate was far away and did not seem very important. This caused us some anxiety in the beginning. We tried, by means of our information bulletins and our visits, to keep in contact especially with superiors. Now, during the enlarged council, we have really understood to what extent all the provincials and principal superiors take responsibility with us of the general council for the whole enterprise. We did not spend much time discussing Province X or Province Y. We talked about the Congregation as it was evident that all the participants in the enlarged council felt that it was their concern.

When I say that we felt isolated at the beginning of our mandate, this also came in part from the very organization of the Congregation. We had the impression of running into well-defined structures of Provinces and Districts, structures of authority, organizational structures. We were, as it were, surrounded by walls which could be easily climbed over. Besides, there was a whole network of circuits which existed and operated independently of us. Now, during this enlarged council, we have discovered that, without changing either structures or organization, we have managed to get beyond them. It was extraordinary to see how important organizational structures were in the long run. When there is a family spirit, when we live in the solidarity, walls fall down easily. We told the enlarged council that we were not asking for any new powers or structures for ourselves—we really wanted the means to do our job. Since we are expected to animate, to coordinate, to make provision to some extent for a common policy, we needed the means to do so. I believe that this enlarged council has given us this generously through the solidarity which it expressed.

Another thing which struck me was the interest in the young. I think we should have to come back again later to the problem posed by an aging group within the Institute and a very small group of younger confreres. However, during the enlarged council, we felt the concern of the leaders of the Provinces for the build-up of the future. There was not much turning back upon the past. The greatest concern was not the worry over the best possible way of organizing the things as they are now.

It was rather a look into the future, with great attention given to that small group of young men which we have among us. It was also a seeking of ways to make them feel at home and able to work creatively within the Congregation

And then, perhaps, I should have begun with this, but it serves just as well as conclusion, this is the secret of the meeting—it was a spiritual experience. We wanted it to take place during the Pentecost Novena. It was not by chance that this was in our minds from the very beginning. We wanted it to be an experience of openness to the Holy Spirit, because it becomes more and more evident that we cannot operate like an organization does, by using powerful means; more and more we recognize that we are "poor fellows." What we wanted was to have a lived experience of prayer. We wanted to be there with the Mother of God, like the Apostles, waiting for the Spirit who would speak to us and reveal to us what the will of God is for all of us and for the mission. Everybody agrees in recognizing that the Spirit did breathe during that week. Some say that things happened which could not have been foreseen and which were not the logical conclusion of the way our meeting had been going or of the things which had been said. It has to be admitted that something like that did happen and that certainly it had a strong effect upon all who were a part of the meeting.

NOVEMBER 1976

Dear Confreres,

With this No. 8 of I/D, the general council takes up again the series of study themes begun last year. We spent October and half of November going over the reports of Provinces and Districts and of the provincial chapters held during the summer, as well as working at the implementation of the decisions of the enlarged council. Our annual retreat provided an occasion for us to meditate in a special way on the missionary charism of the Venerable Founder. You will be finding echoes of our work together in the various issues of I/D foreseen for this year. (We'll try to catch up after our slow start).

I would like to give a few impressions of the eight provincial chapters held last summer. I was able to attend personally four of them (Ireland, England, Belgium, Nigeria East), in whole or in part, and to make a quick visit to the one in France. Four Chapters, one after the other, is rather a frightening prospect, but it was a very enriching experience and a particularly good opportunity to get to know a Province and participate in its life. One can be present at an evaluation of a whole ensemble of activities, commitments, options, and at the making of plans for the future. In every case there was the same fraternal atmosphere, the same willingness to work together. I don't mean just a superficial agreement. The Chapters went through moments of crisis in which various tendencies and proposals were in conflict and when faith in the future didn't come without a struggle. Sometimes unity can be had only at the cost of some disappointments and suffering, as when we are faced with limitations and don't dare close our eyes to them.

I shall stress only two points:

* what seem to me to be the essential results of these Chapters;
* some options which have been taken and which the general council wants to put before the whole Congregation as priorities.

The 1976 Chapters were not just theoretical debates. Most of the Provinces were faced with concrete problems, some of them very serious, which had to be the main topics of discussion: different missionary outlooks; internal tensions; in some cases, the question of survival itself. For example, Nigeria East, emerging from six difficult years of the war's aftermath, had to clarify things and re-define its religious and missionary vocation so as not to go off in the wrong direction. As I think back on all those meetings, I think I can best characterize them as:

1. the effort to achieve unity around a precise objective—what we are and what we have to do: the missionary appeals which the Province accepts as addressed to it; the kind of religious witness to be given;
2. the re-grouping of personnel to do the job;
3. a turning towards the future, without false optimism but with confidence, by deciding upon a definite course of action—an act of faith in the future.

This act of faith has a two-fold basis. First, there is the conviction, renewed in an atmosphere of prayer and openness to the Holy Spirit, that the mission is still alive, not only for the church in general but that our Congregation still has its part to play in it.

The many appeals that come to us from all sides furnish adequate evidence of this. Then, there is the feeling of the unity and solidarity of the entire Congregation which has been shown since the 1974 Chapter and which also characterized the enlarged council.

From among the many recommendations which came out of these chapters, here are the ones which the general council and I particularly want to stress:

1. *The need of bringing about a renewal in depth.* It seems beyond doubt that our Institute has reached the end of an important epoch in its existence and that we have entered upon a new one. History teaches us that we must face the new era with creativity and inventiveness—otherwise we're finished. As we are living in a new world—even in the older "mission territories," a new type of witness is demanded of us. The situation in the mission has changed, so there are, and will continue to be, new appeals making themselves heard. Renewal must be spiritual: the constant replenishing of our religious and missionary vocation by recourse to the mystery of Christ and the church, the renewing of ourselves (individually and as community) in the Holy Spirit, the deepening of our life of prayer, and of the service we give to our brothers in the faith. It must also be a renewal of our mentality, our attitudes, our outlook on the mission of today. It is a matter of regret that there are still confreres who are hostile to any idea of renewal or change.

2. *The need to strengthen the solidarity and spirit of "belonging" throughout the Congregation.* We need to enlarge our immediate horizons. It will require the thinking of all to find how best to utilize all the available strength and vitality for the work of the mission. We have not done enough of this. The "internationality, mobility and universality" the chapters have been speaking about must little by little be given realistic and practical form so that we may serve the mission well.

It is my wish that the Chapters will provide the inspiration that we need.

DECEMBER 8, 1976

Dear Confreres,

Christmas has come round again, so to all of you I send my warmest greetings, along with those of the general council. Christmas, "when the kindness and generous love of God our Savior appeared" (Tit 3:4), is for us also the day on which we think specially of each other and unite ourselves in particular with those who are suffering or in difficulty, the day on which we try to give more than usual importance to "*cor unum et anima una.*"

The list of crisis situations has grown longer since last year. Angola remains a problem. We send out regular news bulletins on it to the major superiors. Two of our confreres are still in the hands of the rebels somewhere in the forests of central Angola. Another is in prison. Many others have had to leave their mission and are waiting in nearby centers. The growing uncertainty is even worse than the lack of material goods, which is also part of the picture.

Then there is South Africa, from where the news has not been so good. As can be imagined, the recent upheavals have not been without repercussions on the work of the missionaries.

In Paraguay, a small group tries to hold the fort, also in difficult circumstances, while hoping for reinforcements.

Can we not say that it is especially in these countries that the Congregation is at the service of "the poorest and most abandoned"? The joy of Christmas—which I wish you all in abundance—is thus tempered by the trials of these confreres. And there are other difficult situations too, in which one must hold on, come what may, to one's unconditional missionary faith. It is especially with confreres in such situations, and with their faithful, that we feel united on this feast of Christmas.

But this union of minds and hearts opens out also onto a great hope: that of today's new missionary perspectives. A few days ago, we received at the generalate some young people belonging to one of the many groups which, in Italy, are looking for new ways of religious and missionary commitment. One of them will be leaving for Cameroon in January. He expressed his motive as follows: "to go and live the love of God and men where there is a call for help, whatever the conditions or guarantees might be." This motive will also be ours, more and more, and in fact is already ours, as it was in the time of our pioneers. Isn't it precisely in this way that the joy that we wish each other at Christmas is born: in the missionary faith that we all share and from which we derive our enthusiasm, dynamism, and spirit of service?

The incarnation will always be inseparable from Easter, which means both death and resurrection. Our personal problems and crosses as missionaries take their place among those of the communities and peoples for whom we work. And, in wishing you joy and peace, I pray the

LORD that, through you, this joy and peace will also be radiated to those around you. May God grant that there be many such sources of light! Happy Christmas to all, and may God keep you and guide you in 1977.

January 1977

LIBERMANN—MISSIONARY

> The charism received by the Founder finds its true expression in the attitude of those among us who are willing to carry further his religious experience and his apostolic intuition. The voice of the Holy Spirit manifested in our common aspirations and concerns shows us how we have to live out this gift in the church of today (XXth Chapter of the Carmelites of Vedruna).

Dear Confreres,

Every year the second day of February prompts us to recall the stature of the man we call "Our Venerable Father."

His life was a great spiritual adventure. Taken hold of by God—and giving himself up to God, the prisoner of the Jewish ghetto discovered an unusual freedom—one which transcended the physical, psychological, social, and cultural conditioning which had been his. With his companions he took up the project of the evangelization of Africa.

His experience was one of advancing step by step on this path of freedom progressively, leaving behind the different stages of his journey— Saverne, Paris, the seminary, Rennes, the vicissitudes of his early foundation, the African projects, the fusion . . . His horizons grew wider and wider as this pilgrimage of his went on, passing beyond barriers and frontiers.

His understanding of God, of men, and of life grew deeper and deeper until he attained peace in total abandon to the action of God, and his sense of the inalienable dignity of every man—especially the poorest— found expression in meeting, accepting, loving, and liberating them by means of a respectful service which was nothing other than a total giving of himself.

That was his *charism*. He was so marked by it that he was among the greatest missionary figures of the last century, and was able to communicate his ideals, his vision, and his missionary dynamism to an entire religious family which is conscious of drawing upon this source even today.

But a charism, the experience of a life, is a unique thing, something original which cannot be reproduced.

If we Spiritans are attached to our origins, it is because we recognize in our personal missionary vocation the ideal he proposed and communicated. It is because his experience helps us to deepen and give direction to our own experience and because it stimulates us to travel the road together so as to respond creatively to today's call. "It is only when remembrance of the past is not totally alien to our own deepest experience that there is a chance of something being done" (A. Willems, *"Quelle place donner aux souvenirs"?*)

In this issue of I/D we have traced out for us a part of the journey of Father Libermann the missionary. I hope that it will help you to grasp its relevance for you, for I believe that in our missionary experience of today we are meeting again the experience of our Founder at the crucial moments of his life, and that the choices he made can shed light upon the path we must walk.

Like him, we live today at the beginning of a new missionary era. It is very different from that of the last century, of which it is the final stage as well as being a new beginning. Just as in the former age, so now too we do not know where the Spirit is leading us. So many things still have to be discovered and a challenge is given to our capacity for openness and for interior mobility, both of which are component factors of our missionary fidelity.

Circumstances are constantly leading us more and more to go to the heart of our vocation which is to give witness to Jesus who died and is risen again, and to the hope he brings to mankind by being ready to reproduce in ourselves the traits of the suffering Christ.

The beginnings of the Spiritan work in Africa were marked by such trials and many such failures that it ought not to have survived. There were so many things which did not seem to work out, so many projects which seemed illusory, so many missionaries lost after a few years. The unity of the Congregation threatened to dissolve from within.

So often I think of those days when I witness today painful experiences or apparently insurmountable obstacles. There is light to be gained from the faith and the ability to surmount difficulties which we find in those early days and which was drawn in great part from the inspiration given by that man of faith and hope in Paris. We too need to have a missionary mystique.

Like Libermann in his day, we are witnesses today of an exploitation of humans by humans, but on an infinitely greater scale than in the case of the liberated slaves of Bourbon, Reunion, and Haiti. All of you, wherever you are, you see it and suffer from it. How can we contribute to the liberation of persons today? Among so many answers offered, which is the best? Which should we choose and commit ourselves to? How are to translate into action our solidarity with the poor and oppressed?

The circumstances are different. We cannot find in the past the solutions for today. But, what we can find there is the dynamism coming from a view of things which is illuminated by God and which penetrates to the heart of things and the acceptance without compromise of the exigencies of our vocation.

> Two marching orders sound out from our entire Spiritan history.
>
> *Mission is the work of God.* Let him act, be open to his action, to the promptings of the Spirit. God has his hour, he has his plans, he has his ways.
>
> *Mission is the work of a community.* Let us draw our strength from a faithfulness shared with others. Let us rediscover and strengthen community spirit. Let us help one another, give mutual support to one another, encourage one another, work together.

"It is important to create a life environment in which the great memories of the past form an integral part. Then there will be present an atmosphere of solidarity and confidence where we receive from the past, spontaneously and from within, what we recognize as important for the future. Thus, the past will inspire us. It will awaken in us experience which we scarcely recognize and will make us discover our own potentialities and what we have to do . . . "

Fraternally yours.

October 1977

SAY IT IN LATIN

My dear Confreres,

The opening of the Synod suddenly brought me face to face with something I had forgotten for a long time—Latin as the common language at a meeting.

Every day there are meetings held all over the world. People come together to exchange ideas. They have language problems but usually solve them by means of simultaneous translation systems which get better and better all the time. There is such a system at the Synod too, and most of the fathers make use of it to have the Latin translated into one of five living languages.

So we might ask: Why Latin? We must admit that even the best simultaneous translation systems cannot guarantee that people will understand one another. Could it be that Latin has some magic power to siphon off the causes of misunderstanding? Can the venerable classic language of the church reconcile the all too evident differences of culture, cool down the heatedness of debate by means of its timeless character, and give every statement some historical significance?

Perhaps it can, but at the cost of using an archaic medium and losing the forcefulness of contemporary expression. So, it is not surprising that by the second day the chairman was announcing that those who wished could be dispensed from using Latin.

That may seem to be a minor decision. In reality, it is a living symbol. As you know, the Synod is discussing catechesis. To speak Latin or not to speak Latin therefore constitutes a symbol: the whole issue is one of language, of communication.

The same could be said of our Information Service. Neither this new format nor our other proposed improvements will remove the difficulty. Sometimes an issue of I/D is well received in one Province or District, not so well in another. The following month it may be just the other way round. Our reflexes and our sensibilities differ, they are conditioned by our own culture. Added to that are our personal ideas, our personal choices, our personal leanings.

Every time I have to write this letter to all the confreres, I am faced with the same problem: What should I do? Say it in Latin? Only say things that everybody will accept without difficulty? Avoid saying anything that might be a personal challenge to anybody?

There are three reasons why I feel I cannot "say it in Latin," why I must speak out clearly.

1. In France, in England, in the United States, in Guyana, in Madagascar, as well as in other places, recent Chapters have given rise to genuine hopes. Why? Because they asked the real questions: Who are we? What choices do we have to make? The genuine hopes are based upon a commitment to real renewal: a conversion of ourselves and the courage to make the hard choices where our works are concerned. "Say it in Latin"—to drown all that in compromise—would be to strangle the genuine hopes that have been raised. Sometimes, on the occasion of our visits to a province or district, we have seen a rising of hopes, but then, sad to say, the good resolutions remained a dead letter and nothing was changed. Disappointed hope can be worse than no hope at all!

2. The recent Meeting of Young Spiritans in Spain—we'll have more to say about it next month—gives great promise for the future of the Congregation. It is more than just the euphoria of a few weeks spent together as brothers; it is also the vivid recognition of how valid the Spiritan and missionary vocation is for today; it is a return to the basic spiritual and apostolic insights we inherited from Father Libermann and the great missionaries who followed him: the gift of ourselves to work for the poor and abandoned in the setting of community life taken seriously. When it comes to things like that, we dare not "say it in Latin."

3. The Synod of Bishops is a challenge to the church. She is supposed to teach the faith. Why does the message not get across better? Because the church, in order to evangelize, must first evangelize herself. Like her, we too are called to a conversion. Can it be that the gospel gets across badly because we do not rise to the level of our vocation? We do so many things and often do them very well indeed. But the heart of our vocation is in what we are: we are supposed to be the leaven, we are supposed to be prophets! Here, too, let's translate it all clearly—let's not "say it in Latin!"

These three points are a challenge to us in the general council as we enter the second half of our mandate and take stock of how we are serving the Congregation. We want to do our best to point the way ever more clearly and ever more persistently towards what is essential in our vocation and towards the choices that have to be made.

We count upon every one of you.

November 1977

"THE WORD OF GOD IS LIVING!" (HEB 4:12)

Dear Confreres,

The Synod has just ended. By this time, you will have read the analyses and commentaries in newspapers and reviews, so I do not need to give a complete account of it. However, I would like to share with you what it meant to me to be there as one of the ten representatives of the Union of Superiors General.

Certainly, the Synod was an experience which I shall remember for a long time. It strengthened and deepened my love for the church. It gave me a better understanding of how Ministry and Charism, Institution and Mystery, meet there and compenetrate one another.

For a month, in the midst of 200 Bishops from all over the world, I was able to "experience the church" in its diversity and uniqueness gathered around the Pope, the sign and guarantee of unity. It was, of course, an exercise of the magisterium, but what I saw was a group of men humbly gathered together with the Word of God as their center. I met pastors who let themselves be challenged, be questioned about *"their genuine fidelity to God and humanity in Jesus Christ"* (Final Message, no. 9). For the participants, the Synod was truly and above all a pastoral experience.

THE WORD OF GOD IS LIVING, yesterday and today. This could be taken as a summary of the 1977 Synod on Catechesis. Several reports were drawn up on the state of catechesis in the world today, on the de-christianization and secularization which are going on . . . There were plenty of scholarly statistics. The preparatory study, which had taken two years and involved the entire church, was embodied in more than 40 Reports from Episcopal Conferences. The prophets of gloom were proved wrong. True, in the past, even the recent past, there were errors and exaggerations. They were pointed out and remedies indicated. But the renewal of catechetics was judged favorably: " . . . the Christian need not be afraid. With the grace of the Holy Spirit, 'strong in faith,' he will succeed" (Message, no. 16). We are confident " . . . in the grace of the Holy Spirit. The greater our faith as it grows to maturity, the more readily can he draw out the fruits of sanctity. There are many problems in the world, but the future belongs to believers, whose hope will not deceive them" (Message, Conclusion).

Did the Synod change anything? Cardinal Cordeiro of Karachi remarked that Synods don't usually have immediate spectacular results; they bear their fruit over the long term. They do not propose solutions to the specific problems of a particular country—the diversity of cultures and situations is too great for that. Synods bring about changes at the level of the participants themselves.

If we are to believe the Bishops, one does not leave a synod the same as one came. Cardinal Thiandoum of Dakar gave this answer in a press conference: "What the Synod changed was my heart. Do you think that is a small result?" Archbishop Bernardin of Cincinnati said: "When a Synod ends in Rome, that's when it begins. Then there can be no more spectators; we all have to get down to the task of translating its directives into action." The previous Synod, through the medium of *Evangelii nuntiandi*, has become a source of inspiration and revival. We all hope the same will be true of this one.

THE WORD OF GOD IS LIVING. And we who represented religious Institutes at the Synod, what was our contribution? In return, what message does the Synod have for religious?

We brought to the discussions the experiences of religious and their communities, as well as the things they try to do. Basing ourselves on the reports and testimonies of our confreres and of Sisters from all over, we were able to clarify the place and role of religious communities in the catechesis of the local churches. Relations between Bishops and men and women religious require constant study and evaluation in an atmosphere of charity and truthfulness. Sisters particularly, but Brothers also, who know they are partners and collaborators of the Bishops, are clearly aware that their role and their aptitudes are not always sufficiently recognized by pastors or integrated into the pastoral plan of catechesis. On the level of Christian education in the schools, they are often crippled by lack of clear directives.

It was not always easy to get such questions into the discussions, still less into the Reports. The post-synodal document will certainly take them up. For the moment, the Synod's message for us religious is primarily this: "WE ARE ALL CATECHISTS IN THE CHURCH." Religious men and women, enter fully into the catechetical efforts of your local church, especially by the witness of your lives. May the Word of God become tangible in your life and your example. Live with joy the witness of your communities which are the leaven of the Christian community.

During a discussion about the specific role of the religious, an African Bishop said to me: "May they live the thirst for God in the midst of our communities. The people need to see in the heart of their Christian community Brothers and Sisters for whom God is everything." Similarly, the Synod reaffirms its "hope in the great spiritual richness which is witnessed to by a life lived in the spirit of the Beatitudes" (Message, Conclusion).

THE WORD OF GOD IS LIVING for all humankind. For that Word is for humanity, through our mediation. A recent survey in France shows that Jesus Christ "is accepted," God "is accepted, but less so," the Church "is not accepted at all." The same is true of many other countries. Why? In spite of its study of the need for "inculturation," for a catechesis based upon real life, the Synod did not come up with a ready-made answer. The question remains as a challenge.

How do we take up the challenge? By being, like the prophets, in the heart of God and at the same time in the heart of the mass of people. That is the role of prophets: to interpret the situations in which men are suffering in order to build up the new world; to break the bonds that keep them turned in upon themselves and let God speak to them.

Then, and only then, will we perhaps reach the hearts of young people. "They are often victimized by false shepherds who would profit from their generosity ... [They aspire] to creativity, to injustice, to liberty, to trust" (Message, no. 3)

To want to be a prophet—is that too pretentious? Are there any prophets among us? Perhaps we can take as a messianic promise the words of Joel: "I shall send forth my spirit upon every creature" and they will all be prophets!

The Synod is over. We cannot remain spectators. The Word of God, living in the church, must "be accepted." It depends upon us too. We must believe it, first of all, and never cease being converted.

December 1977

SEASON'S GREETINGS

Dear Confreres,

As I send you my best wishes for Christmas and the New Year, I feel present to the great Spiritan family all over the world. I should like to say a fraternal word to each of you, a word of joy. You live in so many places and in such different situations. Whether you are alone for these feast days or celebrate them in community, whether you are very active or are in retirement, full of enthusiasm and joy in the mission, or tired and perhaps tempted by discouragement, I wish you all a Holy and Happy Christmas and a New Year filled with God's blessings. I would hope that at this season we might re-awaken in ourselves the feeling of belonging to our large Spiritan community in which each one of us has his rightful place, in which each one of our brothers is "a gift from God and a sacrament of His presence."

Reasons to Be Thankful

During the year which is ending we have seen important events which are like milestones along our road.

Chapters were held in United States East, in South-West Brazil, in Madagascar and in Guyana. A new Province was erected in Angola. In Puerto-Rico, eight young men decided to enter the Congregation.

There was a meeting of principal superiors in Bangui, as a result of which the Spiritan Foundation of French-speaking Africa was established and a new novitiate opened in Yaoundé.

In August, the Young Spiritans held their great meeting in Spain. The Church of Bethlehem in South Africa received a new bishop this year after waiting for more than a year and a half. For our 23 confreres who work there and for their Christian communities this marks a new departure.

Then there was the Synod of Bishops in which, through my presence, so many confreres participated by sharing with me their experiences in catechesis or giving information about the life of the people with whom they work. I thank them and I hope to use all that material later in our study of pastoral activity throughout the Congregation.

We have also been able this year to take important steps in the realization of our three mission priority projects: in Paraguay, three new confreres are now at work and four more are preparing to go; the first international team has arrived in Angola; three young confreres will be leaving for Pakistan any day now.

It is only right to thank God for these events which, along with so many others, are signs of his presence among us and promises that the Spirit can still do great things in us for the service of the kingdom if we remain open his action.

It is only right also to remember that some of our confreres share with their Christian communities and the people where they work difficult situations and much suffering. There are those whom I have just visited in Angola, as well as those in Ethiopia who have close acquaintance with war and heartbreaks in many forms. Our community in South Africa, small in number and advancing in age, is faced with increasing labor and bracing itself for even more difficult times. They urgently appeal to the solidarity of the Congregation.

Poverty of Spirit, Unity, Peace

Against this background, dear confreres, my good wishes are for these things I wish you with all my heart—poverty of spirit, unity, and peace.

Poverty of Spirit.

This is a theme which recurs frequently in our general council meetings. We feel that we are poor in so many ways. We have experience of our poverty every day in the engrossing service of the mission.

> We are poor when so many of our commitments, both in Provinces and Districts, are put in question.
>
> We are poor when the means of action we counted upon are taken away from us.
>
> We are poor in the face of the need for "inculturation" and "incarnation" of the faith, as the Synod reminded us so insistently.
>
> We are poor in the face of the growing influence of the forces opposed to the church.

May the Feast of Christmas give us a strong reminder that the mission is not a question of techniques or methods, but rather of a mystery of life, that of the kingdom of God, the kingdom which grows and develops like a seed buried in the soil, "like yeast which a woman took and mixed in three measures of wheat until the whole batch was leavened" (Matt 13:33).

But the kingdom manifests itself also in so many signs of vitality. He who does not accept this kingdom like a little child, with the heart of a poor man, will not enter into it.

Unity.

How blessed we are that so much attention is being given to community life and its needs. We are re-discovering that community life is at the center of our Spiritan vocation—witness the recent Chapters, the meeting in Spain, and the things being tried in the Provinces and Districts.

The Synod re-affirmed the importance of Small Christian Communities as centers and agents for catechism. It asked religious to make their communities a sign, a yeast, a vital nucleus at the heart of the Christian communities. The Feast of Christmas reminds us that we must gather around Christ who came to heal all divisions. It is my wish that our fraternal unity may grow and that our communities become more genuine, that they renew themselves and occupy a more important place in our Spiritan life.

Peace.

This wish comes from the bottom of my heart as I return from Angola, where I found peace in the midst of war. The confreres there told me they have the impression that the news we give out about Angola is sometimes too negative, that we put too much emphasis upon the difficulties and suffering. "We wish you would highlight more the fact that the church here is alive and that our missionary work is a source of joy."

That was the most striking impression I received there: a living Christianity, full of hope, and missionaries happy in their ministry. That is what I wish for you as I send along this message of peace: the joy of being a missionary, the joy of being received by a people who are eager to hear the word of God, the joy of sharing with them the best of what we are and what we have.

February 1978

A BROTHER AT OUR SIDE

Dear Confreres,

We had a premature announcement two years ago, but now the news is sure and "official": On Mission Sunday, October 22, the Holy Father will declare before the whole church that "The Servant of God," Jacques Laval, a member of the Congregation of the Holy Ghost and of The Holy Heart of Mary, and from now on be called BLESSED. This happy event will shed light upon the entire year 1978. It will be an occasion of thanksgiving, of pride, of interior renewal.

A Shining Presence of God among Us

What is a beatification? Or rather, in a very real sense, what is a saint in the midst of the Christian people? Few of us will have the privilege I have had of experiencing this in Mauritius: a saint is a person who has become so pliable in the hands of God, so transparent for him, so taken over by the Holy Spirit, that the presence of God—the saving God—shines through him in an extraordinary way. The veil is lifted and we get a glimpse of what can happen when a man opens himself to the Holy Spirit who makes all things new. It is in this way that the LORD becomes present through Jacques Laval, our brother. In such a case, death is a small matter; it simply means that God's power has come and broken open the shell.

A hundred years after his death, Father Laval is still God's witness, missionary, sign of hope, peace-maker, bond of unity, God's messenger to hundreds of thousands of men who for generations have never stopped coming to his tomb. In a country which has suffered from social and ethnic tensions, he alone succeeds in bringing together in peace and prayer around his tomb, Christians, Muslims, Hindus, Animists. As a witness to the gospel, and after the example of Christ, he "brings together the scattered children of God" (cf. John 11:52). His prayers—so fervent during his life—and his love for men still seem tangible in that spot. That is why they come. The intuition of the poor is not mistaken.

Beatification is only the solemn recognition of a shining presence of God among us and an invitation to thank God for that presence.

A Companion on the Journey

The community of saints is a reality of our faith which does not enter into the field of our experience every day. A beatification also means that "He who presides over our visible communion here below" says to us: "Your brother is living with God and among us!" We would do well to meditate upon this, we who have such great need of one another in our meeting with God and in our service to the mission. Father Laval lived according to the Spiritan missionary charism which is all ours. He drew from the spiritual spring that Libermann is—that same source that many Spiritans are rediscovering in our own day with great eagerness.

Father Laval lived out his mission in the midst of social and political changes which are not without some resemblance to those we live through today. His times, like ours, were the dawn of a new epoch, full of promise and of uncertainty.

Father Laval is truly "a brother at our side," in whom we can find inspiration, in whom we can discover the Spiritan adventure in all its freshness and all its demands. What is more: he can take us by the hand and lead us towards intimacy with God, because he lives there himself.

A Prophetic Vision

Sometimes we need a celebration of a feast to help us bring out the true colors which day to day remain in the shadow and can appear dull and faded. As a Spiritan family we have had our "crises." Who can say whether our days of trial are now over? This feast of the beatification does not have its principal reference to the past, but much more to the realities of *today* to the *future* that God holds out before us—with Laval, alive and walking on ahead of us.

"The charism of a Founder places much less in the past than in the future: it has much more to do with a plan, a hope, than with a memory. It is by this prophetic gift that a Founder remains alive among his sons."(I/D no. 15, 3).

We are invited to allow ourselves to be challenged by that charism so that we may better live according to it. It is *prophetic* because it unveils for us what the will of God is for us at present. It displays before our eyes how the various elements which constitute our world come together to form a whole, how they take on a meaning "for us" which becomes our true vocation. That meaning, that vocation, comes less from a call in the past than from the unknown in the future. It is dynamic and challenges our creativity and our ability to be renewed. It is enlightened by our heritage, but today it acquires new vigor from the existence of Laval, from the existence of Libermann who inspires it, from the existence of many others among us.

A Call to Interior Renewal

This beatification also calls upon us to be converted, to renew ourselves interiorly. If that does not happen, it will have little meaning. This is a time of grace in our Spiritan history which we must recognize and take advantage of. I ask all of you, dear confreres, to listen to this call. *I hope that every Province, every District, every community, will take appropriate steps to respond to it.* By this interior renewal, I mean that we need to deepen our appreciation of the Spiritan charism made up of abandonment of self to God and unreserved service to the poor, made up of that sort of "Exodus" spirit which prevents us from permanently installing ourselves anywhere and which keeps us in the stance of interior mobility that *Libermann* taught us and that *Laval* lived by in his own personal way.

"Without such a personal experience of the LORD deep within us it is not possible to understand Libermann's idea . . . " (I/D, no. 15, 1)

We are all welcome to this *rendezvous* with the goodness of God.

March 1978

SPIRITAN VOCATIONS

My dear Confreres,

The morning mail often brings surprises, many happy ones like the news recently received from the Eastern Province of the U.S.A. They have just launched there a Spiritan Year of Prayer and work for vocations. The program is a varied one: a day of fast and abstinence throughout the Province on March 15; on April 16, World Vocations Day, families are to be encouraged to reflect upon their own particular commitment in this respect. The theme of all Spiritan Retreats during the year will be vocations; all communities in the Province will join in the Novena of Preparation for Pentecost in this same spirit. Other highlights of the year are Mission Sunday and the Sunday before February 2.

In carrying out this project, the members of the Province are invited to be sensitive and creative in their approach; they are especially encouraged to be particularly open to young people and to welcome them into the community; as far as possible the communities should themselves radiate the spirit they seek to inspire. The vocations director is responsible for co-ordinating the various projects.

This initiative is not the only one of its kind in the Congregation. Several other Provinces also have had concentrated periods of spiritual renewal and missionary inspiration which are equally worthy of mention. Still, this plan of the United States is significant for two reasons.

First of all, the whole Province is mobilized in view of a common effort to awaken vocations to the Spiritan life. Too often, unfortunately, this seeking, this welcome, which should be the concern of all is peripheral to the general interest, one or two confreres are chosen for vocations work and treated as "specialists." This effort by contrast is set down as a priority for the consideration and action of every confrere. The encouraging of vocations becomes "my speciality and that of all my fellows: it is my responsibility, my job. Do I really believe that? What impression of the Spiritan missionary vocation is built up in others as they see me in my everyday life? Do I live with such zest and conviction that I burn with the desire to suggest to others that they too embrace this way of life? There is no doubt whatever that it is not in theories or in books that young people discover vocation; the spark of vocation that sets a young heart on fire is always personal contact with one who is himself committed, with a community which is a living witness to the ideal.

Secondly, the present program is a call to the whole Province to unite in prayer. In a world where the vocation to the religious and missionary life finds itself face to face with new difficulties and where so much effort has been without result, we are driven back to the essential: vocation is a gift of the Holy Spirit. It does not just happen, neither is it a call to a state of life like any other; it is a grace received. It is necessary to pray for it. Thus, we are brought back to a realization of our duty. Prayer and fasting: that is the answer of the humble Christian when faced with a situation where he has relied too much upon his own resources, his own prerogatives.

In many Provinces at the present time vocations are scarce; in some cases, completely absent. This leads some to conclude that our work is finished and that it remains only for us to prepare to die with dignity. That is not how we see it. Faced with what we are too easily tempted to call factual reality we should on the contrary find strength in prayer, in personal conversion, and leave the future confidently in the hands of the LORD of the Vineyard.

I would wish the whole Congregation to organize itself in a great movement of prayer that would renew us in purity and fidelity. Who knows what an Easter might follow such a Lent?

Two months from now the Enlarged Council meets at Knecksteden in Germany. Prayer, spiritual renewal, the problems of vocation, Spiritan formation will be discussed as well as our priorities, urgent missionary calls, and how to meet them. Why should this meeting not be an occasion to launch a great movement of prayer throughout the Congregation? Then indeed the Congregation in its turn would draw much benefit from this council. It is towards this that I have wanted to direct your prayers in this letter. What better time than Easter and Pentecost.

To all I wish a happy Easter and a happy Pentecost to follow.

September 1978

LAVAL: A SIGN-POST FOR THE FUTURE?

My dear Confreres,

All is now ready: on Mission Sunday, October 22, our newly-elected Holy Father will declare Jacques-Desiré Laval Blessed.

That great event will be celebrated in the Island of Mauritius with a joy and ceremony even greater than that usual to traditional feasts in the Indian Ocean. All Mauritius will that day rejoice that the veneration they have shown for "their" saint for nearly a century, has received the recognition and approval of the church and has been proclaimed to the four corners of the earth from the Chair of Peter.

Our Spiritan joy also will overflow this Roman ceremony of beatification and our thanksgiving on this great missionary occasion will rise wherever a Spiritan finds himself on this day. The few hundred of them present in Rome for the ceremony will be representative of the thousands of Spiritans celebrating the event with their people in the Provinces and Districts—members of the one Spiritan family united in thanksgiving. For that reason, I pause briefly to unite myself with you, my confreres, and to dwell a moment on the significance of this beatification for us.

Thanksgiving to God is the first sentiment that rises in my heart, thanksgiving for the privilege of being associated with the great missionary movement begun barely 200 years ago in the Islands and in Africa and Madagascar and now drawing to its close. I thank God also as one era of missionary endeavour ends and another seems to open before us. This day gives us assurance that, useless servants though we be, we can go forward humbly but confidently under the impetus of the Holy Spirit into whatever the future holds for us; as it was in the beginning, so now.

Our Spiritan charism is the same as that received by Laval; ours a heritage the nobility of which shines forth with rare brilliance on this day. Legitimately, we may pause and bask awhile in the reflection of his glory before returning renewed to continue our humble labor in the service of the church.

The secret of Father Laval's extraordinary missionary vitality and zeal is his union with God. The Lord he welcomed in the deep intimacy of his own heart, he discovered and recognized in the hearts of his fellowmen. Conversely, living always close to others and giving himself to them without reserve in dedicated love and service, he found it easy to draw near to God and renew his spirit—in the conversation of prayer.

He gave himself without reserve to the poor and the oppressed. He raised them up to the sense of their human dignity, their dignity as children of God. He fought also that others too might respect that dignity and give them what was rightly theirs. Like all truly holy and committed men before him, he paid the price in the hatred and misunderstanding of the children of this world. It made no difference. Poor man's champion though he was, Laval rose above all classes; a man of God and of the church, his unique desire was to break down the walls of prejudice that separate man from man. With his Master, he gave himself up for every person and prayed that they all be one. He made himself all things to all to win all to Christ, but the poor he loved first of all because their need was greatest.

A man of simple life and needs, a suffering servant ever available where the need was greatest, he is indeed a model of the true Spiritan. As today we rejoice in his triumph, let us not forget, however, that he too experienced the tension arising out of his identification of himself with one particular milieu, the human and Christian community to whose service he was dedicated, and the loyalty that called him, in the Congregation, to unite himself with other calls, other horizons.

On this glorious day in the history of our Congregation, may I invite you to unite with me in joy and thanksgiving that we too share the same charism as Laval and to pray with me that like him we live worthy of our Spiritan vocation. Is this to ask another miracle? Perhaps it is, but what better occasion to ask our brother, the Blessed Jacques-Desiré Laval, to make intercession on our behalf.

Christmas 1978

TO YOU, MY SPIRITAN BROTHER

My dear Confreres,

I send today a warm and sincere greeting: "May your Christmas be a holy and happy one." This Christmastide, I want you to feel that I am with you in spirit, sharing with you wherever you are.

Whether you are amidst a Christian community in the heart of the African bush or in North Brazil; whether celebrating the hope of liberation amongst poor outcasts in city slums or sharing the sufferings of the innocent victims of war and violence; whether giving yourself wholeheartedly to the future of young people in school or college or seeking to improve the quality of life of the workers amongst whom you minister; whether, finally, your mission now is acceptance of the infirmities of age or sickness, and prayer offered for those called to harvest where you once sowed, wherever you are, whatever be your situation, may you find peace and joy this day. May you be a radiant and welcoming witness to Christ's love of men, your brothers and sisters, a joyful witness to his gospel. "Behold, I proclaim to you good news of great joy that . . . For . . . a Savior has been born for you who is Messiah and LORD!" (Luke 2:10, 11).

I should like also to speak to you in this letter of many things which occupy my attention at the present time. Recent months have been most eventful and have, we hope, sown deep in the heart of the world seeds of promise of new evangelical fruitfulness. I speak of the death of Pope Paul VI, then the "meteoric" passage of John Paul I, the election of John Paul II, and these early days of his ministry. Each of these in succession, like so many electric impulses, would carry to the ends of the earth a sermon in sight and sound, a challenge to action, which still resounds. Each in its own way was an opportunity to measure the universality of the church and to live it intensely, raising us up out of our concern for the immediate to a broader and deeper vision of reality. These events were also to provide us with the opportunity of renewing unconditionally our expression of loyalty to Peter.

More modestly too, but none the less really, these months have been enriched by what we have experienced in living and speaking with you, either individually or in groups, during our visits to you, in various parts of the world. We have brought back with us valuable ideas and insights which we are already maturing and which will in time bear fruit for the whole of the family.

More recently we have spent together a month of prayer, study and exchange as a general council. We have passed in review the state of the Congregation, its strengths and its weaknesses, seeking to discern in the light of the Spirit the way in which the Master of the harvest wished us to advance.

And now, it is the General Chapter of 1980 that looms up on the horizon, calling us to mobilize and concentrate our forces in view of renewal. With the chapter in mind, I am also led to raise with you some questions which occur to me, in the light of recent events.

I/D no. 18 and the accompanying "Supplement" have already announced this Chapter; I invite you to re-read these documents. The theme proposed was: Spiritan Life. Many of our confreres re-acted to this, some favourably, others with greater or less reserve. At this moment in which we are about to actively prepare for the Chapter, it is well to be clear about what is in question. Read again the quotation from the Prefect of Religious, Cardinal Pironio, at the end of I/D, 18—it expresses perfectly what we wish for our Chapter.

In Chapter we wish to live in depth two realities—a sincere approach to conversion and a creative facing of the future, under the inspiration of the Holy Spirit going forward in hope. This we shall undertake in an attitude of prayer, poverty, and fraternal charity. Conversion: that is something that concerns us all most intimately, that disturbs our comfort, and is more than a word on the lips.

"What have you done about that wholehearted renewal of life, on which we have been insisting so much in the last three years, because it is our number one priority"? That is the question I put to myself, to you, my Spiritan brother, as you read this today and to your community. Where do we stand?

When John Paul II received the superiors-general the other day, he said to us:

> On each community, on each religious, there falls a particular responsibility for together making Christ, meek and humble of heart, authentically present in the world today. Christ dead and risen: Christ living in the midst of his brothers and sisters.

The Spirit of total evangelical generosity. [Where do we stand, you and I?]

Do not be afraid to remind your religious that a pause made for true adoration has greater value and bears greater fruit than the most intense activity, even apostolic activity. That is the most urgent challenge the religious has to make in a society where efficiency has become an idol on whose altar the very dignity of man is so often sacrificed.

Your houses must be, above all else, centers of prayer and recollection, of dialogue, personal and communitarian, with him to whom we are principally answerable as is right for the passing of our days of labor.

Is there a message here—for you, for me, for our community?

The Pope also spoke to us of "maximal availability" for the service of the church. Again I ask: What is our stance on this? Are we not inclined sometimes to consider as availability to the church what is, in fact, the realization of a personal project? And your community: is it a group of individuals who happen to live under the same roof or a unity in which each is actively interested in the work of all the others? And you yourself: have you this attitude to your community?

Whether it be mission for tomorrow or mission for today: you should be available when needed elsewhere or if asked to blaze new trails. At the same time, you should be equally ready to persevere faithfully in a work begun, to show life-long fidelity to the "church of your first love."

Our service of the church must necessarily be judged against the background of contemporary society. Someone said to me recently: "Nowadays, many *are so anxious* to *know whether we will reach the year 2000 that they haven't time* to *ask about heaven.*" That remark hurt. It is a direct challenge to any Congregation in Chapter. Do you feel challenged by the great questions that agitate society round about you? And, what are you and your community doing about justice and peace?

Once more, in the same audience, it is the Pope who reminds us: "Whoever lives in habitual union with God understands in the true light of the gospel the choice made in favor of the poorest and of everyone who is a victim of human egoism [and] knows how to be involved with people without harm to the specific originality of his own vocation—poor, chaste, obedient."

These then are the questions I pose. They should lead us—you, me, the whole Congregation—to be converted and renewed. Because that conversion will make us available to God's creative action, we may hope it will give rise to a creativity amongst us that will make all new again.

May 1979 bring you joy and deep fulfilment. May you find among your Spiritan brothers and sisters the comfort, support, and living witness which will encourage you to go forward also in the way of the LORD. And, may God walk always with you.

Christmas 1979

SPIRITAN NEWS, No. 26

My dear Confreres,

Each year, when I send you my Christmas and New Year greetings, I try to think how I can make it more personal. I have met most of you by now. And, as I write to you, so many memories come to mind of what I have lived with you in such and such a spot in Africa or Latin America: meetings with Spiritans and with so many other people whom I have met through you. From being unknown names in a "missionary situation" (how we like to slip into jargon!), many of these too have now become faces that will remain engraved in my memory, along with what they have told me of their countries, their churches, their lives.

I remember our conversations, during which many of you opened your hearts to me. I remember the joy at efforts that had succeeded, as well as the obstacles that sometimes led to discouragement; the search for missionary renewal, as well as the slowness of some in adapting to change. I think also of my visits in Europe and North America, with their experiences of light and shade, of bursts of new life alongside routine and immobility. But, as I think of the different situations, it is always the human faces that emerge, the faces of people I have come to love.

In sending you my greetings, I feel a strong sense of gratitude for each Spiritan I have met on my way. In these past five years I have really learned that each confrere is a gift of God. With his talents, and also his limitations and weaknesses, he brings to the community the most precious thing he has—his life, whether he is still in his youthful vigour and enthusiasm or at the end of long years of service. And, because of this, he has a right to be held as a brother in each one's heart. May no one, ever, be treated badly by his brothers and sisters!

Such is our Congregation. The missionary community that we hope to be tomorrow starts from what we are today. The preparation for our

Chapter too should begin with this respectful regard and affection for each other and a willingness to welcome and listen to each other.

To keep to the theme of the Chapter, a number of reactions to the precapitular document have already reached us. Thanks to all who have written.

In these reactions, the joy of being a Spiritan comes through, along with the desire to be faithful to the local church, the will to be personally poor and unattached, the determination never to betray the underprivileged and the outcasts. Some have expressed their regret at seeing so few Spiritans working at the frontiers of the faith, among those to whom the Word of Life has not yet been preached.

One or other has stressed the urgency of decisive choices, even at the risk of leaving behind those who cannot or will not follow.

Some fear "an arbitrary diminution of the apostolic vision of our founders."

Others, finally, are mistrustful of theories that justify comfortable situations and put minds at rest.

These observations, coming from the heart, all bear witness to a deep involvement in mission and a sense of urgency. "Time is short. Let us not waste our energy in trifles."

Who would not feel challenged by these voices? It is up to the Chapter to give answers to them, rather than for me to try to answer them now in this letter.

However, I would like from now to make this comment. Our call for the next Chapter to be a celebration of our Spiritan life has been misunderstood by some confreres. They fear that this directive will lead to satisfied self-contemplation, whereas tomorrow's mission calls us instead to go out of ourselves, it calls for an "exodus." Is there a contradiction in this? Isn't our task precisely to examine and question ourselves, to decide how to make our Spiritan life more authentic, more faithful, more holy— a real living of the Good News, a readiness to die like the grain of wheat?

The Chapter will be a moment of truth, and we should not be afraid of the truth. Truth brings freedom, not rejection of some confreres by others in the name of principles or schools of thought. Let us gather all our strength and personnel resources for tomorrow. There are different tendencies and schools of thought in the Congregation; let each one's voice be heard and let us dialogue with each other in a fraternal spirit of discernment—a discernment in the Holy Spirit that will lead to definite decisions. In this way no one's gifts will be lost to the community.

Yes, time is short, and decisions must be made in the name of mission. The signs of true renewal are still not clear enough, still too few. Let us wake up. Let us decide, once and for all, to get up and go. We cannot allow ourselves the luxury of not facing up to the demands of our vocation. And who will help us to see our way, who will "lead us to the full truth" about our life, our commitments and the spirit that should animate us, if not he to whom the blind man cried, "Lord, that I may see"?

So may the new year, the year of our Chapter, be a year of light and discernment: discernment in the study of the questions facing us, in the renewal of our spiritual life and prayer, and especially in our attitude to God, who must always come first. Speaking one day of God's works, Fr. Libermann said: "God does not want them to be attributed to man's power; he wants them to be recognized as his own" (ND, XI, 160).

Happy Christmas and Happy New Year.

DOCUMENTATION
Numerical Decline of Religious Institutes since 1964
The December 1979 issue of I/D gives some reflections of the Generalate Team on the Congregation as it is today.
The Information Service would like here to extend these reflections by placing the numerical evolution of the Congregation in the context of the other religious Congregations of men.
We base ourselves on an article in the French missionary magazine *Missi* (no. 412, April-May 1978), entitled "Some Striking Statistics," which highlights 1964 as the turning point for virtually all the religious Institutes of men. It was in 1964, in fact, that our own Congregation reached its numerical peak (5,141 members). In 1964, the 62 religious Institutes of men that had more than 1,000 members each, totalled nearly 300,000 religious. Since then, all, except one, have decreased in membership, and the total in 1977 was about 230,000 (a decrease of 24%).
With permission from Missi, we reproduce their list of statistics, along with a translation of the article that accompanied it (p. 3).
We would point out, however, that the statistics in *Missi* are taken from the *Annuario Pontificio*, which is published in January each year by the Holy See, but in which the statistics for Congregations are sometimes up to three years behind time. Thus, for our own Congregation—Spiritans, in Line 17—the real figures were 5,008, 5,141, 5,060, 4,081, for a difference of -1,060 (instead of 5,200, 5,200, 5,060, 4,081, for a difference of—1,119).
The slight discrepancies, however, do not detract from the validity of the overall picture or of the reflections based on it by the author of the accompanying article.

We should note, too, that in the French list in *Missi* the names of the Congregations are in alphabetical order within each subdivision: over 9,000 members, over 4,000, over 2,000, over 1,000. In the English translation of the names of the Institutes the alphabetical order is lost.

If, on the basis of the list, the 62 Institutes are classed according to their percentage of decrease in the 13 years 1964-77, the Spiritans are found to be in the middle, with a decrease of 20-21%.

* One institute had a decrease of more than 40%: the Third Order Regular of St. Francis.
* 11 decreased by 30-40% (including the Marist Brothers, De La Salle Brothers, Premonstratensians, Marianists, Assumptionists, Calced Carmelites...).
* 9 decreased by 25-30% (including Maryknoll, the Vincentians, Redemptorists, Paris Foreign Mission Society, Brothers of St. John of God, Poermel Brothers...).
* 18 decreased by 20-25% (including the Montfortans, Priests of the Blessed Sacrament, Brothers of St. Gabriel, Trappists, Claretians, S.M.A, Jesuits, Spiritans, White Fathers, Capuchins, Franciscans, Salesians, Scheut Fathers...).
* 16 decreased by 10-20% (including the Benedictines, O.M.I., Mill Hill, Cistercians, Marist Fathers, Dominicans...).
* 6 decreased by less than 10% (including the Society of the Divine Word, the Consolata Missionaries...).

The author of the article in *Missi* (p. 3) focuses on the "refusal of life" as the major cause, as he sees it, of the decrease in religious personnel. Each one is free to form his own analysis of the causes of the decline. We live in a complex world, and the factors in such a situation are also complex.

One would have to be bold indeed to claim to have the full explanation. Many sociologists have studied the phenomenon, and have admitted that they cannot explain it fully. One factor in it seems to be a collective subconscious feeling of uneasiness and insecurity in the face of a future in which too many elements that were formerly stable and reassuring have become uncertain.

Those who see the basic factor as a "refusal of life" understand it in a broad sense. The refusal of life is not merely the contraceptive mentality (though this is one of its manifestations). It means also a loss of confidence in values hitherto recognized, a hesitation to commit oneself, a distrust of structures, whether family structures or those of institutions, including religious institutions; it means uncertainty in the face of a future that one cannot predict and that will in any case be difficult.

> However, the phrase "refusal of life," even if it is the explanation, does not take account the new values that people are looking for. Many do not "refuse life," they just want it to be different. All cultural change—and we are living through a period of cultural change—entails rejection and rupture but also the need for new values or the rediscovery of old values, perhaps in a new guise.
>
> Many "traditional" values are far from being rejected. Recent opinion polls have come up with sometimes surprising conclusions. What has taken place, in our modern climate of protest and permissiveness, is that certain values have been reappraised, while others, just as essential and maybe more important, have been emphasized.
>
> In any case, what has taken place is a cultural crisis that began well before the 1960's when it crystallized. Its consequences in the religious world are only one aspect of a wider crisis that affects all sectors of life—in the West and in fact throughout the world. A different kind of world is in the process of being born, and it is futile to sigh for the "good old days." It is better to try to understand the new world and help it to grow, by committing ourselves to it with the hope and strength of the gospel.
>
> J. Godard, C.S.Sp.

MAY 1980

My dear Confreres,

Chevilly will soon be opening its doors to another General Chapter, *parata sunt omnia*. We are grateful to all of you who have reflected with us and have sent in so many replies to the pre-capitular Document.

More United

In reading the summary of these replies in the accompanying issue of *Spiritan News*, you may well be surprised at so many contradictory affirmations, proposals, and requests. Are we such "separated brethren"? My experience of the past six years points in the opposite direction. The unity of the Congregation has, in fact, deepened since the 1974 Chapter. But your responses show that the situation is a complex one and that simplistic, cut-and-dried solutions cannot be expected of the Chapter. The intuition of the 1974 capitulants, which became a program of action, was correct: "united though different."

We have been more united than before through the solidarity that showed itself so often in sharing and cooperation: for Angola, Paraguay, the solidarity fund, etc.

We have been more united through our common reflection on what internationality can mean for us in our missionary service. The larger Provinces especially, and the main cultural blocs of the Congregation, can no longer live in isolation. We must unite in facing up to today's missionary priorities.

In speaking of "cultural blocs," I think especially of the Spiritan Foundations in Africa and Latin America. In my meetings with them three things became clear.

They want to be missionary: their aim is to train African and Latin American missionaries, and give them a structure and a spirituality that will help them to live this vocation.

They want to be Spiritan: to live in full communion with the whole Congregation and share its spirit and traditions.

They want to be themselves: to be recognized and accepted for what they are, with their own characteristics, which are different from those of their brothers in Europe and North America. They know that they can bring something new and original to our long tradition. They know that someday they can transform it and bring a new dimension to it.

Have we the courage to accept this challenge? Or will our Western character make us yield to the temptation to assimilate them, to dilute what is still a rather tentative search, a promise that has not yet come to full flower?

We are also "united though different" in the variety of our apostolic commitments. And the acceptance of both unity and diversity is surely a fruit of the real, though often still too timid, renewal in our circumscriptions.

During the past six years, the general council has tried first of all to recognize this diversity, to appreciate what is being lived and accomplished by our confreres. We have tried to eliminate the frustration and suffering that comes from unjustified conflicts and divisions, while recognizing that conflict can also play a role in the growth of a community.

But we cannot stop there; the time has come for us to try harder to look together in the same direction, towards a common goal that unites us and binds together the whole range of our commitments.

Immobility

From my meetings with Spiritans in various countries, I can only thank God at the sight of so many confreres living fully their apostolic witness in circumstances that are often difficult. But on the other hand, it is impossible not to notice signs of immobility and an incapacity to regroup and mobilize for new tasks.

Why do we find it so difficult to reassess our past apostolic commitments, either to improve them or to redirect them towards new choices? Are we lacking in criteria for this? Our criteria can be defined only in terms of the main needs of the church and the world today. Do we not sometimes live, as it were, apart, closed in ourselves, more concerned with what we have built up than with the cry of those "who are in greatest need"?

In the various situations in which we find ourselves, can each one really say that he is there in the name and the spirit of the Spiritan community? Don't too many consumer-style comforts hamper at times our spiritual and apostolic vigor, as well as our credibility?

What I would like to see from the Chapter?

First of all, I would like us to be able to see more clearly where God wants us today and for what service. We are often told that we are living at a time that is of great importance for the future. And events on all sides confirm this. We have to proclaim the Good News, through our preaching, our commitments, our involvement with people, and our carrying of the cross, along with those who are suffering. What is our own share in this task today? I hope that together we shall discover the criteria for taking stock of our ministry and making the necessary choices. I would not like long declarations from the Chapter, but rather practical, concrete decisions.

I hope, too, that together we shall be able to plan the direction that the Congregation should take in the coming years. We accept the fact that there must be great diversity in our international community, but this does not dispense us from trying to define the broad lines of a common project and a common spirit. There are new insights today on mission, on universality, on solidarity, and we must study and clarify these insights, so as not to go off in different directions to the detriment of our missionary efficacy. The Chapter should help us unify our resources by proposing a number of attainable goals and by strengthening the co-responsibility of the major superiors.

And above all, I hope and pray that the Holy Spirit will be there among us. May we live this Chapter more committed to constant renewal in our lives and in our communities. If the Chapter were to be merely a forum for the exchange of ideas, it would not be enough. It should be a meeting of brothers, listening to and welcoming the Word of God that will fill us with the Holy Spirit.

September 1980

"PUT OUT INTO DEEP WATER AND LOWER YOUR NETS FOR A CATCH!" (LUKE 5:4)

My dear Confreres,

We are at Assisi, the town of St. Francis, now luminous and beautiful in the autumn sunshine, and from the peace and calm that reigns here I write you this first letter since the Chapter. For the past few years the previous general council had taken up the custom of doing its annual retreat at Assisi, where one of the most extraordinary renewal movements in the church had its source. Year by year we have come here, seeking at the tomb of the Poverello the inspiration and drive that we would like to communicate to the Congregation. The new general council in its turn is beginning its ministry with a retreat at Assisi.

A New Team to Build

Just as we did six years ago, we must undertake the slow and patient work of building a team. Already we are beginning to know each other and discover each other's gifts. Already we are sharing our faith in the LORD and in the future that he is opening up to us; and from this sharing must spring the credibility of the animation work that you have given us as our task. We are beginning a new adventure together. For each of us this means a break with the past that is not without pain: the new members have to give up their previous apostolic activity and their companions in it; the old members have to say goodbye to some of their former colleagues, with whom they shared so much. For all, it is the challenge of a new beginning, of a new community life to be created, of a real joy at so many gifts to be shared.

"Poor, Universal, Religious"

These words from I/D, no. 25, seem to us the keys that will open the future. From the start we have chosen them as an ideal, as a sort of motto for the community that we want to build. They will be like seals placed by the Lord on the book of our six-year ministry that is beginning. What will await us, as one by one they are opened?

Post-Capitular Animation

This new adventure is not merely ours: the whole Congregation shares in it. The Chapter has prepared us for it and has traced out its paths. It is up to all the capitulants, along with the general council, to pass on to you, as far as possible, what we lived, shared, discovered, and decided.

The post-capitular animation has now begun. What will the capitulants tell you on their return home? How will they judge the intense and laborious experience that they lived? There will no doubt be as many reactions as there were capitulants. There will no doubt be also, as after every Chapter, a sort of post-operative shock, when one wakes up and compares one's dreams and expectations with the Chapter texts that were supposed to embody them! How can we communicate, to those who did not share it with us, an experience that marked us all? It will need creativity and faith, with so much at stake for the Congregation. And there is, indeed, much at stake.

First of all, the Chapter has brought us to the threshold of a new future. We have had a glimpse, together, of the mission that the Lord is calling us to today and tomorrow. New stress has been laid on certain areas and new priorities defined. Our work will be to deepen and clarify our understanding of these, along with you, in the course of our visits and contacts. There is, here, a strong call to go beyond ourselves, along ways already indicated, for example, in the general council's Report to the Chapter, copies of which you will soon receive, and in I/D, no. 25, "Put out into the deep and let down your nets." We very much wanted to send out to the Congregation, not so much documents, as a message of hope and a realistic, positive vision of the future.

In spite of weaknesses in method and procedure, a strong dynamism revealed itself at the Chapter—a firm unity among us, a unity that is not a sort of lowest common denominator but real mutual trust, going beyond our differences, with a view to a common task. This unity is rooted in fertile soil: we felt it very strongly on the occasion of our pilgrimages to

Saverne and to the tomb of our Venerable Father. It was felt very strongly too at the election of the superior general and his council. This dynamism is a grace that will support us in the coming years. Thanks again to all of you who have expressed such confidence in us, promised us your support, and prayed for us on the occasion of our election to the service of the whole Congregation.

The Chapter has also opened up the Congregation, more clearly than ever, to the universal. The "mission countries" have really become partners in the mission. The Congregation welcomes and recognizes its new Foundations in the southern hemisphere and hopes that they will leave a strong mark on its history and lead it along new paths.

These are a few thoughts on what we hope to undertake, along with you, during the coming six years. "LORD, at your command, I will lower the nets."

Christmas 1980

"JUSTICE AND PEACE WILL EMBRACE"

My dear Confreres,

I still have before my eyes at this moment the televised pictures of a group of Haitian refugees on one of the Bahamas islands, being beaten and pushed like cattle on to the boat that would take them back against their will to the country they had been trying desperately to leave. These pictures, along with my memories of the other Haitian refugees that I recently met in Brooklyn, mark for me the feast of Christmas 1980.

They are not the only ones in need. The statistics are piling up in our offices: 20 million refugees in the world, with 6 million in Africa alone; 200 million men and women living in dire poverty; 4 million children dying of hunger . . . Figures, figures . . . Human suffering reduced to figures!

I receive letters from confreres giving names and faces to some of the suffering millions: in the United States, Brazil, Angola, Ethiopia, South Africa and elsewhere—letters that are often cries of helplessness, appeals for aid that cannot be provided, accusations that will never come to the ears of those really responsible for the suffering.

Christmas: a crib, a young mother looking in vain for shelter, a poor family, the exile of a new-born baby, already a refugee. But also an angel proclaiming peace, in the name of a God who saves. Their history repeats itself forever in the refugees, the persecuted, the oppressed, the marginalized of our time and of all times—with the promise of becoming salvation history. Through them, the Lord challenges us.

Our last Chapter was vividly aware of this challenge and reminded all Spiritans that Justice and Peace should be a key element in our apostolic life. Solidarity with those who suffer and whose dignity is trampled upon should be one of our major concerns. *At the heart of his apostolic life the Spiritan today must face up to the terrible injustices that oppress so many. It is in this world* of *ours that the Good News of liberation must be made a reality* (cf. Chapter Document, 69-77).

At this feast of Christmas, I make a personal appeal to all my Spiritan confreres to enter fully into the orientations of the Chapter. If the cry for justice becomes so pressing today and becomes a cry of revolt, hatred, or simply despair, the voice proclaiming peace must also be heard. Christ the refugee, homeless, and persecuted from his birth, has said: "Peace I leave with you, my peace I give you" (John 14:27); and it is he alone that can give it. It is only by identifying ourselves with him that we can hope that our struggle for justice will bring about the peace of the Good News.

I thank all those among you who, through your own daily commitment, give life to this world. I would like to support and encourage you—you who are in the forefront of the struggle for the poor, you who, at times alone in danger zones, share the risks and insecurity of the dispossessed and the persecuted, you who help ward off famine or who merely give the support of your presence. Sometimes you may feel that you are out of the mainstream of the Congregation. I want to assure you of the solidarity of the whole Spiritan community. Don't give up, don't be discouraged.

Every Spiritan cannot be in the forefront. But I ask you all to undertake the conversion requested by the Chapter.

> Each Spiritan is invited to ongoing conversion towards vital involvement in favour of the poor and oppressed, and away from an unduly comfortable and easy way of life. Every Spiritan must know the urgency of inculcating and maintaining in his whole way of life a great sensitivity to justice and peace. Witness must first of all be given by Spiritan communities (Chapter Document, 79-80).

On the occasion of Christmas, let us try to develop "a spirituality *in which being with the poor and oppressed (with the insecurity and risk which this involves) leads* to *being poor like them and resembling Christ more closely"* (Chapter Document, 78).

All this may seem new, even upsetting. Let us discuss and reflect together on how to put it into action. In the times in which we live, we must shake ourselves out of our habits and be inventive and imaginative.

Yes, "Justice and Peace will embrace." I pray that this embrace will take place first of all in your hearts and bring you happiness, in the renewal of your spirit.

Happy Christmas. Happy New Year 1981.

Christmas 1981

6,000,000 REFUGEES IN AFRICA

Dear Spiritan Confrere,

This letter brings you my sincerest good wishes for peace, hope, and joy. Times are hard and there are problems of all sorts, but Christmas comes to remind us that God is there and that his name is Emmanuel, God with us. This should give us courage to begin the new year with confidence. Whatever it may bring us, He will be there to help us. Assured of this help, you should yourself be a sign of it and a support for others.

This letter must take the place of the visit that I would like to make you. We would certainly have much to share with each other. A missionary's life is not his own. He has to share it with others, to give to others, always available and welcoming and continually crossing frontiers—poor with the poor in Christ's name, on the road to a better world. Must we not all be missionaries, at least in our attitudes and in the goals and lifestyle of our commitments? This is not easy, and we need the support of each other. So, in wishing you the peace of Christ, I pray also that you will always find a confrere and a community that listens to you, friends who understand and encourage you. For my part, I assure you that I include in my prayers the brother that you are to me along with your projects and your work.

As I write this, I think back over all the missions, the situations and the works in which I have shared a little in the life of Spiritans and seen the many faces of mission today. If at times you are discouraged by your problems, if you cannot always easily see how what you are doing contributes to the advancement of the kingdom, I can tell you that from my vantage point it is easier to see the overall picture and to tell you: keep on, it is worth the trouble, it is worth the gift of your life.

As the kingdom of God is built up through the paschal mystery, it is not surprising that the cross is always part of it. For many of our confreres, especially the old and the sick, it is even the main part of their contribution. And there are also so many situations today in which the missionary can hardly do otherwise than share the suffering of the poor, in a solidarity that I hope will become always closer. Be assured that the cross leads to life and light.

Last Christmas I spoke of some frontier situations in which Spiritans are engaged in difficult, even dangerous, ministry.

This year I would like to call attention to one of the most important challenges today: the suffering of 6,000,000 refugees in Africa (and of so many others in other continents). Why should I mention this in a Christmas letter? Because meditation on the mystery of the incarnation, in its concrete historical context, should stir us out of our settled ways and help us to see more clearly what the incarnation means for the poor today. And I would like to provoke a response from the Spiritan community. For we too are concerned—in Algeria, Angola, Cameroon, the Central African Republic, Ethiopia, Gabon, Kenya, Nigeria, Senegal, Tanzania, Zaire, Zambia. In these countries, in all of which we work, there are nearly 2,000,000 refugees.

Reports and magazine articles give statistics and facts, and there are some excellent documentary films in which images speak even more clearly. Surprisingly, perhaps, it is not the physical conditions that the refugees find hardest. The moral suffering of being uprooted and removed from their milieu remains even when their material needs are met. Insecurity, loss of identity and of self-esteem, a feeling of being unwanted, distrusted, and rejected by those around them—these are what cause them to suffer most. And it is this suffering that challenges us as missionaries. What they need from us is not so much material aid or reception centers, but a friendly and fraternal presence. "We need another kind of help," said a refugee woman recently, "we need leadership, spiritual help, a pastor, someone in whom we can trust, with whom we can speak, to whom we can confide our fears and our discouragement." A film that we have just seen at the generalate showed us the hope that the mere presence of a missionary brought to a refugee camp in Zambia.

Here are two practical questions that were recently put to superiors general. I pass these questions on to you, for your prayer and reflection

Are there any of your missionaries, working in the countries of origin of these refugees, who would accept to join them in their exile and so help them to feel that the break with their country is not total and definitive?

Have you any volunteers who would undertake to work, even for six months or a year, in a refugee camp, to provide this fraternal presence?

A happy and holy Christmas and every blessing for the New Year.

June 1982

ARE WE GETTING TIRED?

Dear Confreres,

I was talking recently to a confrere who had come home for a refresher course and, while speaking about his mission and his plans for the future, he suddenly said to me: "You know, I find that the Congregation is slowing down. Are we getting tired? Are we losing our energy? How can we recover our strength?" And he added: "For my part, I am willing to pay the price."

It was a strange coincidence, for I had just been thinking of putting the same question to you. We have just finished our third Enlarged Council, an account of which is enclosed along with this. Several Provincial and District Chapters are about to be held—it is a time for reflection and evaluation. Is it true that we are getting tired?

I do not want to come back to the question of aging and diminishing personnel. This is a fact that we are trying to live with, but it should not be an excuse for taking up defensive positions. Bernard Shaw has said that how we behave does not depend so much on our past experience as on our future expectations. The remedy for weariness of heart and soul is belief in the future and in our capacity to build it together.

Thanks be to God, we still have high expectations. The members of the general council see this in their visits, and at the recent Enlarged Council we have heard moving accounts of how Spiritans live today in certain difficult situations. We know many confreres who are no longer young but who continue to give of themselves without counting the cost and without looking for security, even when not in good health. Others who have been forced to retire by old age or ill health make of their lives a ministry of sacrifice and prayer.

To say that we are getting tired would be unjust to so many who, day after day, put into practice the words of Libermann: "Apostolic life is that life of love and holiness lived on earth by the Son of God . . . by it He continually sacrificed Himself thereby glorifying the Father and saving the world" (SRL, no. 3; cf. ND, X, 505).

All this is true, and yet there are signs of a certain tiredness. Even at the Enlarged General Council we felt them: there are many problems, and the animation of a District or Province can be a heavy task for superiors and their councils. Should these problems, with the questions they raise, mean that we must push into the background such new realities as the rapidly growing Foundations, the recently founded mission in Pakistan (which was presented with such enthusiasm and commitment by its representative), or the calls on us from other urgent situations? I do not think so.

The provincial of one of the large Provinces reminded us that, in spite of the problems ("and God knows how many we have," he said), the accent must be placed on hope; no circumscription has a right to turn in on itself; we should remain open to new calls and to solidarity.

Thank God, our solidarity is genuine and far-reaching. The general council, for its part, has felt itself encouraged to go ahead resolutely with the priorities that were so clearly defined by the 1980 Chapter. The "march of Providence" is a forward march. I am reminded of the letter that Libermann wrote to M. Briot in 1845: "Give things a chance to mature and don't seek to gather fruits before they are ripe . . . in all things, at all times, and under all circumstances, learn to follow the movements of Providence . . . After the case has been well examined, fearlessly make your decision and then put it into execution with great confidence in God"[2] (ND, VII, 191).

To go forward means diagnosing our tiredness and prescribing remedies. It is something that you must do together in your meetings and also in your personal self-examination and prayer.

The following are some signs of tiredness that I have noticed: I feel sad sometimes when I see confreres still at the height of their powers choosing easy and comfortable parishes when there are so many urgent situations for which we are looking in vain for personnel. (Obviously I

---

2. *Letters to Clergy and Religious*, vol. 1, 215-216, 215.

am not talking here about aged or sick confreres nor of those who have been explicitly sent by their provincial.)

I get worried when I see some confreres being too concerned about financial security as they get older, with personal bank accounts to back them. Then there are the "untouchables" whom no provincial would dare to approach, those who have not done a retreat for years, those who resist any suggestion that they should do an updating course, those who turn in on themselves, those who are incapable of standing back to take a good look at their life and work. These are all signs of tiredness. I know, as you all do, that they are a small minority. But they make their weight felt, and they are a sort of unproductive capital, which in these times of inflation is a matter for concern!

No doubt, we ought to have maintained, under one form or other, the tradition of a recollection month after ten years of ministry, as other Congregations have done. In any case, the general council will continue its efforts to promote the renewal of confreres by updating courses, retreats, and other forms of animation. All the major superiors at the Enlarged Council committed themselves to continue their animation for the renewal of community life and to evaluate apostolic engagements and seek out new paths—within each circumscription but also in the context of a wider solidarity.

Have we a right to be tired? No! On the contrary, let us give each other a hand and, with renewed hearts, let us walk resolutely forward "in the ways of Providence"!

Christmas 1982

A STAR TO LIGHT THE WAY FOR THE POOR

Dear Confreres,

Every year at Christmas I pay you this little visit which I like to make as personal as possible. There is something I want to say as one brother to another, something I want to share with you that means a great deal to me and is at the very heart of our Spiritan life.

When I come to write my Christmas letter, I usually find myself re-living the various encounters I had during the year which is coming to an end, and I find myself travelling in spirit in order to be with you where you are and to take up a quiet moment of your time in the midst of your Christmas preparations. I feel very close to you and I remember you in my prayers—all your joys and cares, your projects and your questionings, the cross that is yours to carry. Peace be with you, my brother! May the LORD visit you today and let you feel the joy of belonging to him.

First let me speak a word to my elder brothers. We shall soon bring to a close the "Year of the Elderly." Probably that sounds strange to many an older person! These grand themes proposed by the United Nations sometimes seem a bit artificial. And yet wouldn't it be too bad if we didn't pay at least some attention to them? I should like to ask you: during this year, have you felt that your place and your role in our community has been better understood? Have you yourself understood how your ministry has changed but not ended? There is still much to be done. As the number of our senior citizens increases, it is becoming more and more urgent that we pay particular attention to that stage in our Spiritan life. What do you have to tell us about it? What message do you have for your younger confreres?

Last year I spoke about refugees. Their number has grown ever larger. Their needs are still great. These refugees are one category of victims among so many others. Can we say that the earth has become a more livable place this year? Look around you: there are so many signs of a broken world. Who will dry the tears of so many innocent sufferers this year?

> "Peace on Earth. God among us. A Savior has been born to us:
> good news which is for all people . . . "

How are you going to announce that peace? How preach that Savior? How many poor people will see, through your mediation, the light of the Star which will show them the way? Did we not say one day, like Isaiah: "Here I am, send me" (Isa 6:8)? You cannot escape that question. Nobody can. "Peace on earth" is not a vague promise or a pious wish. It is a Word of God which makes what it announces become a reality. But not in a miraculous way. That Word became flesh in Jesus. Similarly, it must become flesh in you and in me. That Word calls for a choice, a conversion.

Jesus lived that choice in his preaching, in his declarations to the scribes and the doctors of the law, and above all in the giving of his life on the cross so that they might have life: the poor and the little ones first of all.

One day you and I made the same choice: a choice for him, a choice for his message—"Here I am, send me!"—a choice for his favorite people, the poor. How many times have we repeated and renewed our "Yes"? Well, if you want to announce his peace today, renew your choice once again.

There is no other Word which can comfort and heal, reconcile and raise up. But Jesus wants his Word to be read, not on the pages of a book, but in your heart. The Star which announces the light is you. You and I have to be the first to pick up the challenge of John the Baptist: change your heart, your ways of thinking, your habits. Give up your compensations, both little and great. Shake yourself out of your lethargy. Be converted!

Then we shall have good news to announce at Christmas and many tired eyes will see and marvel at the light which drives out the darkness.

May God grant this grace to you and to me!

October 1983

"REMEMBER YOUR LEADERS . . . IMITATE THEIR FAITH" (HEB 13:7)

Dear Confreres,

Within a few weeks two of our former superiors have died, Father Griffin and Father Lécuyer. While recalling their memory with gratitude and affection, I should also like to highlight what each of them has left us as a last will and testament.

Father Griffin had a strong personality and tended to meet problems head-on. Always a man of action, he spent half his priestly life (29 years) in the general administration. He combined great personal piety with a strong consciousness of authority—this latter tempered, however, by his sense of humor and complete lack of affectation. All his exhortations insisted upon fidelity to the Rule and the personal discipline everyone needs to go on to the end in his commitment and allow nothing to be lost to the kingdom. He led the Congregation at a time of great missionary expansion, a time when structures were strong and unchallenged. It surely was a great suffering for him to see the crumbling away of so many things that seemed destined to remain unshakeable.

Father Lécuyer was more of an intellectual and research man. He spent his entire priestly life in teaching and in the formation of priests, without any experience in the foreign missions nor previous acquaintance with administration in the Congregation. His culture was broad and deep and his talents were fully developed. His theological studies had led him to a great love for the tradition of the church, without closing him off to the new questions of our day or to the new values emerging from the confusion of rapid change. Jesus Christ the Mediator was the great love of his life and he never ceased to deepen his knowledge of the universal priest through study of the Sacrament of Orders (his specialty in theology). Being a considerate person, he found that dialogue with others came naturally to him. His long years in Rome and his indefatigable work for the Second Vatican Council, as an expert and as a "confidant" of Paul VI, gave breadth to his horizons and opened his mind and heart to the universal.

These two men presided over the Congregation in two epochs which had little in common, though their mandates were only separated by six years.

Father Griffin came to the general administration in 1933, at the beginning of a period of rapid growth of evangelization in Africa and a mass movement of people towards the church. Then the war came with its destruction and its suffering. It was then that there began to surface a certain confusion between the missions and the colonial powers. After the war, the church began to grow again. Those were the years that saw most of the African countries gain their independence. This posed a great challenge for the mission: how to free oneself of all traces of colonialism, how to present the gospel as a seed of life sown in the hearts of those peoples so that they too might add their treasures of faith to the common patrimony. Father Griffin understood this. We see it in his *avis du mois*, in his insistence that his missionaries pay attention to Libermann's words: "Forget about Europe, its ways of thinking, its customs, its conventions. Be a Negro with the Negro."[3] A difficult challenge indeed—one which, because of the very success of the missions, could be forgotten by missionaries at times.

Six years after Father Griffin, Father Lécuyer became superior general in 1968, and how times had changed! Now came the years of questioning everything. It was the death of the old uniform world modelled upon norms and values once considered universal and built around Europe and its culture. For many, it was only a time of crisis and the only way out was to rebuild the old structures as quickly as possible. We can thank God that at that time he gave us Father Lécuyer as our guide. He tried to get us to understand that it was not simply a crisis—that there were also new opportunities, new calls—and the challenge of finding a new synthesis. He pointed out to us the road into the future: openness to the universal at the precise moment when the cultures of Africa and

---

3. To the Community of Dakar and Gabon, November 19, 1847: ND, IX, 324-332; *Spiritan Anthology*, I, 281-287, here 287.

Asia were beginning to play their part fully in the symphony of human values. The true understanding of evangelization now became: to go to meet those cultures with great respect, to let fall there the seed of the gospel so that it might ripen and bear fruit. He never tired of explaining the Second Vatican Council to us and urging us to welcome it and assimilate it with joy. His presence at a time of internal tensions helped to heal our divisions and reforge our unity.

There are so many other things that could be said about these two men. Both were men of God and each in his own way incarnated Father Libermann's ideal: "Fervor, charity, sacrifice." "Reflect on the outcome of their lives, and imitate their faith" (Hebrews 13:7). The end of their lives was a confirmation of what they had taught to their brethren: for the one, a long old age passed in peace and serenity; for the other, the martyrdom of incurable cancer endured in that same peace and serenity.

Each of them has a personal message for us, two messages that seem to be different, but which flow from the same source and are drawn out of the common treasure which both of them tried to make fruitful for us: our Spiritan heritage, God's gift to us over the centuries.

One of them calls for uncompromising fidelity to the exigencies of our religious life through austerity and self-denial. The other asks us to enter confidently into the new era, to meet our so-called post-Christian culture and the cultures of the other continents as messengers of the gospels in such a way that they can say: "We hear them speaking in our own tongues of the mighty acts of God" (Acts 2:11). Now that the Congregation has grown roots in the southern hemisphere through the young Provinces and foundations, it has definitely committed itself to this challenge.

These two messages go well together. Different as we may be from one another, let us try to live according to this testament in all our various situations. Thus, we shall take unto ourselves what was best in their lives and make it bear even more fruit.

May the Father welcome them into eternal joy!

Christmas 1983

PEACE AND RENEWAL OF HEART

My dear Spiritan Confreres,

Christmas 1983. Already! Where have these twelve months gone that seem to have hardly begun? Another year has passed, with its joys and sorrows. And the feast of Christmas comes to close each of our years. As we look around us and within us and take stock of the past months, perhaps with anxiety and pain, there comes the feast of Christmas to restore our certainty that God is with us, Emmanuel. "I come to bring you tidings of great joy for all the people: today a Savior is born for you." And this good news brings us across the threshold of the new year and allows us to wish each other a truly happy New Year.

Yes, my dear confrere, I hope you will be able to celebrate Christmas "strong in faith and joyful in hope." Welcome with the heart of a child the God who made himself a child for us, and draw strength from the gift he offers you: "Peace on earth to those who are his friends."

There are so many things I would like to speak to you about in this letter. The past year has been rich in events for the Congregation, and we can be grateful for so much. The centenaries in Cape Verde and the Congo remind us of the abundant harvest in places where we have helped to sow. God gave the growth and in ways that we would never have dreamt of. In the past year we have been able to send out about fifteen young missionaries, some of them to very difficult missions. Others, less young, have accepted to go out to strengthen Spiritan teams in priority situations. The Foundations continue to grow. And then there is all the day-to-day work, often in the silence of humble tasks, in which confreres give themselves generously to the service of the kingdom. How many of you live poorly, in deprivation and insecurity. How many of you accept, in a spirit of obedience, tasks that you would never have chosen yourselves. Allow me to say at least once a year how happy my visits make me and how grateful I am to the LORD when I see so much generosity and missionary spirit. I thank each of you personally for your effort in the common task.

Among the events of this year, there has been one that has impressed me in a special way and which brings me back to that promise of peace that I have just mentioned, namely the Synod on conversion and reconciliation, in which I was able to take part. It is true that the Synod was largely ignored by the mass media. However, as Cardinal Etchegaray remarked: "The Synod took up one of the most relevant topics of our times: the crisis of spiritual conscience. Because people today have lost, or have never had, the sense of sin, they don't know what to do about the morbid and widespread feelings of guilt that pervert cultures and ideologies. When these feelings of guilt are ignored, they explode in acts of violence that try in vain to re-establish the original purity that humankind still hankers for. In this Synod what is at stake is the question of salvation, which is of concern to every human destiny."

How true and deep this analysis seems to me. All around us we see how peace eludes the hands reaching out so avidly for it. And do we not often feel the ground shifting beneath us, powerless as we are before the torrents that sweep away the men and women of our time? In our own flesh we experience the forces that depersonalize, dehumanize, and enslave. Where is our own responsibility in the evil that surrounds and penetrates us? How are we to fight and conquer it? And how find peace?

At the end of the Synod the Pope reminded us that "penance and reconciliation are a fundamental aspect of Christianity. They belong to the very roots of Christian existence in the world today." And he added: "The crisis of penance today should disturb us deeply; it goes far beyond the crisis of the sacrament of penance. It is a question of the fundamental, interior attitudes of Christians." All the difficulties, injustices, wars, and crises of the world are connected with it.

This throws light on what the Bishops tried to do during the Synod. They analyzed the evils and crises that beset the world. They considered how these crises are lived by our contemporaries: in the post-Christian world of the northern hemisphere and in the differing situations of Asia, Africa, and Latin America. Against the background of these various contexts, they listened together to the word of God: on the roots of evil, on the Father's merciful love, on the call to conversion and reconciliation. Then they sought together, again with these differing contexts in mind, how the church should teach and celebrate conversion, pardon, and reconciliation so as to bring out clearly the link between the evils and crises of the world and the salvation that is proclaimed in Christ.

A bold undertaking. It is too early to judge how far they succeeded, but I feel that this Synod could have, in the long run, a far-reaching influence on the church's life and that it could be compared to the Synod on Evangelization, which found expression in the document *Evangelii nuntiandi*. Personally, I feel profoundly challenged by it, for it has helped me realize more clearly how "penance, conversion, and reconciliation belong to the very roots of Christian existence" (John Paul II).

1. I cannot begin to understand what sin is if I do not have a real and deep experience of the love of God in my life. When I accept God's pardon, in and through the community which is always wounded by my sin, it is a deeply personal encounter with God, which restores me to myself.

2. We are always challenged to "be converted and believe in the gospel." There is no true conversion unless we accept the Beatitudes as the basis and program of our life. And the fruit of the Beatitudes is peace.

3. We are not powerless in the face of evil, even the great evils of the world around us. The testimony given by Bishops and by groups of lay people who came to address us confirmed this by examples. Individuals must first be converted, and then they must unite in faith and hope, without faltering and with determination to go on to the end.

I am happy to be able to share these thoughts on the Synod with you, and I hope that you too will listen to God's call to conversion and will work for the peace that the world needs so much.

June 9, 1984

THE BEATIFICATION OF FR. DANIEL BROTTIER

My dear Confreres,

The news that many of you have already heard is now official: this morning the Holy Father signed the decree for the beatification of our confrere, Fr. Daniel Brottier. The beatification will take place in Rome on Sunday 25 November. Sister Elizabeth of the Trinity, a French Carmelite, will be beatified at the same ceremony. I am very happy to be able to communicate this good news officially to you, and I invite you to offer thanks to God.

The beatification of someone whom many of us have known, and with whom some of us have lived, is a rare event. Fr. Brottier died on 28 February 1936, less than 50 years ago. Since his death, there have been so many extraordinary signs—cures, conversions, help for the work of

Auteuil—that nobody can doubt that he is still attentive to those who turn towards him. A popular veneration has grown up quietly around his tomb, not as massive as that of Fr. Laval, but strong enough to have culminated in so short a time in this solemn recognition of his sanctity by the church.

Who was this Spiritan, Fr. Brottier, this man of many activities in the Congregation and in the church? What does he mean to the people of our time, and especially to us of his religious family? Like Fr. Laval, he was a secular priest before he entered the Congregation. He became a missionary in Senegal, then, during the 1914-18 war, an army chaplain of outstanding courage and apostolic zeal. He was organizer of the fund for the memorial cathedral in Dakar, a general assistant of the Congregation, and finally a father of orphans. A varied career indeed!

He never chose his work himself, but, "*paratus ad omnia,*" accepted in obedience whatever task the Congregation entrusted to him. And he devoted himself to the limit in them. After the war, his life was marked by a great devotion to St. Theresa of Lisieux, which later at Auteuil transformed itself into a sort of complicity with her, almost tempting Providence in a thousand ways in the development and running of the work for the orphans. In the tradition of Libermann, the "little way" of St. Theresa was a way that became familiar to him. Man of action though he was, he knew how to live a life of deep interior "practical union" with God in the midst of his exhausting activity. What I have seen in the life of so many Spiritans in the course of my travels, he lived to a heroic degree. For his Spiritan confreres, the message of his life is a simple one. At this time, when the general council is calling all the members of the Congregation to deep personal renewal, Frs. Brottier and Laval are there, given to us by God in his kindness, as models to follow and as helpers to encourage us on the road to conversion.

Fr. Brottier's message for our time I see as especially his deep faith in God's Providence and his abandonment to it. For even religious look too much for a security which at times prevents them from being witnesses. And our anxious world of today has such need of a trusting faith in the love of God our Father. In a world in which so many are lonely, marginalized and exploited, Fr. Brottier's warm humanity and his boundless commitment to the poor radiate the gospel and show the way to reconciliation. Open to the action of the Holy Spirit, he was always able to see what had to be done, and his methods, though audacious for his time, were humble and without any search for prestige. May he show us too the road to apostolic sanctity.

In Rome and in Paris, the program for the beatification is being prepared. The French Province and Auteuil have set up a coordinating committee which is looking after publications, religious objects, photos and cards, and organizing the celebrations in Rome and Paris. The chairman of this committee is Fr. Christian de Mare, 40 Rue La Fontaine, 75781 Paris, Cedex 16, and information may be obtained from him. A special joint issue of *Pentecote sur le Monde* and *Ecoute* (the magazines of the French Province and of Auteuil) will be brought out on the life of Fr. Brottier—in French, English and Portuguese.

We hope that many Spiritans will join us for the celebration on 25 November. Welcome in advance!

Let us all prepare ourselves in prayer for this event, and let us allow ourselves to be challenged by this life that was so simple, so extraordinary and so humbly Spiritan.

Christmas 1984

"AT THE SERVICE OF THE DIGNITY OF THE POOR"

My dear Confreres,

A very happy Christmas to you all and to each one of you. God loves us. He came to live among us. This year again let us allow ourselves to be amazed at this overwhelming news, which changed the course of history. He sends us to proclaim it to the ends of the earth: "I bring you good news of great joy: today a Savior is born to us." I pray that each of us will experience this reality deeply in his own life and that it will permeate our communities. We will then face the new year with fresh courage, and those who listen to us will see the joy that is ours and will realize that we are indeed bearers of good news.

Emmanuel: God with us as our travelling companion, the companion of our destiny, to the end of the road. The light that shines: Jesus comes to enlighten a world which for so many millions is still a world of darkness. But each year we are reminded that "those who sit in darkness and in the shadow of death have seen a great light." As at Bethlehem, the condition for receiving it is to have the heart of the poor. Will we have such a heart and be bearers of the light to others? St. Paul said of his Christians in Corinth: "God has shone in our hearts to bring to light the knowledge of the glory of God on the face of [Jesus] Christ" (2 Cor 4:6). This text reminds us of where the light comes from: it is the reflection of that which shines on the face of Christ when our faces are turned towards him in prayer.

While meditating on our mission to be bearers of the light, I remembered how a confrere once summed up Fr. Libermann's missionary vision: "revealing to the poor their dignity as children of God." And when one thinks of some of the situations of darkness into which we Spiritans are sent to bring the light, this phrase takes on its full force. Ethiopia (the television has been showing us harrowing pictures of the famine there); the Sahel; Angola, whose problems we know so well; Brazil with its millions of exploited people: these are just a few of the afflicted areas in which the Congregation is working and in which we are therefore each of us to a certain extent involved. Nor should we forget the work of Auteuil, with its thousands of underprivileged boys, now that we are celebrating the beatification of Fr. Brottier.

These situations are typical of what we were especially founded for the evangelization of the poor. Situations of distress make immediate demands on our sense of solidarity: they require urgent assistance, and emergency programs have to be put into effect. But we should not forget the deeper reality underlying such extreme cases: what we see each time is human dignity being trampled upon in these men and women living in subhuman conditions. In the mystery of Christmas God tells us: "These men and women are my children. I want to set them on their feet again." "The glory of God is in the living person": this is the dignity of the children of God. Our vocation is to say "Get up and walk" in the name of Jesus of Nazareth—a vocation that should make us happy and proud and that should set free all the resources of our generosity.

Our missionaries in Ethiopia, Angola, Brazil, Auteuil, tell us that when men and women and young people get up, take their destiny in their own hands and set off, everything changes. Hope springs again in their hearts, communities are built up, and the impossible becomes possible.

These same missionaries tell us how faith develops and the Body of Christ is built up when people can stand on their own feet. Then the light spreads and goes out towards other areas of darkness. The life and work of Fr. Brottier is an outstanding example of this.

The general council, in keeping with the recent General Chapters, frequently sends out calls for all Spiritans to recognize this mission to the poor as being at the heart of their vocation. Some of you reproach us for it, some even say that we are betraying the heritage of our Founders. This saddens me, as it is so obvious and clear to me that this is the road the LORD wants us to take.

God wants us to be at the service of the dignity of the poor. This holds for those who are living in what are called "frontier situations." But those working in other situations—parishes, schools, universities, wherever they may be—should also have this as a priority in their ministry: that the dignity of the children of God, and especially of the poorest, be recognized and respected.

Devote your whole strength to it again this year. If you have difficulty in seeing clearly in the area of "justice and peace," which is still relatively new for some of us, then take as your motto this phrase that is so Libermannian: "at the service of the dignity of the poor." And you will be bearers of light, helping Christ to be born again in a world in which he wishes to be present as Liberator and Savior.

Happy Christmas and Happy New Year.

> Fr. Brottier tells us:
> "If Providence exists, if God takes care of orphans and the destitute, if the birds of the air and the lilies of the field are dear to him, if, as the church teaches us, the communion of saints is not a myth and the merits of some can go to help others, then we should act in accordance with our faith. We must never doubt Providence. With prayer and action we can level mountains. We must go ahead blindly and put our trust in God."
>
> "Either we have faith or we haven't. If we have, we should act like believers, and hope in God with our eyes closed."

Christmas 1985

"DO NOT LET YOUR HEARTS BE TROUBLED" (JOHN 14:27)

My dear Brothers,

What shall I say to you this year in this last Christmas letter that I shall be writing to the Congregation?

Each year, when I send you my Christmas greetings, I meditate on the great and wonderful gift of peace that the angels proclaimed at Bethlehem. And I think of different events and situations that I have come across in the course of my journeys during the year, and which call in a special way for the peace that we wish each other at Christmas. I see again some missionary in his lonely outpost, some country torn apart by turmoil, those refugees, "those who hunger and thirst for justice." This year again there are so many difficult situations, and I have to repeat to so many among you: take courage, be strong, rekindle your hope, "comfort my people" (Isa 40:1).

This year I think especially of those of you who bear some wound received in the course of your Spiritan life, and which refuses to heal. My ministry has brought me into contact with some of these, and I have always been distressed at this suffering, coming from within the Spiritan family itself and leading at times to bitterness and sadness. The causes can be many. One confrere might feel he has suffered an injustice from his community; another that his qualities have not been recognized and that he has been kept down by a narrow-minded superior. Someone may have thrown himself into his work with great generosity, only to find that his intentions have been misunderstood; another may have worn himself out in an exhausting ministry and, at a moment of crisis, may not have found confreres to support him and help him make a fresh start. Sometimes, normal tensions that arise from a legitimate pluralism of options harden into conflicts based on false assumptions. And sometimes one finds it hard to adapt to an old age that one was not sufficiently prepared for.

Whoever may be at fault and whatever—the objective reality of the injustice suffered, the wounds are there and lead only too often to solitude, withdrawal, and bitterness. This can become in its turn an excuse to shut oneself up in one's own world, to go one's own way, to become a cynic and criticize everything.

Some confreres have the tact, when they notice the solitude of another, to be able to offer him their hand. But how many others, even when they see the difficulties of a confrere, are not able to find the right word or gesture to help him, and that in spite of good intentions. How many times have I myself failed to find the right word in my contacts with you?

A new General Chapter is approaching, with its invitation to a fresh start, a return to the enthusiasm of our origins, an acceptance of the challenges before us. As I write these lines, the Extraordinary Synod is taking place here, twenty years after the end of Vatican II, and calling for a revival of the marvellous energy released by the Council. For how many will this be merely rhetoric? How many will wearily shrug their shoulders and let others go ahead while they turn back to their own past?

To these confreres I say today: do not let your pain turn to bitterness, or your suffering to sadness. For then you would let your life drift away, and condemn to sterility the gifts of the Holy Spirit within you. Get up, pray, come with us, and be prepared to forgive. We do not want to go without you. And to the others I say: are we able to recognize the wrongs that we do, and are we prepared to ask pardon and pay the price of reconciliation? Do we really pray for each other? Do we stop and take a real interest in our confreres, instead of forging ahead on our own, or getting irritated with them and shrugging them off?

Christmas means new life from the crib each year by the grace of God. It is as a child that he comes to visit us. In order to grow, this child will need the tenderness and affection of those around him.

With all my heart I pray that peace will be reborn in all hearts and that we will know how to share it in joy. To each and every one of you: a happy Christmas and a happy New Year.

January 2, 1986

"FERVOR, CHARITY, SACRIFICE..."

My dear Brothers,

As the Chapter approaches, I often look back over the past eleven years, during which I have been so closely associated with the life of the Congregation. And this evening, while meditating on the death of our Venerable Father, I wondered how he himself saw, on that evening of the 2nd February 1852, the eleven brief years of the history of his Congregation.

No doubt he felt how much this little Congregation, and the work it had accomplished, was a part of himself. An intense spiritual experience, which little by little became a missionary call, had given birth to an extraordinary adventure that he had lived in company with his brothers. This work was his whole life; he had sacrificed everything to it, without reserving the smallest part for himself or his personal interests. Everything is said in the spiritual testament that would point out the road to those who would continue the adventure: "Fervor, Charity, Sacrifice..."

Around him were his companions of the first hour. As he looked at them he must have thought of those who had set out with enthusiasm and generosity, many of them to meet an early death that they accepted as a sacrifice in union with the paschal sacrifice of their Lord. He must have thought too of the young men whom he could hear singing Vespers in the neighbouring chapel. A young community surrounded him, full of life and vigor, already tempered by trials and suffering, inspired with faith in the mission, borne along on an impulse of love. "Fervor, Charity, Sacrifice..."

He certainly thought of the immensity of the task, the chronic lack of personnel, the constant requests for more workers. So many cares had filled his days and nights and caused him anxiety: the missions in rapid expansion, the tensions one after another, the painful disasters... And then there were other worries: the loss of spiritual vigor in some; the abandonment of community life in the name of a mistaken apostolic zeal; the loss of a sense of the Congregation in others, with a false opposition between Congregation and mission; the danger of losing one's sensitivity to the action of the Holy Spirit by throwing oneself into unrestrained activity.

Perhaps he remembered letters that had been written to him in the heat of anger or in discouragement or opposing directives and decisions that were misunderstood or unpopular.

In the midst of all this he had remained the soul of his young community patient, peaceful, trusting in Providence, always present to his confreres, encouraging them, bringing them back to the essentials, urging them to go forward with no fear of the unknown.

He would no doubt recognize many of the problems and cares that are ours today. He would tell us not to be afraid, not to give in to fatalism, which so often disguises itself as realism. He would say to the small groups on the frontiers: think and plan your action, without dispersing your resources; above all, draw new strength from prayer and community life. He would advise the defeatists to trust completely in Providence, without looking for assurances; he would remind all of the need for apostolic zeal and of the importance of paying attention to the signs of the times.

He would perhaps find it difficult to understand that it has taken us nearly six years to draw up a Rule of Life when his own rule flowed from his pen in less than a month—but then he had the special grace of a Founder. He would no doubt congratulate us on the many good things we have drawn from our heritage and from the church's life today, and would ask us to live them generously for the glory of God, at the service of the world.

Many of you ask me: at what stage is the cause of our Venerable Father? Indeed, what an encouragement would his beatification be for us, what a powerful recall to our spiritual and missionary heritage as a way of apostolic holiness. We must certainly continue to pray for his beatification. The postulator of his cause will contact the major superiors to make concrete suggestions in view of the Chapter. But the essential point remains this: that we should accept with all our heart his last testament, which is a summary of all that God gave him to live, understand and share: "Fervor, Charity, Sacrifice . . . especially Charity, Charity above all . . . Union in Jesus Christ."

June 4, 1986

"JESUS SON OF GOD, SANCTIFY YOUR BROTHERS"

My dear Brothers,

The time for the General Chapter has come. It has been well prepared—we entrust it to the grace of God and the guidance of the Holy Spirit.

For myself and the rest of the general council, our term of office is drawing to an end. And, before handing over this charge, after twelve years of contacts with you and sharing in your concerns, I would like to address myself once more to all my brothers. Above all, I feel the need to say thanks to you. During these long years I have always found trust and loyalty and a great deal of friendship. In the past few months many of you have written again to express these same sentiments, along with your good wishes to the whole council for the future—a future that will take us on different paths but with the same goal as yourselves, in the service of the gospel. Thanks to all who have written, for your words of friendship and encouragement. And the thanks that you have expressed to us we will share with all our collaborators in the different services of the general administration.

To leave Rome and this ministry at the center of the Congregation is bound to cost something, as you can well understand. I have exercised this ministry with all my heart and made many friendships. From this privileged position, I have discovered mission as I would never have suspected it. I have come to know the Congregation as few get the chance to do, having personally met nearly all the confreres, of whom so many have become my friends. What a richness there is here! My parish has been the world. I have been able to go and meet most of you, in all parts of the world, discovering the infinite riches of the life of all those churches. Every time I got back to Rome there were letters waiting for me from various countries, widening still further my horizon. All of this we shared in the general council, trying to pick out common directions in the midst of this diversity, and the orientations to propose. Many times, during our visits, we have been able to note how our exchange of ideas with you concerning the action of the Holy Spirit in so many churches, and in our own confreres, has encouraged you by allowing you to make a clearer judgment on your own contribution to mission, sometimes in the midst of great difficulties.

And then there were the contacts and exchanges with other superiors general, during the many meetings and study sessions organized by the Union of Superiors General and the Union of General Assistants.

I shall always consider this as a particularly rich period of my life and an extraordinary grace. My only regret will be that I did not make it bear more fruit for my brothers. To leave Rome will be a deprivation, but a salutary one and one that is necessary in the life of a missionary, which must be a life of mobility, with a willingness to give up things for the sake of the kingdom.

At such a moment of departure, one makes an inventory, an evaluation, and this I will be doing in a long report to the General Chapter. Here I will limit myself to two personal confidences: my happiest memory and my greatest worry.

My happiest memory is without any doubt that of personally knowing nearly all of my Spiritan brothers. The thought of all these contacts fills my heart with joy and gratitude. How many times have I admired the faith, courage, simplicity, and poverty of so many of my brothers!

And also what a capital of friendship has been accumulated in the course of these twelve years! In my first circular letter I said that I wanted to listen to each of you. I have honestly tried to do so, though I recognize that I have often failed. I have frequently summed up my work in the words: "to unite, motivate, and encourage." To animate so many confreres and especially to be a "spiritual father" to them—what an enormous task! I am only too conscious of my poverty. Thank God, I was not alone, and I thank my confreres on the council and in the other animation services for complementing me so well. And I know that it is through poor instruments that the Holy Spirit works to accomplish his designs.

My greatest worry is that of the interior renewal of our community. I see it so clearly after these twelve years. "Revive in you the grace you have received," St. Paul wrote to Timothy. When I see new commumities being born and developing around me, it is their fervor and their spiritual energy that strikes me most. It is like that that I imagine our Spiritan beginnings. It is true that history gets the better of the collective fervor of beginnings, of the drive that lifts up a whole community and gives it a special attraction. I have often been told that one must be realistic. Certainly there are many signs among us that the Holy Spirit is at work. But let us not hide the fact that there are also signs of weariness, of an excessive search for security, of a lack of interior mobility, of a turning in on oneself. This becomes a dead weight. It is not the will of God for our community. We all need to open ourselves to the Spirit of apostolic holiness, so that he may inspire us and raise us above ourselves. I dream always of this return to a spirit of foundation. Have we prayed enough together for the Chapter of our Constitutions to commit us more firmly to this road?

Once again, thanks to each and everyone of you. I hope that I shall be able to meet many of you again, and I will remember you in my prayers. May the LORD keep you all in his love, and may he renew our energies with this Chapter. I entrust you all to the maternal Heart of Mary, and I ask your prayers for myself and for all the members of the outgoing council.

CHAPTER THREE

VERY REV. FR. PIERRE HAAS, C.S.Sp.

Superior General, 1986-92

VERY REV. FR. PIERRE Haas, C.S.Sp., hails from Alsace in eastern France. After philosophical and theological studies in France and then military service, he was ordained in 1964. He did further studies in Canon Law in Rome and Catechetics in Paris, and was sent to Senegal in 1969, where he first taught in the major seminary and then did pastoral work on the outskirts of the capital city, Dakar. He was appointed District Superior of Senegal, Mauritania and Guinea in 1976 and then in 1979 was elected Provincial Superior of France, a post he held until 1985. After one year studying sacred scripture in the University of Strasbourg, he was elected Superior General of the Congregation at the General Chapter held in Chevilly in July 1986, a post he held until 1992. During his time in office the gradual shift in the center of gravity of the Congregation from Europe to Africa became more evident; there was an increased awareness of the importance of work for Justice and Peace and of the need for good relations with the Islamic world. Fr. Haas returned to Guinea later on and was involved especially in the training of priests and religious. He is at present in retirement in Wolxheim, France.

Christmas 1986

AT THE SERVICE OF OUR BROTHERS IN UNITY

My dear Brothers,

In this first letter, I would like to greet you all—those of you whom I know personally through having travelled part of the road together, and those of you whom I shall get to know in the months and years ahead. I would like to express, to all of you, my fraternal friendship and my desire to be at your service during the six years to come.

In the *Spiritan Rule of Life* (our new Constitutions), which you will receive in a few months' time after it has been approved by the Holy See, the ministry of the superior general is described as follows:

> He confirms his fellow members in their Spiritan calling, in keeping with the spirit vocation in accordance with the spirit of the Founders and in the living tradition of the Institute. He makes the unity of all Spiritans a reality. He assures the unity of all with the church. He strives for the for the common good and the vitality of the Congregation (no. 193).

To Confirm one's Brothers in their Spiritan Vocation

This is a duty of every member of the Congregation in virtue of his profession; it is mine in a special way through the responsibility entrusted to me by you and by the LORD. Our Rule of Life—our way of living the Gospel today—has its roots in a gift of God to his church: our Founders. Claude Poullart des Places and Libermann, with their individual and complementary charisms, were chosen by God for a particular mission in the service of the kingdom. It is in fidelity to their inspiration and our living tradition that this gift of God reaches us today.

I thank the LORD for this Spiritan Rule of Life, which, placing us at the service of the men and women of our time, and in response to their deepest needs, is based on Scripture, on the living tradition of the church (especially as expressed in the Second Vatican Council) and on our Founders.

The writings of our Founders are quoted several times in the Rule, as a source that unifies our apostolic life and our spirituality.

I have to admit in all simplicity that my first encounter with Libermann, twenty-five years ago, did not awaken any great enthusiasm in me. I was in fact somewhat repelled by the deficiencies of his style, the outmoded expressions and the 19th-century theological setting. In the past ten years, I have come to a better understanding of this treasure that had remained hidden from me, as it perhaps still is for a certain number of us. Without wishing to fall into the exaggerated zeal of the newly converted, I am convinced that Libermann's message, his passion for the coming of God's reign, his recognition of the dignity of every human person, his openness to the inspirations of the Spirit, and his serenity in the midst of trials are a way of apostolic holiness for us Spiritans and for all men and women today. I am also convinced of the need for us to study the deep links between Libermann and Poullart des Places, links which correspond to a definite intention on the part of the LORD to point out a way for our Spiritan family.

A Ministry of Unity

My ministry is also, according to our Rule, a ministry of unity. This service of unity consists first of all in recognizing our diversity. In drawing up the final text of the Rule, we became more aware than before of the impossibility of arriving at a complete consensus, which would in fact be a sort of lowest common denominator, concerning our mission and Spiritan vocation. The texts recognize a legitimate plurality in our commitments, in view of the diversity of local churches and missionary situations. We noted too how our practice of religious life bore the mark of different cultures, with their values and at times even their counter-values.

> How are we to live in unity without getting rid of legitimate diversity? How are we to live in true communion?

Our differences are not obstacles to unity, but can on the contrary become a way to achieving a unity that is living and dynamic, if they allow us to challenge each other and lead to conversion and a deepening of our life and activity. If we can joyfully accept the missionary experience of our brothers who live in ecclesial situations different from our own, and if we allow ourselves to be challenged and stimulated by them, then our differences will become a great source of richness and will be perhaps the most striking aspect of our missionary witness in the world today. In the midst of a human society that is searching for unity, have we not a duty, at our own level, to be a sign of communion, as we seek, along with others, a "new way of living as a church"?

It is the mission of the superior general and his council to promote an ever-deepening communion through their animation, their visits, and their various meetings.

Our Spiritan Rule of Life is certainly a privileged means for achieving this unity. It was approved by the Chapter in practically unanimous voting. Our Congregation can thank the LORD for this unity, which was achieved when it was not at all evident at the beginning of the Chapter, at certain stages of it, and during some of the preparatory period. We learned in fact to live, before writing it down in our texts, this deeper form of unity that I mentioned earlier, and which is called communion. It required a good deal of listening to each other, and at the same time, a determination not to give up anything that was essential to our vocation.

This unity that has been written into the texts must not remain a dead letter; we must bring it into our lives. Each of us, personally and in community, must check the quality of his apostolic commitments, his spiritual life, his religious life and his prayer, in the light of this Rule.

I hope that it will stir up in our Congregation a new youthfulness and enthusiasm; that it will renew in each of us the joy of our Spiritan vocation in its first flush of generosity. "Here am I, send me . . . "

You will be receiving this letter on the occasion of Christmas. In this feast Christ wishes to be reborn in the lives of each of us and in this part of his Body that is the Congregation, so as to be more present in the world today.

In the name of the general council and in my own name, I wish you all a Holy Christmas and a Happy New Year.

Fraternally.

March 10, 1987

PROGRESS REPORT ON OUR SPIRITAN RULE OF LIFE

Dear Confreres,

During these past few weeks we have been frequently asked, orally and by letter, what is the position with regard to our new Rule of Life. The inquiries about the Rule show a deep interest in a text that concerns us all in a vital way and are a sign that it will be well received. They also express a desire for information on the stages leading to the definitive approval of the Rule—information that the present letter will try to give.

In the month of September, a commission of four (Frs. Manuel Goncalves, Francois Nicolas, Vincent O'Grady and Georges-Henri Thibault) began work on corrections of form, style, and presentation—corrections which were then examined in detail by the general council, as it was important that a correction of form should not betray or obscure the meaning of the capitular text. On 15 November, I submitted five copies of the text to the Congregation for Religious, accompanied by a letter to its Prefect, Cardinal Hamer.

The Rule was examined by members of this Congregation, who made their comments on it—this being the first stage in the process of approval. Three months later, on 13 February, I received a letter from Archbishop Fagiolo, Secretary of the Congregation, the essential points of which are as follows.

> The Congregation for Religious and Secular Institutes has attentively examined the draft of your Constitutions submitted to it. It has appreciated this document, which so clearly presents the fundamental values of consecrated life and the way in which these are lived in your Institute.
>
> Before the text is presented to the Congresso, our Congregation communicates to you, in the following pages, some remarks concerning complements or modifications to be made to certain articles. As you will see, it is requested especially that several dispositions laid down in the Code of Canon Law be transferred to the Constitutions (Book I) from the less permanent regulations (Book II), where they are at present.
>
> When you have made the opportune modifications, please send in eight copies of the resulting text to the Congregation, for examination by the Congresso, which may itself request further corrections.

This letter, with its positive and encouraging view of our Rule, was accompanied by about sixty requests for modifications of various kinds, most of them asking for the transfer from Book II to Book I, of texts referring to canonical dispositions, which in fact cannot be modified by a subsequent General Chapter. Certain remarks bring an opportune precision to our text; others ask for a few additions that figure in the Constitutions of all religious Institutes dependent on the Congregation for Religious; a very small number ask for a change in our text. We have examined these requests at length in council, so that the new formulations might be as close as possible to our original text.

We then undertook a normal process of dialogue with the Congregation for Religious, with a view to negotiating these changes, while taking the wishes and options of our Chapter into account.

After this preliminary phase of examination and consultation, our text will be studied by the Congresso, i.e., by the group of permanent members of the Congregation for Religious, with a view to its final approval. We are now well on the way to this, but we shall have to be patient for a little while longer.

When the Rule is approved, we will send you, along with the text, the points where modifications were necessary. In this way we will give an account of the mandate we received at the end of the Chapter:

> The General Chapter gives the Superior General and his Council a mandate to prepare, in its final form, the text of the Constitutions to be presented to the CRIS (the Congregation for Religious), and to make the corrections that may be required by the CRIS.

From the outside, the process of approval may seem to be a procedure with a certain human weight. The same could perhaps be said about the successive stages that went into the drawing up of our Rule of Life. In both cases, however, there is a true discernment: a human procedure certainly, but to be lived and read in the light of faith. Faith assures us that the Spirit of the Lord uses human mediations—our own and those of the Congregation for Religious, which has received the mission in the church of guaranteeing the authenticity of apostolic religious life.

For an Institute like our own which wants to find its place as an ecclesial community within the church, as our Rule of Life asks, this approval is necessary. It is the church that gives us our mission and authenticates it. We have only to recall how careful Fr. Libermann was to obtain the approval of Rome for his project for evangelization.

Our Rule of Life calls us to a radical commitment to the proclamation of the gospel, through a life of poverty, chastity, and obedience in the footsteps of Christ. It is this radically evangelical path that we propose to the young men who want to join us; for them and for all of us, the church will give it the stamp of its approval.

You will be receiving this letter around Easter—an occasion that gives the general council and myself an opportunity to invite you to live in a still deeper way this central moment of the liturgical year. Let us resolve already to make together the passage to a renewed life: our Rule of Life will be the evangelical path that the LORD will open to us to place us still more at the service of his kingdom.

To all of you, a very happy Easter.

Pentecost 1987

APPROVAL OF OUR RULE OF LIFE

Dear Confreres,

I am writing this letter to you on Pentecost Sunday from our community at Gentinnes in Belgium. With the confreres of the Belgian province and of neighbouring Provinces, we have recalled at the Kongolo Memorial the sacrifice of our confreres at Kongolo 25 years ago. Members of their families, who came from all parts of the country, were intimately associated with this celebration.

Our confreres paid with their lives for their willingness to stay with their people, afflicted by war. They knew the danger of such a choice and they accepted it, in keeping with Christ's words about the good shepherd. "They died," wrote Bishop Nday of Kongolo last year, "because they chose to continue their work as pastors, in the midst of great difficulties. They could have left their flock without a shepherd. But they preferred to follow the example of Christ, the Good Shepherd."

Twenty-five years on, this witness of our Spiritan brothers continues to challenge us: the total gift of our life is a fundamental parameter of our missionary vocation—whether this life is given day by day, or required of us suddenly, in the prime of life, while generously fulfilling our duties.

Two years ago, on Pentecost Sunday, a 29-year-old confrere, Fr. Jean-Etienne Wozniak, was shot down in Angola on the road from his mission to an outstation to celebrate Mass. A few weeks ago, in similar circumstances and in the same country, Fr. Nicolaas Ligthart also paid with his life for his dedication. Among his papers in the car were found the significant words: "A boat is much safer in port, but boats are not made to stay in port."

On this day dedicated to the Holy Spirit, who inspires our apostolic life, my thoughts turn in a special way to my Spiritan brothers who are working courageously in difficult situations for the coming of the kingdom of God, in countries troubled by war, drought, famine, apartheid.

I think also of our confreres working among refugees and sharing their insecurity. I think of those who are worried at the thought that what they are doing will not be followed up, because of lack of personnel to take over. I would like simply to say to them: take courage, in hope and joy, in spite of all difficulties.

If I am writing this letter to you today, it is because today, which marks also the opening of the Marian Year, our Spiritan Rule of Life has been approved by the Congregation for Religious. Here is the text of the decree of approval:

> The Congregation of the Holy Ghost under the protection of the Immaculate Heart of Mary has proceeded to the revision of its Constitutions, in accordance with the requirements of the Motu Proprio *Ecclesiae Sanctae* (II, 6), and has submitted to the Holy See the text drawn up by its 1986 General Chapter.
>
> After an attentive study of the document, to which certain modifications have been brought, the Congregation for the Religious and Secular Institutes recognizes that this "Rule of Life" commits Spiritans to respond to the needs of evangelization in their time, in living fidelity to the charisms of their Founders, Claude Poullart des Places and Francis Libermann. The preaching of the good news, the practice of the evangelical counsels, and life in a fraternal and praying community, are the three essential elements that give their apostolic life both its basis and its unity. They participate in the Church's mission, according to their proper vocation, by evangelizing the poor, going more especially to those who have not yet heard the gospel message and to those whose needs are greatest.
>
> By the present decree, the Holy See grants, then, the approval requested. This measure does not derogate in any way from the requirements of the Church's universal law.
>
> May Spiritan religious observe these Constitutions with love, so as to have "one heart and one soul" and be totally available for the service of the gospel. May the Holy Spirit, dwelling in their hearts as in the Heart of Mary, be the fruitful source of their missionary spirit.
>
> Notwithstanding all things contrary.
>
> Given at Rome, on 7 June 1989, the Solemnity of the Pentecost and the opening of the Marian Year.

It is particularly significant for us Spiritans to receive our Rule of Life from the church on this day of our patronal feast. The Holy Spirit has indeed been the invisible guiding hand in this Rule of Life, through all the stages of its preparation. And it is he who will inspire us with the fidelity needed to make of it a true Rule of Life.

This day of Pentecost 1987 is also the beginning of the Marian Year. Mary has a special place in our Rule of Life, as the following article, among others, shows clearly:

> In every facet of our lives, but particularly in what has to do with prayer, Mary is our model of docility and of faithfulness to every inspiration of the Holy Spirit. We offer her veneration and prayer that after her example the Holy Spirit, who dwelt in her Immaculate Heart, may come to be in us too an abundant source of apostolic spirit" (SRL, no. 89).

We hope to get our Rule of Life to you, in its French, English, and Portuguese versions, by the end of the year.

During this Marian Year, let us ask Our Lady for the grace of a great openness to the Holy Spirit. In committing ourselves to this new way of life, we shall be able to collaborate more than ever with Christ for the coming of his Kingdom.

Christmas 1987

"IN DOCILITY TO THE HOLY SPIRIT"

My dear Confreres,

The Feast of Christmas gives me an opportunity to visit you wherever it is that your mission to bear witness to the Emmanuel, God with us, has brought you. Together with you I am looking forward in this season to the coming year. I share with you, on the threshold of the new year, those secret hopes each one has in his own heart—that a plan will become a reality, that the hope we have for our daily living may be fulfilled, that there will be a turn for the better in our world, our church, our Congregation, our community, our own life.

Many such hopes are accompanied by a sort of uneasiness, an anxiety that feeds off experiences in the past. What does the coming year hold in store for the people with whom I am working, with whom, in solidarity, I seek freedom, a better living, peace, justice, and human dignity? What is our church to become, as it seeks to be, in spite of obstacles and obstructions, a church that is communion, a church that is poor and at the service of all?

We know even before it begins that this year will bring us the usual joys and sorrows. We are sure that there will be unforeseen and unforeseeable events, which we shall find hard to accept when they come knocking at our door. How are we to turn such things to good account? How can we have them speak as God's word to us in our own life, how let them bring about in us an attitude of "docility to the Holy Spirit," a "state of habitual faithfulness to what the Holy Spirit inspires" (SRL, no. 5).

May I say how often I am struck, in talking with one or other of you or in a letter that comes to me, by the way that certain confreres remain marked by some event in their lives that happened during their years in formation perhaps, or even before then. Maybe it is an injustice done them, a lack of delicacy shown them as persons, a failure to appreciate their gifts or to value their abilities . . . These are things that have, so to speak, stuck in their throat, a foreign body lodged in them that affects them even today and almost paralyzes their life.

In order to face up calmly to the events of both the past and the present and to prevent them from weighing us down, we must try to integrate them into our lives and to see their meaning.

What sort of meaning? Let us not be too hasty in calling this thing or that a word from God. It is too easily said and too soon. Many an event in our own lives—as indeed in the lives of others—lies open to various interpretations. The essential attitude is prudence, then, lest we run the risk of attributing all sorts of words to God.

Sometimes we interpret events in accordance with our natural inclinations or our current preferences. Should we succeed in some scheme that gives us satisfaction, we easily see this as God encouraging us to follow up the enterprise. Should the opposite come to pass, a hold-up in some mission that we find less attractive, how quickly is it God's hint that we alter course. We tend too readily to put into God's mouth what we want to hear. To say without discernment that everything is God's word is to risk taking the easy road.

Other things that happen to us—let us have the courage and humility to admit it—result from what we ourselves do. They are not done to us by anyone else. For example, there are failures that are the fruit of the sort of men we are, the lives we lead, the way we behave ourselves. Many a time there is a sort of complicity between the manner of men we are and what happens to us. How salutary to admit that some of what life does to us but mirrors what we are. May we never charge to God's account, nor that of anybody else, what we should mark down to our own.

An event does not become God's word to us and a sign of his Spirit until we have interiorized it and reflected on it in prayer. Jesus speaks to us in the gospel of "signs of the times" to be watched for, to be understood, and he himself gives an example of how to read the Father's will in hours of prayer and meditation. Mary, who is put before us by our Rule of Life as a model of docility to the Holy Spirit, was able to face up fully to things that shattered her life, thanks to that "pilgrimage of faith" (to use the expression of John Paul II in *Redemptoris mater*[1]), in which she "pondered these things in her heart" (Luke 2:51), thus gradually discovering their meaning and mystery.

The events of life are capable of being words of God in so far as their impact on us immerses us deeper in those values that belong to the Gospel, the world of the Beatitudes; in so far as their impact opens our mind and heart to others and does not make us self-centered; makes us serene, not stressed; leads to reliance upon God rather than hesitancy and doubt, to forgiveness and not bitterness, to constancy rather than a succession of changing loyalties . . .

It is in this sort of interpretation, often with the help of a community, a confrere, a friend, or a spiritual director, that "the Spirit too comes to the aid of our weakness" (Rom 8:26). When we let the Holy Spirit direct us in life's lesser as well as its great events, then little by little we enter that state of "practical union" Fr. Libermann talks about as "this condition of habitual fidelity to the inspiration of the Holy Spirit" as our Rule of Life expresses it (no. 5). In one of his last spiritual talks to the novices (ND, XIII, 697-702), Fr. Libermann speaks of practical union as "acting in everything in conformity with God's will, in a spirit of faith and love." He goes on to say (and it is here that we see that the spirituality he wishes to inculcate is one that is deeply rooted in the daily life of the apostle), "a missionary's joys, his troubles, his sufferings, the work his zeal drives him to, his very failures, are all of them lived in the Spirit of God." This practical union as a habitual way of living is more than merely human good will; it is the gradual growth of God's own life in us: "we will come to him and make our home with him" (John 14:23). To one who is an apostle, this means the contemplation of the mystery of God in his plan of salvation for the world.

> We live out our mission in willed obedience to the Holy Spirit, taking Mary as our model. This condition of habitual fidelity

---

1. John Paul II, *Redemptoris mater*, 1987.

to the inspiration of the Holy Spirit is the "practical union" of which Libermann speaks. It is the wellspring of our apostolic zeal and leads us to being completely available and making a complete gift of ourselves (SRL, no. 5).

With sincere good wishes to you, and to those who are celebrating Christmas with you, for a Happy Christmas and a happy New Year 1988, lived out in docility to the Holy Spirit.

Pentecost 1988

AT THE HEART OF OUR SPIRITAN VOCATION
The "Apostolic Life"

My dear Confreres,

Before becoming a charter drawn up by our combined efforts, the Spiritan Rule of Life was already written in the existence of each one of us, with different accents and at levels whose depths only God himself knows. Indeed, this is why our whole Rule is written in the present tense: it does not say of Spiritans that they "will do" or "will be," but it says, "we are," "we do." What it requires of us already exists, at least up to a point, and we are on the way to fulfilling it still further; in this, the Rule of Life is a source of dynamism, not of paralysis or discouragement.

In the course of our visits to circumscriptions, the general assistants and I are happy to discover how the Rule of Life is already inscribed in our lives. During the past few months, meeting our confreres in Zaire and Angola and taking part in their respective Chapters, I was able, for instance, to realize once more how the "solidarity" that the Rule mentions so often is not a vain word.

In Zaire, there is solidarity with people living in difficult social and economic conditions, and solidarity with a church which, in spite of the vitality of its Christian communities, is in urgent need of apostolic workers.

In Angola, I could feel the joy of Spiritan vocations lived out in solidarity with the dramatic situation of a people continually faced with insecurity and poverty as a result of the widespread war. Here too our confreres are deeply united to a church in which many Christian communities are without a priest because of the war or of lack of personnel.

It is through such solidarity that we give meaning in our lives to what our Rule calls the "apostolic life."

The "apostolic life," as understood in the first chapter (SRL, no. 3), is a life in Christ's footsteps, with three essential dimensions: the proclamation of the Good News, the practice of the evangelical counsels, and a life in fraternal and praying community. It is thus a good deal more than simply apostolic or pastoral activity; it is the consecration of our whole existence to the service of the kingdom. There is a whole dynamic of creative tension between these elements that constitute our Spiritan life.

It is in this perspective, of becoming better apostles in accordance with our vocation, that the evangelical counsels are presented in their apostolic and social dimensions: chastity, as a form of opposition to all forms of degradation of love; poverty, as bearing witness to a new world of justice and sharing; obedience, as freedom from the thirst for power, so as to be able to serve the poor. It is also in this perspective that there is question of the inculturation of our religious life, its practice taking on "different forms among different peoples or in various cultures." The progression of the subtitles, within certain chapters of the Rule, itself suggests this dynamic unity of our life: "called to live in community . . . for the apostolic life"; or "prayer in our apostolic life . . . moved by the Spirit . . . with Mary."

This unity of Spiritan apostolic life that we see in our confreres during our visits finds its echo in what has been told us by young men in formation whom we have met in Africa. Several have told me that they discovered their Spiritan vocation through seeing such and such a confrere (citing names) preaching the good news to the "poor" while living a fulfilled personal life in a truly fraternal community.

However, if the Spiritan Rule of Life is already inscribed in our lives, it invites us to go still further, because the Holy Spirit, under whose guidance it places us, always goes beyond the letter of the law.

What do we mean by going still further? It means opening ourselves to what the Spirit has to say to us in the new challenges to mission today, such as inculturation, inter-religious dialogue, ecumenism, hunger in the world, injustice, the problems of youth, especially in large cities, unemployment, and so many others. It means opening ourselves to what the Spirit has to say through certain new communities in which lay people, men and women, find the fulfilment of their baptismal vocation and their mission; in which ministries are diversified and harmonized for the building up of the people of God, of the Body of Christ which is the church. To go still further means opening ourselves to the Spirit, who reminds us of our preferential mission to "those who have not yet heard the gospel message or who have scarcely heard it; those oppressed and most disadvantaged, as a group or as individuals; where the church has difficulty in finding workers."

To go "still further"—does that mean to go elsewhere? Sometimes, yes. But, wherever we are, it means listening to new calls, whether this implies shifting our commitments to bring them more in line with our specific vocation (the Rule asks all Spiritans, you and me, to undertake, in discernment, this kind of reassessment), or becoming more docile, where we are, to the voice of the Spirit, who challenges us through the people among whom we work, the church in which we live, and through what the Rule refers to as "prophetic voices." To go still further means rooting our lives ever more deeply in the life of the Blessed Trinity, which is the source of all mission, of all sending. It means rooting them especially in "that life of love and of holiness lived on earth by the Son of God in order to save and sanctify people, and by which he continually sacrificed himself to the glory of the Father for the salvation of the world" (cf. SRL, no. 3).

With all good wishes for a happy feast of Pentecost.

Christmas 1988

SOLIDARITY

My dear Confreres,

Christmas time is a time for renewing contact with one's family and friends. Together we make up a large family, and I would like you to feel linked, through this letter, to your 3,400 brothers and sisters at work in more than 50 countries in the five continents, and animated like yourself with the same missionary ideal. Whatever your situation in the Congregation, whether a young Spiritan in formation, a missionary in full apostolic activity, a senior member, or an invalid engaged in a mission of prayer and suffering, I greet you with all your confreres and wish you a very Happy Christmas.

Along with this greeting there comes also an assurance of my friendship and prayer. These expressions may seem conventional, but our union in prayer is very real: every day there are Spiritans who offer Mass for the superior general's intentions, and every day I ask the LORD, who knows, better than I do, the needs of my brothers, to help those in special need and sustain them in their life and work. These Masses and prayers may have supported you in the past and I hope will continue to help you give of your best.

This leads me to a subject that I think is an important one: SOLIDARITY. Our Rule of Life speaks of it several times: solidarity with the poor, with the Congregation . . .

An issue of I/D will soon be reaching you, on the subject of *solidarity with the poor* and the promotion of justice and peace. I invite you to read it attentively: it will help you, as it helped us who worked on it, to examine where our true solidarity lies, to see if we are truly sons of Claude Poullart des Places and Francis Libermann. Christmas time is a good time for deciding to take the side of the poor and oppressed, with the insecurity and risks that this entails, knowing that in doing so we will be more like Christ, the child of Bethlehem who is also Emmanuel, "God with us."

Another form of solidarity is *solidarity with the church*: the local church in which we work, and the universal church. This solidarity has its joys: that of helping in the foundation of a church, sharing in its development, or awakening its missionary spirit; and the joy of living in the church of the Second Vatican Council. It also has its difficulties: in adapting to certain changes; or, more usually, of impatience with the slowness, reluctance and lack of boldness on the part of the church in accepting the challenges of today. And there are also tensions, such as those that grow out of our solidarity with the poor. If sometimes we have to suffer in, or even because of, this church, we wish to renew it from within, so that it may become more faithful to its mission and help us to become more faithful to ours.

Our Rule of Life presents us with this form of solidarity as an ancient tradition in our Institute. And so, we were saddened last June to see one of us separate himself from communion with the church and take others with him in a refusal of Vatican II and of the church that emerged from the Council. I had written to Archbishop Lefebvre, begging him, in the name of all Spiritans, not to break this communion. The witness of fidelity from the rest of us may help to compensate for the breach of solidarity on the part of one of our former members, for there is truth in the Chinese proverb: "A great tree that falls makes a lot of noise, but the immense forest grows in silence."

A solidarity that will be more and more important in the years to come is *solidarity with the Congregation*, in personnel and finances. Circumscriptions that traditionally relied on certain Provinces now call on the Congregation as a whole, as the Provinces, for lack of sufficient new personnel, can no longer meet the needs of "their" Districts. The Congregation's solidarity has thus been able to respond to some urgent missionary situations by diversifying the personnel in such circumscriptions as Angola, Southern Africa, Haiti, Kongolo, Paraguay . . . . Some older Provinces are benefiting from, or are hoping to benefit from, an injection of younger blood from the Foundations or young Provinces. Spiritans applying for their first appointment are showing an openness to the missionary priorities of the Congregation and a great willingness to respond to them. Thus, many of us are rediscovering that, over and above our membership of a particular circumscription or Province of origin, we are members of the Congregation as a whole.

Financial solidarity is also a reality in the Congregation and has enabled the Foundations to develop considerably. It is a form of solidarity that I hope will continue to grow. Basing myself on the Spiritan Rule of Life (especially nos. 21, 70.1 and 72.4), I recently wrote a letter in the name of the general council to all superiors and bursars of circumscriptions, with a view to setting up a more effective system of sharing within the Congregation.

I count on you to help the Congregation advance in these different forms of solidarity.

May God bless you during the coming year.

Ogoja, Nigeria, 1930. Frs. Biechy and Soul visit parishioners

Christmas 1989

TOWARDS THE FUTURE

Dear Confreres,

On the threshold of a new year, we like to look back at the year that is ending, to evaluate it and set new objectives.

The year 1989 has been marked, in our Congregation, by several important meetings. At the beginning of July, in Dublin, there was a meeting of Spiritan novice masters—a time of sharing that had been looked forward to and was much appreciated, enabling the participants to discern better how to help their novices "deepen the grace of their Spiritan life" (SRL, 110): During the same month of July, a meeting was held in Dakar for Spiritans working in countries with a strong Islamic presence, or engaged in dialogue with other religions. This was an occasion for reflection on the way we live "mission as dialogue"—one of the aspects of mission that the church is currently stressing and the importance of which, for each Spiritan, the Rule of Life also stresses (SRL, 13.1)

However, the meeting with the greatest impact on our Spiritan family was that of the Enlarged General Council in Arusha, Tanzania. All those who took part in it would agree that Arusha opened up a new way of living unity in diversity; in an atmosphere of frankness, loyalty, and openness, it was possible to express our diversity, at times our differences, our deep feelings, even our frustrations, without a majority imposing its decisions on a minority. By understanding our diversity and accepting it as a richness, at times as a challenge, we were conscious of living a dynamic unity and of progressing towards the *"Cor unum et anima una"* that was written in ten languages on the main wall of the assembly room.

At the end of the meeting, one of the participants wondered whether the religious life could not become a prophetic sign and word, not only through the evangelical counsels, but through this unity lived in diversity: is the church today not seeking, slowly perhaps and with difficulty, a communion in which the diversity of local churches can better express itself?

Arusha invites us to turn our gaze towards the future. During its September-November plenary session, the general council, taking account of suggestions at Arusha, decided that the next General Chapter, in 1992, will be held in Brazil. More precisely, it will be held at the Itaici Center, about 70 kilometers north-west of Sao Paulo, where the Brazilian

Episcopal Conference usually holds its meetings. Why Brazil? Several reasons influenced our choice:

* The Spiritans of the southern hemisphere are becoming more and more important in our institute. To hold a General Chapter in that hemisphere is a way of acknowledging the profound change taking place in the Congregation.
* Latin America will be celebrating, in 1992, the fifth centenary of its evangelization. Should this not be an occasion for us to question ourselves in this context on the value of our evangelization today (its goals, its strengths, and weaknesses), while profiting from the lessons of history? It will also be an occasion to question our Congregation on its fidelity to the "preferential option for the poor" that inspired our Founders too.
* On 2nd February next year, Brazil will become a new province in the Congregation. The General Chapter will be a sign of encouragement and support for this province, and for all Spiritans working in Brazil and in the neighbouring countries of Paraguay and French Guiana.
* The 1986 Chapter asked the general council to limit expenses on General Chapters and to consider other locations. Among the possible locations studied at Arusha, the financial conditions offered by Brazil were by far the most advantageous. This was one of the reasons, and not the least, that guided our choice.

A change of 'scenery', as we know from experience, often brings about a change within us. We would like this change of scenery to be also an occasion for changing our style of chapter. We now have our Rule of Life, the fruit of 20 years of reflection in the Congregation. It enlightens our Spiritan apostolic life and invites us to open another book: that of our experience and our concrete missionary commitments.

Using a more inductive, more pastoral, method, we would like, at the next chapter, to start from some of our more significant missionary experiences and widen the field to other experiences of Spiritan life as it is lived. Reflection in depth will enable us to make a sort of "reading of experience". Comparing this with our Rule of Life, we would hope to arrive at some new guidelines for action, with missionary orientations for the Congregation as a whole.

This review of our life, and discernment undertaken in common, will be possible at the next Chapter only if, already from now, each of us, each community, each circumscription, begins to evaluate its missionary experience with openness to the Holy Spirit, as he calls us especially through the cry of the poor.

Are not the most significant experiences those that put us in contact with the poor, who are the privileged ones in the preaching of the Good News? With them alone can we welcome the God-with-us, Emmanuel. And He alone can make us one with those who seek a home for their family, with those who struggle for recognition of their dignity, with the hungry and the strangers.

It is in this spirit that we can welcome the mystery of Christmas.

And so, a Happy Christmas to you, and a Happy New Year.

Pentecost 1990

"BEHOLD, I MAKE ALL THINGS NEW" (REV 21:5)

Dear Confreres,

The experience of my visits to the different circumscriptions helps me discover the very varied ways in which the Holy Spirit challenges our Congregation to "respond creatively to the needs of evangelization of our time" (SRL, 2).

It is usually Events themselves that become a "Sign" to Us

In the older Provinces, the decrease of personnel is one of the factors that lead us to make choices among existing commitments.

In the Districts, this decrease (most have dropped by half in the past 25 years) is largely compensated for by the increase in local priestly and religious vocations. But this new situation raises the following question: "What is our place, our Spiritan mission, in a particular local church?"

The Foundations and young Provinces also have choices to make, for the opposite reason of their own rapid growth, and ask themselves: "What is our mission in our church of origin and in the churches that ask for our missionary collaboration?"

All these choices, and many others, require from us a careful discernment in the Holy Spirit. This is not always easy, and we have no guarantee of infallibility! But we can at least avoid certain dangers.

The danger that would result from lack of adaptability in the face of events, allowing ourselves to be dominated by them. We could, for example, give up or undertake works, not as a result of a mature choice, but with our backs to the wall—or in a forward flight—through the force of circumstances or lack of personnel ... It could happen then that fall back positions that were badly thought out and badly prepared for create discontent or put a strain on confreres who have to take on too much work (some confreres end up doing the work of two or three).

The danger of remaining in the past and refusing to move forward. Libermann reproached the clergy of his time with this, and it would be a pity if today's Spiritans "held on too tenaciously to what has served its time." Let us avoid closing ourselves into forms of mission that are ending, taking as criteria for our action the past choices of a Province or District, even if we have historical responsibilities to a particular local church or work.

The danger, finally, of thinking that we are the only ones who can continue or begin works entrusted to us. More and more we are called upon to share our work with others: priests, religious or laity. It is in fact a great grace of our time to be able to count on the participation of laity, many of whom are happy to take on responsibilities and to cooperate with us, in the same missionary spirit. Perhaps, while insisting too much on the crisis of vocations that we are well aware of in certain countries, we neglect to read the positive signs and calls that are hidden behind this reality.

The Rule of Life helps our Discernment

To help us in our discernment, the Rule of Life proposes quite a wide range of activities (cf. especially nos. 18 and 18.1). It makes room for the diversity of situations in the 70 circumscriptions that make up the Congregation. It is clear that the choice is not always easy and that one cannot always have unanimity when certain decisions have to be taken in the Districts, Foundations and Provinces.

However, the fundamental criteria for our choices are well indicated in our Rule (no. 12). These are the following.

> Situations of first evangelization: to be discerned in consultation with the local church, which implies a recognition both of its missionary priorities and of our own charism, guiding us to choose one priority rather than another.

Those whose needs are the greatest, and the oppressed. It is through our commitment in situations of oppression and injustice that the LORD can reveal himself more truly as a Savior.

Where the church has difficulty in finding workers.

It seems to me that respect for the above criteria implies a certain preference for structures that are light rather than heavy; preference also for poorer means, a poorer and simpler lifestyle; and willingness to accept posts that may not be easy.

As our Rule of Life requires (no. 25), in discerning the signs of the times, we have to "re-examine periodically the reasons that underlie our present commitment and our present apostolate." On this feast of Pentecost, I would like to invite each circumscription to continue this discernment in a spirit of great openness to the Holy Spirit.

Christmas 1990

"FREED FROM THE NEED TO OWN" (SRL, 74)

Dear Confreres,

A religious who was teaching Christian doctrine in a secondary school often used the word "sharing" to express certain aspects of Christian life. When his students asked him about the meaning of his religious life, "sharing" was also one of the words he used to explain it. One day, after Mass, he found that his office had been emptied. In place of his radio, his camera, his tape recorder ... he found a card with the words: "Brother, we have done a bit of sharing."

"Before becoming a religious," said a young Filipino, "I used to live in a poor milieu, but now I often find myself seated comfortably at table with others, discussing the option for the poor."

Words and Deeds

These two examples—a true story and a wry comment—show that poverty is one of the aspects of our religious commitment in which there is at times a considerable gap between our words and our deeds. Moreover, it is not easy today to be a sign of a reality that is viewed quite differently according to the different social and cultural contexts in which we may live.

In wealthy countries, poverty is considered as a rather marginal phenomenon. In fact, these societies are discovering more and more that they are the cause of the marginalization of the poor, and they also give birth, within themselves, to a new dispossessed class, which is growing more and more numerous and which will never have access to the benefits of consumerism.

In economically disadvantaged countries, poverty—apart from a few privileged people—is the lot of nearly everyone, and takes the form of a daily experience of hunger, privation, sickness, insecurity, dependence. It is endured as a hard fact of life, of which everyone says: "We must get out of this."

Living in these different contexts, with their various economic, social, and cultural conditions, what meaning do we wish to give to our witness to poverty? Like all Christians, and religious in particular, we would like to give witness to the ideal of evangelical poverty, and we know with what insistence Jesus spoke about it and how he himself lived it. In accordance with our own vocation, we want to be a sign of this evangelical poverty especially in its "apostolic" dimension, putting all that we have and all that we are at the service of the proclamation of the kingdom. It is in this sense that our Rule of Life opens with the quotation from Luke 4:18-19, summing up the missionary program of Jesus: to live a form of poverty that signifies liberation and good news for the poor.

This means that our way of living poverty will be marked by the cultural context of the people among whom we live: with them we shall try to welcome, with different modalities, the Good News through which we learn to "live poverty while fighting it."

Signs and Challenges

Several circumscriptions, in recent times, have been taking up the challenge of the great increase in the number of destitute people in industrial and urban societies. In the spirit of Poullart des Places and Libermann, they have been undertaking initiatives adapted to the needs of today: pastoral and development work in underprivileged urban areas; work for refugees, migrants and the homeless; rehabilitation of drug addicts; prison chaplaincies; human and spiritual assistance to young offenders and children from broken homes, etc.

While supporting confreres engaged in such work, we should allow ourselves to be challenged by them, so that our lifestyle may come closer to that of the poor and increase our solidarity with them (SRL, 71). Sometimes, almost without our being aware of it, our lifestyle gets further and further from that of the poor and becomes that of the relatively well-to-do: religious houses similar to those of the rich in exclusive areas inaccessible to the poor, personal comfort which at times has nothing to do with the normal demands of pastoral efficacy. Sometimes we have inherited such community situations from those before us, but let us not create them and hand them on to others by our own choices and decisions.

In any case, there are many ways in which our communities could give a more meaningful expression of their sense of poverty: for instance, in not withdrawing behind their walls, especially if these are of a cultural, ideological, or even religious order, and in working along with others for a better distribution and safeguarding of the earth's riches.

Prophetic gestures in this direction find an echo in the hearts of young people searching for a meaning to their life; several of our young men in formation have told me that they found their vocation through witnessing such initiatives.

We must admit, however, that, in spite of all our efforts to live closer to the poor, we shall never be like the destitute. Because of our knowledge (studies, travels, contacts), our possessions (land, houses, cars), our power and social rank, we can be considered among the privileged ones. One of the first ways of living our poverty would be precisely to accept this fact that we can never be really like the poor, if only because of the security and solidarity that we have through belonging to a religious family. But the poor do not ask us necessarily to be like them; rather they ask us to be at their side in their struggle to bring about "a new world of sharing and of justice" (SRL, 70). Many of our communities, in fact, do take part in the uncertainties and hopes of the peoples among whom they work.

Our Relationship with Money

Whatever our commitments may be with respect to poverty, I would add that they always require a clear attitude on our part towards money. Poverty requires from us, both as communities and as individuals, a relationship with money that is both responsible and respectful. Money is at times referred to as "dirty," when one thinks of money from drugs, prostitution, and various forms of exploitation.

But, apart from such deviations, money is respectable. The Senegalese peasant who has worked hard for the three months of the rainy season receives with respect the money he has earned: it is his livelihood and that of his family until the next harvest.

The poor person's money is very respectable indeed; our own money, which comes more from widows' mites than from the crumbs that fall from the tables of the rich, is respectable. Also respectable is the money earned by the work of our confreres, whether salaried or not, and which, in accordance with the logic of the vow of poverty, they put into the common fund; and the same goes for money which they inherit from their families, possibly the fruit of the toil of several generations.

Money that is entrusted to us is particularly respectable, inasmuch as it is intended for the evangelization of the "poor" and their liberation.

In many ways, we should question ourselves today on the way in which we live our poverty. It is more difficult than before, no doubt, because we are more conscious of the demands of authentic poverty in a world undergoing rapid change and plagued by growing inequalities. The challenge of poverty is one of the aspects of our life in which we have to show real creativity and to "discern" the calls of the Spirit. To help us answer these calls, we have the living witness of Christ, which is brought so strongly to mind in this Christmas season: "he became poor although he was rich, so that by his poverty you might become rich" (2 Cor. 8:9).

I wish you, fraternally, a very happy Christmas.

Pentecost 1991

THE HOLY SPIRIT, THE PRINCIPAL AGENT OF MISSION

Dear Confreres,

In this Pentecost Letter, I would like to point out some passages in the recent Encyclical *Redemptoris missio* which should especially stimulate and confirm our Congregation in its missionary orientations. The theology and praxis of mission will still have to meet many challenges in the future, and the Encyclical does not dispense us from continuing a research that is difficult as well as fascinating, but it confirms us, at least, in our vocation and in our present choices.

A Vocation that is more Relevant than Ever

Pope John Paul II encourages us, and other missionary Institutes, to be faithful to our specific vocation: "now, as in the past," he says, "missionaries hold a place of fundamental importance" (RM, 65). These Institutes, he continues, "remain absolutely necessary, not only for missionary activity *ad gentes*, in keeping with their tradition, but also for stirring up missionary fervor both in the churches of traditionally Christian countries and in the younger churches" (RM, 66).

The Encyclical states on more than one occasion that "missionary activity is only beginning" (RM, 30). It recalls the fundamental importance of lifelong missionary vocations, which are a sign of the missionary vocation of every baptized person: "To say that the whole church is missionary does not preclude the existence of a specific mission *ad gentes*, just as saying that all Catholics must be missionaries not only does not exclude, but actually requires that there be persons who have a specific vocation to be lifelong missionaries *ad gentes*" (RM, 32).

Mission, therefore, is not a thing of the past, even if certain forms of it now belong to history. We are particularly happy to see the importance given to the missionary role of the young churches. Our Foundations and new Provinces are an expression of the growing place that these churches are taking in mission. At the same time, this new impulse to mission should reawaken in the older churches the desire to renew their faith by sharing it with others. May our Provinces in the northern hemisphere keep up their confidence!

An Invitation to re-read our Rule of Life

We find that the Encyclical confirms the main aspects of mission that we highlighted in our Rule.

The Proclamation of the Gospel to the Poor

Pope John Paul II quotes with approval the words of the Latin-American Bishops at Puebla: "The poor are those to whom the mission is first addressed, and their evangelization is par excellence the sign and proof of the mission of Jesus" (RM, 60). Likewise, the Encyclical invites Christians "to carry out a sincere review of their lives regarding their solidarity with the poor" (RM, 60). Our Rule of Life stresses on several occasions the need to live out this solidarity in a practical way, and in my last Christmas letter I pointed out some of these demands.

Mission as Inculturation

Inculturation "means the intimate transformation of authentic cultural values through their integration in Christianity and the insertion of Christianity in the various human cultures" (RM, 52).

We must confess that in the field of inculturation we still have some way to go in passing from good intentions to acts. The meeting, next November in Chevilly, of a score of confreres engaged in situations of first evangelization should help us to get a better picture of concrete initiatives in this area. The coming African Synod should also help us to make progress here, and the fact that many basic Christian communities have been asked to express their opinion on this matter is a good sign.

Mission as Dialogue

"Dialogue does not originate from tactical concerns or self-interest ... It is demanded by deep respect for everything that has been brought about in human beings by the Spirit, who blows where he wills"—in persons and in religious traditions (RM, 56). I think that it is in this area of dialogue that a great deal of theological research still needs to be done and that a number of challenges still have to be met. The Encyclical mentions the main questions to be faced here.

The Spiritan meeting in Dakar in July 1989 enabled confreres who were particularly engaged in religious dialogue to exchange their experiences with each other. And, in two recent I/Ds, we have discussed various ways in which these confreres and others, throughout the world, are trying today to live mission as dialogue.

Mission as Service and human Liberation

Here too, the Encyclical quotes Puebla: "The best service we can offer to our brother is evangelization, which helps him to live and act as a son of God, sets him free from injustices and assists his overall development" (RM, 58). This leads us to ask a double question: to what extent are our missionary practices truly evangelizing, and to what extent is our way of evangelizing truly liberating?

More and more, our activities at the service of local churches (cf. SRL, 18) are in areas of evangelization that are stressed by the Encyclical (RM, 37).

Urban apostolate: "efforts should be concentrated on the big cities, where new customs and styles of living arise."

Youth apostolate: "the young, who in many countries comprise more than half the population."

Work with refugees, immigrants and those on the margins of society, with people living in "situations of poverty, often on an intolerable scale."

From the beginning, the Encyclical notes that "the commitment of the laity to the work of evangelization is changing ecclesial life" (RM, 2); it recognizes that "ecclesial basic communities . . . are a sign of vitality within the church, an instrument of formation and evangelization . . . and a source of new ministries" (RM, 51). These guidelines encourage us to continue to give priority to our efforts at "fostering Christian communities and the education and training of a committed and responsible laity" (SRL, 18).

An Invitation to entrust Ourselves to the Holy Spirit

As Spiritans, we are particularly sensitive to the way in which the Encyclical stresses the Trinitarian foundations of mission and the Holy Spirit's role in it. He is "the principal agent of mission" (RM, 21), and it is he who "opens people's hearts" (RM, 46).

Missionary spirituality is a spirituality of the Holy Spirit, who leads us to live a life of complete docility to the Spirit and commits us to being molded from within by him, so that we may become ever more like Christ (RM, 87). Is there not here an invitation to follow still more closely the example of our Founders and to find again in the writings of Libermann the ways, which he describes so well, of "habitual fidelity to the inspirations of the Holy Spirit"?

A Challenge to give Ourselves radically

Like our Rule of Life and like our Founders, the Encyclical reminds us that a missionary vocation presupposes the total gift of oneself: "mission derives . . . from the profound demands of God's life within us" (RM, 11), and "we are missionaries above all because of what we are . . . before we become missionaries in word or deed" (RM, 23), for "people today put more trust in witnesses than in teachers" (RM, 42, quoting *Evangelii nuntiandi*, 41). As a result, engagement in the service of evangelization "involves the missionary's whole person and life and demands a self-giving without limits of energy or time" (RM, 65). We could renew this radical gift of ourselves on the feast of Pentecost, asking the Holy Spirit to make us, like the Apostles, totally and forever committed to the mission that he has given us.

The Congregation as a whole will also be called upon to renew its missionary commitment on the occasion of the coming General Chapter. In just over a year, in fact, the Chapter will be an occasion for us to reflect on our missionary orientations and our witness.

This feast of Pentecost is, for me, a privileged occasion for officially convoking the General Chapter, in accordance with our Rule of Life:

> "The General Chapter is convoked by the superior general, with the consent of his council (SRL, 217); the convocation is published at least one year before the opening day of the Chapter" (SRL, 217.1).
>
> I confirm that the Chapter will be held in Brazil, at Itaici (near São Paulo), from 18 August to 18 September 1992.

I invite all the confreres to pray personally and in community that this Chapter may be a new Pentecost for our Congregation.

Fraternally.

Christmas 1991

BALANCE, THE FRUIT OF RENEWAL

My dear Confreres,

In a few months our General Chapter will take place. For the whole Congregation it will be a special opportunity for "responding in a creative way to the contemporary demands of evangelization." (SRL, 2) It becomes increasingly important for us, in a world of immense political, social, and cultural change, to renew ourselves continually. Thus, we shall be faithful to the spirit of our Founders and to the spirit of the Church of Vatican II.

Along with this Christmas letter, you will receive another document in which the general council explains how we wish to prepare with you for the coming General Chapter: it will be an event of great importance, six years after sharing in the revision of our Rule. It will allow us to interpret our missionary experience in the light of contemporary events in all their diversity, so as to understand better our Rule of Life and to go forward from there.

Will we be able to discern the "signs of the times," to interpret them correctly according to the gospel and to react appropriately? That will depend to a great extent on the manner in which each one of us participates in such a process of discernment and shapes his daily life accordingly. Chapters are a bit like the highlights of renewal programs: experience shows that, if they are not to be merely barren interludes, they must relate to everyday life.

Our Rule of Life lays it down that this personal development is a serious duty for each Spiritan. Each one of us is called to make use of his time according to a daily or weekly schedule, having regard to his abilities or tastes, to ensure his personal development: by reading, seminars, lectures, TV programs, private study—all related to the responsibilities which have been entrusted to him. I well recognize that it is not easy for many of us to disentangle ourselves from the demands which are made on our time. Sometimes we have to overcome a certain scruple: that time devoted to our own development is time stolen from others.

Nevertheless, one of the best ways of being open to others and of understanding them consists in striking a balance between all the aspects—human, spiritual, theological, professional, pastoral—of our vocation, described by our Rule of Life as elements of our personal development. (SRL, 142.1) This is also an excellent way of fulfilling our vocation as servants of mission. There is sometimes a danger that one element of our Spiritan charism may take over to the exclusion of all the others. For some of us, the apostolate is paramount; it may even completely dominate our activity, in which perhaps we have become too narrowly specialist. For others among us, it may consist in a rediscovery of the spiritual, accompanied however by a disregard for intellectual content; this may derive from a quest for easy security and a fear of enquiry. For others again, intellectual activity may serve as an excuse not to communicate with our confreres or with God.

Balance is said to be a particular virtue of Spiritans, a legacy of our Founders. They desired that the community should be to some extent a guarantor of this balance. It is up to the superior and to each of us to ensure that we find a just balance in the use of our time. It is said that the great contemporary challenge is the management of our time, that we are continually in danger of losing control of it.

After the Synod on the Laity, Jean Vanier paid us a brief visit at the generalate. He told us about a religious who had come to the community of mentally handicapped people at L'Arche for a sabbatical. In the beginning, this man had felt himself adrift, deprived of his usual anchors: language, scholarship, etc. However, on coming back from a holiday he made an unexpected discovery: the handicapped people were looking forward to his return and greeted him with open arms. Hitherto, in his large religious community, his comings and goings went largely unnoticed. Some of us too may have had the experience of being reminded of human values by those who are deprived in some way. The places and communities in which we live are important for our own balance: they are not simply "jumping off points." And we do not necessarily improve the standard of living of a community by means of material comforts.

We should all be ready to deal with change. For each of us such change can come about in an unexpected manner: a transfer, a sickness—old age, which always seems to come as a surprise. But what commonly causes us the most surprise is the events of everyday life. And yet they, in common with our own personal life, constitute those "signs of the times" referred to by the gospel and by Vatican II. In this area we never cease to learn. And we must learn to absorb these experiences, not only peaceably, but confidently and creatively.

Experience indicates that the more "open" our interests are—not simply restricted to our immediate work—the better we will deal with change. These interests will include cultural activities, manual labor, an involvement in art, sports, or a hobby. Provided they do not in turn become all-consuming, such activities help us to remain creative and adaptable.

Awareness of the past is important to help us accept coming events both in the world at large and in our own lives. Today's events often have their origins in the remote past. That is true for our own lives, as well as for mission, church and world. A frequent look in life's rear-view mirror is a good way to help us drive safely into the future.

In this connection each of us should be capable of returning with ease to the wellsprings of his vocation. On the day of the Annunciation, Mary had a spiritual experience which she continued to rediscover throughout her life in ways both identical and different. She was able to live her pilgrimage of faith both actively and creatively by ceaselessly referring back to the mystery of God's original involvement in her life.

This Christmas let us ask Mary for that human and spiritual balance which enabled her to place herself continually at the disposal of her Son's mission. Let us make that request for each one of us and on behalf of the whole Congregation. In this way the Lord will be able, during the coming Chapter and throughout our lives, to do great things in us.

With fraternal good wishes for the feast of Christmas.

CHAPTER FOUR

VERY REV. FR. PIERRE SCHOUVER, C.S.Sp.

Superior General, 1992-2004

FR. PIERRE SCHOUVER, C.S.Sp. was from Lorraine in eastern France and followed one of his uncles into the Congregation. From an early age he was possessed of an intelligence higher than the average. After studies in Rome he returned to France and taught theology in our seminary at Chevilly-Larue for seven years, where as a lecturer he was greatly appreciated. He then spent eighteen happy years as a missionary in the Central African Republic. A good theologian and exegete, he was also a good pastoral man. From the John XXIII Center in Bangui, his influence reached the whole country because of the formation given to catechists, liturgical animators, and leaders in rural areas. He was elected superior of the confreres in Central Africa from 1988-92 and was then secretary to the country's Episcopal Conference. He was chosen as Superior General at the General Chapter at Itaici, Brazil, in 1992. He fulfilled this post for twelve years during which time the Congregation expanded its outreach in Asia in countries such as Taiwan, Philippines and Vietnam. He returned to Central Africa in 2005, but his health deteriorated and he returned to France where he passed away at Wolxheim on 13th September 2010.

May 1993

THE SPIRIT WHO BREATHES IN OUR MIDST: TRUE WEALTH

My dear Spiritan Brothers,

Recently, about twenty of us made a trip to Monte Cassino, the place associated with St. Benedict, the man who set off one day in search of God, forsaking everything with only an intuition to support him.

Today, Monte Cassino is the site of a great, majestic monastery, splendidly cloistered. But the search for the one thing necessary still goes on. Unless the Spirit underlies everything as it did fifteen centuries ago, those stones remain what of themselves they are: mute and meaningless.

We heard a teacher, leading a group of children through this shrine of art and spirituality, tell them authoritatively: "That's the left-hand door, there's the central door, and that over there is the right-hand door."

We need to show practical respect for our missionary tradition, so as not to reduce it to a caricature. It is a wonderfully varied tradition from which we can draw forth things both old and new.

Spiritans in many places are setting down the record of aspects of our history. Far from directing our gaze back on the past, such studies help us to sharpen our vision as we seek to know where the Spirit is leading us in our own time.

The only real wealth that we possess is the Spirit of Jesus Christ from which we draw life. This Spirit is not at our beck and call, neither is his presence to be taken for granted. But when he passes by, he leaves precious signs of his passing, signs which we attempt not only to preserve, but to follow.

The Spirit breathes among us.

As we celebrate Pentecost this year, let us also celebrate the Spirit breathing among us. Ever since the Chapter, I have been deeply and repeatedly impressed by what I have seen and by the reports I've read. I ask myself: Where did they get that idea from? What drew them to that issue and what keeps them going in those difficult circumstances? What makes them so happy?

The majority of us continue our work in conventional missionary circumstances. But, moving out from these steady reference points, the

Spirit is profoundly renewing the work that we are engaged in. Others among us feel themselves urged on by the Spirit out of their accustomed groove in order to carry the Good News to the alienated and the disadvantaged.

We see the most astonishing convergence between old and new experiences. One of the pleasant surprises has been the way in which the Congregation as a whole has accepted things which would have shocked us a few years ago. There is no doubt that, almost unawares, we have changed.

Specific Examples

Three middle-aged Spiritans live in a poor and disreputable part of Dublin. They live in an apartment indistinguishable from the others, in a public housing project whose walls are covered with graffiti and drawings. Their mission is right there amongst the people, in the midst of their concerns, being in contact with them and with their activities, reflecting with them on their lives, holding prayer meetings, counselling, putting out a little local bulletin of news and comment. In a setting which might be described as hopeless, they befriend their neighbors and give them a shoulder to lean on. They reminded me of other Spiritans working in a Muslim environment. This is mission in the truest sense: even though there is little sign of results in terms of organized communities or the celebration of the sacraments.

One of the two groups working in Ethiopia (the other one was presented at the Chapter) has lived for twenty years among the Borana nomads, sharing the dangers of war and tribal rivalries, adapting the Good News to the local culture, investing heavily in the means of doing so.

When one of our Belgian confreres died in Lubumbashi at the age of sixty, a Zairian scholastic wrote: "He was a man of deep humility . . . He always knew how to deal with people in the most respectful way . . . He was youthful with the young people, striving always to put a human face on his pastoral work, trying to produce a real effect on the lives of his flock." One who assisted at his deathbed wrote: "He knew he was dying. His death was beautiful."

Project Notel has been set up on the ground floor of the provincial house at Cologne in Germany. This is a reception center under Spiritan auspices where professed and lay Spiritans receive drug addicts for up to two weeks at a time so that they can try to get their lives together in a drug-free environment. There is a cafeteria open all day, specialists available for consultation, an invitation to share eventually in the prayer life of the Spiritans.

The recent Chapter of the East African Province has renewed its top-priority commitment to serve the poorest members of society, especially the AIDS victims in Uganda. The news we receive from Angola tells of the generosity and courage of Spiritans there.

During my visits to the houses of retirement, I was touched by the gestures of friendship between members of those communities, by their openness to the new developments in the Congregation, by the signs I saw among them of how their own lives are marked by their lifelong commitment to mission in its essentials.

Danger Signals—Reviewing the Quality of our Life

There are also the warning signs of our weak points to be considered: for instance, the problems some of our young confreres have at the start of their missionary work, raising the issue of how we receive them, of our community life, of the support we give them; then there are the missionaries who are burned out, discouraged, and so on.

I've just been reading the continuing education program of a missionary Institute. They make provision for a period of retraining at crucial points in the religious life— at age 40 and at 50. We too should assess the quality of our own personal and community life. Under the pressure of our work we can easily neglect ourselves. I've learned the word "workaholic" which applies to some of us. In order to allow the Spirit to guide us, let's take the time and the measures which will allow us to live and to breathe at every level of our being.

A joyous Pentecost to each one of you!

December 1993

OUR CONGREGATION IN THE LIGHT OF CHRISTMAS

Dear Brothers and Sisters,

The one living in Rome knows he is brother to the one who lives in India (St. John Chrysostom). My thoughts are with each one as I write this Christmas Letter, wherever you may be, some so very far. We may well be scattered over the whole world, priest, brother, associate, young Spiritan, novice—yet a deep community makes us one.

Great Joy

We shall recall Bethlehem, but celebrate also today's quiet arrivals of God in our missionary activities or our enforced inactivity. Luke has the identical term for the shepherds' rejoicing around the crib as for the elation of the lame man Peter and Paul cured at the Temple gate. That word speaks the joy of one face to face with God's manifest presence. May each of you share this deep joy. Christmas can flash out from the direst poverty. In Maasailand, at Esilalei, I saw a youth bring fire out of a mere two sticks, spinning the softer in a hollow of the hard one.

In an inhuman World

In the very season we are celebrating, the manifestation of divine goodness and God's love for men and women (*philanthropia*, Tit 3:4), how horrible it is to watch hatred unfurl across the face of the earth, to see the misery of an immense number of men, women, and children, outcome of a warped usage of the world's wealth; conflicts, resolution-proof, resisting mediation; atrocities, rampaging racism, people shut out; entire peoples suffering horrors unheard, day after day, year following year, their children mere skeletons, scarcely living, looking out at us through huge agony-clouded eyes, questioning: "why have I no right to life, to know love"?

Hope to the Hopeless

We are all, in the person of our fellow Spiritans, present in these zones of violence, conflict, distress, in Angola, Croatia, Haiti, southern Africa. There they elect, despite all risk, to stay. "In conscience, I have to remain whatever happens. I am Spiritan. I accepted appointment to Huambo, to share the good times and the bad with this people. The risks are high, but how could I not stay? I count on your understanding, your prayers, your solidarity." Networks of support form around such suffering peoples.

Innumerable examples could be given of Spiritan people committed to defending human rights, to peace and reconciliation, to education and to development. The job of the coordinators of Justice & Peace is to keep us all on our toes, so we are "the advocates, the supporters and the defenders of the weak and the little ones against all who oppress them."

In them we see our suffering LORD. "Jesus Christ is in agony until the end of time, until then none must sleep" (Blaise Pascal).

The Strength of our Weakness

Is all we can offer just a drop in the ocean? Don't we exaggerate the impact of what we achieve? Are all our commitments but feeble protests? Let us never forget our limitations. We grow old and numbers drop in the countries of the North, our South is young as yet, our set-ups are ill-adapted for what is needed, we are not trained for it . . . can we pick up the challenge of the forces of death in the world of today?

The fact is our Congregation is not behaving like a helpless, aging company. Where Itaici blazed a trail, succeeding Chapters in Provinces, Foundations, Districts and Groups have displayed an *astonishing dynamism*, not just to make shift with problems as best may be, but to re-create, to go for start-ups. Our young men, when they request First Appointment, do not ask for tranquility, but for the challenging post.

We are reminded too that we are never on our own. With *lay people* we are working out new ways, sharing the burdens, our motives and our spirituality with them. In mission, they are not mere stand-ins. They have their very own witness to bring, one portraying the church more truly, extending to ways beyond our reach.

Imagine my astonishment on seeing, where first evangelization still ran, responsibility for development activities and training already passed into the hands of new Christians and catechumens. Their Christian initiation and their education and training as men and women had been given fullest scope from the start.

Whatever we do is primarily *witness*. Over and above immediate tangible effect or outcome, our commitment is a sign that shouts and strikes home, triggering transformation from the inside out. Those things Spiritans, from North and South, which many another person of good will does that the face of the earth be renewed, may very well look tiny. It is the tip of the iceberg, of a great hidden quest for justice and peace, for brotherhood, coursing through the hearts of men and women everywhere. The little limited witness of a mere few, sheds the light of today on the power Our Savior came to bring us. Here we touch on that force our witness has to parent others in responsibility, rather than be ourselves directly effective.

Our Congregation, the church too, as situated at present, hold the potential to set *the Gospel's true power free*, "for it is when I am weak that I am strong" (2 Cor 12:10).

Harbingers of Hope Preaching the Good News

We have ample evidence in present-day society of the forces that evil and materialism unleash. Four clear major lines induce oppression of the poor and the sundering of peoples.

> the *market's hidden hand*: economic life is geared for profits, not for people;

> the North's *cultural domination* has it posing as superior to the South, which resents this, so relationships and cooperation become soured;

> *unsettled relationships* between cultures and nations that differ; fear and rejection of peoples who are other; exclusion; genocide.

> And as ever in history, *the side-effect of the dominant powers*. Power is sought for power's sake, in the so common idea that without domination there can never be order.

We begin to grasp that no system, recipe, power holds the cure. Only quite a different sort of force can get *at the root of the evil*, the quick of inhuman structures. The meaning of the Good News then blooms for us in a fresh light. This strength is ours with the discovery of Jesus, the witness of his life and his death, a strength we try to pass on. When this happens the deepest direction of our lives changes.

So, explicit Gospel preaching, catechesis, animating church communities, all take on new meaning from a commitment to justice and peace. The renewal of pastoral ministry is a watershed in serving the poor.

Growing more Free—a new Style of Life

To shore up a strong and lifelong commitment, we no longer have the manifest evidence of the value of Christian living or the worth of mission. Our world is cosmopolitan and ever-changing. We have to refresh our conviction as we go, constantly reset the foundations. They are not laid once for all. We realize we too are part of the death-dealing systems. How fragile are the lives even of the most generous unless they be fed by personal spiritual journeying and a dynamic life lived in community!

This Christmastide, with God arriving to set us free, an infant king, poor, without power or privilege, we must seek to be freer persons.

> More free in how we look upon money and how it fulfils our longings. We know intuitively the power poverty represents to free us from the sick hold of the economy of selfishness, not so we look better, nor win, but like St. Francis of Assisi electing poverty to be with Jesus, in order to have some share in the experience of the poor.
>
> In the age of cultural prejudice and xenophobia, the challenge is to let go all pretension and resentment, wholeheartedly to trust others different in culture and religion. What we are tempted to do is work out a *modus vivendi* with other people, fixing things so we get by. Now we know the price we have to pay in terms of our cultural prejudice if we are to give or withhold our trust.

The Spirit leads us to being completely open with all others, to living in "international" community in real fraternity. It is a way that will not let us down. If we go working in foreign fields and think ourselves superior, it were better to stay at home. For nothing good is to be achieved in the way of life we are trying to follow by one who sets off with feelings of superiority. We are made ridiculous and unbearable for others by our pretension. If dying to our pride of race is rejected, our common living is not going to result in a rising afresh to greater freedom and nearness to God.

Let us recall how humbly Jesus entered in to work to set men free. On the cross, with no support and no means, he loosened love and trust, the great power to set creation free. We look then to see what of dominance, of strength, may linger in our attitudes or behavior.

We are not living through tranquil times. That the seeds of justice and of love the Spirit sows in men and women may spring to life in our hard times, robust experiments and iron commitment are called for. To reach out and grab attention for evangelical living, only bold signs will do. It is going to take witnesses who play for keeps, give their lives in one great gesture or in plain life-long faithfulness.

May I wish each one of you, in the name of the general council and the community of Clivo di Cinna, the Joy and the Peace of Christ.

Pentecost 1994

ANIMATING THE CONGREGATION: THOUGHTS FROM PIERRE SCHOUVER AND THE GENERAL COUNCIL

Dear Confreres,

At Pentecost, a year and a half after we first came to Rome, we think it is good to tell you at what point we are in our mandate.

For all of this first period of our term in office we have made it our task to get to know the Congregation. Our duty is, above all, to look, to listen, to meet the confreres and at the same time to interpret amongst ourselves, we who are from different backgrounds, and also with you. Our frustration is that we do not feel that we are "on active service."

We tried to organize ourselves with help from Father Thomas Farrelly who came from Pittsburgh to work with us for a month.

Taking the guidelines given us by the General Chapter as points of reference, we centered our reflections on them, and we were able to define projects and work out plans of action. Mostly these are proposals made to circumscriptions asking for their collaboration. Frequently it is more a matter of building on and coordinating initiatives from the grassroots.

After a time of "seeing" and "judging" (Itaici, the beginning of our term), we are now giving more attention to "action"! We are, however, still making discoveries and our convictions are still taking shape. We present them briefly.

How do we see Things now?

1. In a world which is daily more and more characterized by violence,

    * confreres are living in solidarity, even putting their lives at risk;
    * Spiritan communities are intercultural and international;
    * and Spiritans are committed to ecumenism and to dialogue.

2. In a secularized world, with the values and inhumanity which that implies,

    * confreres, reviewing their faith and action while remaining genuinely committed to their true vocation, are at the same time open to new ideas.

3. In spite of the fragility and aging of our Congregation and some of its works, yet

   * confreres manifest great hopefulness as well as great realism;
   * young people ask to live the religious-missionary life with us as we interpret it.

4. Where local churches have taken responsibility for our former "mission territories,"

   * Spiritans are trying to discover their new proper place, are taking on new commitments, vocations growing in these areas.

Some Convictions

1. Without prejudice to what is traditionally Spiritan, we see our mission in the future, as having the following orientations:

   1.1. Announcing the Good News through dialogue and inculturation. This would presuppose that while communion is safeguarded, autonomous church structures are set in place.

   1.2. Announcing peace and justice in solidarity with those who are "excluded" by our lives and our pastoral choices.

   1.3. Denouncing all that hinders justice and peace.

   1.4. Going beyond the limits of race and nation, through a community which bears witness to the possibility of living together.

   1.5. Living on what is necessary (poverty), in a world which glorifies abundance and appearances. Taking on board the historic reality of our world of today—a world which lives on appearances, and being committed to persons and to concrete realities.

2. Mission today positions us in more radical(!) fashion beyond the frontiers of the established church.

   In so far as we live in communion with men and women of other cultures, in a secularized world, we are all being led to look for a new faith experience for ourselves, to announce the gospel through dialogue, collaboration and sharing of life with others—without proselytism.

* In encounter with others, in bearing witness to the gospel, we are finding a new source of life.

3. Lest we stray in our search or lead others off the way, it is vital we should "make our own the mind of Christ Jesus" (Phil 2:5-11), allow ourselves to be guided by his Spirit (Gal 5:13-25), "be joyful in hope" (Rom 12:12), discern things by the fruits they yield, sustain a personal practice of the spiritual life and an effective community life, remain freely and humbly in visible communion with the church.

4. If we seem frequently to refer to those who are in frontier situations of first evangelization, in danger zones, in contexts where Christian communities hardly exist, it is not to canonize them nor forget the others. It is because we are persuaded that their experience can teach all of us, things about our mission today.

Lines of Action

1. Broadly speaking, we are seeking to:

   * be in solidarity with our confreres and the peoples they are committed to:
   * accord each confrere his true worth and urge him to take part in the life and the mission of the Congregation;
   * encourage those who are in frontier situations and at the same time are living a community project that bears witness to the kingdom (cf. First Appointments, means of communication).

2. With Regard to our Task of Animation

   2.1. We regard the general council as a sort of sounding board for the experiences of our confreres throughout the world. We see the Spirit already at work. Our task of animation is to promote the dynamism that exists in the Congregation at this point in its history, so that no one should feel marginalized, and so that each one may draw enrichment from what all the others are living.

   2.2. We submit our ideas, our projects and our plans for action, to the superiors of circumscriptions to ask for their advice.

2.3. We try to re-read our history so that on the one hand it should inspire us, and on the other help us discern the signs of the Spirit today. SRAC (Spiritan Research and Animation Center) has launched efforts to follow up on no. 41 of Itaici, with regard to the Spiritan anniversaries due in the years 2002 and 2003.

3. Regarding our Policy in missionary Commitments

    3.1. We support what is being done for Justice and Peace and it is our wish that every one of us should have greater critical awareness. SRAC is involved in promoting this. We share in trying to define what this option entails and to propose lines of action.

    3.2. Along with confreres who are involved in education, we are actively reviewing ways in which we can undertake this mission today, a mission essential for the promotion and evangelization of youth, in keeping with a Spiritan understanding.

    3.3. We are also studying possible commitments in new countries: Asia, Eastern Europe, other African countries that invite us ... We are trying to draw up a plan for investment of our human resources for the coming 10 to 15 years.

    3.4. We have worked out the way we make First Appointments. Among other steps, we send out an annual reminder of our missionary orientations and a list of requests for personnel to the superiors of circumscriptions and to houses of formation, so as to guide the choices our young confreres and others are making, towards our priorities and the actual needs.

4. The structures and the organization of the Congregation are among matters that keep recurring, in our dealing with questions arising from the development of Foundations, "Groups" of various kinds, and of regionalization. We are working on a new version of chapter 7 of SRL.

5. Regarding Spiritan Personnel

    5.1. We are working on initial and ongoing formation so as to impart dynamism to our houses of formation and to foster unity.

We have published a draft Directory and organized meetings of formation personnel.

5.2. We are examining different forms of association with our Congregation for lay people.

6. We are working on an improvement in communications

    * within the Congregation, in keeping with our style of animation;
    * and outside the Congregation, for purposes of missionary animation and a commitment to truth and to justice.

7. "Finances and Solidarity" are a key Theme!

We have begun a review of the management in Fribourg, and of COR UNUM, and we are trying to set up a retirement scheme for circumscriptions that do not have one.

We take this opportunity to reaffirm our friendship towards you all, our willingness to be at your service and our oneness with you in prayer.

Christmas 1994

STEPPING DOWN FROM OUR PEDESTAL

> "He emptied himself, taking the form of a slave, coming in human likeness; and found human in appearance, he humbled himself, becoming obedient to death, even death on a cross. Because of this, God greatly exalted him . . . " (Phil 2:7-9a).

My dear Brothers and Sisters,

Besides the set curriculum of our years of training, each one of us, and our Congregation as a whole, has private lessons given us by the LORD himself. What he would seem to be offering us nowadays is tuition in gospel availability. It is a subject we find difficult to grasp: "If you knew the gift of God and who is saying to you . . . " (John 4:10). Let us be on the look-out in this Christmas season for the signs of a call, aware that it is going to take courage to be able to answer it.

Family

A new spirit breathes through our communities. Together we are working out new ways to live and to do our work, discerning what God's will for us is, attending to what each of us has to say, sharing responsibility and giving space and recognition to the cultural traits of every individual.

Regulations and authority exist, but fraternal charity takes precedence over all.

We are trying to organize in solidarity, as they did in the early days, when " . . . all who believed were together and had all things in common . . . " (Acts 2:44). We stand by each other in our ordeals. It is my hope that those among you who are living in situations that are testing will, this Christmas season, have the certain feeling that you are being supported by the prayer and the friendship of all.

There is much we still have to learn. And in this favorable time "if you bring your gift to the altar, and there recall that your brother has anything against you, . . . go first and be reconciled with your brother . . . " (Matt 5:23-24).

We must appreciate all we have already, which is not merely the fruit of the times in which we live, but comes from God's free gift and by our self-giving too. It is Christ's own love taking flesh, lighting up our lives and the lives of those round about us.

At the Service of Others

The way we think of mission today is as a total openness to the other, in a process of inculturation and of dialogue (cf. the Synod for Africa). We ourselves are being evangelized as we share our faith. We do not look first for the good of our Congregation. We seek life in its fullness through justice and peace for all people.

In the biblical perspective, we are never called for our benefit alone but for a mission. Our Institutes were born of awareness of the needs the people had (cf. the Synod for the Consecrated Life). The dynamism of our origins will not be revealed to us by navel-gazing but by:

* a renewed interest in the poor, discerning in their lives the signs of God and their needs;
* deepening our spiritual compassion and developing, with the poor, action that is effective.

This new commitment, as we go back over it in our prayer will renew our faith in Christ and our love.

At School with the most Deprived: the Refugee and the Migrant

Today there are millions of refugees, of persons displaced inside their countries, of migrants who live in precarious conditions. Such people should, for us Spiritans, be our brothers and sisters in Jesus Christ. Over and above the material things for which professional organization is necessary, they are in want of pastoral care to give them back some confidence. There are already several confreres committed to this. Could we not be doing more? Could some circumscriptions not plan something along these lines? The general administration, insofar as it can, stands ready to give its backing.

It can be salutary for us to live with refugees. They can teach us trust in the midst of insecurity, steadfastness in suffering, the solidarity of the widow giving all she has.

Moved to the Depths of our Being

A missionary Institute shaken by the drama of Rwanda has asked itself, "faced with such an unleashing of hatred and violence, the temptation to lose faith, to doubt the strength of the gospel, is great indeed. Has our mission been a total failure?" These are questions for us too. The process of their meditation allows them to see, in slaughtered innocents, Jesus on the cross, to ask pardon for themselves and accept once again to be sent on mission "but poorer yet, and humbler still".

Other lived experiences penetrate to the roots of our being, making us look at how personally poor we are and calling us to radical trustfulness in the love of God:

* when our life is at risk;
* when we have failed, are weak, are misunderstood;
* when we are fatally ill;
* when our Province has no young people to replace us;
* when an Angolan Bishop and two of our confreres, at the end of months of fighting, must quit their ruined town with nothing but the clothes they have on and make their way on foot to the nearest mission.

Stepping down from our Pedestal

When in our own or our Congregation's life there comes such a shock, it is not a time to try self-justification, to grapple tight to all the baggage we carry along life's road. "This now is the time to live by faith" (Libermann).

Such private lessons must never, ever be forgotten. What they do is place us, our very being, in prayer. They restore to us the trustfulness that enables us once more to commit all our capacities to the serving of Christ.

Evdokimov, the Orthodox writer, describes a vision in which the mouth of the complaining Job was covered by a crucified hand. And Job, looking through the pierced palm, finds fountains of light flowing over him (from a homily of Cardinal Etchegaray given at a Mass for deceased religious men and women, victims of violence).

Christmas is an invitation to each of us to step down from our own pedestal, so we may find new strength, new happiness in gospel availability. The wishes of the community of the generalate are that the LORD may give us, one and all, such grace.

Christmas 1995

WITNESSES THROUGH OUR SOLIDARITY

> "You know the gracious acts of our LORD Jesus Christ, that for your sake he became poor although he was rich, so that by his poverty you might become rich" (2 Cor 8:9).

Dear Spiritan Brothers and Sisters,

Since my Christmas letter of last year, I have been able to meet many of you. You received me very well everywhere I went, even though I carne *empty handed*. We recognize each other as members of the great Spiritan family. I think it is worth investigating the true meaning of this solidarity between us and trying to understand the price we have to pay for it.

Our Mission is One of Solidarity.

Quite a number of young Spiritans say that they joined our family because they saw or heard that Spiritans were on the side of the poor. Perhaps the most characteristic aspect of mission as we live it today, is this movement towards those who are far off, who belong to another culture, another church, another religion, and, strongest of all, towards the poor and marginalized.

In this we are reflecting the movement of God himself who takes up the cause of the widow and the orphan. His promise has been realized, "God with us." When we visit a remote village, when we organize help for refugees or search, in prayer, for some words of comfort for the afflicted, it is the same spirit that inspires us and echoes in us the song of the angels at Bethlehem: "Glory to God in highest heaven, and on earth peace to all in whom he delights."

At a time like ours, when people pay more attention to the way the message is announced than to its contents, we must study the approach of Jesus: "He was rich, yet for your sake he became poor, so that through his poverty you might become rich." Our aim is not to seduce people, nor to sort out all their problems or bring them the truth on a plate. We go to them with *empty hands,* but our respect and interest, our trust and compassion, can perhaps be the first witness of the Good News, and a call for them to become more supportive of each other. In this way, our poor words and limited service take on something of the brightness of the glory of God, just like the mite of the widow whom Jesus admired so much.

Solidarity between Ourselves, in the Service of the Poor

This movement, which directs us towards the poor and those who are far off, is what unites us more strongly than anything else. It is our *"charism."* In practice, one sees that as soon as some confreres get involved in a work for the most neglected, many others are ready to come and help them.

The Provinces of North America are giving their help and support to the confreres of Haiti in many different ways. During this last year, the East African Province decided to come to the aid of Rwandan refugees in Tanzania, and when they made an appeal, others joined them. Some circumscriptions have sent money. During the long years of war in Angola, European Provinces sent men and material to sustain the mission of the confreres there. Let us not forget the confreres who look for financial help, send out containers, and take different practical steps to help missionaries in every continent.

We lean on each other in our great common undertaking. Everybody plays his part. Our older confreres pray for us, like Moses on the mountain while the battle was going on in the plain, and those who look after them are helping them to keep their arms raised.

But it is not just a question of an efficient use of our different capabilities. Solidarity amongst ourselves comes from the same spirit that has taken us towards the poor. Sometimes, it is true, we do not show our confreres the same concern that we have for those who are further away. Sometimes the most dynamic groups are not the most united. As companions in the same mission, our solidarity must develop into a genuine fraternity. Our confreres who are starting out on their mission need to be listened to, and those who are going through a period of crisis rightly look to us for delicacy and tact.

Solidarity between Circumscriptions

More than in the past, solidarity is developing between circumscriptions. Their situations are very different. They are sharing their various capacities for a mission that has become much more complex.

As regards financial solidarity, Cor Unum and bilateral help, setting up reserve funds and funds for retirement—all these have their place in the perspective that we have been explaining. It is not as if we were giving alms to each other, doing away with the need to act ourselves; rather we are supporting one another in an undertaking that belongs to us. Cor Unum is meant, above all, for the formation of young confreres for the announcing of the gospel. This solidarity is not just practiced in view of its usefulness. It has to be inspired by an evangelical attitude. With us Spiritans, we are far from the idea of an imposition or a tax. Rather, the superiors and their councils are interpreting the wishes of those they serve to show solidarity with others. The contributions have grown considerably in the last few years.

Regarding solidarity of personnel, it is in the hands of each circumscription. A member is only transferred with the agreement of his major superior. Yet Provinces are still sharing, even in their poverty. Each year we make known the personnel needs of different circumscriptions, especially to those who are coming up for a first appointment. We do not make these appointments following a preconceived plan.

Whether it is a question of solidarity in finance or personnel, we put our trust in the generosity proposed by the gospel. We do not base our hopes on good management. We are not discouraged by statistics and shrinking bank balances. Sometimes a sort of miracle comes about when we make this witness to solidarity; we receive more than the sum of what each person brings along. Generosity attracts companions to us whom we never even thought of. A lay associate said to one of the visiting councilors, "I have discovered the heart of the gospel with the Spiritans!"

To inspiration, of course, we have to add planning and organization. For the whole to produce a harmonious sound, the various instruments of solidarity have to be tuned to each other. The meeting, "Finance and Solidarity," which takes place in March 1996, will try to do just that. The general council will waive the baton!

I wish you all a happy Christmas, as you come together to celebrate that day when it all began, a small light in the night, a song of peace in the midst of the world's cacophony.

Pentecost 1996

NEW FRONTIERS TO BE CROSSED

> "You will receive power when the Holy Spirit comes upon you, and you will be my witnesses in Jerusalem, throughout Judea and Samaria, and to the ends of the earth" (Acts 1:8).

Dear Spiritan Brothers and Sisters,

In remembering the original Pentecost, we also celebrate our life today as witnesses of the Gospel. As in the Acts of the Apostles, we can detect the mysterious presence of Christ and the power of his Spirit in his witnesses. Think of those who are living constantly in danger or in chaotic situations, those setting out again for a new task, those who are struggling to overcome lack of understanding and opposition. Think of those who are trying to learn and understand, to remain faithful, creative, humble.

We lift our eyes to the extremities of today's world, to the horizons of contemporary mission. In Christian times, the Gospel left the shores of Europe to go to what then appeared to be the ends of the earth. But this picture is turned on its head when we look at the missionary appointments of the present generation of Spiritans: a Nigerian leaves for Papua New Guinea, an Australian for Kenya, a Mauritian goes to Pakistan, a Zairian to Brazil, a Brazilian to Senegal.

So for us who are called to bring the Good News to the poor, right to the ends of the earth, where do we look for the horizon today? What are the new frontiers that have to be crossed?

Today's Horizons

What hopes and what threats does our present world bring for the future of humanity and, in particular, for the poorest people? Technology and the law of the market have created a world of abundance and instantaneous communications across the planet. It seems as if globalization must suppress all frontiers. The future would see the extension of this prosperous society to the outer limits of humanity, and cultural and religious differences would no longer be of much importance. But some discernment is necessary here. We are not talking of a neutral area where the possibilities opened up by technology and market forces would simply play a benign role. A former director of the IMF put it like this: the taking of a particular financial decision can mean a sentence of death for the poor.

We know the results only too well. Statistics show a widening gulf between rich and poor on this planet. "In a world controlled by rich and powerful nations, Africa has practically become an irrelevant appendix, often forgotten and neglected"[1] (Apostolic Exhortation *Ecclesia in Africa*, no. 40). The earth, which was created for us to live in, is being disfigured by the demands of production and the struggle for survival of the poorest.

In the struggle for the Gospel, we have to find out where the enemy lies today: "The enemy batteries must be attacked where they are presently placed; we must not give them the chance to dig in by looking for them where they are no longer to be found" (Libermann). There are false roads to progress just as there are new possibilities of freedom and cooperation. Analysts are more and more finding fault with a type of development that ignores people's roots and seems to reduce them to mere producing and consuming beings. There exists today a civilization from below that demands that priority be given to the quality of life, sustainability, equity and, above all, shared happiness, the only kind of human happiness.

Our new Frontiers

The horizons of today's world give meaning to involvement in justice and peace. As well as action in particular cases, we have to look for the source

---

1. *Ecclesia in Africa,* no. 40.

of the continuing impoverishment of half of humanity, of exclusion, of violence. At this level, action is inevitably long-term and on a big scale. We make our contribution. Our new frontiers are those which have to be crossed to reach the poor: slum-dwellers, street-children, drug addicts, victims of AIDS, abandoned rural peoples, the young who cannot find work...

We also have cultural frontiers to cross in order to meet people in their own world, like the Maasai, the Borana, the Hamer, the Pokot, the Pygmies, the Bassari, the Manjaks, the Bassa, the Marwari, the Melanesians, the Guarani, the Huastecos and the Nahuatl... Elsewhere, in those places where the church has been established for a long time, we are far from having brought the Gospel right to the heart of their cultures. Nobody can say that cultural frontiers are no longer relevant, that we are wasting our time learning languages and local customs. After 500 years of evangelization in Latin America, and despite all the changes that have taken place, CELAM has chosen "pastoral ministry to the indigenous peoples" as a priority. The African Synod sees inculturation as an indispensable key for reaching the hearts of the people.

> So even in facing up to contemporary challenges, we must be faithful to our missionary tradition of learning languages and taking root amongst a people.

We should not feel guilty about limiting our work to a specific human group. Let us not be over-impressed by the large-scale performances. The fruits of an evangelization that is too rapid, simply in order to occupy an area, can be swept away by the first storm that comes along. I think we are on the right track wherever we are working with people from the heart of their unique cultural experience, from which God calls them by name. In our mission, we are not looking for immediate results. We put our trust in the slow and lasting fruits of the witness given by communities inspired by the Gospel.

We are trying to cross the Frontiers of the secularized World

Particularly in parishes, we are helping people who are hungry and thirsty for spiritual nourishment. We are helping lay people to prepare themselves to get involved in society in a Christian way. It is also a good thing to turn back to the first steps of primary evangelization, to go looking for the people of our villages and Districts. Their life is like a closed book: perhaps so far we have done no more than just flick through it. This is also true of those who, in education or other ministry, have to go through a learning process to come to grips with the world of young people.

We are used to seeing the proclamation of the Gospel being followed by entry into the Christian community.

Today, in certain situations, there are scarcely any baptisms. But in coming into contact with witnesses to the Gospel, some people deepen their religious sense, grow in freedom and devote themselves to helping the poor. In fact, the front line of present-day mission is often in those places where different kinds of generous people are coming together, beyond the frontiers of religious or other allegiance. In the face of distress, urgency, danger, our differences while not being destroyed, are relativized. We feel at one with others in those places where the love of God liberates and brings together.

Finally, we are still looking for new geographical frontiers to cross, as for example, Mozambique, and perhaps soon new Asian countries. We are receiving pressing requests which are in line with our vocation. We see in all this a source of enrichment for our Institute.

A Frontier that has to be crossed in our own Lives

If we wish to remain faithful to our vocation, we cannot just follow the style of life of the consumerist society and the television culture. Much discernment and conversion are needed if we are to be present in today's society while at the same time staying in close contact with Christ who is our unique and universal source of life. This is one of the main elements in ongoing formation. Mission itself is an opportunity for our renewal. The poor and people of different religions and cultures help us to become more profoundly Christian. We are also called to a greater openness to our confreres in our communities, often international and inter-cultural. Going out towards others involves crossing a frontier within ourselves, and this is a sort of death and resurrection.

On all our front lines, despite everything, the Spirit of the Lord is going to incite us to celebrate Pentecost. The feast gives expression to the hidden joys of everyday ministry; it reveals the splendor of our daily work, which does not go unnoticed by people of good will.

Best wishes for our beautiful feast.

Yours fraternally.

A missionary crossing a log bridge

Christmas 1996

AN INVITATION TO HAPPINESS

> Do not be afraid; for behold, I proclaim to you good news of great joy that will be for all the people. For today in the city of David a Savior has been born for you who is Messiah and LORD. And this will be a sign for you: you will find an infant wrapped in swaddling clothes and lying in a manger (Luke 2, 10-12).

Dear Spiritan Brothers and Sisters,

I am happy that the coming of Christmas gives me the chance to write to you once again, and I want to use the opportunity to tell you about our new initiative in Asia, not to make a special advertisement for this project, but rather to look at it as something that reveals the nature of our Spiritan mission today.

Mission impossible?

It was not without a certain questioning that we followed up the wishes expressed by our last General Chapter. How could we take on the challenge of mission in South-East Asia with such small means at our disposal? Would we not be better using them in areas where we are already established and have experience? Are we going to send young confrères to an impossible mission where they will soon get discouraged?

But we are already committed in many places to a "mission impossible," faced with the indifference of secularized societies, fundamentalists, social degradation, the ravages of conflicts as in Mozambique where we are beginning another new missionary adventure. It seems to be a basic characteristic of our mission at the moment. Confreres stay in impossible situations despite their helplessness. They see the needs and they feel called to respond to them, for that is their Spiritan vocation. We have reacted to the call of Asia in the same way, despite our meagre resources. Rather than reckoning up "how many divisions we have," we are relying on a widening of our hearts.

Thoughts on our Weakness

In his Rule of Life for the Christians of Milan, Cardinal Martini reflects on the weakness of Jesus. By not looking for an escape when faced with the threat of evil, Jesus showed what strength and freedom can be drawn from a belief in the love of God. Our feeble presence in a difficult situation is our first witness. *"The face of Jesus Christ on the cross is the casket wherein the meaning of life, of history and of the world are treasured in silence."*

During a concelebration in Chinese, the old priest beside me simply smiled when I asked him where we had got to in the liturgy. Later I learnt that he had spent all his life as a priest, more than forty years, in prison in China and that he had just been released a few months previously. He could only speak Chinese. There was no sign that this experience had destroyed him, yet he had waited so long for the walls to crumble.

Such a life gives food for thought. When we entrust ourselves into the hands of God, we are liberated from fear; our hands which were clinging to all sorts of illusory life-belts have become free to hold on to that secure life-line which is the protecting love of God.

Our own Mission

A Taiwanese Bishop told us that his church was stagnant and that he looked to the Spiritans to inject a new missionary dynamism into it. A Bishop of the Philippines, having outlined the new organization of ministries in his diocese, admitted that all these structures could remain empty shells. It is not our vocation to run established churches. *"The church is for those who are outside it."* What we try to do is to be with the people, to share their joys and sorrows, to strive with them for the fullness of life, for justice and peace. We live with this vision of the church, and we try to promote it in Christian communities.

A Community of Witness

Each day, each year, our confreres in Asia will have their community life to help them renew their trust in the love of God. The Bishops there have agreed to respect it, knowing that it will benefit the quality of their ministry.

In Asia, we also received an extraordinary welcome from the local churches and other missionaries. The sorrow expressed when a young African missionary died suddenly showed how much the people had come to appreciate him. It is this sort of atmosphere that makes sense of our decision to take on a commitment so far away. Our teams will be a part of a large network of witnesses to the Gospel in those places.

In the course of our brief visit, we were edified by meeting many devoted and enthusiastic people. In the Philippines, some catechists, men and women and mostly young, follow a formation course which consists of four periods of two months during the school holidays, after which they are appointed to parishes. We met one young woman of 22, in a very remote village without a priest, leading a life of prayer and fraternity with the people, serving several different villages. In Taiwan we were impressed by the generosity of a young worker in charge of the Y.C.W. who was about to leave for Taipei to follow a full-time course in theology for three years. It is in this milieu that our confreres will offer and receive their inspiration.

At the Feast of the Kingdom with All the People

Mission beyond frontiers is open to us over there. Some things have stuck in my memory: a Franciscan in the mountains of Taiwan who had taken to the local people like a duck to water; a group of Muslims and Christians on the island of Mindanao who meet every month *"to become friends"*; a Jesuit who had devoted himself for forty years to dialogue and friendship with Buddhists to such an extent that the Bishop was in admiration of the power of the Holy Spirit which had prevented him from becoming a Buddhist himself; a large number of young men and women who are entering Buddhist monasteries *"to find a real spiritual life,"* as some of them told us.

By being in contact with such people, searching for the fullness of life and fraternity, the Spiritans will experience this atmosphere of joy that so much impressed me. At the same time, they will have to face up to the difficulty of patiently getting to know the languages and cultures of these people. Even during our life on this earth, we are invited to share the banquet of the kingdom with all the peoples of the earth. We are invited to happiness at the price of dying to everything that turns us in on ourselves. It is not a feast for the powerful. We met religious living in poverty in the large cities, under the pressure of a communist regime. Their *"bedrooms"* were a portion of a long corridor, divided up by curtains. I asked them if they had anywhere to go to replenish their forces. Their reply was "*No but we are encouraged by living with the poor. We are poor like them and we are happy to work with them.*" This is the happiness to which we are being called, not to an easy life. Our joy is the same as that which Jesus brought us, so as to be "God with us".

I wish you all the joys of Christmas, whatever the circumstances in which you will be celebrating.

Pentecost 1997

A TIME OF COURAGE, A TIME OF GRACE

Dear Spiritan Brothers and Sisters,

Greeting to you all from Rome! Special thanks to those who have been my hosts over the last few months. As we approach Pentecost, I will try to record those things that have inspired me from my visits to different parts of the Congregation.

A Challenge for Africa

Even if we are undertaking a new initiative in Asia, even if the Congregation is undergoing new developments in Latin America, and even if the Spiritans of Papua New Guinea and Australia have just held an assembly to organize their presence and mission in Oceania, there is no way in which we are lessening our efforts in Africa. We have heard the cry of the refugees. We have responded to the call of the Church of Mozambique where the international group is already getting down to work and study.

Faced with the upheavals that are shaking some countries and the structural difficulties against which others are struggling, we are all trying, along with our African confreres and the local churches, to discern what plans the LORD has for this continent. We are looking there for lessons that the Spirit might wish us to apply to our mission throughout the world.

A Challenge for our Congregation: a Lesson in Courage

Our brothers and sisters in Africa, including our confreres, have a lesson for us as we come up against obstacles and an awareness of how weak we are. We sometimes hear people who are handicapped in some way being referred to as "challenged" by their condition. Such people often make huge efforts to overcome the limits imposed on them by such difficulties. They draw upon hidden resources that they have never used before.

Many people in Africa are faced with incredible difficulties. It is a constant struggle to keep themselves and their families alive. In seeing this courageous suffering before their eyes, Spiritans from Africa and elsewhere find unsuspected reserves of strength within themselves, just as it was for the first Spiritans who arrived on the continent with a very short expectancy of life. Many confreres, both young and old, willingly put their own lives at risk. Many are struggling to continue their missionary work, to form new members in difficult circumstances, and even to respond to new appeals.

They are teaching us all the meaning of courage. We are challenged by them to give of our best, like them. The Spirit is gently blowing for us through their example. Being sent to those who are broken, we know that we can never let ourselves slip into discouragement or an easy style of life. Even if we are coming up against many difficulties and temptations in these times, we must never give in and just take up any sort of work, as if it no longer matters what we do. More than ever, we are being called to stick to our own Spiritan type of commitment.

Some Ways in which those faced with their Weakness show great Courage

There are many places where our official jobs are more modest than in the past. Out of respect for others, we often have to take a back seat. If old age forces us to slow down, that does not prevent us offering ourselves, body and soul, to the "God who brought joy to our youth." Msgr. Fretellière, our local Bishop who died recently at Chevilly, used to say: "I try to take a step forward each day, however small it might be".

Courage can take the form of patience and perseverance when we are learning the language and culture of the people to whom we are sent, a thing which is a vital ingredient of missionary life.

Courage does not just consist in persevering but also in searching and taking on commitments. All circumscriptions are called upon to take part in the effort of creative fidelity towards which our Rule of Life leads us. Now is the time to use the gifts of each one of us to the full, to share responsibility and to seek collaboration beyond the limits of our own Institute.

At this time, when people are "more willing to listen to witnesses than experts," we are called to be courageously authentic concerning our prayer, our relations in ministry and community life. The buffetings we experience in life do not leave us unscathed. It is not enough just to find a new theology; the old need to dominate can raise its head once more in the way in which we push forward our new ideas. Libermann warned Levavasseur to be very wary of his emotional reactions and unconscious prejudices, so as to be able to examine situations as objectively as possible, under the influence of the Spirit, and to look at the world like a child, with eyes that are new and a heart that is free. Ongoing formation and sabbaticals can give the Spirit of truth a chance to get to work on us.

A Time of Mercy

In these changing times, the LORD shows us his mercy in so many ways. He does not abandon us, but comes to look for us when we are in danger of getting lost. His mercy is not just pity. He helps us to get up again. Just like the priest who said to a dedicated doctor, saddened by not being able to believe in God, "What matters is that God believes in you." God shows his love for us by trusting and challenging us. This realization should impel us in the same way to believe in every human being, not being frightened to give fraternal correction but always sprinkling our relationships with a good dose of mercy.

May the Spirit of the LORD give us his gifts in abundance and continue to guide each one of you along the path of courage and humility.

A Year devoted to the Holy Spirit
Christmas 1997

WELCOMING THE IMPORTUNATE FRIEND

> If you then, who are wicked, know how to give good gifts to your children, how much more will the Father in heaven give the holy Spirit to those who ask him (Luke 11:13).

Dear Brothers and Sisters,

As Christmas approaches, I want to send you greetings from myself and the community at Clivo di Cinna. I look back on my meetings with you over the last years with feelings of pleasure and gratitude. Your practical missionary witness, that I have seen in brief visits, meetings, and celebrations, or in reading your letters and news bulletins, is the best thing about the Congregation, that which is beyond doubt when we come to take stock of ourselves.

We are never better than when we are totally involved in our own type of mission. Some of you said the same when replying to the preparatory questions for the Chapter: *"The vitality of the Congregation depends on how closely it follows its specific mission."* There, above all, is where we will renew our enthusiasm. It was in seeing the needs and the capacities of the poor that our Founders started on their journeys. This is how their vocation was born and their plans were carried out with the help of their friends and the poor themselves. Let us try to look closer at this experience, which is an experience of the Spirit.

Pay Attention to the Spirit

In this letter, I want to echo the call of the Holy Father to celebrate the Holy Spirit in 1998, the Spirit to whom we are all consecrated (SRL, 6). Although he plays such a central role in our world, he works so quietly that we can easily miss him. We must make ourselves aware of him, because we believe that it is he, like the invisible sap, that is constantly giving new life to the old tree which is our Congregation. The Spirit relentlessly sends us out on his mission, impelled by a powerful wind—a wind that we are not sure where it comes from or where it is going. So, the best way to continue our preparations for the Chapter will be to fix our attention on him, trying to locate that underground stream which irrigates our life and our work.

Will People find the Holy Spirit when They come to see Us?

One day, a person came to see us here, expecting to find something strange because of the name of our Institute. During the coming year, we could discuss amongst ourselves where we detect the presence of the Holy Spirit and what we have discovered about his action, so as to help others to find him. We could take a new look at:

* our ordinary religious life: liturgy, daily personal prayer, as indicated in SRL; *lectio divina,* that very old spiritual approach to reading Scripture;
* our pastoral work that brings us examples of sanctity amongst the people;
* the adventure of missionary undertakings: the Spirit is always there before us in the diversity to be found in churches, religions, and cultures, often amongst the most disadvantaged peoples;
* the brotherhood lived in diversity in our Spiritan communities;
* the charismatic renewal, which warns us against creating a church that is dehydrated through an excess of discipline, ritual, emphasis on action.

Open the Door to the importunate Friend

The parable of the persistent friend (which Cardinal Martini of Milan comments on for the year of the Holy Spirit) draws our attention to a key point for Spiritan life today. The friend is already in bed with his children when the knocking starts. In the time of Jesus, people used to sleep on mats placed on the floor behind the main entrance, so if somebody arrived late at night, it meant disturbing everybody to be able to open the door. Perhaps we are sometimes a bit like such a family, asleep in a house where everything is in perfect order and the doors are firmly closed.

What it really means to be Available

The conclusion of the parable, which I quoted at the beginning, brings us to the mystery of availability in the Gospels. In the persistent friend, we can recognize the one who will say at the last judgment: "Whatever you did to the least of my brothers, that you did unto me." When we make time for others, we lose something of ourselves and meet the LORD, sharing the same forgetfulness of self. The risk that we take is like an act of confidence. It has its own prayer: "God has sent the Spirit of his Son into our hearts: the Spirit that cries, Abba, Father." The Father listens to this prayer in action when we are carrying out the mission that is our own: "The evangelization of the poor is our purpose . . . we take for our motto the words "One heart and one soul '" (SRL, 4 & 7). The gift of the Spirit will come in answer to our availability.

Where will We recognize this importunate Friend?

* As a new option in the service of refugees or work in an abandoned rural area?
* In more frequent changes of appointment made necessary by the evolution of the Congregation and the taking on of new initiatives? The demands of availability are never easy: having to leave when we have become so attached to a particular work; sticking to our job when we were planning to do something else.
* Will we recognize him in the time we are asked to put aside to listen to each other in community? Or in the sharing of responsibility with a new arrival, making space for his ideas, his spirituality, his way of doing things?

As in the parable, our house does not have a limitless capacity, but with a little ingenuity, generosity and courage, we can always look around to see if there are some things in the house that are no longer useful but just taking up valuable space. If we get rid of them, we can find room for this persistent visitor in our personal agenda, our plans for the community, circumscription, Congregation.

When the Spirit releases his creative Force

After the enthusiasm of early days, difficulties are never far behind. The Spiritan comes up against opposition, perhaps criticism; he soon realizes his limitations. Perhaps he looks around for excuses: an unsuitable formation? Bad organization? Maybe. But remember how upset the first disciples were when they found that the cross persisted even after the resurrection of their Master. Difficulties are a sign of reality; it is only in dreams that there are no problems. They challenge us to attain a deeper conversion, a more genuine communication.

It is here that we see the Spirit as he really is. Certainly, he is the artist who arouses our sensitivities and our imagination and plays on them to produce an infinite variety of expressions of trust and friendship. But he acts much more profoundly than that, in the heart, at the very source of our decision, and thus creates a story. He wrote his definitive story in the life of Jesus, who loved until the end. But he wants to write in our story as well when "he makes us partakers in the death and resurrection mystery of Jesus and prepares us to make the total gift of ourselves for the kingdom" (SRL, 10). This is why we must walk close to Jesus while living in our church, our community. We set out with him now on the road of a new liturgical year, while remembering his birth in poverty. Let us try to be ready for the unforeseen.

A happy Christmas to you all, and safe journey!

Pentecost 1998

THE SPIRIT OF YOUTH

> I have come so that they may have life and have it to the full (John 10:10).

Dear Brothers and Sisters,

At this time of Easter, when we celebrate the fullness of life that sprang from the death of our LORD, our sessions in the general council have shown us signs of vitality in the Spiritan mission at the same time as signs of a civilization of death. One such sign struck me very forcibly during my ministry in Africa, and I have continued to find it in many other places over the last six years: it is the sad fact that so many children and young people today live a diminished sort of existence. In this letter, I would like to focus attention on the place given to young people in our missionary orientations and in the life of the Congregation itself.

Young People are a Priority of Spiritan Mission

The parts of the world where Spiritans have their mission today are getting younger. Those under 15 years of age make up 44% of the population of Africa, 42% of Papua New Guinea, 38% of the Philippines, 33% of South America—while they are no more than 22% in North America and 19% in Europe. If we really want to work for the future, then our efforts must be directed at these young people. Spiritans are working amongst them in many different ways; their experience will help us to find new approaches.

At Itaici, young people were referred to as "a new continent," with so much in common despite their different nationalities. Even where a Christian tradition exists, they have generally had little contact with Christian life, and ministry to them becomes a sort of first evangelization. In a civilization where points of reference are so fluid, they have to be helped to forge their own convictions and to remain faithful to them. They must not be seen as passive receptacles for a ready-made education, but rather as creative partners in their own formation. The ministry and education that we offer them should not separate them from their family, their milieu, and the rest of the church. They have to find their own place there and take on their own responsibility. In such a mission, lay people bring us their experience and competence and we can contribute a moral and spiritual formation.

Concern for the least Fortunate

Faced with the crying needs of education and formation, our mission will not exclude any category of young people. But our vocation does call us to make a special commitment to the least fortunate. In the poorest countries and milieus, policies of structural adjustment very often result in a rise in unemployment and a diminution of health and education budgets. Whence the spectacle of young people wandering aimlessly around the streets, frustrated, with nothing to do, weakened by under nourishment and neglect. Often one of their greatest handicaps is the instability they experience in their family background.

Some drift to the margins of society. Their feeling of helplessness turns them towards violence or different avenues of escape. The world market leads logically to the exploitation of young people and even children—as a cheap source of labor, or to their manipulation as yet another promising market. Even worse, they are sometimes compelled to fight in civil wars. Yet in the plan of God, they also are called to happiness and the fullness of life. The Spirit, which is given to us to bring happiness to the poor, will surely be close to those confreres and circumscriptions who try to find new ways of serving young people—to educate them, introduce them to an authentic spiritual life and defend their dignity. It is so important that we keep in touch with the young and give them special attention. We need more confreres to specialize in this ministry, to understand young people, to analyze their problems with them, to find ways to help them towards integral human growth—and to help us all in our efforts to relate to them.

As with every mission, working with young people is enriching for us, as long as we are prepared to listen to them and trust them. Being close to them will rejuvenate our own heads and hearts—an essential condition if the Congregation is to remain vibrant and attract young people to join its ranks.

Young People in our Congregation

Like Abraham, our Congregation, which is almost 300 years old, has been blessed by the arrival into the family of many young people, who in their turn are sharing in the blessings of our missionary religious life. Since 1992, 414 have joined the Institute, of whom 321 are from Africa. We have devoted most of our solidarity funds to their formation. We must do our best to improve this formation further and prepare more qualified formators, particularly in the area of personal accompaniment.

We should ask ourselves if we have really understood the effort that is required of us to make young people truly welcome to our family and to allow them to use their creativity. There was a congress in Rome, last September, that brought together 840 young religious from 69 different countries: they came from 230 orders for women and 150 orders for men. One of the contributors to the meeting said the following: *"The relationship that an Institute establishes with the young people who join it and its attitudes to their expectations is usually indicative of the age of a religious family, its psycho-spiritual youth, or the degree to which the original inspiration is still to be seen in its present-day creativity."*

We were founded on a Pentecost Sunday, in 1703, by a theology student aged 24 and a few friends who were even younger. Have we kept something of our youthful origins? What sort of relations does our Institute have with young people today? The days of imposing outdated models on them have long since gone; this is the age of freedom and trust. And we are convinced that the Institute and the older confreres have something essential to offer them, something to do with freedom and witness.

Under the impulse of the Spirit, both children and old men became the main actors in biblical history. Experience has shown us that it can be very good to have young and old members in the same community with a view to producing a creative fidelity. The generosity of the man advanced in years, who becomes young at heart through the deprivations of a life of service can combine with the generosity of young people to produce a very creative cocktail.

May the Spirit help us to journey together towards the fullness of life!

A happy Pentecost to you all!

Christmas 1998

AT THE ENTRANCE TO THE YEAR OF GOD OUR FATHER: ANOTHER JOURNEY

> In the middle of the journey of our life I found myself astray in a dark wood where the straight road had been lost sight of ... How I got into it I cannot clearly say for I was moving like a sleepwalker the moment I stepped out of the right way. "Why do you not climb this beautiful mountain which is the beginning and cause of all happiness?" (said the man who met me) ... Look at the beast for whom I left the way; save me from him, for he makes me tremble ... "It is good for you to take another road," he replied, because he saw that I was crying (Dante Alighieri, *Divine Comedy*, Hell, Canto 1)

Dear Brothers and Sisters,

Once again, this letter will reach you at the four corners of the earth. It is an invitation to rediscover the deep joy of Christmas, despite the difficult circumstances in which you may be living out your vocation at the present time.

Staring out on a new spiritual Journey

The invitation of the Maynooth Chapter to make our Spiritan life into a sort of pilgrimage finds an echo in the opening lines of Dante's *Divine Comedy* quoted above. It was written at a time of change and troubles which made people worried and prevented them from "climbing the mountain" of the accepted way of doing things. Dante sets out on a spiritual journey, guided by witnesses who have passed through death, wise men and poets from antiquity and Beatrice, the love of his youth.

We are living through a similar period. The rapid changes in today's world and the fact that Spiritans are coming from such different backgrounds and situations mean that a simple continuation of our tradition will not suffice to give us light and encouragement on our journey. We are all looking for new approaches in many ways. The experiences that were related at the Chapter, the input for the retreat and the messages from guest speakers were all an inspiration for us, and the fact of sharing all this together produced a great unity amongst us.

So, it is good that we also should set out on a new journey. We took as a symbol for our pilgrimage the figure of a boat, which was used to represent mission beyond the seas in ancient Irish art. It is not an incitement to escape; it represents the current direction of our own lives, our work and our relationships, lived under the breath of the Spirit. Pope John Paul II invites us to see the final year of preparation for the Jubilee as a journey to meet the Father, who draws us to himself while he continues to guide the world's course: "As a wheel that turns smoothly, free from jarring, my will and my desire were turned by love, the same love that moves the sun and the other stars" (the last lines of the *Divine Comedy).*

Meeting God our Father

"A child is born to us, a son is given to us."

The humble beginning of the life of Jesus, God-with-us, has something in common with the characteristics of our present experience, which are signs for us of a new inspired journey that is beginning. The fragility of this baby is what makes him close to us. The joyful Gospel of Luke, which wraps this birth in the light of the love of God, is echoed by the joy and the strength that we feel today in our personal lives; in humble work in the service of the most abandoned, in our simple relationships where we are not looking for our own advantage, where we learn from others like Jesus did, where our witness is all the stronger when we do not seek to impose it.

Jesus set out on his earthly pilgrimage with very little luggage; for the difficult journey ahead, he simply relied on his trust in the love of his Father and his Father's trust in him. At the moment when he felt most abandoned, he cried out *"Abba, Father,"* and so emerged victorious from the trial of death. We gradually learn this same filial trust as we interpret the course of our lives with the Spirit of Jesus, guided at the same time by those who went before us, whether they were Christians or not, and by so many examples of wisdom, beauty, and love. We can then be ready to face up to the prospect of death which prevents us from sinking into superficiality.

We likewise learn to appreciate the confidence that the Father has placed in us by making us responsible for those who have not yet discovered his love. Poullart des Places and Libermann are great examples of this humble trust, which led them to such bold initiatives and untiring activity.

"Yes, I shall arise and go to my Father."

What is it that holds us back from setting out on this pilgrimage? Leaving aside those who have gone through painful family experiences, contemporary civilization seems to have a problem with a concept of God as Father—or Mother, because the Bible also uses maternal imagery. Being steeped in a culture that has taught them to measure the universe and affirm their individual liberty, some of our contemporaries are suspicious of a paternalistic domination or a childish abandonment of responsibility in this father-son relationship, and see a relationship to God the Father as a dependence that is not worthy of them. Behind this refusal to accept God as Father, there may lurk an unconscious and illusory desire to make the reality of death disappear, that death which ruins all the foundations of our claims to be masters of our own lives.

Like the Prodigal Son, we are tempted to look for our autonomy and pleasure far away from our Father, until that moment comes when the experience of suffering and failure leads us back towards him and he comes running to meet us as soon as we take the first step. But the atmosphere in which we live also encourages the attitude of the older son, who feels he has done nothing wrong but is in fact much further from his Father than is his younger brother. He seems to be closed even to the possibility of understanding the love of his Father. Perhaps it is only through acknowledging our sins that we can reach the heart of the Father, and exercise a genuine forgiveness towards our brothers and sisters.

Our Father and the Father of All

Today, we ourselves have a new interest and respect for those who are different to us and a new sense of the unity that exists in that difference. We can see in this a reflection of the Spirit of the Father, who is awakening in us a desire for dialogue and inculturation, and a movement towards international and inter-cultural communities.

In this way, we are moving forward in the discovery of God our Father throughout our history and in our lived experience, which nothing can replace because it is a unique experience. We want to encourage everybody to make the same discovery in the story of their own culture and personality. But at the same time, we will help each other by communicating in humility and without fear. We are learning to trust each other, not on principle but by the attention we give to the signs of the Spirit at work in the life of each one of us.

May this feast of Christmas help us all to set out once more to meet the Father, the source of all love, and may our songs of joy and praise join together across the distances that separate us and drown all sounds of lamentation and mourning.

Pentecost 1999

THE REALITY OF PENTECOST

> They were all filled with the holy Spirit and began to speak in different tongues, as the Spirit enabled them to proclaim. Now there were devout Jews from every nation under heaven in Jerusalem ... they gathered in a large, but they were confused ... they asked, "Are not all these people who are speaking Galileans? ... What does this mean?" But others said, scoffing, "They have had too much new wine" (Acts 2:4-5, 12-13).

Dear Brothers and Sisters,

In these days leading up to Pentecost, I want to be with you by means of this letter in all those different countries and situations where the Congregation has sent you to bear witness to the love of God. We can confidently celebrate the very concrete coming of the Spirit into our Spiritan life. We should not see Pentecost as a purely interior event, nor should we reduce the reality of our mission to what is acceptable to the philosophy of the dominant civilization of our time.

Pentecost in a precarious World

Despite disappointments and sometimes losing their way, the disciples placed all their hope in Jesus and followed him right up to the moment of his passion and death when everything seemed to fall apart. Our hope as Spiritans has become identified with the mission and religious life of the Congregation, often in the context of a particular mission that has become our pride and joy, to which we have given ourselves heart and soul. Today, some of the northern Provinces feel that their very existence is threatened. Elsewhere, in areas of war and social chaos, there are confreres who are literally sharing the privations and insecurity of refugees. They find it impossible to work with any hope of continuity or to draw up projects that have any hope of survival.

The whole Congregation is going through a period of great uncertainty. In recent times, we have had to say goodbye to many things of which we were proud and in which we placed our hope. So here we are on the eve of another Pentecost perhaps a little poorer, a little closer to the destitute. We feel less sure of ourselves, less protected and less esteemed by others. Our mission is leading us into the full force of the gale, exposed, like the Apostles, to the hostile reactions of people who do not share our convictions. Sometimes our presence is a source of confidence, but it can equally provoke perplexity, skepticism, indifference, or ridicule.

For us, all this is not a sign of death, but an indication of new life. "It is not by perfecting the art of dying but through the resurrection of Jesus Christ that a new and purifying wind will blow through our world."[2] It was the unexpected appearance of the Spirit after the resurrection that brought the church to birth, by generating a witness of faith in Jesus Christ, dead and risen again, and creating a fraternal community. Where today can we find the living and inexhaustible source of our missionary joy and of the pleasure of living together as brothers and sisters? What form will our witness have to take to reply to the challenge of a world that sees itself as realistic and demanding authenticity?

Inspiration and Realism—the Reality of Pentecost in our Day

In our Mission

The Chapter of Maynooth drew from our lived experience and our tradition certain guidelines of faith for our mission today: a new missionary beginning, a new style of mission, fidelity to our priorities of first evangelization and the service and defense of the weakest and most vulnerable. These are not the options of human wisdom; they betray rather a genuine breath of the Spirit. At the same time, the capitulants did not lose sight of the human reality with its potential for good and bad. In mission

---

2. Bonhoeffer, *Letters and Papers from Prison*, 240. Letter of April 30, 1944.

situations, the confreres who stay put when violence and war break out often lasting for years, give witness to the action of the Spirit of the LORD in concrete terms.

These choices are at the same time a source of encouragement and a challenge. They strengthen our trust in the love of God and in others. On the other hand, the attention they draw to the realities of the human condition reminds us to be on our guard against an exalted idea of our own importance. A good dose of human realism can lead to an increased spiritual realism by making us more open to others.

In our Life together

The Central African Foundation and the four Districts of the region have decided to merge into a single Province from the feast of Pentecost this year. This option will now have to be translated into the realities of daily living. It will call for much wisdom and know-how, but the generosity of the original decision leads us to believe that the Spirit will be there to help.

International and intercultural communities, as well as formation communities, are places where communication must be guided by a special sensitivity. They place a responsibility on all to cultivate an evangelical spirit, a sense of humor and a willingness to learn how to appreciate and live out a genuine unity in diversity. This will create a spirit of friendship and joy.

Losing and putting on Weight—a spiritual Journey

The precarious situations in which our present-day mission places us, our decision to really go out to meet the most abandoned, to live together in our diversity—all this results in our being more directly exposed to others. It has the added effect of giving us a better knowledge of ourselves in our human reality, with all our gifts and shortcomings.

Fear of these situations can tempt us to turn inwards or hide ourselves in our little clan, or perhaps seek refuge in asserting ourselves over others. But the Spirit of the LORD gradually gives us confidence, esteem and compassion for others, and teaches us how to put ourselves at their service. Those who do not learn to welcome this gift of the Spirit will find it difficult to be at home in the mission of today.

By investing all our human talents in the Spiritan venture, by making ourselves ever open to the suggestions of the Spirit, we will certainly lose weight in the direction of self-promotion, but we will replace it with what the Bible calls "the glory of God," in other words, with an outburst of love. *"He must increase and I must decrease."* The Spirit of Pentecost is the Spirit of Easter. He helps us to experience the joy of self-giving and thus to discover the beauty of the LORD: "O night, how resplendent you are!" (Easter Hymn).

A happy feast day to everybody.

Yours fraternally.

December 13, 1999

JUBILEE SPECIAL: AN APPOINTMENT FOR THE YEAR 2000

"LET YOURSELF BE RECONCILED"

My dear Confreres,

The eclipse of the sun last summer created a great public interest; some newspapers referred to it as *"an appointment between the sun and the moon."* People searched out the best vantage points so that they could also be present at this incomparable meeting. In many places at the moment of total eclipse, chattering crowds were reduced to complete silence; as the light gradually returned, some people had tears in their eyes. Was this because of the unique opportunity of experiencing the cosmic order on which our life depends?

We are about to celebrate another such appointment. After 2000 years of civilizations strongly influenced by Christianity, new "planets" have appeared that have somewhat eclipsed the light of Christ. But this has also led to a new interest in him: people have been deeply affected by his radiance, both inside and outside the church.

We would like the meeting of the year 2000 to be a completely new experience for us of the benevolent presence of Christ. It is the whole point of the celebration of the Jubilee.

The Jubilee

In the Jewish tradition, a Jubilee is above all else an expression of great hope. After seven weeks of ordinary years, the Jubilee Year celebrates the sovereignty of God over the world and its history. During that year, the justice of God will reign, that justice whose basic law is that of merciful love. So, in Israel, land is returned to its rightful owner, debts, offences, and punishments are all forgotten and slaves are set free. Even nature is not left out; fields are given a rest from growing crops. It is a time for justice for the poor, for rebuilding relations with outcasts, enemies, and God himself.

Jesus saw himself as the one who gives meaning to the Jubilee year and brings its hope to fulfilment: *"The Spirit of the* Lord *is upon me, because he has anointed me to bring glad tidings to the poor. He has sent me to proclaim liberty to captives, and recovery of sight to the blind, to let the oppressed go free, and to proclaim a year acceptable to the* Lord.*"* And Jesus adds, *"Today, this scripture passage is fulfilled in your hearing"* (Luke 4:18-21). The challenge before us is to rediscover this same vivifying presence, after 2000 years of history, in the human relations of our own day, to welcome this Spirit of liberation, peace, and reconciliation and to communicate it to others. A Jubilee is not designed to produce a feast of nostalgia for the past or to fill us with fear of what is to come; it is above all an experience of Jesus Christ living today. It is a time for bringing our calendars up to date and for re-setting our watches. This is what Libermann meant when he said: *"The world is moving on and we have to follow it, while continuing to live by the spirit of the Gospel. We must do good and fight evil in the reality of the world as we find it today."*

Where are we, as Spiritans, to find our inspiration for this? What sort of a conversion do we need to go through so as to recapture our confidence in the love of God? How can we heal our memories, how can we find a new heart to praise the beauty of the Lord and a new enthusiasm for the mission we have been given? With the general council I would like to invite you to look at some ways in which we can begin this journey of discernment.

> *What sort of an authentic Jubilee can we celebrate with the poor and with our confreres? The reply to this question will depend on the Jubilee that each one of us will celebrate in the intimacy of his own being.*

1. A Balance Sheet of the Past

A World of Progress

Over the last few centuries, human achievements have multiplied. Science and technology have provided the instruments for our control of the world: management of the earth, unprecedented growth of the economy, the planet reduced to a big village by advances in communications, a deeper understanding of the human reality. Education and the media, infused with their own particular spirit, have spread this new knowledge throughout the world. The thought of these phenomenal changes should not lead us to feelings of impotent resignation, because human prowess is all part of the plan of the Creator (Gen 1:26—2:24). We remember the way the Psalmist puts it:

> *You have made him little less than a god, crowned him with glory and honor. You have given him rule over the works of your hands, put all things at his feet ... O* LORD, *our* LORD, *how awesome is your name through all the earth!* (Ps 8:6-10).

An Inheritance of Conflict and a critical Spirit

But progress has often been achieved at the price of a conflict that has left scars and open wounds in human relations. New ideas of the autonomy of reason and freedom were aggressively asserted in the face of traditional ways. The tensions thus created continue in our day and are also found within the churches. Social improvements were only attained through fierce struggles and these struggles continue.

The movement of colonization caused immeasurable damage. Despite the symbolic challenge of the Conference of Bandung[3] in 1955, despite its official ending at the time of independence, the domination of the great powers still remains

Some poor countries are crushed by the weight of their debts and the competition of the market. Frustration and anger increase as the media spread the dream of a life of abundance. Economic migrants come

---

3. A meeting of Asian and African states, mostly newly independent, which took place on 18-24 April 1955 in Bandung, Indonesia. The twenty-nine countries that participated represented a total population of 1.5 billion people, 54% of the world [Editor—from Wikipedia]

face to face with the walls built up by rich countries fearful for their own security.

Progress has produced unimagined ways of waging war while new ideologies sometimes lead to new kinds of hatred. Marxist revolutions and fascist movements resulted in the violent seizure of power, totalitarianism and genocide. Nuclear arms threaten the very survival of the human race. In some countries that are emerging from a colonial or totalitarian past, the political leaders now play the card of nationalism or tribalism. Neo-liberal economies drag young people who see no future for themselves into thankless conflicts. With "progress," the worst has now become possible!

Profit and Loss

This picture of the dark side of modern struggles must not obscure the positive gains: the end of the cold war, social progress, the triumph of democracy (at least as an accepted ideal), the United Nations with all its limitations, humanitarian movements insisting on the rights and duties of intervention, networks for the safeguarding of rights and the resolution of conflicts, movements for the protection of nature. Their influence is felt by decision-makers, even though such initiatives are often being taken by ordinary people rather than by the big names in politics and economics. Their intervention forms a strength of public opinion which finally opens the eyes of those who preferred to keep them closed.

2. The Question of Human Relations
Paths that Lead Nowhere

What effect does all this have on human relations? Men and women today have cut many of their traditional relationships, either deliberately or in the wake of movements such as the exodus from the countryside, which has cut them off from the world of nature. Their changed lives have perhaps brought them an increase in personal liberty and a greater capacity for facing up to new challenges. But they have also experienced new constraints, and, sometimes, a diminution in the quality of their relationships, or even an experience of isolation.

The extreme competition of the world market subjects workers to an exhausting rhythm of labor. Their relationship to their work is often precarious and lacking in interest. They feel exploited. In the cities, heterogeneous populations are lumped together without any plan or preparation, often in a climate of great insecurity. The resultant stress creates tensions that are felt in society, in schools and in families. Individuals, especially those who have no stable work, feel fragile, exposed and distraught. For recreation, they seek escape from the stark reality of their lives, sometimes by way of a display of violent emotion and noise.

Some fall back on the appeal of nationalism, tribalism, or various religious movements in order to escape from their isolation and their fears. Extremist movements have no trouble in finding recruits. As they seem to offer the last hope, their adherents are willing to do whatever they are asked, even going as far as violent crime.

In being separated from their roots, many people also lose their principles and values. When such principles are detached from the experiences that formed them (often religious), they can easily be reduced to no more than empty rhetorical phrases to be used in the service of politics or other interests. The exposure of corruption, found even in the highest public offices, ruins all confidence in authority. Lacking any genuine experience of the transcendent, it is easy to make something sacred out of a commitment that is taken up through passion or despair.

Our world of excessive competitiveness seems to engender endless tensions, suspicions, hatreds, and conflicts. Who will bring us reconciliation?

Seeking new Relationships

On the positive side, new types of relationship grow up to answer the needs of individuals who are isolated and under stress. Groups are formed around different interests and establish ties that are sometimes akin to those of a family. Many people are active in support associations—to defend people's rights, to protect the environment, to promote various peace movements. They are delighted to discover a new sort of relationship that is genuinely open to the poorest. These are signs of hope for human relations in the Third Millennium; this is especially so for we Spiritans who in the last General Chapter identified the quality of our relationships as the key to a new style of mission and religious life.

One of the aspects of the ministry of Spiritans in refugee camps is a commitment to peace and reconciliation. It is an essential dimension of our social ministry, in the same way as is our work for justice. We can identify with the Franciscan approach, which sees peace as a part of justice in that it strives to rebuild relationships that are "just." A Department of Studies for Peace and Conflict Resolution has been set up at Duquesne University in Pittsburgh. In a recent article, the confrere who started this initiative described the process that led him to center his commitment to Justice and Peace on peace *and reconciliation.*

We are challenged by all kinds of conflicts, but before speaking of the way we can respond, we should first of all take a good look at ourselves.

3. A new Look at Relationships in our Spiritan Life and Mission

In our Congregation, we can find similar examples of these new initiatives that are emerging in society. The Jubilee is a time to thank God for such blessings. But it is also a good moment to direct the light of the Gospel on some of the darker areas in our lives. As a starting point in the journey that needs to be undertaken by the whole Congregation, we would like to talk of some of the less attractive aspects of the witness we give as Spiritans.

Difficulties in communicating at a personal Level

We enjoy living and working together, but it is sometimes difficult to share our more personal joys and sorrows even when it would be good for us to do so. It is as if we do not fully trust each other or are frightened that we will be misunderstood. This is even more so today when many of our communities and most of our circumscriptions are international or inter-cultural. It can happen that there is a blockage in relations between confreres, or that there are strained relations between different groups. It gradually dawns on us that the tensions and antagonism that grow up between different human groups are also to be found within our own family.

We can detect signs of a loss of personal assurance amongst ourselves regarding our Spiritan commitment. In different ways, we share a common poverty. Confreres in the northern Provinces sometimes feel they have no future. They are accustomed to overcoming problems with the support and prestige that they formerly enjoyed, but now they feel there is not much they can do. There is a tendency to focus on their own fate and that of their institutions rather than on their vocation and their mission. Confreres in the south are living in situations of poverty, war, and even chaos, which make them acutely aware of their vulnerability and sometimes tempt them to abandon efforts which seem so futile. It seems that we all have a need to be reconciled to ourselves.

We have to get to work on ourselves in order to heal those wounds that go to the depths of our personal being. In the spirit of Libermann, we must look for a better understanding of the difficulties that are harming our personal relationships today. We should turn to the mercy of the LORD who is the way that leads to our reconciliation.

"All are equal, but Some are more equal than Others!"

These words of George Orwell express the feeling we sometimes have—that there are different categories of confreres in the Congregation: those who are chosen as delegates to Chapters and those who are never elected; those to whom we always listen attentively and those whose voice is rarely heard. In our own family also, the voiceless need to be heard.

Today there is a line that goes through the life of the Congregation between North and South. It is sometimes said, half-jokingly, that the North, with few vocations, finances formation and mission while the South, which is poor and insecure, provides the personnel. It is a simplistic image: there are still vocations in the north and confreres from the north are working in every continent. In the south, circumscriptions are doing their best to find their own resources. Nevertheless, both hemispheres are experiencing the frustration of their own particular kind of poverty and this should lead us all to humility and mutual understanding.

Despite such feelings, our North-South relations have become more positive as we have increasingly lived and worked together. The year 2000 presents us with an unrivaled opportunity for true reconciliation.

Our Relationship with Authority

Authority sometimes meets with a certain lack of confidence, a suspicion about the sincerity of those who preach to others. There are confreres, perhaps wounded by some of the attitudes of those in charge, who seem to have a constant anger within them against superiors. For those of us in authority, it should not be too difficult, at this time of honesty and truth, to admit that we have made plenty of mistakes. At times, we have not paid enough attention to those who are less visible; at others, we have not listened carefully enough because we were too sure of our own convictions and too determined to put them into practice at any price.

It is much safer to admit our limitations and weaknesses rather than trying to give the impression that we are always beyond reproach. The great obstacles to our ministry of authority (and evangelization) are not so much our faults as our pretensions. In trying to appear always perfect, we are obscuring the light of our witness. On the other hand, those in authority sometimes get the impression that once elected or appointed, everybody leaves them to carry the burden alone. Or, as somebody put it at the General Chapter, the Congregation can at times resemble a soccer match where everybody is playing with his own personal football! It is not easy to be in authority and those who accept this service need to be supported in order to accomplish their ministry. They sometimes feel that confreres do not appreciate their efforts.

That which restores Sense and Meaning to our Commitment

In the past, we were strengthened and protected by stable structures and a homogeneous culture. Nowadays, the changes, the migrations and mixing of peoples, the invasive media, all tend to destroy our socio-cultural foundations. Firm, long-term commitments become more difficult. Superficial relationships leave us isolated and unsure in our attitude to others. This, no doubt, partly explains a certain lack of enthusiasm for mission.

We tend to take our emotions, our personal comfort, our bodily appearance and our social success as the ultimate reference point. But such things are ephemeral and leave us feeling vulnerable. We can easily become aggressive towards those who seem to threaten the insecure foundations on which we have built our lives. We look for scapegoats. We find it difficult to accept even the mildest of criticisms. Our struggle for justice can easily conceal a struggle for our own advantage at any cost. If we allow ourselves to be enmeshed by such emotions, we will end up with feelings of deep dissatisfaction and guilt.

We can face the present-day challenges of mission and religious life if we establish interpersonal relationships that are built on deep respect and steadfast friendship. Each of us is unique. At this level, what brings us assurance is not impersonal things but interpersonal relationships.

Instead of allowing the new possibilities afforded by technology and communications to close us in on ourselves, exploiting and dominating others, we must follow the Spirit who leads us outwards towards others, giving ourselves, body and soul, to God and to our brothers and sisters.

The Jubilee opens up a path that leads from slavery to freedom. If we want to *"bring the spirit of the Gospel to the reality of the world as we find it today,"* we must be aware of the wounds that our times inflict on the personal lives of so many people, and of the deep longings that they have for a life which is free and worthy of humanity.

4. New Paths to Reconciliation

We have spoken of a world torn apart by many conflicts, where the cold logic of the global market leads to the degradation of nature while at the same time introducing into society and international relations the deadly pressure of competition and the threat of death for the weakest. We see a world where men and women are wounded by the stress of isolation and fears.

As followers of Christ, what good news do we have to offer for this meeting of the year 2000? What sort of an authentic Jubilee can we celebrate with the blind and the captives? What sort of Jubilee can the Congregation celebrate? The reply to these questions will depend on the Jubilee that each one of us will celebrate in the intimacy of his own being.

God with Us at the Center of our Freedom

It is evident that it is not simply a question of drawing up sensible conclusions for the future of our Institute in the context of present-day global strategies. Nor are we just looking for an answer to philosophical and theological problems.

"Let yourself be reconciled by God" means letting him penetrate into your being for an interpersonal dialogue between your spirit and the personal Spirit of God. Our life together in the Congregation, in our communities and circumscriptions, that sometimes goes through periods of tension, will never attain that joyful and radiant peace of fraternal life unless we open ourselves to this dialogue of reconciliation with God our Father and Creator. It is in the light of this meeting that our wounds from the past can be healed. This is how we will be set free to go out and meet

those who are different to ourselves, to meet the poor to whom we are cent by the Spirit. We must never close the door.

Progress and struggles for liberation can be given a new direction through the witness of those who have seen or approached the Burning Bush where another freedom has penetrated into the hidden place of their own freedom. The Bible explains this meaning of freedom: the one who is truly free is he who listens to the living Word of God, he who is united with God and his brothers and sisters. "You were called for freedom, brothers. But do not use this freedom as an opportunity for the flesh; rather serve one another through love" (Gal 5:13). Our relationship with God is at the very heart of our personal freedom: "we will come to him and make our dwelling with him" said Jesus (John 14:23).

This way of looking at things is also in line with African traditional wisdom. Human beings are seen as members rather than as individuals. To be completely ourselves, we have to be authentically related to others. Some African religions also have the idea of a personal relationship with God. For the Manja people of the Central African Republic, when the Christians wanted to find a word for the true God, they did not use "*Koro*," who is the God of the sky and the storm, but "*Galē*"—my personal God, the God of my fortune, the God who has a relationship with me.

We can learn from African traditions with their idea of this relationship with God, and from others, an idea that has been somewhat eclipsed in western society but which remains essential for us all. The year 2000 could be seen as the favorable time for a new spiritual meeting of the Congregation with Africa. We would come in our spiritual poverty to experience what seems to be at the very core of the wisdom of this continent.

A Ministry of Reconciliation

Our ministry of reconciliation will be born from our own reconciled life. Let us listen to how the American theologian, Bob Schreiter, describes the Christian understanding of human reconciliation.

He lists five points (from a conference given to the General Assembly of Caritas Internationalis in July 1999):

* *"Reconciliation is first and foremost the work of God, who initiates and completes reconciliation within us."* It is through the presence of the Spirit of the LORD that things begin to change.

* "In the Christian understanding of reconciliation, the process begins with the victim, not with the evildoer": this was so with Jesus, dying on the cross and raised up by the power of the Spirit, the power of love shining through total dereliction.
* "The experience of reconciliation makes both the victim and the wrongdoer a "new creation" (2 Cor 5:17): like the centurion at the foot of the cross, the executioner is moved and converted.
* "What creates this new humanity for victims and wrongdoers can be found in the story of the passion, death and resurrection of Jesus Christ."
* "The Christian understanding of reconciliation reveals a deeper truth about the world itself": we can see from our recent history how much the human race stands in need of reconciliation and we want to be witnesses to him who is its source.

Such thoughts will surely indicate new paths for the life and mission of our Congregation in the next millennium.

5. Conclusion: A Call to all Spiritans

> "Fraternal communities, in the heart of society, of people who speak to God."

This is how an Indian Jesuit, Fr. Amaladoss (who writes for *Spiritus*) described the mission of our institutes in the future, during a talk delivered at SEDOS (*Sedos*, 1996, 235). This could serve as a summary of the initiative that we are asking you all to undertake:

"Fraternal communities"

Let us take steps that will give a new tone to our relationships within communities and circumscriptions and even within the whole Congregation. Inspired by the LORD, we will allow ourselves to be reconciled with those who have something against us, or with whom we have a problem. We will try to give more depth to our life together with all its international and inter-cultural diversity. We must review the kind of relationships that exist between the different types of Spiritan: brothers, priests, and lay associates. It is a time to look again at our relationship with the

Congregation itself, especially if we have distanced ourselves from it in various ways, and to seek to establish ties with those who are far off.

Finally, we must review the way we relate to each other in initial formation: those who have the responsibility of initiating young men into our Spiritan life and the young men themselves, who today often come from different countries and cultures.

"In the heart of Society"

In line with our last General Chapter, our mission must make a new journey towards those who are far off, those who are weak and small, those who are excluded. We must examine our attitudes, our style of life, our structures to see if they are helping us towards an authentic encounter, if they are a credible witness to the Good News we preach and the ministry of reconciliation that we practice.

"People who speak to God"

Let each one of us listen attentively to God and open our intimate life to his Spirit for a dialogue of praise and supplication. Let us re-examine the way we speak to him. Let us allow the Spirit to heal our memories, so that we will accept ourselves with all our past history. Let us be reconciled with ourselves.

This appeal will reach you during Advent or Christmas time, when God comes to visit us and speak with us as a friend talks to a friend. A joyful and peaceful Christmas to you all!

Blessed Daniel Brottier, Army Chaplain

Pentecost 2000

BEARING FRUIT

> "It was not you who choose me, but I who chose you and appointed you to go and bear fruit that will remain" (John 15:16).

Dear Brothers and Sisters,

The rapid changes in missionary situations in recent times have led us to make many readjustments in our approaches. As Pentecost comes upon us once again, the feast that celebrates the beginning of the acts of the disciples of Jesus, let us take another look at the inspiration behind our initiatives and actions in the service of the Gospel, which are lived out in a world where progress and efficiency are all but deified.

Some Questions on the real Nature of our Mission Today

Several factors can explain the lessening of enthusiasm for mission that we are experiencing today. Its very meaning is no longer clear for many people. In the past, in line with the ideas of the time, great importance was attached to the number of baptisms carried out and the rites and ceremonies of our ministry were seen as having an almost automatic efficacy; this approach poses some questions for us today. In preparing for the Synod for Asia, the Bishops of Japan did not reply to the questions sent to them regarding statistics; they preferred to make an evaluation of the impact that the church was having as a witness to the Gospel in society. The idea of a mission of presence and dialogue can be frustrating for those who have not been trained for it or who have not yet experienced it in practice. Moreover, we are suspicious of a spirituality or a pastoral approach that is too much reliant on feelings and emotions.

The situation in many countries where we are working and the movement of globalization seem to condemn in advance our efforts for justice and peace. In some areas, the aging of personnel and the lack of vocations can lead circumscriptions to a mood of resignation. We can be tempted to surrender to a feeling of sterility, doubting ourselves and our Spiritan brothers and sisters: "we no longer have the necessary strength, resources or personnel; we have nothing more to give." The worst of all would be if we begin to doubt the power of the Gospel as a channel of fruitfulness for humanity and seek instead a more significant and effective commitment outside the church.

Perhaps a short *lectio divina* could throw some light on the question.

"Have you Nothing to eat? — No! — Throw out your Nets" (John 21:4-6)

In a meditation on John 21, Cardinal Martini of Milan draws a picture of the fishermen on the lake of Galilee, worn out after casting and pulling in their nets all night, fed up with finding the net empty every time, getting on each other's nerves and blaming Peter for the lack of results. It could remind us of some moments in our own ministry when the repetitive and mechanical nature of what we are doing begins to get to us. Martini describes the feeling like this: "Actions which are empty and unauthentic, words of kindness lacking kindness, greetings devoid of genuine welcome, acts of love that are loveless, words of life that are sterile" (*"Témoins du Ressuscité,"* 40).

In the morning, Jesus appears on the shore, just as God did on another morning to help the Hebrews when they were in trouble at the Red Sea. Jesus asks these disappointed and exhausted fisherman, *"Have you nothing to eat?,"* as if he was saying to his disciples, "Is there something in your life that brings you strength and helps you, in your turn, to bring life and strength to others?" To this disturbing question, we could also answer "no!," recognizing that we have nothing of value to offer of ourselves! Admitting this humble truth is both an act of trust and a cry for help. In making us face up to our limitations and failures, it opens us to God and to others and prevents us closing ourselves in our own solitude and working in a void.

Jesus says, *"Throw out your nets,"* in other words, "Shake yourselves up, there is work to be done!" And the first thing to be done is to listen to the Word of the Lord, to trust him and to work with him. Jesus tells them to do something that they have done so often, but which now has a new meaning and is permeated by the strength that comes from confidence in love. It is at this point that the power of the Word and of faith shows itself clearly. The disciple whom Jesus loved says to Peter, *"It's the Lord!,"* a cry of joy to which each member of the team reacts in his own way. Peter jumps straight into the water to reach Jesus as quickly as possible; the others, more practical and down to earth, concentrate on pulling in the nets and the catch.

When they are all together on the shore, Jesus invites them to eat something (and asks them for their contribution) before talking to Peter alone. He asks him about his love, an essential question for a pastor who must have something worthwhile to offer to others.

Like a gentle Breeze

This is a text which is full of enlightening symbolism. The enthusiasm of the disciples is born again from the concrete experience of meeting the risen Jesus, with his new way of presenting himself and challenging his friends. It is a presence that is strikingly discreet yet it produces amazing effects: the brightness of this presence, unseen by eyes and yet plainly visible to the heart, a new commitment to work with the miraculous catch, the fraternal meal, mysteriously prepared by Jesus, the precision of the vocation of Peter as it is purified by love. The presence of the Lord, perceived in the context of our daily life, brings great peace, especially when things are difficult. When he appeared to the apostles in the middle of a storm, the sea suddenly grew calm. He shares his Spirit with us, the Spirit that allowed him to cry out in the garden at Gethsemane, and continues to cry in our own hearts, "Abba, Father!"

And so the creative and liberating Spirit, the protagonist of our mission, comes to live in us. Peter, having already made his profession of faith at Caesarea, now makes his triple profession of love from which springs the radiance and fruitfulness of his ministry.

Perhaps you might say, "but where is this Spirit to be seen at work in *our* day?" We can see him in the many vocations which have flowed from the witness given by Spiritans in the countries where they worked, countries where many of their bodies still lie, worn out by the difficulty of their tasks. He is at work in the new breath of life brought to us by young Spiritans; the fifty students who spent Holy Week together at Gentinnes, coming from Europe (North, South and East), Africa, and Latin America, somehow seemed to be harbingers of a new style of fraternal life, collaboration and solidarity in the Congregation. We can see signs of the presence of the Lord's Spirit in the new movement of lay collaborators and associates, in the departure of yet more confreres to serve the most abandoned, in the fidelity of those who continue to bear the heat and burden of the day in our different circumscriptions.

The work and life of our confreres and friends seem to denote a desire for a spiritual renewal, like a gentle breeze that wakes pilgrims in the morning to set out on another stage of their journey.

With the general council and all the generalate community, I wish you a very happy feast of Pentecost in this year of grace, which for all of us must be a time for renewal of hope.

Yours fraternally.

Christmas 2000

THE FACE OF THE LORD IN A NEW HUMANITY UNDER CONSTRUCTION

> "The Lord bless you and keep you! The Lord let his face shine upon you and be gracious to you! The Lord look upon you kindly and give you peace!" (Num 6:22).

Dear Brothers and Sisters,

I want to send you my best wishes for Christmas and the New Year with this Old Testament prayer that was adopted by St. Francis. When we first set out to witness to the Gospel throughout the world, we wanted, somehow or other, to bring the blessing of the Lord to our brothers and sisters who were forgotten by society or living far away. In what way can we convey that blessing today? The Chapter of Maynooth put the emphasis on presence, closeness, and sharing of life, and dialogue with those to whom we are sent.

When God himself came amongst us, he did not come like a high priest presiding over the life of religion, nor like a learned scribe, nor like a rabbi championing the practice of the law. He came into a colonized people with the face of a man, the face of a child, the face of poverty. This is the face that the shepherds came to see, and they left full of joy, singing the praises of God. They were followed by the Wise Men, led by their guiding star; they gave him presents and they went home having also experienced a great joy, anxious to protect this little child who was already being threatened.

A Face both unique and multiple

Our mission has a lot to do with faces. The missionary exhibition currently in Rome for the Jubilee Year begins in the open air with an evocative portrait of human history, with all its tragedies and its outbursts of generosity. Then one enters the abbey church of the Trappists of Tre Fontane as if to receive a revelation. A video entitled, *"From the Face to the Faces,"* shows how the unique face of Jesus of Nazareth has multiplied itself through the different cultures of the world. The icons from Africa, America, Asia, Europe and Oceania bring us a richer understanding of the face of Christ, and make that same face more recognizable to the different nations. A new review of art and spirituality in Italy has chosen the title: *"Il Volto dei Volti"* (The Face of Faces).

Caught in the Net of Globalization

At the recent meeting of the Superiors General in Rome, we reflected together on a document prepared by our Theological Commission, with the grandiose title of *"Inside Globalization: towards a multi-centered and an inter-cultural Communion. Ecclesiological Implications for the Administration of our Institutes."* These grand-sounding words need not be taken too seriously. The intention was to see how, in the context of globalization, those of us committed to religious life and mission can live out our humanity to the full and make it an image of the loving face of God.

With the development of an ever more efficient network of communications, the Congolese, the Chinese, the Brazilians, the Americans, the Australians, and the Russians have all become neighbors. Behind this media-web are hidden (but only partially) the world market, multinationals, banks, and stock-exchanges. One thing is becoming clear, something that is in line with the idea of the Gospel: that henceforth, all human beings, for better or worse, are going to be closely linked to each other. But with all these networks, the system is still working badly: pictures of incredible luxury flash onto the same television screens as scenes of insupportable misery; conflicts are born, multiply, and seem to be deaf to those who cry out for peace; old hatreds are still alive and well despite all the progress. People look for leaders who will do something about it all, but behind the Heads of State are the anonymous international networks which undermine their authority. We hear talk of "the invisible hand of the market." One looks in vain in this great labyrinth for those who are *actually* responsible for the degradation of our planet, for the pollution of our seas and rivers, and for the warming of our atmosphere.

The human race is being shaken to its foundations by the technologies and upheavals that it has set in motion. But let us not look for false solutions to real problems. The remedies are to be found in the system itself, in our capacity to communicate on a large and small scale, in the experience of our diversity which makes us conscious of our own limitations, while at the same time discovering the abilities and qualities of others. It comes like a revelation: despite everything that separates us, we are all human beings, ready to help each other and capable of loving each other.

The document of the Superiors General points to the emergence of the "local" alongside the "global." More than in the past, people are growing in personal liberty and responsibility. "People power" is emerging as a spontaneous growth, developing both at a local and a wider level, where it is whittling away at the powers that were traditionally invested in larger centers. Thus, towns and Provinces are claiming a greater autonomy vis-à-vis the central authorities, while the growth of new cultural structures and innumerable associations witnesses to the increased power of the ordinary people. These new centers of society are increasing their common action, even at the international level.

Our Institute — a Laboratory of a new Humanity

Our Congregation has also put on a new face in the global net. It is present on all the continents with many centers of decision-making and communications which are becoming more up to date. Its members, coming from all corners of the planet, live and work together. The missionary movement is no longer coming from just one continent. Missionary relationships are now based on reciprocity — as seen in intercultural communities, cooperation between professed Spiritans and lay Associates, friends, and collaborators.

In line with this, we will have to look at some very concrete questions, like the inculturation of our Spiritan charism. These problems are on the agenda for the next Enlarged General Council at Pittsburgh: Formation — Interdependence — History and Anniversaries as sources of inspiration. So we can finish with a well-founded declaration of hope: today, the face of the LORD, with all its blessings, is present in our mission and our Congregation. Even if many things are still under construction, even if we are still going through the pains of giving birth, we are convinced that in the world as it is, we have a future as witnesses to love and reconciliation, as *"a living memorial of the passion of Jesus for the Covenant and his struggle on its behalf"* (Working Document, 41).

By our striving to live out our freedom in a creative and fraternal way, by our continuing presence amongst people in difficulty, by our working and living together with our many cultures, our Congregation can be a laboratory for a new life so that the reign of God may come.

"May the LORD look kindly on you and give you peace!"

Yours fraternally.

Pentecost 2001

SET OUT INTO THE DEEP ONCE MORE

Dear Spiritan Brothers and Sisters,

Does the Spirit of Pentecost still blow in our day? We are sometimes tempted to doubt it. But looking back over the period since the last General Chapter, we realize that it is the Spirit who has put life into our plans and activities, who has helped us to keep going when things got difficult and inspired us to live and work together as brothers and sisters. As we face new challenges, all the signs indicate that he is still very much with us. He inspires us to leave behind our prejudices and fears, so as to move ahead once more.

I remember some years ago in Africa, I used to see a woman who had been wandering around the town every day for many years. One day, she was knocked down by a car but she continued her perambulations with a limp. She used to carry a little bundle which she would open when she sat down beside the road. But in this bundle, there was just a pile of rubbish — empty boxes, pieces of cloth, tufts of grass. What could have happened to make her like this? Another woman would constantly sweep the surroundings of the cathedral each morning. Was this some sort of purification?

We also can end up going round in circles, avoiding exposure to new challenges, attached to useless things while perhaps being plagued with feelings of guilt. *"Put out into the deep!"* said the Pope at the end of the Jubilee year in *"Novo millenio ineunte."*[4]

Moving ahead in our Missionary Commitments

With the development of local churches, a fresh look at our charism is leading us again to first evangelization, for which we will need to learn new approaches. The media keeps reminding us of the suffering, injustice and conflicts throughout the world. We have no choice but to turn to the most disadvantaged and to undertake new initiatives for and with them. Current debates are helping us to clarify our vision of mission. It is not, in the first place, to seek new adherents: our Christian sensitivity would make us shrink away from any kind of proselytism. Our desire for dialogue is not a low-profile strategy for enticing people; our social works are not aimed at alluring the unsuspecting. At the very heart of mission is the free gift of beauty and love. We are united through the radiance of the love of God with peoples of different cultures and religions, with those who are bowed down under the weight of suffering. No matter what stage of evangelization we have arrived at, the essential thing is that we, as missionaries, allow the face of the LORD to shine out in all its brightness.

A Step forward in our Life together

Those who have experienced a positive inter-cultural community life discover a new dimension, a new gift. By getting to know people who are different, we affirm our own identity. From the way the Congregation is developing, it seems evident that such experiences will become much more common and we will surely find the sources of inspiration to take this step forward in our tradition of *"Cor Unum et Anima Una."* Institutes are feeling the need to inculturate their charism: people from different

---

4. John Paul II, *Novo millennio ineunte.*

origins must find their own way to live out the same vocation, enriching rather than dividing the Congregation.

The great Challenge of Spiritan Formation

In this changing world, we must look again at our formation program. The *Guide for Spiritan Formation* made a good evaluation of the changes following the criteria of our Spiritan vocation. One of the big challenges is to find a good educational relationship between young confreres and those responsible for their initiation. The authority, which must exist, should have the character of a "witness," like an elder in the family structure. The young people in turn must create fraternal relationships among themselves.

Our Life-style and our Solidarity

Maynooth drew our attention to our economic situation. Each of us has a responsibility to look for the means which enable us to live and work. We are not paid because we are religious. Many of our predecessors worked with their hands (SRL, 72.1; Maynooth 6). Each community, each circumscription should aim at financial autonomy, even if in many cases it can be no more than partial. We should also look for people and organizations who will support our work. At the generalate, we have established a new post to promote and organize fund-raising.

Financial solidarity in our Congregation is remarkable, but such are the present needs of formation and mission that we are proposing another appeal to the whole Congregation to set up a fund for our mission (in addition to *Cor Unum*, which remains dedicated to formation needs). This necessary appeal is an invitation to go on a sort of economic diet, to "re-examine our current life-style in the light of the spirit of poverty and simplicity envisaged by our founders" (Maynooth 4.24). This simple way of life is a path of freedom, that leads us to the peace and joy of God.

A Time for Inspiration and Discernment

Today, we can no longer simply follow the traditional ways of mission, no more than we can allow ourselves to be swept along unthinkingly by modern currents. More than ever, we are constantly obliged to make our own discernment and judgements. If we are not to lose our way, we must be open to the inspiration that comes from our sources and habitually review things with our communities. In this way, our life will develop its own unique richness; it will become a new pilgrimage. But this supposes that we will be contemplatives, that we will so arrange the style and rhythm of our life that contemplation will be possible.

May the LORD, who is calling us to push out once more into the deep water, grant us his Spirit. I wish you all a very happy feast of Pentecost.

December 2001

A MESSAGE FOR THE SPIRITAN YEAR: WITH THE POWER OF THE SPIRIT

Dear Brothers and Sisters,

We are about to embark on the celebration of key moments in the history of our Spiritan family. This special year, decided upon by the Chapter of Maynooth, presents us with a unique opportunity for spiritual renewal. We attempt to rediscover the inspiration of our beginnings by responding creatively to the challenges of our own day. The meaning of this sort of re-foundation is encapsulated in the logo above. It refers us back to the boat of the Maynooth document, inviting us to get on board for a new voyage. The sail is filled with the breath of the Spirit. We are not leaving for a cruise among our archives; if we look back to the past, it is to prepare ourselves, with the power of the Spirit, to set out into the deep for a long journey ahead.

A storm-bound Ship

> "One day he got into a boat with his disciples and said to them, 'Let us cross to the other side of the lake.' So they set sail, and while they were sailing, he fell asleep. A squall blew over the lake and they were taking in water and were in danger. They came and woke him saying, 'Master, Master, we are perishing!' He awakened, rebuked the wind and the waves, and they subsided and there was a calm. Then he asked them, 'Where is your faith?'" (Luke 8:22-25).

Jesus leads his disciples to the other side of the lake, which is regarded as a pagan area. In all three Synoptics, attention is focused on Jesus: he is the first to enter the boat and his disciples follow him (Matt 8:18-25); he invites them to launch out into the deep. When the storm is raging while he sleeps, they cry out *"Master, Master,"* with the trust in his authority that the Greek word used implies. He shows his power and calm is restored.

The narration is a reflection of the period after the paschal events, when Jesus has passed through suffering and death to enter into the fullness of life. For Luke in the Acts, Jesus continues his presence and action through his disciples. With him, by the power of his Spirit, they too can pass through trials and become his witnesses in the worst of situations. In the same way, he will be with Paul and the other missionaries of the early days. Is he also with us? Are we ready for a new and difficult journey? Are we able to call on him with all our heart? Where is *our* faith?

A Search for the Truth

Now is the time to seek out the truth, beyond the routine and superficiality of our daily lives, and to live it to the full. In the wake of the EGC at Pittsburgh, we in the general council have shared together our assessments of the current state of the Congregation and the way in which we could make use of the Spiritan Year as an occasion for renewal. We have tried to dig into the everyday life of the Congregation to see what inspires it. Below are some of the impressions that we have gained from our visits. In a world of quickening change, cultural diversity, complexity and specialization, we feel at times that we are losing our footing. But it is a situation that gives us the chance to exercise freedom because it calls for personal choices. We must get rid of all self-delusion: it is only when we really know ourselves, with all our strengths and weaknesses, that we can integrate our Spiritan vision into the reality of our lives. So much of our life has been cerebral: the old style of formation tended to put the accent on grand ideas, to the neglect of the reality of the way we are, with all our needs and wounds. Some confreres have left the Congregation; we have been affected, to an extent, by the question of pedophilia. This brings home to us the reality of our vulnerability.

We have to learn to make our personal choices with integrity while at the same time being supported by a community and the Congregation. We cannot become free all alone; we need the help of others. But there is often a lack of personal communication between us and we sometimes know little about the confreres with whom we live. If we are to have a common spirituality which touches our lives and our work, we need to interact at a deeper level.

We could ask questions about the role of faith in our lives; does it have incisive repercussions, for example, in the way that some confreres deal with difficult situations? How far does prayer help them to react in the right way? Each of us has to fall back on our well-tried sources: personal and community prayer, Bible reading, and celebration of the Eucharist in the light of what we are living, the example of other witnesses. We must let the LORD speak directly to our hearts. A practical spirituality is vital, especially for those who are deeply disappointed and depressed by situations of war and opposition. We should look for ways of reviving our confidence, like displaying texts from our Founders in our communities. Others have been inspired by elements of the missionary vision of Libermann. In seeking the truth, we must pay much attention to our life of faith.

Where is *our* Faith?

Our Congregation made its *aggiornamento* after Vatican II by successive Chapters and the writing of our new Rule of Life. But the challenge of the contemporary world is an on-going thing. As we try to help those who are forgotten, the world today gives the impression of a boat that is out of control, driven by the anonymous force of the law of the global market, the law of the strongest. The media tell us of some societies that are suffering from stress and the excesses of consummation and others that are wracked by misery, chaos and fear. Recent events have spread the suffering to the whole world. We feel so helpless when we try to act against or draw attention to the forces of the globalized world. It can happen that we begin to have doubts.

The difficulty can also come from ourselves. Perhaps our *aggiornamento* has remained superficial and we have ended up by simply rediscovering our old weaknesses instead of producing something new. We can feel there is something essential lacking in our attempts to live a genuine Spiritan life. In the milieu in which most of us live, we act as if everything depends on us, as if we are perfectly capable of finding the right course of action by ourselves. The Christian tradition is often seen as an inherited package of convictions and values where each can draw out what is needed and make his own menu. We are all, to a greater or lesser extent, marked by such an attitude.

But at the heart of the original tradition, Jesus is there, after the paschal events, as a real and living presence in the faith of the disciples, in their relations with each other, in the witness that they give of him before men and women. He is the one who propels them towards an adventure beyond those horizons they have known so far. The power of his Spirit is real and creative in their lives. We, in our turn, must live with confidence in God's unconditional love in our own present experience. Beyond our own strength and competence, there is something that we could never have given to ourselves: the living presence of Jesus amongst us. Are we able to call on him with all our heart like the apostles?

This thought leads us to identify a source that is the origin of everything. Faced with the huge variety of cultures and religions, we have to discern, more than we did in the past, what is the real origin of things and how it relates to us. We must not allow the face of Jesus to remain indistinct and blurred. Trust in him is lived at the level of the heart, at where we make our decisions, and in the actions and attitudes that come from them. The presence of the LORD does not just come to us through what happened in the past: he reveals that he is still with us in the lives of those who testify to him. He continues to inspire us by the charism of our Founders, but he also shows himself through the witness of the confreres with whom we live and work.

The Testimony of our Founders

We discover the strength of the Spirit of Christ in the lived experience of those who have made our history up to the present day. Libermann and Poullart des Places are examples of total trust in God and openness to the Holy Spirit. Poullart let himself be led by unexpected events as he moved forward humbly in the presence of God. He wrote in *Reflections on the Truth of Religion*:

> Let others say what they please; let them approve of me or make fun of me, treat me as a visionary, a hypocrite or a righteous man! All this henceforth must leave me indifferent. *Ego Deum meum quaero* [I am seeking my God]. He has given me life only that I may use it to serve Him faithfully ... God alone loves me sincerely and wants what is good for me. If I can please Him, I shall be exceedingly happy. If I displease Him, I am the most wretched man in the world. I have won everything if I live in grace. Losing it, I lose everything.[5]

---

5. Koren, *Spiritual Writings*, 81, 83.

For Libermann, God is present throughout our history; even if things seem to roll on without him, he is always there with his merciful goodness. He wrote to the community at Cape Palmas (January 15, 1844).

> Have no fear of the difficulties you are going to meet. They must never discourage you. You have not gone out in your own name; it is not you who are doing the work, but the One who sent you. You are not alone, and he will always be with you if you remain faithful. So do not be faint-hearted or allow your faith to weaken. An apostle of Jesus Christ cannot be downcast when faced with obstacles. Bear them manfully with peace and patience, and always persevere with any of your projects which are definitely useful for the glory of God and the salvation of souls. Stop a while in front of obstacles and difficulties which for the moment seem to be insoluble, and wait for God's moment with confidence. Be faithful, and that moment will surely arrive (ND, VI, 3-8).[6]

The Power of the Spirit of Christ amongst Us Today

Although the Congregation is faced with numerous difficulties, as well as its own limitations and weaknesses, many confreres are giving an example of calm strength, perseverance, new initiatives despite obstacles and disappointments, a simple presence amongst the people, of fraternal life amongst different cultures, of a sense of responsibility and a deep concern for spiritual renewal. Their witness is strong and it renews our own faith when we meet them in the course of our visits. These tangible fruits of the Spirit are convincing evidence of the enduring presence of the Master throughout the storm.

We also see the presence of the Holy Spirit beyond the frontiers of the church before the Gospel is ever preached. Just as Jesus is recognized in the Scriptures and the breaking of bread, so the Spirit speaks to us through other peoples. He appears to us in the guise of the poorest of people and touches us deeply by their humility and trust. The Spiritan Year is an opportunity to experience the unswerving love of God in our lives and to build a greater confidence in him. It is the time to learn once more how to celebrate each day the newness of life that Christ gives us through his Holy Spirit. Our joy is not just that of the feasts that come

---

6. *Anthology*, I, 226-32, here

and go: it springs from a new-found interior freedom, from friendship and forgiveness given and received.

During this year, the decisive question of Jesus will be put to us again: "Do you also want to leave?" Will we give the same reply as Peter, "Master, to whom shall we go? You have the words of eternal life. We have come to believe and are convinced that you are the Holy One of God" (John 6:67-69). Are we genuine disciples who are going to be his witnesses? How can we communicate this faith to all those who are joining our Congregation? How can we deepen our own sufficiently to face up to the challenges of our day?

Some practical Suggestions for all Spiritans

We invite every Spiritan to set aside "a desert time" during the first weeks of the Spiritan Year — at least one day — to look at his or her life in the presence of God, to give thanks, to ask pardon, to renew confidence, to ask for needs and look to the future.

After that, confreres could come together in community (if it is small) or in small groups for the larger communities, in order to exchange your reflections of faith with each other. The sharing could then be extended to the whole circumscription on the occasion of other meetings or celebrations.

Such a sharing could begin by considering our Founders: how have they influenced my life, in one way or another?

These two stages seem to be a good way to proceed towards the indispensable renewal of the whole of the Congregation; the Spiritan Year lasts for 16 months so it is good to spread the program over several steps.

We should not allow the process to lose itself in minor considerations; it should focus on our basic experience and the big challenges that we are meeting at this time.

In our meditation, let us not forget the essentials of our vocation: How can we live in solidarity with the poor, in our personal context as well as on the larger scale? How can we bring about our spiritual renewal? How can we promote greater friendship and fraternal sharing in the life of our Congregation which is ever more international and inter-cultural?

We must thank God for our Congregation and for all that it has accomplished, for all our confreres and what they are and have been to us. We share all the joys and hopes, the worries and anxieties of the men and women of our time. Our vocation is not to withdraw from this world but to love it and to live out God's loving plan in it under the breath of his Spirit. But to do this, we must also obey his call to draw aside at times to be alone with our Master.

May the LORD be with each of you and give you the power of his Spirit.

On behalf of the general council.

Pentecost 2002

AFRICA IN THE STRENGTH OF THE SPIRIT

> "I believe in the Holy Spirit, the LORD and Giver of life" (Nicene Creed)

Dear Brothers and Sisters,

Libermann encourages us to be like a feather under the breath of the Spirit, but we must be ready to catch this breeze. Where does our inspiration come from today? The Spiritan Year is an act of faith, rooted in our experience that in looking back at our history we can often be moved, encouraged and revitalized. The Spirit breathes when we remember our Founders and other witnesses from former times. As we approach Pentecost, we look again at our past and present in Africa, the continent where we have made our biggest investment in the course of our history.

Commitment for Life and Death

Africa is no longer simply a place where Spiritans go on mission: this continent has entered the ranks of our Congregation with about 1,000 members. And, particularly since Libermann, mission in Africa has left its mark on our religious family, as can be seen in *The Spiritan Anniversary Diary* which will appear shortly and in other historical publications. A Spiritan from Brazil told us at the Enlarged General Council of Dakar that the Spiritans he had met were permanently affected by their African experience, of which they talked incessantly.

There has been something of a love affair between the Congregation and Africa. Libermann committed himself to an apparently impossible venture there, despite his chronic lack of means: he had bad health, no money, no personnel and, at the start, no support. But without even setting foot on African soil, he became possessed by a passion for the people which was a vision of faith: "My heart belongs completely to you and to all Africans ... I wish to spend my whole life trying to bring about their happiness. And not only in this world, but above all to prepare them for the immeasurable and endless happiness ... in heaven."[7] He enjoined his men to respect African culture with great humility; writing in 1847, he told them to relate to Africans "as servants relate to their masters."

Our missionary experience has taught us that *"to submit to the breath of the Spirit"* does not mean that we are just going to float around: the graves of some of our young missionaries would soon teach us otherwise. On a visit to the old cemetery of Huila in Angola, one of the catechists from the formation center took a Bible and read us this extract from Mark: "there is no one who has given up house or brothers or sisters or mother or father or children or lands for my sake and for the sake of the gospel who will not receive a hundred times more in this present age ... and eternal life in the age to come" (Mark 10:29-30).

The very first page of the *Spiritan Anniversary Diary* refers to the massacre of Kongolo.

Other confreres have lost their lives in Angola, in Sierra Leone. Our recent history in Africa has been punctuated by civil wars and wars of independence. As Africans took over responsibility for their future once more in Church and State, it proved to be a difficult time for many confreres but was ultimately a purifying experience. The departure, imposed or judged to be opportune, of many confreres was a time of great suffering for them: but many set out again for other horizons in Latin America, North America, Australia, Papua, and other parts of Africa. The suffering experienced in Africa became a source of blessings for other missions.

"If the Grain of Wheat dies, it will produce much Fruit" (John 12:24)

The local churches in Africa were born from the mystery of death and resurrection lived in this way and we have been blessed by vocations which are bringing new life to our Institute. Our mission in Africa is increasingly being led by African confreres in five Provinces and several Foundations. The number of confreres from Europe is rapidly diminishing; sometimes, no more than 2 or 3 remain as witnesses. Their presence is important both for their experience and for the links it gives to another continent. At the same time, African confreres are involved in

---

7. Letter to Eliman, King of Dakar, 1848. ND, X, 22-26, here 24; *Spiritan Anthology*, I, 303-306, here 304

new Spiritan initiatives in all continents. Some are working in the old circumscriptions of Europe and North America where they are witnessing in their turn to a new vitality coming from Africa. A similar movement is taking place on other front lines of our mission in Latin America and the Caribbean. In this complicated turn in our history, springing from Africa, we can see the work of the Spirit; we do not know where he comes from or where he is going (cf. John 3:8).

In recent times, our Congregation has changed a great deal, with a new organization, a new source of recruitment and new areas of apostolate in all continents; but our greatest commitment is still in Africa.

The Holy Spirit who is LORD

The most important thing is that wherever we are, we do not fall into superficiality, doing what is easy, keeping up appearances, but that we follow the example of our predecessors, in the strength of the Spirit. Many confreres did not escape unscathed from the upheavals of Africa, but they finally rode out the storm and kept their feet. Their strength was not so much in their physical power, their multiple abilities, their wisdom or their temperament behind all these things, there was a life lived through the Holy Spirit, learnt gradually in the school of Libermann, reinforced by prayer, community life and the service and defense of the poor. The silent strength of the Holy Spirit was at work in them; "He prepares us to make the total gift of ourselves for the Kingdom" (SRL, 10).

The ambient culture in which we live can easily direct us into a path of self-fulfillment, simply developing and using our own human energies. When we talk of "the spirit," are we perhaps referring to our own? But the Spirit of the Christian tradition has a capital letter. In the Azores, there is a popular devotion to *"O Senhor Espirito Santo."* Real spiritual strength is that which comes from this Spirit; his assurance and authority come to us as a free gift through the witness of others, which bears no relation to what we are capable of doing when simply left to ourselves.

"I believe in the Holy Spirit who is LORD." He instills into us that same confidence that he gave to Jesus, that allowed him to say *"Abba, Father"* in the garden of Gethsemane (cf. Gal 4:6). In the same way, he gives us confidence in others and makes us see them as brothers and sisters. He is the Spirit of sonship, who proceeds from the Son. From this confidence is born the energy of an active service, the internal freedom to love without reward, to forgive, to undertake. He is the creative Spirit who proceeds

from the Father. The Blessed Virgin inspires us with the faith of her Immaculate Heart, ready for the unforeseen and the total gift of self.

May this feast of Pentecost lead us all back into the breath of the Holy Spirit, who is the LORD and giver of *real* life.

Yours fraternally.

Christmas 2002

STARTING AFRESH IN HOPE

Dear Brothers and Sisters,

First of all, the community of the generalate would like to wish you all a very happy Christmas and New Year. We are all one family, even though we are working in 58 countries and come from 52, not to mention the multitude of cultures which only God could enumerate. In this year when we are celebrating the anniversaries of our Congregation, it is also good to think about our future; one confrere was heard to quip recently, *"We've certainly got a past, but have we got a future?"* Advent is the right time to insert the "principle of hope" into our visions, our plans, and our preoccupations.

New Vitality and new Worries

In the northern countries, there are signs of a new vitality in Christian communities and many people, especially the young, are giving their services to the most neglected people and to the causes of justice and peace, reconciliation and the protection of the environment. But at the same time, in our older Provinces we are suffering because we know there is hardly anybody to continue the work after us. In Latin America, the Caribbean, and, above all, in Africa, we have been blessed, like Abraham, by the arrival of many young people into our Spiritan family. But this wonderful vote of confidence in our Congregation, which is getting old like Sarah, is not without its own problems. Where can we find enough experienced formators and how can we build the necessary structures? We are experiencing the positive side of an international and intercultural community life that is spreading everywhere, but some still find it difficult to relate to those who are very different to themselves in age and culture

Despite many positive initiatives, we are still worried by the way our societies are developing. Confreres from the north are saddened by the present religious indifference of the countries where their vocations were born. They are not at ease with the scramble for material satisfaction or with the negative attitudes towards immigrants fleeing the chaos in their own countries. Those in the south see some of their countries falling apart as a result of poverty, disease, violence, world-wide injustice or bad government.

A Lack of Hope

What people can believe in and hope for changes at different times and with different cultures. But in today's environment, hope is often limited in its perspectives and weak when it is confronted by obstacles. It is as if there is a lack of hope. This seems to be especially true for the richer countries, which head the lists of the number of suicides as a proportion of the population. And in these same countries, young people dice with death as if they want to put their lives to the test. There are philosophical ideas in vogue which see life as controlled *"by chance and necessity";* the wheel of fortune turns and we disappear from the scene. The final word rests with the rhythm of the universe. But what if the opposite were true—what if the first and last word was not controlled by destiny but by a primordial act of love?

We run the danger of becoming obsessed with a sort of global sub-culture, made up of superficial and inferior substitutes for ancient philosophies. Preoccupied or fascinated by the present, many of our contemporaries seem to skirt around the most important questions. This also affects us and our hope is in danger of crumbling, like old rocks worn away by the weather, even if we try to put on a brave face. We want to keep alive the fundamental questions of life and give witness to everybody of the hope that is within us.

Return to the Source of Hope

When our hope is threatened in this way, not just by the accumulation of problems and uncertainties but by the whole climate of our societies, it is not enough just to start repainting the furniture. We have to dig into our lives to rediscover the source, which in our case means to return to Jesus this Christmas. For the source is in Jesus, who appeared in human descent as Emmanuel, God-with-us.

Jesus appeared, in time, in a little village *"without pomp or majesty"* (Pascal). According to the dominant criteria of our civilization, he would have had no future. He was crucified, he died and he was buried. Even in his final agony, he continued to say *"Abba, Father,"* his extreme prayer of hope.

The theologian, J. Moltmann, distinguishes between "the future," which flows from the natural evolution of things, and "what is to come," which is neither natural nor evident but which we can only wait for or hope for from somebody else. In this sense, hope was made flesh with all its power in Jesus on Golgotha. This is where his witnesses find their hope, including our Founders and the other great figures of our history. Therein lies the secret of their extraordinary strength both to withstand and to launch out courageously.

The excellent Symposium on 300 Years of Spiritan History, which recently took place in Paris, proved to be very instructive. Our past teaches us never to be resigned to things, never to be impatient in the face of obstacles or to look for superficial results but, whatever the situation, to start afresh in hope.

Starting afresh in Hope

The Congregation for Institutes of Consecrated Life published an Instruction last Pentecost for the mission of such Institutes in the third millennium, under the title: *Starting afresh from Christ*. During our Spiritan Year, we also want to start afresh in hope. It is not a step backwards; it is a grace born from confidence, worked out in a life of fidelity, which becomes a source of creativity (SRL, 2). What we receive when we look back on the past is not a pre-established plan, nor an assured result, but an inspiration. It is not something that is given to us all at once but over a period of time and through our meeting with many witnesses.

As Spiritans, we find it in our Founders, in our confreres today and in many other people whom we meet on our missionary journey, often poor and of other religions. As our recent Chapters have shown, our missionary life is a pilgrimage which each day renews hope, our source of innovation and commitment. The season of Advent and Christmas is a favorable time for us to learn this lesson again and to live it in patience.

A very happy Christmas to you all.
Yours fraternally.

Pentecost 2003

"GIVE THANKS TO THE Lord FOR HE IS GOOD!"

Dear Brothers and Sisters,

In Europe, the feast of Pentecost falls when nature is bursting out in its fullness and the liturgy seems to echo the same idea of plenitude: "The Spirit of the Lord fills the whole earth, Alleluia!" We can now ask ourselves whether the Spiritan Year, the aim of which was to *"encourage a renewal of the Congregation and to make our Spiritan missionary spirituality better known"* (Maynooth 8.1) has helped us all to live a real Pentecost experience.

It would be presumptuous of me to make such an assessment for the whole Congregation; perhaps it could be attempted once the circumscriptions have made their own. In any case, only God knows what happened in the heart of each one of us. So let us just try to identify some examples of vitality.

The Treasury of our History

Historians have been delving into our past with a new enthusiasm, revealing what riches still lie in our archives. At the start, a committee of experts stimulated and organized research. After Maynooth, a commission drawn from the different regions of the Congregation carried the movement forward, encouraging the interest of confreres and planning meetings and celebrations throughout the Spiritan world.

It was decided to focus not just on our Founders and great figures but on the totality of our history. Our historians were in great demand for retreats and conferences. The celebrations and pilgrimages were inspiring for ourselves and helped others to discover our spiritual and missionary heritage.

Missionary Vitality

Some of our old missionary projects were given a face-lift while new ones saw the light of day for the first time. Latin America sent a team to Bolivia and the North American/Caribbean region started preparations for an insertion in the Dominican Republic. The work for the education of young people in Congo Brazzaville (Sala Ngolo) in the Province of Central Africa has undergone further expansion in the wake of the violence and destruction of the civil war. After many setbacks, the agricultural college at Kasumo in the diocese of Kigoma (Tanzania) will finally open its doors at the end of this year. And during its first Chapter, the circumscription of Australia decided on the mission to the Aborigines as its first priority. Missionary vitality is also seen in our fidelity to older commitments which are clearly Spiritan in nature as, for example, in African countries afflicted by war, social injustice, and extreme poverty.

In trying to work for justice, peace, and the protection of creation, we often feel we are engaged in an unequal struggle against the injustices of this world and the violence which they generate, a bit like David confronting Goliath with only a sling in his hand. But our history teaches us that victory ultimately goes to David.

Paths to Unity

In our societies torn by violence and accelerated change, we have taken up the challenge of living in communities that are international and intercultural. We are making progress down this road, even if misunderstandings can sometimes bring hurt and tensions. The time of grace we have just lived prompts us to reconciliation with one another if we are living in an atmosphere of discord. I also ask pardon from those whom I may have wounded. May the motto of our Congregation become even more true as we reach the end of this year.

In this way, we will make our contribution to that peace and reconciliation which seems to be the greatest need of the world in our time. We have been called to live a life of truth and this has been given further precision in the area of our affective life; you will all be receiving the document that the general council has prepared on this subject.

Learning Again to give Thanks

I told one confrere, who could be somewhat excitable on occasion, that he now seemed to be much more at peace; he told me that he had relearnt the prayer of thanksgiving in a community to which he went from time to time.

During the Spiritan Year, we have rediscovered the multiple signs of the love of God in our history and in our present life. The greatest blessing we could draw from this time of grace could be the prayer of thanksgiving and praise. Through the joy that it awakens in us, it helps us to straighten out our deviations and heal our wounds.

I wish you all a share in this great joy of Pentecost.

Yours fraternally.

Christmas 2003
"LET US GO OVER TO BETHLEHEM" (LUKE 2:15)

Dear Spiritan Brothers and Sisters,

I am writing this letter at the conclusion of the First Chapter of the South Central African Foundation (SCAF). It was held in the diocese of Bethlehem in South Africa from the 1st to the 10th of December, 2003. It consisted of delegates from the Foundation and the superiors of the five circumscriptions from which it was born: the Districts of South Africa and Zimbabwe, and the Groups of Zambia, Malawi and Mozambique.

Taken together, these five countries cover 3,280,000 km2 and have a combined population of about 90,000,000 inhabitants. The 85 confreres working in the area are of 17 different nationalities. There were 20 capitulants in all, as well as several invited confreres.

Even if the name of the town of "Bethlehem" has only a tenuous connection with the town in Palestine, the SCAF Chapter strikes me as having a special significance for the whole Congregation as we approach Christmas. While not wanting to canonize it, I see it as a humble witness to Spiritan authenticity.

Concern for Unity

In our human family, where so many people are uprooted, upset, and worried about what lies ahead, it is hardly surprising to find a tendency to fall back on oneself, one's country, one's ethnic background and one's own group. Before the Chapter began, it would not have been unreasonable to expect such tendencies to show themselves in view of the vast territory covered and the great diversity of the Spiritans who are working there. But the exact opposite was the case. The Chapter showed great unity and openness. When it came to the fundamental question of the structures to be foreseen for the future, several models were suggested; but the capitulants decided to choose the most common model which is closest to our Rule of Life, the one which moves in the direction of an eventual single Province.

Mission in the Service of the Poor

The sense of unity shown by the capitulants, who readily agreed to follow the view of the majority, sprung, no doubt, from the central element of our mission, the whole reason for our presence and all our efforts. As

Spiritans, we do not look for personal achievement nor the dazzling success of a particular project: we work together in a shared witness to the Gospel on priority commitments in the region that has been confided to us, as a service to the poorest of people. Our confreres working in the South Central African Region are concerned by the ravages caused by AIDS, the widespread violence, the catastrophe of a countryside reduced to poverty by recurring drought, the lack of worthwhile education.

The formation, to which the SCAF and the circumscriptions are devoting so much of their human resources, is a guarantee for the future of a truly Spiritan mission.

"It is the Spirit who gives Life"

The dynamism of a Chapter flows, above all, from an inspiration. Fidelity to praying together is an essential help in this area. At a time in human history when people and groups are less open to belief, to hope, and to love, we have to be ready to row against the tide. It is when we are praying, alone or together, that the LORD talks to us, beyond anything that we could imagine by ourselves.

At this stage in its development, the SCAF Chapter did not concentrate on structures: it gave guidelines for the future, rather than lay down the exact nature of what must be achieved. The important thing is to keep going forward in the unity of our charism.

The fact that the Chapter was held in South Africa surely brought something of the dynamism of this country, renewed by the outstanding witness of Nelson Mandela and the democratic inter-racial elections of 1994. In the other countries too, the mission has a look of youth about it and a Spiritan presence that is still fresh.

Return to Bethlehem. The Seal of Humility

Each year, Bethlehem turns our attention once more to the spring which has given life to this world. Christmas is the time when we learn again the lesson of humility, the seal that gives unity to the Congregation, dynamism to our mission and to our Spiritan inspiration. Christmas, with its gift of humility, gives authenticity once more to our life and missionary commitment. And with humility, we rediscover joy.

In the center where the Chapter was held, each cottage had the name of a virtue written in Zulu: the one where Michael Onwuemelie and myself were lodged was called *"Boikokobetso,"* which means "Humility."

This is the blessing that we can wish each other at this Christmas time, to increase our joy: "LORD, direct our heart towards the joy of such a great mystery" (Prayer for the 3rd Sunday of Advent).

With fraternal greetings, on behalf of the general council and the whole community at Clivo di Cinna.

Pentecost 2004

DECISIVE MOMENTS IN OUR LIVES

Dear Spiritan Brothers and Sisters,

Pentecost and our 19th General Chapter both present us with an occasion to authenticate our lives and to welcome the Spirit. We have enjoyed the blessings of our Spiritan Year; what can we now expect from these meetings with the Spirit? I am sure we would like some effects that are more visible and lasting. In any case, our vocation calls for a vitality which does not automatically sustain itself.

"Vatican II was just the Beginning of a Beginning" (Karl Rahner)

Let us take a look at the Second Vatican Council which was a providential moment (*kairos*) for the whole church. To mark the centenary of the birth of Karl Rahner, Vatican Radio played some extracts from the conferences given by this great theologian. One of the points he made was that "Vatican II was just the beginning of a beginning." And yet nobody could say that they skimped on the resources: 2,400 bishops and a host of experts and observers sat through four sessions from 1962 to 1965, which produced extensive theological texts and decrees, renewing the constitution of the church, its liturgy, its mission and the nature of its presence in the modem world. All this needed to be assimilated and the orientations put into practice.

But in the light of the progressive fall off in religious practice and the lack of vocations (particularly in Europe), it became evident that secularization was seriously weakening good habits, respect for authority, and the acceptance of the convictions passed down to us by our ancestors. The Council was accepted, assimilated and put into practice by a minority, but a new strength is now called for in some societies which are increasingly individualized and critical. In addition to the fresh evangelization which is breathing new life into Christians and attracting others of good will, a large part of the world's population requires nothing less than another first evangelization. In this sense also, one can say that Vatican II was the start of a beginning, and our own General Chapter of 1968-1969 committed the Congregation to a new mission.

"Zacchaeus, make haste, and come down" (Luke 19:5)

The statement of Rahner is even more true if we look at it from a fundamental perspective of faith, an area where we are all concerned. Let us start with the story of Zacchaeus (Luke 19:1-10). Crowds of people are following Jesus through the town of Jericho; Zacchaeus is intrigued, but because he is not very big, he runs ahead of the crowd and climbs a sycamore tree from where he can get a good look at this Jesus who will pass by. He wants to have a good view but he also wants to be able to discuss the event later on with his friends and neighbors.

Zacchaeus has a lot in common with the people of today. Like him, we are often content to remain spectators and commentators on the events which are happening in the world and closer to home. Faced with the complexity of many situations and aware of our own powerlessness — and perhaps also because of our lack of strong convictions — we run the risk of never really becoming involved. In this way, we join the ranks of a generation which is being reduced to childhood through the power of the mass media.

The rest of the story is also challenging. When Jesus arrives at the tree, he looks up and says to Zacchaeus, "Hurry and come down, for I must stay at your house today." During the Spiritan Year, we were invited to take some time apart to allow the LORD to enter into our most intimate life — to *"go into your room and shut the door"* as it is described in the Gospel of Matthew (6:5-6). Zacchaeus, who up to this point has been strictly an observer, commits himself to Jesus, saying, "Behold, half of my possessions, LORD, I shall give to the poor, and if I have extorted anything from anyone I shall repay it four times over." Jesus replies, "Today, salvation has come to this house."

"The Spirit . . . prepares Us to make the total Gift of Ourselves for the Kingdom" (SRL, 10)

A meeting similar to that of Zacchaeus is the beginning of real Spiritan life. Confronted by Our LORD, who suffered, died and rose again, we take life seriously and are ready to give our whole selves to him. It is then that we experience the new life, along with the great joy that accompanies it. The Spirit of Pentecost comes upon us and gives us the strength to go to the very ends of the earth. This is the true beginning which we have to re-live continuously. It is then that we become real missionaries. As our Rule of Life puts it so well: "The Spirit calls us to continual conversion, shapes our personal and community lives, makes us partakers in the death and resurrection mystery of Jesus and prepares us to make the total gift of ourselves for the Kingdom" (SRL, 10).

For our mission today — a mission of first evangelization, work for justice and peace and the integrity of creation, the service and protection of the poor, inter-religious dialogue — as well as for our fraternal life between confreres who come from all points of the compass and our duty to testify to the love of God throughout our lives, it is important that the LORD remains with us always "to the end of time" (Matt 28:20).

"The Church lives by the Eucharist" (Pope John Paul II)

Once again, the Holy Father has drawn our attention to the Eucharist by his encyclical *Ecclesia de Eucharistia*.[8] The Eucharist is how we experience Jesus in his death and resurrection. It is indispensable for us if we are to be true missionaries and religious, capable of renouncing ourselves to go beyond the frontiers of our particular diversities. It is the key to our authenticity, which is not just a question of being correct in our relationships, but of learning to love authentically. If we are only superficially committed, our weaknesses remain and we are incapable of launching into the deep.

In this final letter, I want to give my sincere thanks to the general council, the confreres working in the services and the members of the generalate community who have helped me even more since I have been handicapped with bad eyesight. I am also indebted to all of you who have welcomed me in the different continents throughout the world. I always returned from my visits with renewed strength. I ask forgiveness of all those whom I may have hurt in these 12 years of leadership. May the LORD give us a large measure of his Spirit at this Pentecost which precedes our General Chapter, so that we may be more free and happy as we travel along the paths of our mission.

Fraternally.

---

8. 2003.

CHAPTER FIVE

VERY REV. FR. JEAN-PAUL HOCH, C.S.Sp.

Superior General, 2004-2012

Fr. Jean-Paul Hoch, C.S.Sp., hails from Alsace in eastern France; after gaining a license in philosophy from the Gregorian University in Rome and spending one year teaching in Congo-Brazzaville, he gained a Master's degree in mathematics from the University of Strasbourg where he also completed his theological studies. After ordination in 1978 he worked for ten years in the Central African Republic being at one time chaplain to the Young Christian Workers in the country and also chaplain at the university of Bangui. On returning to France he was vicar provincial for a time before being elected provincial superior there for six years up to 1997. After this, he took up a new challenge of learning Chinese in order to join the confreres in the new mission on the island of Taiwan, where he remained until 2004. At the General Chapter of Torre d'Aguilha that year, he was elected Superior General and completed his mandate in 2012. During his time in office, the unions of circumscriptions were created as a means of facilitating greater co-operation in formation and mission among Spiritans living close to each other geographically. Returning to France he was superior of the community at Wolxheim until 2017 and is now in retirement there.

Christmas 2004

"PEACE ON EARTH TO THOSE WHOM HE LOVES"

> "Peace be with you!" Today, when the angels hardly speak again in public (weary, no doubt, of getting such small human audiences) and the risen LORD has gone to sit on the right side of the Father, who is going to tell men and women about this message of peace and reconciliation?

Dear Spiritan Brothers and Sisters,

On the day of his birth, the Child Jesus was still too small to be able to explain the meaning of the coming of the Word of God in our flesh. Mary and Joseph had far too many worries at that moment to think about calling a press conference. So, it was the angels who, as so often in ancient times, were given the task of enlightening us: "Glory to God in the highest and on earth peace on whom his favor rests" (Luke 2:14). But on the evening of his resurrection, Jesus did not leave it to others to remind the bewildered disciples of this same Good News: "Peace be with you!" Today, when the angels hardly speak again in public (weary, no doubt, of getting such small human audiences) and the risen LORD has gone to sit on the right side of the Father, who is going to tell men and women about this message of peace and reconciliation? You, me, all of us who have put our trust in him through whom it has pleased the Father to reconcile all beings to himself, "by making peace by the blood of his cross" (Col 1:20).

In our Congregation, we are increasingly aware of the urgency of this mission of peace and reconciliation. From as long ago as 1987, there has been a "Justice and Peace" service at the Generalate to support those confreres throughout the world who want to be "artisans for peace." More recently and in the same spirit, coordinators have been appointed for relations with Islam and ministry to refugees. At our recent General Chapter in Torre d'Aguilha, four confreres shared their experiences of mission in situations of conflict or post-conflict: Oscar Ngoy for Congo-Kinshasa, Barnabe Sakulenga for Angola, Gabriel Luseni for Sierra Leone, and Pierre Cherfily for Haiti. Vedastus Babu talked of the practical difficulties of ministering to refugees in the diocese of Kigoma (Tanzania). There are many confreres and Lay Spiritans who have given themselves totally to these works of justice and peace, dialogue and reconciliation—sometimes putting their lives and health at risk, often in the face of incomprehension or opposition from those around them. They are to be found in the North and the South, in ministry to parishes, schools, prisons and hospitals; they are working directly with the poor or in the world of communications or in the area of reflection and teaching. Let us not forget them in our prayers, let us tell them of our support and friendship, for these brothers and sisters are truly the "great throng of the hosts of heaven" who bring men and women the good news of reconciliation and peace on the Christmas nights in these times.

When we study the history of mission, we can sometimes be surprised by the words and attitudes of some missionaries in the past. While admiring their zeal and courage, we feel that the way they thought and talked was more relevant to the political and cultural imperialism of the time than to the values of the Gospel. We tend to judge them harshly.

But when we look at ourselves, should we not be worried that the historians of tomorrow might make exactly the same harsh judgments about us? Are our ways of thinking sometimes infected by retrograde nationalist and "communalist" prejudices, or influenced by destructive theories about the clashing of civilizations? Our hearts, our communities, our circumscriptions—are they really places where reconciliation comes about, where peace is built up?

Why does our Spiritan tradition, our Rule of Life, our Chapters, both general and in circumscriptions, put so much emphasis on community life? Is it simply because it brings us support and encouragement, making our ministry more efficacious? What the LORD demands of us, his disciples, is that we love one another as he has loved us, so that we may be one and the world may believe (John 17:21). It is precisely for this reason, and no other, that we attach so much importance to community life and to internationality: to witness, in a world that is divided and torn apart, to the possibility and reality of that peace and reconciliation that the Father offers us through his Son, Jesus. It is not because peace is possible that we believe: it is because we believe that peace is possible. The recent General Chapter reminded us insistently of the primacy of spiritual life and convictions, making "the spiritual renewal of the Congregation" the principle theme of its reflections and guidelines.

Pope John Paul II has declared October 2004 to October 2005 as the year of the Eucharist. Before we receive the same bread and the same cup in communion, we pray for peace in the church and the world and give and receive the sign of peace.

Is it not in the daily life-giving and fervent celebration of the Eucharist, "the source and summit of Spiritan living" (SRL, 93) that we can find the light and strength to overcome our small and greater differences and a mutual forgiveness for the wrongs we have done so that we can continue to build up that peace which can never be taken from us, both in ourselves and in those around us?

In the name of the general council and the whole community at Clivo di Cinna, a happy Christmas and a joyful New Year.

Pentecost 2005

SOME THOUGHTS ON OUR SPIRITAN CHARISM

Dear Spiritan Brothers and Sisters,

The General Chapter of Torre d'Aguilha gave us a pressing invitation to renew our spiritual life: "Reflecting on our charism is not an exercise of wishful thinking and dwelling on the past for its own sake, but of rediscovering the charism and intuitions of our Founders in the context of the contemporary world."[1] Some of the reading I have done recently has been a great help to me in understanding our Spiritan charism as applied to the world of today and I would like to share some of these thoughts with you. In his recent book on Bishop Edward Barron, Fr. Sean Farragher reminds us of the important role of this first pioneer in the mission to the west coast of Africa.[2] Also, in *Memoire Spiritaine*, no. 19, you will find a critical edition of the famous Memoire written by Eugene Tisserant in 1842, in which he describes the origins of the Society of the Holy Heart of Mary. In looking at these "heroes," known and unknown, of whom these two texts speak, I was struck by three qualities which they seem to have had in common and which, even today, are part of our Spiritan charism.[3]

The first thing I noticed was that our founders, directly or indirectly, were all possessed by *a deep feeling of compassion* for suffering humanity.

---

1. Torre d'Aguilha, no 1: "Spiritual Renewal of the Congregation."

2. Farragher, *Edward Barron*. Francophone readers refer to Morel, "Mgr. Edward Barron (1801-1854)," in *Memoire Spiritaine*, no. 15 (2002) 53-80.

3. In referring to Bishop Barron as one of the inspirers of the Spiritan charism, I am not trying to annex him to a Congregation to which he never belonged; rather, I am attempting to illustrate how our charism, like the river Nile, has many different sources.

It is true that some contemporary authors are rather critical of this feeling of compassion; but it is even more true that it is backed up by many ancient and solid biblical references. There are so many of them that they are firmly fixed in our memories: the story of the first apparition of the LORD God to Moses in the Old Testament; the occasion when Jesus was full of sorrow for the plight of the widow of Naim and told her, "Do not weep" (Luke 7:13); the description of Jesus visiting the tomb of Lazarus when he burst into tears (John 11:15); the passage where we are told that "at the sight of the crowds his heart was moved with pity for them because they were troubled and abandoned, like sheep without a shepherd" (Matt 9: 36).

At this time, when the Spirit is urging us to take up new commitments in Asia, it is encouraging to think that even long ago, Chinese philosophy looked on a spirit of compassion as the foundation and basis for moral conduct. Menicus, in the 4th century put it like this: "All men have a mind which cannot bear to see the sufferings of others. My meaning may be illustrated in this way: if men suddenly see a child about to fall into a well, they will, without exception, experience a feeling of alarm and distress—not so that they may gain the favor of the child's parents, nor to seek the praise of their neighbors and friends, nor from fear of a reputation of having been unmoved by such a thing." It is this same feeling of compassion that, from the start, has moved generations of Spiritans to commit their lives to following Christ, the Good Shepherd, bringing to suffering humanity the most precious gift of all—the Good News, but always combining the preaching of this Gospel with concrete and tangible signs of the gentleness of God. More recently, it is this same feeling of compassion that has given some of our confreres, especially in Africa, the strength to commit themselves to the service of AIDS victims. During and since the General Chapter, several confreres have told us how much they feel that this commitment in the domain of health seems to be one of the new missionary priorities of the Congregation—an area in which a new generation of Brothers and Lay Associates can find an absorbing amount of work.

I see another characteristic of our Founders as a repetition of the miracle of the *"sharing of tongues of fire."* To begin with, each of them independently experienced a deep concern for those whom we call in our tradition, "the poorest of the poor." But before long, and surely providentially, they found the opportunity to meet together and compare, share and validate their apostolic dreams—with one another and by referring their ideas to Rome. In this way, they discovered that their personal feelings all had the same origin—the Holy Spirit, the Spirit of Pentecost, who inspires us to speak as much as to listen. We see this in the coming together of Tisserant, Levavasseur and Libermann. It is also evident in the meeting of Bishop Barron, the Prefect Apostolic of the Two Guineas, with Libermann on December 20th 1842. His only helpers were an American priest, John Kelly, and a young layman, Dennis Pindar, both of Irish origin, like himself.

Our Spiritan charism has never been, and can never be, something of a purely personal nature; in one way or another, it will always relate to community. There are many meetings scheduled in our Congregation for the months ahead: regional gatherings, circumscription Chapters, enlarged councils. Each of these is like a repeat of the first great Chapter, that of Pentecost; we see again what appear to be tongues of fire, which spread and settle on each of the participants. The confreres who are preparing to take part in these meetings could well benefit from this advice of Father Libermann:

> When we know beforehand what will be brought up in the council meeting, we would do well to examine the background of these questions in the presence of Our LORD; but we should never prepare in advance the way we will put forward our opinions or reasons. For that, we should allow God to lead us and follow the inspiration of the moment. In examining the questions in advance, we must not adopt a stance that is too rigid; we must be ready to adapt or change our opinions in the light of what we hear during the discussions[4] (ND, II, 339).

When we reflect on the biography of Bishop Barron and the Memorandum of Eugene Tisserant, they seem to read like a *Way of the Cross*. For those who committed themselves to *"the poorest of people and the most abandoned in the church of God"*[5] (ND, II, 236), nothing was easy. Libermann and Barron both died relatively young: the first in 1852 at the age of 50, worn out by his commitment to the "Work for the Black People"; the second in 1854 at the age of 53, having contracted yellow fever while visiting the sick in Savannah (Georgia). The Cross is inseparable from our Spiritan charism. At the last General Chapter, we drew up a list of all the trials and difficulties that we come up against today: personal and

---

4. *Provisional Rule.* Part III : The Government of the Congregation, chapter 8 : the councils ; Art. 6 [The English translation lacks Part III. Ed.].

5. *Provisional Rule*, 37.

community weaknesses; a lack of personnel and finance; an organization not well adapted to today's realities; cultural, political, and economic environments that are not encouraging, etc. But are we not sometimes too much the children of our times, when we look on "crosses" as obstacles to be overcome, difficulties to be surmounted, problems to be resolved. Are we, at times, somewhat naive in thinking that the "centralization of second cycle formation" or the just sharing of the property, capital, or reserves of circumscriptions will solve all our problems in the areas of formation and finance? In defining our concept of the Spiritan charism, have we sufficiently integrated a sharing in the mystery of the death and resurrection of Jesus, which prepares us to make a total gift of ourselves for the kingdom? (cf. SRL, 10). Speaking of the newly converted Saul, the Jesus tells Ananias: "go, for this man is a chosen instrument of mine to carry my name before Gentiles, kings, and Israelites, and I will show him what he will have to suffer for my name" (Acts 9:15-16).

A few days after his election, our new Pope, Benedict XVI, was keen to visit the Church of St. Paul outside-the-Walls. While there, he strongly encouraged us missionaries, reminding us of the vocation of Paul: "To make Christ the center of his life, leaving all things for the sublime knowledge of Christ and the mystery of his love, and then committing himself to revealing him to all, especially the pagans." May the Spirit of Pentecost, who is also a spirit of listening and obedience, revive this same vocation within us, which, from our earliest days, has driven us for the sake of Christ to have "a concern and tenderness especially for the poorest and the most unfortunate, as they appear to the eyes of the world"[6] (ND, II, 255).

CHRISTMAS 2005

Dear Spiritan Brothers and Sisters,

Some time ago, when I was consulting the website of UNCTAD (The United Nations Conference on Trade and Development), I came across the list of the 42 poor countries which are heavily indebted, drawn up in 2002. Reading it attentively, I noticed that our Congregation is present in 23 of these 42 countries. Here they are in alphabetical order: Angola, Benin, Cameroon, Central African Republic, Congo, Democratic Republic of Congo, Ethiopia, The Gambia, Ghana, Guinea, Guinea-Bissau, Kenya,

---

6. *Provisional Rule*, 107.

Madagascar, Malawi, Mauritania, Mozambique, Tanzania, Senegal, Sierra Leone, Uganda, Vietnam and Zambia. Other countries could be added to this list. Many confreres are also living and working in neglected areas of other countries which do not appear on the list. It is with all these confreres in mind that I am writing this Christmas letter to you.

Daily and prolonged contact with people, men and women, children, and the aged, who live, or rather, survive, in extreme poverty and insecurity, is a psychological and moral trial that is sometimes very difficult to bear. Lest such a trial should crush the missionary, he must be able to count on the dual support of a real community and an authentic spiritual life. It is important to have brothers and sisters around with whom one can speak spontaneously and freely, without fear of being misunderstood or misjudged. Being able to talk with others in a fraternal way is a source of great encouragement and release. It is equally important to maintain a deep and personal contact with the LORD Jesus. In the same way that we recognize, through faith, that he is truly present in the Eucharistic species of bread and wine, we also see him truly present under the human species of the poor, the afflicted and the persecuted of every sort (Matt 25:31-46; Acts 9:3-5).

In normal economic situations, the dioceses and the people can often provide some or most of the material needs of the confreres, but this is not the case when the overall economic and social conditions are too depressed. The confreres are then faced with the problem of their own survival. Solidarity from the Congregation and the generosity of benefactors is not always sufficient. In such conditions, many confreres are obliged to take on work (farming, livestock, salaried work) which will bring in the minimum resources necessary. They adopt a Pauline approach to being a missionary (cf. 1 Thess 2:9; 2 Thess 3:7-9; Acts 18:3).

In such extreme conditions of poverty, ordinary pastoral work becomes more and more difficult, if not impossible: the insecurity of travel on dilapidated roads, the lack of transport and fuel, not having the finance to organize the meetings and sessions that are so useful for the growth of Christian communities and the formation of their leaders. Our confreres have to find other pastoral approaches and rediscover methods which are simpler and less expensive. They often find that just their presence is as efficacious from an evangelical point of view as programs which involve considerable financial and material resources.

Like generations of Spiritans who went before them, the confreres who are living and working with exceptionally poor people show a great deal of courage and ingenuity in bringing them the most necessary material help. They know how to mobilize the generosity of distant friends and organize the distribution of material help so that it will get to those whose needs are greatest. Often at great risk to themselves, they are not frightened of analyzing the basic causes of so much misery and poverty. Here and there, one hears it said that as they are neither social workers nor militant politicians, they should not get involved in such things but confine themselves completely to announcing the Word of God. I cannot hear the voice of the Good Shepherd in such words, he who during his own lifetime so closely blended preaching and miracles of healing, who gave such simple and straightforward orders to his first missionaries—"preach and heal." Neither can I recognize there the voice of Fr. Libermann, who in the Rule of 1848 recommended that his confreres should act as follows:

> Since their divine Master has sent them to those who are poorest and most miserable, their care and special tenderness shall be for those whose misery and destitution are the greatest. They will treat them with special love and kindness, and will obtain for them all the help and solace they can, without asking whether they deserve it or not[7] (ND, X, 516).

So when we hear these voices which would like to divert us from the real sufferings of people, we must have the courage to refute them, because what they are saying is contrary to the gospel, contrary to the teaching of Fr. Libermann, and contrary to our long Spiritan tradition.

In the 23 countries listed above, there exists, or soon will exist, a Spiritan Province or Foundation, which means that more and more confreres will be coming from these countries. We can see the enormous financial task that the support and training of young Spiritan candidates will lay on the superiors, bursars and formators of these circumscriptions. Our recent General Chapter was very much aware of these problems; we must now try to resolve them in a rational and efficacious way. Next spring, the General Council intends to launch the enquiry into the moveable and immovable goods of circumscriptions that was requested by the General Chapter (Torre d'Aguilha 7.3). Normally, an examination of economic and financial affairs does not receive high priority in our preoccupations; we tend to put it at the end of our official documents or the last place on the agenda of our councils. But I am convinced that

---

7. *Règlements*, in Daly, *Spiritan Wellsprings*, 119 (Part II, chapter III, Art. 6).

the good health of our Congregation rests equally on the wellbeing of our spiritual life, our community life, and our financial life and sharing. These three aspects depend closely on each other. If, throughout the day, I am not in practical union with the LORD, where will I get the grace and the strength to love my confreres and to share everything with them? If I do not love my confreres tenderly, how can I want to share everything with them and claim that I love the God whom I cannot see? And if I am not seriously concerned with the financial state of my community and circumscription, of what value are my beautiful speeches about community and spiritual life?

I wish you all a holy feast of Christmas and a fruitful New Year in 2006.

Pentecost 2006

GLORY BE TO THE FATHER AND TO THE SON, AND TO THE HOLY SPIRIT

Dear Spiritan Brothers and Sisters,

Article 6 of our Rule of Life, under the title "Dedication," reads as follows: "We are dedicated to the Holy Spirit, author of all holiness and 'source of the apostolic spirit' (ND, X, 568). We place ourselves under the protection of the Immaculate Heart of Mary, who was filled beyond measure by the same Spirit 'with the fullness of holiness and apostolic zeal.'" This special consecration to the Holy Spirit and this filial devotion to the Immaculate Heart of Mary should always be lived and understood in the light of a deeper and more fundamental consecration—a consecration to the Holy Trinity.

When, in 1840, Fr Libermann drew up in Rome what we now refer to as the Provisional Rule, he began his long text with the following heading: "All for the greater glory of our heavenly Father in Jesus Christ, our LORD, through his divine Spirit and in union with the Holy Heart of Mary." In answering the question which he poses for chapter 2, "To whom is this Congregation consecrated? Who are its Patrons?," our second founder leaves us in no doubt: "The Congregation is consecrated first to the Most Holy Trinity, as having existence only in order to establish Its glory in its own members, and then among all men with whom they will establish relations, and above all, among those for whose benefit the Divine Will especially calls them"[8] (ND, II, 235-237).

One hundred and twenty-five years later, the Second Vatican Council approved the Decree on the Missionary Work of the Church, *Ad gentes,* restoring once more the idea of its deeply Trinitarian character: "The Church on earth is missionary by its very nature, since, according to the plan of the Father, it has its origin in the mission of the Son and the Holy Spirit" (*Ad gentes*, 2). As we celebrate the 40th anniversary of this decree, it would be a good idea to look at it again, and ask ourselves if our concept of mission still sees the Trinity as its source and its end, or whether we have unconsciously put ourselves in the place of the Father, Son, and Holy Spirit, by talking of *our* mission, forgetting that mission is, above all, the *missio Dei*?

Having rediscovered the original insight of Fr. Libermann and following the teaching of Vatican II, our Rule of Life that was promulgated in 1987 has a distinctly Trinitarian character, as can be seen from the very first article: "Sent by the Father and consecrated by the Holy Spirit, Jesus Christ came to save all people. He continues this mission of salvation, of which the church is the sacrament, in the world of today . . . " (SRL, 1). "When he prays, Jesus is giving expression to his union with the Father, who sends him, and the Holy Spirit who consecrates him. This union marks his entire apostolic life, when he is submitting to the Father's will as when he is announcing the kingdom." (cf. John 5:19; SRL, 83).

This Trinitarian vision of our mission and this "practical union" with God, Father, Son, and Holy Spirit, has much to offer us. Faced with our personal and communitarian sins and the sins of the whole world, we run the risk not just of discouragement but, even worse, of becoming cynical and disillusioned. But a continuous union with the Blessed Trinity convinces us that true reality is not to be found in division but in unity, not in hatred but in love. So, we grow in a conviction that does not depend on our qualities or talents, but on the nature of the only reality that really matters: the love of God, given and received in the heart of the Blessed Trinity, which spills out into the world. "The Spirit is also the energy which transforms the heart of the ecclesial community, so that it becomes a witness before the world to the love of the Father, who wishes

---

8. *Provisional Rule*, 53.

to make humanity a single family in his Son. The entire activity of the church is an expression of a love that seeks the integral good of man."[9]

By a continuing union with the Trinity, we can avoid another danger—that of substituting ourselves for God. Of course, we know that everything comes from the Father who created us, from the Son who saved us, and from the Spirit who inspired the prophets of the Two Testaments. But all that is so far away in time, so theoretical for practical purposes; we have to act now! So, generation after generation, we come up with new models of mission, the most recent always claiming to be better and more efficacious than what went before. But we know that God himself is mission, so how can we make a model of mission? Can we aspire to construct a "model" of God, as we can build a model in physics of the atom and its basic elements? Saint Paul said long ago that mission is an inexplicable foolishness, an incurable weakness. In consecrating ourselves to mission, we consecrate ourselves to God the Father, Son, and Holy Spirit so it is always the Blessed Trinity, not ourselves, who takes the initiative.

There is yet another advantage. We know how difficult it can be to balance our convictions and our priorities. The same problems keep recurring: reconciling religious and apostolic life, community and mission, mission ad intra and mission ad extra, parochial and extra-parochial ministry, evangelization and development, announcing the kingdom and commitment to Justice and Peace. But when looked at from the perspective of the mystery of the Blessed Trinity, the divisions between these apparently opposing demands become less clear: is not the Trinity both a reciprocal gift between the Persons and a gift from all Three to the world? Is the Trinity not a perfect unity but, at the same time, a clear distinction between the three Persons? No one can claim that contemplating the mystery of the Trinity will provide us with immediate answers to concrete questions, but it will enable us to see our problems in their true light. The ultimate criterion to which we must submit our convictions, our concrete models and even our types of organization, is their coherence with the mystery of the Trinity.

By our religious consecration, our first commitment is not to a list of particular practices or behavior; much more importantly, we are allowing our whole being to be re-fashioned on the model of Trinitarian love. Through the vow of obedience, we are united in a special way to our guide, the Holy Spirit; through the vow of chastity, we are united

---

9. Benedict XVI, *Deus Caritas Est*, no. 19.

in a special way to Christ, who loved us to the end; through the vow of poverty, we are united in a special way to the Father, who, in giving his Son and sending his Spirit, also offered up himself.

Each one of you, from your own spiritual experience, could surely add to this list of the blessings we receive when we contemplate the mystery of the Blessed Trinity. To conclude, I would like to quote the words at the beginning of a beautiful prayer composed by our first Founder, Claude Poullart des Places: "Most Holy Trinity, Father, Son and Holy Spirit, I adore you by your holy grace with all my heart, all my soul and all my strength. I beg you to grant me faith, humility, chastity, and the gift of not doing, saying, thinking, seeing, hearing or desiring anything except what you want me to do and say . . . "[10]

Christmas 2006

OUR CONGREGATION, A GIFT OF THE HOLY SPIRIT

Dear Spiritan Brothers and Sisters,

In my childhood, as Christmas came near, my grandmother had the custom of taking one of her big gardener's baskets and filling it with all sorts of good things: oranges, mandarins, clementines, bananas, figs, dates, chocolates, sweets, sugared almonds, spiced bread . . .

In those days of relative poverty after the Second World War, we rarely had the chance to savor such delicacies. Our usual dessert was whatever fruit was in season. Our grandmother then placed this great basket, filled to the brim, under the traditional Christmas tree, next to the crib. When we, her grandchildren, went to visit her, she never failed to take us to the crib. After a song and a prayer, she always said to us, "My dear children, from all that is in this big basket, you can take anything whenever you want and as much as you want. You do not need to ask my permission or to say thank you." Year after year, my parents tried in vain to get my grandmother to give up this practice, so contrary, in their eyes, to the principles of a proper education. But my grandmother always held out, to our great delight! I think in this way she really wanted us to understand something about Christmas, almost as a kind of catechesis: in giving us his own Son, has God not given us everything, grace upon

---

10. Koren, *Spiritual Writings*, 23; in French: *Memoire Spiritaine*, no. 4, 317.

grace, with no merit at all on our part? In this way, our grandmother instilled into us, in a very enjoyable and practical way, the idea of "gift."

Calling to mind this lovely childhood memory, I remembered that the most important word used in our last General Chapter was precisely that of "gift," together with its other related ideas of "charism," "grace," "heritage," "treasure." "Faithful to the gift confided to us"—such was the common strand in the Chapter texts. We were invited to "rediscover the charism of our Founders," to "accept, in our communities, the spiritual gifts of patience and respect for differences which are so necessary in today's world"; to be more fully aware that as Spiritans "mission is something given to us and not something we give to ourselves," to make sure that we pass on our charism to future generations . . . Each one of us, in re-reading the Chapter texts, could bring out so many references to this wonderful idea of "gift."

In this Christmas message, I want to emphasize one aspect of this idea of "gift." We are all agreed that the charism of our Founders is like a gift, and that the mission confided to us, as well as our confreres and the poor among whom we live and devote ourselves daily, are also a kind of gift. But are we sufficiently aware of the fact that the Congregation itself is really a gift of the Spirit to the church and, through the church, a gift to the world, and especially to the poorest? To put it another way, I invite you to deepen the idea of how you see your relationship with the Congregation.

Among the beautiful letters I often receive are those from elderly confreres in reply to my letter of congratulation to them, on behalf of the general council, on the anniversaries of their various jubilees. These confreres, when they look back on their long years in the service of the Congregation like a *lectio divina*, rarely fail to underline how happy they are to belong to our religious family and, despite the limitations of their age or state of health, how they still feel a deep solidarity with the mission of the Congregation. They thus indicate to us that the real player in the drama of mission is not so much the individual but the Congregation as a whole.

Generally, this conviction is the result of long years of work, reflection, and prayer, and often also of trials and sufferings. Right at the beginning of our entry into the Congregation, we are above all attracted by the evangelical strength and beauty of the Spiritan charism, seeing in it the means for us to achieve our full human potential. At this stage, the Congregation is seen as a means at our disposal, allowing us to fulfil our own vocation in life. But little by little, we realize that generations of Spiritans have gone before us and have sowed where we can only gather. We also become aware of how the integrity of an institution is necessary for it to create long-lasting results. In the end we do not see any absolute opposition between "charism" and "institution." Thus, the conviction grows in us that our Congregation itself, like all other religious families, is really a "gift" from the LORD which we welcome with respect and gratitude.

In moments of sharing among members of the general council, we sometimes express our regrets at having left active missionary work for what Fr. Libermann regarded as the multiple tasks of government and administration. This feeling is common to all confreres who, like us, have accepted to work in the administration of the Congregation. But the conviction that the Congregation is itself both the subject and the agent of mission, brings us more than a mere consolation. It strengthens and energizes us in carrying out the service confided to us.

At this time when the Congregation is becoming more and more international and rooted in more and more diverse situations, it is important for us to reinforce our sense of belonging. This Congregation, which has been in existence for a long time and yet is ever young, belongs to us all. It is completely at the service of the mission of the church. Throughout this coming year, may all of us accept it as a precious gift, be faithful to it, and commit ourselves to its common good and vitality. In this way the poor will continue to be loved, served, and evangelized.

I wish you all a Happy Christmas and a Good New Year.

Pentecost 2007

20TH ANNIVERSARY OF THE APPROVAL OF THE SPIRITAN RULE OF LIFE

Dear Brothers and Sisters in the Spiritan Family,

It was on the 7th of June 1987, the Solemnity of Pentecost, that the Congregation for Religious and Secular Institutes gave the official approval for our present Spiritan Rule of Life. A few months later, each confrere received a copy of the Rule of Life with an Introduction signed on the 8th September of the same year by Fr. Pierre Haas, superior general at the time. This twentieth anniversary is an opportunity for me to offer you some reflections on our Rule of Life.

A long development in the spirit of the Council. Immediately after the end of the Second Vatican Council, during its Chapter of Renewal held in Rome in 1968-9, our Congregation began a long reflection which would eventually lead to the adoption, by the General Chapter of 1986, of the final text of our new Rule. It was then submitted to the Holy See for final corrections. Our Rule of Life is therefore not the result of the work of just a few experts, but the expression of our common mind. We must be grateful to the generation of Spiritans which has left us such a precious heritage. Circumscriptions whose members took part more actively in the different meetings that put the text of SRL together (as at Carcavelos in 1983, Rome in 1984, the General Chapter of 1986) could very usefully ask them to give some account of the evolution of our present Rule.

Biblical Inspiration. The Word of God is often explicitly quoted in SRL; each chapter begins with a biblical quotation. This is true even in the case of the rather dry chapter VII on the Organization of the Congregation. We are also reminded that the Word of God is clearly our first Rule of Life. We know, for example, what a strong reluctance St. Francis of Assisi had in writing a Rule for his first followers. Is the Gospel "pure and simple" not enough to enlighten us and give direction to our lives? In saying this, I do not want to put any false opposition between Word of God and Rule of Life; it is simply that the Rule of Life is for us the concrete way in which we wish to live the gospel ideal and follow Jesus. If, for example, SRL reminds us clearly of the need for community life, it is not because community life is an end in itself, but because through it and in it, we are able to live the new commandment given to us by Christ. It is also thus, that we are recognized as his disciples and missionaries in the eyes of the world. (John 13:34-35).

Return to our Spiritan Sources. Like many other Congregations, we too have discovered in the charism of our Founder a new inspiration for our mission today. This is clearly stated in SRL,2 and is evident in the many references to our foundational texts, especially those of Fr. Libermann. Neither has the older tradition coming from Poullart des Places been forgotten; this is seen in the last paragraph of SRL, 4 with the reference to "availability." This strong, three-fold inspiration, a basis in Scripture, the Council, and other Magisterial texts, and also in our own tradition, has enabled our Rule to remain relevant for these past twenty years. Apart from the chapter on the Organization of the Congregation, there have been very few changes made by subsequent General Chapters.

A two-fold but single movement. SRL invites us to let the Holy Spirit work in us a twofold movement—towards Christ and towards "the poor." The spiritual and mystical aspect of mission is often emphasized, as for example in SRL, 3, where the "apostolic life" is described, following Libermann, as "the life of love and of holiness lived on earth by the Son of God . . ." This idea is found again in SRL, 10. As regards mission, it is not described in geographical terms (no particular continent is mentioned), but in terms of a movement towards "peoples, groups and individuals who have not yet heard the message of the Gospel, or who have scarcely heard it, to those whose needs are the greatest and to the oppressed" (SRL, 4). In effect, this two-fold movement is only one because the Christ to whom we go, is the one who gave his life for the salvation of the world. In "the poor" to whom we go as well, it is Christ himself who is present.

SRL serves the unity of the Congregation. One of my main worries, which I share with the other members of the general council, concerns the unity of the Congregation, this "great family" as Pierre Schouver called it in his Report to the 2004 General Chapter. The great variety of our origins and our commitments as well as the diversity of legitimate interests of each one, could easily create serious divisions among us. How is the unity of the Congregation not only maintained but strengthened as SRL, 192 and 199.1 demand? The first and principal means to this was strongly emphasized by our recent General Chapter—living together the same Spiritan spirituality. If the same Spirit is in each one of us how can we be divided among ourselves? A second means at our disposal is equally important—a shared respect for our common Rule of Life. I am convinced that many conflicts could be avoided or resolved easily if we were to apply better the Rule of Life. But how do we apply it if we do not know it? And how can we know it if we never read it? The study of the Rule of Life is a necessary and important element at every step of initial formation. The annual retreat provides an excellent opportunity for re-reading it attentively. Every community meeting could begin with the reading of a passage from SRL, or from other important documents, like general or circumscription Chapters. Apart from the excellent *Handbook for the Spiritan Rule of Life* published in 1987, do any studies of SRL exist at all? Our experts, young and not so young, are encouraged to investigate more deeply this area of study for the good of their confreres.

In conclusion, I remind you of what Pierre Haas wrote in the Introduction to the Rule of Life: "Here is the Spiritan Rule of Life which the Congregation, in the church, hands to each of us. By the Holy Spirit's grace, it can become for each one who lives it, in spirit and in truth, a road to apostolic holiness."

May I wish all of you a holy and joyful Pentecost.

Yours fraternally.

Mass under mango tree, Tabora, Kongolo

Christmas 2007

TOWARDS A RENEWED COMMON VISION

Dear Brothers and Sisters, professed Spiritans and Spiritan Associates,

During the recent meeting of new circumscription superiors, many of them asked themselves if our Congregation was still really united by a common vision. We need to take this issue seriously. Times have changed a lot since the time when all Spiritans came from the same cultural milieu, where most of them shared the same theological outlook and devoted themselves to similar apostolic activities. Today, our cultures of origin are becoming more and more varied, and this diversity is increasing. The spread of our ministries is growing at the same rate that we try to respond to the new demands. If we continue to use the same expressions to describe Spiritan life ("announcing the Good News, the practice of the evangelical counsels, fraternal and praying community," SRL, 3), we do not always give the same words the same meaning. How then do we "safeguard the unity of the Congregation" and at the same time respect its diversity (SRL 199.1)?

Each one of the last General Chapters has, in its own way, felt the need to search for a renewed common vision, especially concerning mission (Itaici, 92 and Maynooth, 98) and Spiritan spirituality (Torre d'Aguilha, 04). We are more and more aware of the real need of renewing our common vision in other areas, like that of the vocation of Brothers, initial and on-going formation, the vow of poverty, organization, and finances.

So as not to dwell on generalities, here are some concrete examples. For many years, a circumscription was devoted solely to one type of ministry. Circumstances having now changed, Spiritans see very well that they cannot continue working as before, that they are now in a "transition situation." But what new commitments are to be taken up? There are divergent views about it. Elsewhere, new and young Spiritans bring with them different ways of seeing things and question the common vision which up to now was shared by all in a circumscription. How do you integrate a new understanding without giving up former commitments? Again, there are cases where the whole organization of a circumscription is questioned. Problems become complicated when, as well as the understandable difference of opinions and visions, inter-personal tensions arise which are based on prejudice, hasty judgments, and sometimes an inconsiderate desire for power.

The Congregation does not lack the means necessary to create this indispensable common vision: the Rule of Life, General Chapters, Circumscription Chapters . . . even though, it must be said, the search for a common vision does not depend on producing written documents, important as they may be. Our common vision is never given to us in advance, neither is it given once and for all—it is always the fruit of a process of discernment which is forever being re-thought.

After the "fusion of 1848," not all the former members of the Society of the Holy Heart of Mary were agreed on the advantages of such a fusion. Some of them saw it rather as a deplorable "confusion." It took many years for the Congregation to integrate and harmonize the double charisms of Poullart des Places and Libermann.

At the beginning of the 1970s when the Foundations were being set up, not all the confreres of the old Districts were convinced that this was the right way to go forward. Many years passed before we arrived at the belief, now commonly accepted, that the Spiritan charism is not truly rooted in a local church unless the Congregation has members originating from the same local church.

Around 1990, many confreres foresaw that Europe could no longer just remain as a base for recruiting and sending out of missionaries, but was itself becoming a place of true Spiritan mission. This new situation created much discussion and some reluctance, until, at the chapter of Torre d'Aguilha in 2004 the validity of "mission in one's own country" (TA, 6.10) was affirmed.

Many other examples could be quoted to show that what is now "taken as read" by everyone, has only come about after a long process: the importance of the vocation of the Spiritan lay associates, the need for commitment in the area of Justice, Peace, and the Integrity of Creation, ecumenism, inter-religious dialogue . . .

We wish to go forward in pursuing our efforts towards a renewed common vision. The forthcoming publication of the *Spiritan Anthology*, the celebration of the Enlarged General Council in May-June 2008, the tercentenary in 2009 of the death of Poullart des Places, are as much means as occasions to help us realize this end. Especially important are the different initiatives for promoting Spiritan spirituality: the setting up of the Center for Spiritan Studies at Duquesne University, the opening of similar centers in different circumscriptions, various publications . . .

There is a difficulty with the expression "common vision"—it limits us to the realm of knowledge or the intellect. There is a risk we might forget that we have as much need of a "common feeling" and "fundamental common attitudes." When SRL, 3 speaks of the unity of Spiritan life, it is quoting Fr. Libermann: "The apostolic life" is at the heart of our Spiritan vocation; it is "that life of love and holiness which the Son of Man lived on earth."

We too must reflect the centrality of Christ in our lives and ministry. It is in the person of Jesus Christ himself that we must seek and find this common vision which is so necessary. When St. Paul wrote to the seriously divided community of the Philippians, he advised them to "have among yourselves the same attitude that is also yours in Christ Jesus; who, though he was in the form of God, did not regard equality with God something to be grasped . . . " (Phil 2:1-13).

I pray that this feast of Christmas may be for each one of you, an occasion to put Christ at the center of your lives. I wish you all a Happy Christmas and a Good New Year!

Pentecost 2008

"BUILDING ON THE ROCK" (MATT 7:24-25): TOWARDS THE ENLARGED GENERAL COUNCIL

Dear Brothers and Sisters,

> "The wise man who built his house on rock . . . " (Matt 7:24)

From the 25th of May to the 7th of June 2008, we will celebrate the next Enlarged General Council at Ariccia near Rome. Our Rule of Life defines the aim of this consultative assembly thus: " . . . to check on the implementation of the decisions of the General Chapter; to study new means of strengthening and bringing about the Congregation's objectives; to reinforce collaboration between different circumscriptions both among them and between them and the superior general and his council." (SRL, 206.3) Note that the emphasis is clearly on "practice." In general, we know well enough how to prepare for our various Chapters and assemblies and we know how to celebrate them with dignity. But our weakness is putting into practice the beautiful and noble decisions which have been discussed and voted. That is why the parable summing up the Sermon on the Mount has been chosen to inspire and energize us. Many other parables could have been chosen, like that of the two sons (Matt 21:28-32), the Beatitude concerning those who hear the word of God and put it into practice (Luke 11:27-28), or the Parable of the Last Judgement (Matt 25:21ff). Responding to my Pentecost Letter of last year on the subject of the 20th anniversary of the approval of our present Rule of Life, a confrere sent me his reflections: "In many ways, our Rule of Life lacks realism . . . it would be good if everyone had kept their initial enthusiasm . . . I think that, regarding obedience, many confreres have their own agenda which they follow." Yes, like St. Joseph, we receive "in a dream" (SRL, Chapters, assemblies . . .) all the instructions needed relating to what we have to do. But, in contrast to St. Joseph, we have problems waking up, and when we do, we have lost sight of the divine dream . . . The Enlarged General Council will give us the chance for an honest and realistic assessment, and allow us to verify whether what we have said and decided in the Chapter is being carried out. All of us are invited, personally as well as in community and by circumscription, to participate in this difficult exercise of evaluation. We may not have any lesson to give to anyone, but we can all learn something from each other.

"It is God who has made Everything" (cf. Heb 3:4)

In many biblical texts, the idea of building is used a little differently than that above. It is not a question of insisting on the personal activity of the builder so much as remembering that the real builder is not man, but God himself. Thus, in Psalm 127 we read: "Unless the LORD build the house, they labor in vain who build it." Again, in Matt 16:18, to Simon, son of Jonah, who had just recognized him as "the Christ, the Son of the living God," Jesus does not say that he is the one to build his church, but that he is only the "rock" on which he, Jesus, will build his church. Note too that after the 'Great Commission,' a commitment to action, if ever there was one, Jesus adds: "And know that I am with you always, yes to the end of time." (Matt 28:20) This is evidently not a passive presence! It is because of this continually active presence that we say the protagonist of mission is the Holy Spirit. Another quotation from the letter to the Hebrews: "Every house is founded by someone, but the founder of all is God. Moses was 'faithful in all his house,' as a 'servant,' to testify to what would be spoken, but Christ was faithful as a son placed over his house. We are his house, if [only] we hold fast to our confidence and pride in our hope" (Heb 3:4-6). Between the first meaning of the idea of building and the second, there is a profound link. While we need to be active and enterprising, we always need to ask ourselves whether it is our own house we are building or God's. If we forget that we are just the builders and not the architect, we risk putting up only ruins.

Providentially, two important Spiritan feasts will be celebrated during the forthcoming Enlarged General Council. First of all, Tuesday 27th of May is the exact anniversary of the Foundation of the Congregation. Then Saturday 31st of May is the feast of the Immaculate Heart of Mary. The first celebration reminds us how our first Founder was at the same time a man of action and a man of contemplation. From October 2nd 2009 to October 2nd 2010, on the occasion of the 300th anniversary of Claude-Francois Poullart des Places' death, we will make an effort to know his life and message better, and above all to imitate him in his practice of poverty. The second celebration shows us how the Almighty can do marvels when he finds a heart full of faith, generosity, and availability. Let us pray that in the future, as in the past, the LORD will make use of our Congregation for realizing his plan of love, making of us authentic "builders" of reconciliation and peace.

Rome, 15th March 2008, anticipated celebration of the feast of St. Joseph.

Christmas 2008

AN ORIGINAL ID OF FR. LIBERMANN: "ALMONERS"

Superiors, Bursars and "Almoners"

In the course of the year 1840, when Fr. Libermann was in his little attic in Rome, he wrote the Provisional Rule of the Missionaries of the Most Holy Heart of Mary (ND, II, 235-365). His fundamental idea was clear: "The Missions to which the Congregation will dedicate itself will be among the poor and despised, whose needs are very great, who are the most neglected in God's church, and among whom one could expect to produce much fruit." From what we call today the "preferential option for the poor," Fr. Libermann draws two concrete conclusions. The first is well known to all of us and concerns the demanding practice of the vow of poverty for all the members of the future Society. The second is less well known: it touches on the organization of the communities themselves with the creation of what Fr. Libermann calls "almoners." In his future communities, the Founder envisaged them having a superior, a bursar and, surprisingly, an "Almoner." Here is what he wrote[11]:

> The Superior of each community will establish in that community a council of almoners, which will administer the distribution of money for good works, and the president of that council will be the guardian of that money. All the surplus money that was destined for sustenance of the community and all the gifts and alms that have been received by the superior and by other missionaries will be put in that safe. When a missionary needs money for the poor, he will ask for it from the authorities. The bursar will never be permitted to be a member of said council. When circumstances do not make it possible to have several almoners, there will always be at least one.
>
> The president of the almoners, helped by the council, must also examine the accounts of the bursar every three months. The bursar must give these to the president, together with the surplus money which was destined for the expenditures during the three months. The president of the council of almoners will then transmit to the superior the remarks made by the members

---

11. *Provisional Rule*, 137, 138.

of the council regarding the accounts of the bursar. At the same time the president of the council will give an exact amount to the superior for the use that has been made of the money that was set aside for good works. He will also give a specific description of the principal alms which he himself and the other almoners have distributed personally.

Can we perhaps see in this original idea of Fr. Libermann the inspiration for SRL, 71.1, "In every budget a sum of money shall be set aside for the poor; it will be a symbol of our solidarity with them"?

An Inspiration for Today

I do not know whether these "almoners" were actually put in place in the first Libermann communities. In recalling this idea of his, I am not attempting to resurrect this element in the organization of our communities, but to remind you how seriously Fr. Libermann and his first disciples, just like Poullart des Places, regarded this concern for the poorest. There are many reasons why I call this to mind.

* For a number of years in our Congregation we have been asking ourselves how we could be better organized. Some large Provinces are dividing into smaller circumscriptions and working together in the "Unions of Circumscriptions." Other circumscriptions are coming together. We do well to proceed thus. But let us not forget that all these efforts make no sense if they do not lead us to serve the poorest in a better way. Organization is always at the service of mission.

* For many years we have been concerned about the financial viability of our circumscriptions. It is actually intolerable that in the same Congregation there exist circumscriptions which are "rich" and others which are "poor"; that in the same circumscriptions there are communities which are "rich" and others which are "poor"; that in the same community there are confreres who are "rich" and others who are "poor." But all our efforts towards the financial well-being of our circumscriptions and communities make no sense if they do not lead us to be more effective in helping the poor, in the spirit of Fr. Libermann.

* For many years our Congregation has started up in new countries or taken new commitments in ones we have been in for a long time. We think of new commitments in the Philippines, Taiwan, Vietnam,

Bolivia, and the Dominican Republic, as well as the new social and pastoral initiatives begun in the European or American Provinces. Some confreres ask whether, in acting in this way, our Congregation is not being unfaithful to the fundamental vision of Fr. Libermann. Personally, I think this important question has nothing to do with geography, but with our basic inspiration: the evangelical service of the poor. Whatever may be the place where we live and work, are we truly at the service of the poor? The spirit and ideals of an institution usually die off well before those who are members of it.

* The circular letters of our confreres, and our Visitations to circumscriptions, show us that the plague of poverty and misery is far from being eradicated. The first and principal victims of the recent world financial crisis are not the bankers, but millions and millions of poor people. It is shocking to see how quickly and energetically our various countries came to the aid of failing banks, compared to the slow and half-hearted way these same countries take measures to ease the suffering of the poorest.

Christmas Today for the Poorest

The end of the year is the period when accounts and budgets are examined. When we do this, could we not question the amounts that are designated for the poor? The approaching feast of Christmas, reminds us that Christ, though rich, became poor. This same Jesus Christ, once born in Bethlehem, waits for us on the last day for our final judgment.

Only one sole question will be asked us: what we have done to ease the misery and sufferings of the "little ones" who belong to him (Matt 25:31-46).

I wish you all a Happy Christmas and a Good New Year!

Pentecost 2009

TOWARDS THE SECOND SPECIAL ASSEMBLY OF THE SYNOD FOR AFRICA
Visit of Benedict XVI to Cameroon and Angola (March 17-23, 2009)

> Reading attentively the speeches given by the Pope during his recent trip to Africa, I have noticed that a great number of themes are addressed, with respect and lucidity. These themes are also of interest to our Spiritan missionary life. I have therefore extracted a few quotations that seemed significant to me in order to propose them for the reflection of my Spiritan brothers and sisters. But nothing is better than reading the speeches themselves, which are easily accessible on the site www.vatican.va

1. *Synod.* "And now I myself come to deliver the *Instrumentum Laboris* of the Second Special Assembly, to be held in Rome next October ... Almost ten years before the beginning of the new millennium, this moment of grace is a call for all the Bishops, priests, religious men and women, and lay faithful of this continent to dedicate themselves with new enthusiasm to the mission of the church: to bring hope to the heart of the peoples of Africa and to the peoples of the whole world. "(Yaoundé, March 17, 2009).

2. *Suffering in Africa.* "In the face of suffering or violence, in the face of poverty or hunger, in the face of corruption or abuse of power, a Christian can never remain silent. The gospel message of salvation must be proclaimed loudly and clearly, so that the light of Christ may shine in the darkness in which people are immersed. Here in Africa, as in so many parts of the world, countless crowds of men and women are waiting to receive a word of hope and comfort. Regional conflicts leave thousands of orphans and widows, homeless and destitute. On a continent that in the past saw so many of its children cruelly uprooted and sold across the seas to become slaves, today the trafficking of human beings, especially defenceless women and children, has become a new form of slavery. At a time of insufficient food production, financial turmoil, and climate change disruption, Africa is suffering disproportionately: more and more people are falling into poverty, hunger, and disease. They cry out

for reconciliation, justice, and peace, and that is what the church is offering them. "(Yaoundé, March 17, 2009).

3. *Respect.* "I have a more positive vision of the church in Africa: it is a church that is very close to the poor, a church alongside the suffering, with people who need help and therefore it seems to me that the church is really an institution that still functions, while other structures no longer function, and with its system of education, hospitals, aid, in all these situations, it is present in the world of the poor and the suffering. Naturally, original sin is also present in the church; there is no perfect society and therefore there are also sinners and deficiencies in the church in Africa, and in this sense an examination of conscience, an inner purification is always necessary." (On the plane, March 17, 2009).

4. *Hope.* "Hoping against all hope": isn't this a beautiful definition of a Christian? Africa is called to hope through you and in you! With Christ Jesus, who walked on African soil, Africa can become the continent of hope!" (Yaoundé, March 19, 2009).

5. *To the public authorities.* "Angola knows that the time has come for Africa to be the continent of hope. All upright human behaviour is hope in action. Our actions are never indifferent before God; and neither are they for the development of history. Dear friends, with an honest, magnanimous and compassionate heart, you can transform this continent, freeing your people from the scourge of greed, violence, and disorder by leading them along the path indicated by the principles indispensable to any modern civil democracy: respect for and promotion of human rights, transparent government, an independent judiciary, free means of social communication, honest public administration, a well-functioning network of schools and hospitals, and a firm determination, based on the conversion of hearts, to eradicate corruption once and for all . . . Economic and social development in Africa requires the coordination of national governmental actions with regional initiatives and international decisions. Such coordination implies that African nations should not only be seen as recipients of plans and solutions developed by others. Africans themselves, working together for the good of their communities, must be the primary actors in their development." (Luanda, March 20, 2009).

"I would like to ask that the legitimate realization of the fundamental aspirations of the most deprived populations be the main concern of those who assume public office, because their intention—I am sure—is to accomplish the mission they have received not for themselves but for the common good. Our hearts cannot rest as long as brothers and sisters suffer because of the lack of food, work, shelter or other basic necessities. In order to give a concrete response to our fellow human beings, the first challenge is that of solidarity: solidarity between generations, solidarity between nations and continents, which generates an ever more equitable sharing of the earth's resources among all people." (Luanda, March 23, 2009)

6. *The crisis.* "We all know that a fundamental element of the crisis is precisely a lack of ethics in economic structures; it has been understood that ethics is not something "external" to the economy, but "internal" and that the economy does not function if it does not have an ethical element within it. That is why, speaking of God and of the great spiritual values that make up the Christian life, I will try to make my own contribution to overcoming this crisis, to renew the economic system from within, where the true heart of the crisis lies." (On the plane, March 17, 2009).

7. *Commitment of the church.* "Ladies and Gentlemen, you will always find the church—by the will of its divine Founder—by the side of the poorest of this continent. I can assure you that through diocesan activities, the countless educational, health, and social works carried out by the various religious orders, the development programs of Caritas and other organizations, she will continue to do everything in her power to support families—including those affected by the tragic effects of AIDS—and to promote the equal dignity of men and women on the basis of harmonious complementarity." (Luanda, 20 March 2009).

8. *Family of God.* "In the context of globalization, the church has a special interest in the poorest people. The Bishop's mission leads him to be the defender of the rights of the poor, to raise up and encourage the exercise of charity, the manifestation of the LORD'S love for the little ones. In this way, the faithful are led to understand concretely that the church is a true family of God, united in fraternal love, which excludes all ethnocentrism and excessive particularism

and contributes to reconciliation and collaboration among ethnic groups for the good of all" (Yaoundé, March 18, 2009).

9. *Family.* "In your pastoral concern for all human beings, continue to raise your voice in defence of the sanctity of human life and the value of the institution of marriage, while promoting the role of the family in the church and in society, calls for economic and legislative measures that help families to welcome the birth of children and support them in their educational mission." (Luanda, 20 March 09).

10. *Youth.* "I say to you: Courage! Dare to make final decisions because they are the only ones that do not destroy freedom, but give it the right direction, allowing you to move forward and do something great in life. Life is worthwhile only if you have the courage for adventure and the confident certainty that the LORD will never leave you alone." (Luanda, 21 March 2009).

11. *Women.* "I urge all of you to become genuinely aware of the adverse conditions to which many women have been—and continue to be—subjected, by examining the extent to which men's conduct, lack of sensitivity or lack of responsibility may be the cause. God's plans are different . . . In a civilization such as ours, dominated by technology, we feel the need for this complementarity of women, so that human beings can live there without dehumanizing themselves completely. Just think of the lands where poverty reigns, of the regions devastated by war, of the many dramatic situations resulting from forced or forced migration . . . It is almost always women who keep human dignity intact, defend the family and safeguard cultural and religious values." (Luanda, 22 March 09).

12. *Education.* "Education is another essential aspect of the church's ministry: now we can see the efforts of generations of missionary teachers bear fruit as we contemplate the work accomplished by the Catholic University of Central Africa, which is a sign of great hope for the future of this region."(Yaoundé, 17 March 09).

13. *Health.* "I am also thinking of all the sick, especially here in Africa, those who are victims of diseases such as AIDS, malaria and tuberculosis. I know how strongly committed the Catholic Church is in your country to an effective struggle against these terrible scourges,

and I encourage her to pursue with determination this work, which is so urgent." (Yaoundé, March 19, 2009).

14. *About AIDS.* "The solution can only be found in a double commitment: the first is a humanization of sexuality, that is to say, a spiritual and human renewal that brings with it a new way of behaving towards one another, and the second is a true friendship, also and above all for those who suffer, the readiness, even at the cost of sacrifice and personal renunciation, to be close to those who suffer." (on the plane, March 17, 09).

15. *Fears.* "Today it is up to you, brothers and sisters, in the wake of God's holy and heroic messengers, to present the risen Christ to your fellow citizens. So many of them live in fear of spirits, of the evil powers they believe to be threatening them; disoriented, they come to condemn the street children and also the elders, because— they say—they are sorcerers. Who will go to them to tell them that Christ has overcome death and all the powers of darkness (cf. Eph 1:19-23; 6:10-12)?" (Luanda, March 21, 2009).

16. *Dialogue.* "You can therefore understand how important dialogue among men is to me, because it makes it possible to overcome all forms of conflict and tension and to make each nation—and therefore your homeland—a house of peace and fraternity." (Luanda, March 20, 2009).

17. *Muslims.* "[An authentic religion] rejects all forms of violence and totalitarianism: not only because of the principles of faith, but also because of right reason. Indeed, religion and reason are mutually reinforcing because, on the one hand, religion is purified and structured by reason and, on the other hand, all the potential of reason is unleashed by revelation and faith . . . May the enthusiastic cooperation of Muslims, Catholics, and other Christians in Cameroon be for other African nations a shining indicator of the enormous potential of religion in Africa." (Yaoundé, 19 March 2009).

18. *Vocations and formation.* "In your dioceses, many young people are presenting themselves as candidates for the priesthood. We can only thank the LORD for this. It is indispensable that a serious discernment be made. To this end, I encourage you, in spite of the difficulties of organization at the pastoral level that can sometimes result, to

give priority to the choice and formation of formators and spiritual directors." (Yaoundé, March 18, 2009).

19. *Religious life.* "The spiritual contribution made by consecrated persons is also significant and indispensable to the life of the church. This call to follow Christ is a gift for the whole People of God. According to your vocation, in imitating Christ who is chaste, poor, and obedient, totally consecrated to the glory of his Father and to the love of his brothers and sisters, you have the mission of witnessing before our world, which is in such need, to the primacy of God and to the goods to come (cf. *Vita Consecrata*, no. 85) . . . it is necessary, therefore, that your style of life express accurately what makes you live and that your activity does not hide your real identity." (Yaoundé, Mvolyé, 18 March 2009).

20. *Theologians.* "It would be good today for your theologians to continue to explore the depth of the Trinitarian mystery and its significance for African daily life. This century will perhaps, with God's grace, bring about the rebirth, on your continent, but certainly in a different and new form, of the prestigious School of Alexandria. Why not hope that it can provide today's Africans and the universal church with great theologians and spiritual masters who would contribute to the sanctification of the inhabitants of this continent and of the entire Church"? (Yaoundé, March 19, 2009).

21. *Spiritans.* "We have the joy of meeting together to give thanks to God in this Basilica of Mary Queen of the Apostles of Mvolyé which was built on the site of the first church built by the Spiritan missionaries who came to bring the Good News to Cameroon." (Yaoundé, Mvolyé, March 18, 2009).

Christmas 2009

TOWARDS THE 2012 GENERAL CHAPTER: A TRIPLE INSPIRATION

Dear Brothers and Sisters of the Spiritan Family,

Beginning with this Christmas 2009 letter up to the Pentecost 2012 letter, I want to take the preparations for our next General Chapter as the main theme. As the "supreme authority in the Congregation" (SRL, 212 and Canon 631), a General Chapter must be carefully prepared in order for it to be celebrated properly and have the desired practical results afterwards. For this to happen, all of us, personally, in community and by circumscription, need to play our part in as many ways as possible in the dynamics leading up to it. This letter, like the following ones, will put before you some general reflections on the situation and the mission of our Congregation. I leave it up to you to respond to these reflections ... and also to suggest new ones.

AFRICA

In the month of October 2009, the Second Special Assembly for Africa of the Synod of Bishops was held in Rome. For several reasons this Synod is of interest to us. In our history, Africa has played, and continues to play, a very important role. Africa is, by a long way, the continent to which the largest number of Spiritan missionaries have been sent. Today once again, of the 2,900 members of the Congregation, around 1,200 live and work in Africa, and in the last twenty years Africa has been the continent of origin of most of our young confreres. Each year, about 60 confreres request from the General Council their "mission appointment" and about 50 of these are Africans. Evangelization in Africa is far from being completed. Geographically and sociologically, vast sections of the population are hardly touched by the gospel. As well as this, new demands are being made on Spiritan missionaries: street children, youth ministry, and education in general, health ministry, formation of the laity, Justice, Peace and the Integrity of Creation, interreligious and ecumenical dialogue ...

There are many dioceses asking for our Spiritan presence for the first time or for our presence to be strengthened. The general council is at present looking at the possibility of starting up missions in South Sudan, Liberia, Botswana and Burundi.

The theme chosen for the Synod of Bishops is of special interest to us: "The Church at the Service of Reconciliation, Justice and Peace: 'You are the salt of the earth ... you are the light of the world' (Mt.13:14)." These concerns are those of our confreres on the spot, in Africa and elsewhere. Our Congregation cannot and must not disengage from the African continent on the pretext of the expansion in other countries and continents or other pressing needs elsewhere. It falls to our numerous African confreres and circumscriptions to safeguard the Congregation's historic fidelity to Africa.

> Question: what kind of missionary commitments and Spiritan missionaries does Africa need at present?

SPIRITAN PRIESTS

Providentially, our celebration of the tercentenary of Poullart des Places' death, coincides with the Year of the Priesthood proclaimed by Pope Benedict XVI for the whole church. We know that after a long search for the path God willed for him, the young Claude decided to become a priest. We also know that during his years of preparation for the priesthood, he took an interest in other young people, priestly candidates like him, but too poor to pay for accommodation in a formation house. No-one can deny that the first aim of the infant Congregation was the long and demanding formation of future priests prepared for the most humble service in the church. Subsequently, how many Spiritans devoted themselves in Africa and elsewhere to the formation of the local clergy? How many minor and major seminaries have been built and staffed by Spiritans? This emphasis on the formation of the local clergy—one of Libermann's main ideas—is such that it is sometimes difficult for us today to admit that the formation of Spiritan missionaries, everywhere we are, is as much an urgent and necessary task for the good of the church. Our general council, following on from the preceding ones and encouraged by decisions of General Chapters, will continue to do its utmost to develop the vocation of Brothers and Associates in the heart of the Congregation. For all that, we cannot and must not neglect the vocation of the Spiritan priest. In recent years there have been very few reflections and documents specifically dealing with the vocation of the Spiritan priest, as if there were no problems pertaining to it! Is not now the right time to begin a reflection on what it means to be a Spiritan priest?

> Question: how does the word "Spiritan" help us understand better and live better the vocation of the "Spiritan priest"?

A NEW THIRST FOR THE SPIRITUAL LIFE

In the course of their visits and attendance at circumscription assemblies, the general council members have been struck by the frequent expressions of a thirst for a better spiritual life. Well beyond our communities, this need is also felt among the peoples whom we are called to serve. In answer to this need, there have been numerous initiatives: setting up Spiritan spirituality centers, various articles as much in the written press as in the "virtual" press, confreres doing special studies in spirituality. Our modern world is far from being a spiritual "desert," in fact it is in search of new inspiration. The coming feast of Christmas will once again show how deep this search is. As a Congregation, are we really aware of the size and dimensions of this new desire for spirituality? And we ourselves, do we take the opportunity to "go back to our sources"?

Do we know how to draw from our own sources, the waters that will quench this great thirst that is found among both the young and the not-so young? Is it not the Congregation's mission "to respond creatively to the needs of evangelization of our time"? (SRL, 2).

> Question: In your opinion, what must we do, in our communities and circumscriptions, to respond more creatively to the renewed thirst for spiritual life?

May these reflections and questions inspire us in our shared path towards the next General Chapter!

With all my best wishes for a holy and joyful celebration of Christmas and the New Year.

Christmas 2010

TOWARDS THE GENERAL CHAPTER OF BAGAMOYO (2012). THE OTHER GREAT MISSIONARY COMMANDMENT (JOHN 13:34-35)

Dear Brothers and Sisters of the Spiritan Family,

We all know the great missionary commandment that the risen Christ gave to his eleven apostles on a mountain in Galilee: *"All power in heaven and on earth has been given to me. Go, therefore, and make disciples of all nations."* (Matt 28:18-20). It was this same commandment which, one day, prompted us all to leave home and which still inspires us to undertake new journeys. Perhaps for some of us, as we grow older and are less agile, these journeys are less "geographical," but they still make the same demands on us regarding personal and community conversion. No doubt, at the next General Chapter, we will be looking once more at the quality of our missionary engagements. We should never forget that "the apostolic life is at the heart of our Spiritan vocation" (SRL, 3).

But there is another great missionary commandment that we should always bear in mind: *"I give you a new commandment: love one another;*

as I have loved you, so you also should love one another. This is how all will know that you are my disciples, if you have love for one another." (John 13:34-35). It has much in common with the great commandment in Matthew's Gospel quoted above: it is a commandment of the risen Christ (in John 13 and following, it is the risen Christ who is speaking); it is given exclusively to the disciples; it exhorts them to copy the actions of the "historical" Jesus; it has a universal value, in place and time. Notice the proximity of this commandment to the washing of the feet, which both inspires and illustrates it. Its real missionary nature is shown by the last verse: *"This is how all will know that you are my disciples, if you have love for one another."* We know very well that our missionary dynamism does not primarily depend on our numbers, our financial resources or the efficacy of our organization, but rather on the quality of our discipleship, in other words, on the love that we have for each other in community.

At the Heart of new Evangelization

I am drawing your attention to this other great missionary commandment while thinking particularly of our communities and circumscriptions in Europe and America. In one way or another, the local churches of these large regions of the world are facing the same difficulties: an increasing secularization, a continuing drop in religious practice and in vocations (particularly missionary), and the necessity of a "new evangelization." As Spiritans concerned about the needs of peoples who are furthest from the church, we are obviously challenged by this need. I have seen that the circumscriptions of Europe and America have not waited for official directives before taking steps in this direction. As always, the Spirit is pushing and inspiring us to do something about it, and I feel that this other great missionary commandment can guide us in these initiatives.

One of the great difficulties is to establish our own credibility as evangelizers. Even if these areas of Europe and America are often dechristianized or distanced from the church, the kingdom and the gospel, they are not entirely virgin country: the past, both recent and more remote, has left its traces and not all of them are very attractive. Our great challenge is no longer simply to show the excellence of our catechisms and organizations, but to ensure the concordance of our lives and communities with the words of Christ. As long as we are not recognized as authentic disciples of Christ, we will stand no chance of attracting anybody. But according to John's Gospel, there is no other way, above all today, to be seen as genuine disciples of Christ than to love one another as Christ has loved us. Remember the words of Libermann to M. Collin: "The missionaries see only the souls to be saved and the work to be done. Since community life seems to be an impediment to all that, they throw it overboard."[12] In his homily at the Basilica of Sagrada Familia in Barcelona on November 7th, Pope Benedict XVI said: "This is our great task: to show everybody that God is a God of peace and not violence, of freedom and not constraint, of harmony and not discord." Is there any clearer image of such a God than a love that is shared by brothers and sisters in the same community?

A widespread Concern of the Congregation

The replies we have received to our request for subjects to be discussed by the next General Chapter give prominence to a need for renewal in our community life. You will soon receive a synthesis of the replies submitted so far. Amongst them, you will read remarks like the following:

> *There are some signs of crisis in the Congregation which suggest that it is only by a deep experience of community life that we will be able to overcome the challenges that are threatening our Congregation today.*
>
> *We must look at the problems we are facing in community life in the context of the world today, where there is so much change and instability in institutions, the family, marriage, authority, autonomy and freedom, sexuality . . .*
>
> *It seems that the time has come to make a serious evaluation of internationality.*
>
> *There are some principles which are non-negotiable for community life: treating the community as a hotel must not be tolerated. What is our attitude to our older confreres?*
>
> *We must not sacrifice community life to the demands of the mission.*

Our experience in the general council is that many of our problems would be quickly solved if there was real fraternal love: there would be fewer power struggles and a genuine sharing at all levels, and consequently, we could give a more effective witness to the life of the kingdom of God. The recent restructuring of our Spiritan presences by Unions of supportive Circumscriptions has given rise to some legitimate questions:

---

12. *Spiritan Anthology*, 1, 334-338, here 335.

have we sacrificed our witness to unity and fraternal communion on the altar of cultural, regional, and ethnic antagonisms?

We have always been poor, and to be faced with paucity of numbers in the challenge of the tasks we have undertaken is nothing new for us; but if we let divisions destroy our communion, we will surely have lost everything and we will be dead in our hearts even before we are quenched by our statistics. Should we not make our own the conviction of our recent and deeply regretted superior general, Pierre Schouver: for him, the Congregation was not primarily a complex organization but "one big family."

Through the Christ of peace, in the communion of the Spirit, may the Father help us to celebrate the holy and joyful feasts of Christmas and the new year.

Pentecost 2011

TOWARDS THE 2012 BAGAMOYO GENERAL CHAPTER: "SIMPLY SPIRITANS . . . "

Dear Brothers and Sisters of the Spiritan Family,

A Slow Awakening

I have to admit that it took me a long time to appreciate fully the importance of our consecration to the Holy Spirit. In the past, I regarded the title of "The Congregation of the Holy Spirit" as simply a name without any great significance. Any other title would have served equally well! It is only in the last six or seven years that I have come to understand the importance of our belonging to the Holy Spirit. I have become aware, sometimes painfully, of the great weaknesses and even the sins of our Congregation, both now and in the past: but I have also learnt to admire the energy and holiness of many of our confreres, communities and circumscriptions. How can it be that the same group of people can be both "a bunch of nobodies" (as Libermann put it) and a community of genuine witnesses to Christ—sometimes at the price of martyrdom, as we will recall next year at the 50th anniversary of the Kongolo massacre (January 1st, 1962)? I am convinced that such things can only be the work of the Holy Spirit, which is exactly what we ask for in the second epiclesis of the Eucharistic Prayer II: "May all of us who share in the body and blood of Christ be brought together in unity by the Holy Spirit." Is this not as extraordinary a "miracle" as is brought about in the first epiclesis when we ask that the Spirit, who has come down upon our gifts, should make them become "the body and blood our Lord, Jesus Christ"?

A Widely-held Conviction

For the last few weeks, the general council has been receiving replies from circumscriptions to the second consultation which will enable us to draw up the main questions for presentation to the coming General Chapter. Most of these contributions underline the extreme diversity of our Congregation today and the need for steps to be taken to ensure that this is not just a result of a growing individualism amongst us, but rather an expression of the richness of what makes up our unity. Many suggestions are made to this end and there are many different ways of expressing them: a return to a greater degree of centralization, a deeper respect for the Rule of Life (which also assumes that it is read and understood!), a closer following of the charism of our Founders and a more visible expression of our "identity." But I feel that all the confreres are convinced that our greatest need is for a much deeper unity, that unity which is itself a gift of the Holy Spirit to our hearts and our communities. Many plead for a re-discovery of our shared consecration to the Holy Spirit and, consequently, of the celebration of the feast of Pentecost as the principle feast of the Congregation.

"Hard-working, Competent, and ready for Anything"

In a letter written sometime before 1734, Pierre Thomas said that the aim of M. des Places and his successors in setting up the Seminary of the Holy Spirit was to produce priests who are hard-working, competent, and ready for anything. They are willing to take on the most difficult and unpopular works, such as hospitals, vicars and priests in small villages in the country, missions in France, the colonies and elsewhere, the running of seminaries, the direction of sisters and teaching in rural areas.[13]

---

13. "has for purpose to educate poor clerics in ecclesiastical discipline, zeal and love of virtue, especially of obedience and poverty, who will be ready for everything in the hands of the prelates, to serve in hospices, to evangelize the poor and the infidels, and not only to undertake but to love wholeheartedly and to prefer to everything else the meanest and most toilful ecclesiastical duties for which ministers are found only with difficulty" (in Daly, *Spiritan Wellsprings*. Latin text in Le Floch, *Claude François Poullart des Places*, 586).

Evidently, in less than 30 years after the foundation of the Seminary, the "Spiritans" were already working in a great variety of apostolic commitments. The same situation exists today. Note how in those early days, the Spiritan was surprisingly not defined in the first place by what he did or where he worked but by those three titles: hard-working, competent, and ready for anything. Is it not in these three qualities, in these gifts of the Holy Spirit, that our real identity is to be found, long before the distinction between Priest, Brother and Associate? The aim of all our initial and on-going formation is to help us become "hard-working, competent, and ready for anything" in other words, to become "simply Spiritans."

> "We place ourselves under the protection of the Immaculate Heart of Mary, who was filled beyond measure by the same Spirit 'with the fullness of holiness and apostolic zeal'" (SRL, 6).

Our consecration to the Holy Spirit is inseparable from our devotion to the Virgin Mary. From our beginnings right up to the present day, we have remained deeply faithful to the Immaculate Heart of Mary in all our communities across the world, albeit in different ways according to time and place. Even if we cannot fully explain it, we feel that it is in her example that we find the best model of what a Spiritan missionary should be, rather than in any abstract theories or somewhat aggressive practices. By contemplating, admiring, and imitating the Mother of Jesus we can learn how to overcome our too frequent attitudes of clericalism, individualism, and arrogance. The re-constructed attic of the Venerable Father in the garden of the generalate reminds us that it was by taking her as the patron of the "Work for the Black People" that he finally discovered the inspiration he needed to compose the first Rule of his Society.

When we gather together at Bagamoyo for our next General Chapter, we will have need of a new inspiration to help us continue faithfully to the calls of the Holy Spirit! We pray that through the intercession of Mary, this same Spirit will breathe abundantly on us all.

Happy Feast of Pentecost.

CHAPTER SIX

VERY REV. FR. JOHN FOGARTY, C.S.Sp.

Superior General, 2012-2020

Fr. Fogarty, C.S.Sp. of the Irish Province was ordained priest on 27 September 1981. He obtained a Licentiate in sacred theology from the University of Fribourg, Switzerland (1982). He did pastoral work on mission in Kumasi diocese, Ghana (1982-86), served on the provincial council of Ireland, before returning to Ghana as Rector of the Spiritan Institute of Philosophy in Ejisu (1990-1994). In 1994, he returned to Ireland as assistant provincial till 1998 when he was elected First Assistant to the superior general in Rome. He became the first Director of the Center for Spiritan Studies (2005-2009), then Provincial of the US Province (2009-2012), and is currently the superior general of the Spiritan Congregation.

Christmas 2012

A NEW ENCOUNTER WITH JESUS

Dear Brothers and Sisters in the Spiritan Family,

I am conscious as I write that this is my first Christmas letter to the Congregation following my election as superior general at the General Chapter in Bagamoyo last July. The memory of Bagamoyo is, of course, very much alive in my mind and heart, as I am sure it is for all of you, especially those who had the privilege of participating in this extraordinary gathering. The first such meeting on African soil, the 2012 General Chapter brought us back to the beginning of evangelization in Eastern Africa, inviting us to return to our sources seeking new inspiration and new courage for our contemporary Spiritan life and mission in very different but no less challenging times. The Superior General's Report essentially set the context for our discussions and deliberations: despite many positive developments, we still live in a globalized world driven by neoliberal economic values that take little account of human dignity and further marginalize the poor; an increasingly multicultural world with its attendant problems of alienation, intercultural tension and growing fundamentalism; a secularized world marked by exaggerated individualism, the absence of religious values and the pursuit of personal fulfilment in the present moment. We were deeply conscious at the Chapter of our own fragilities, of the fact that we ourselves are profoundly affected by the philosophy and the values of the times in which we live, and that the primary call addressed to us today is one of authentic conversion, a true conversion of mind and of heart in our personal lives and in our communities.

Bagamoyo was an inspiring experience of communion in the Congregation to which we have dedicated our lives. We shared together our hopes and dreams and tried to capture them in a series of orientations and decisions that you will shortly receive in booklet form. All our discussions, however, were marked by the conviction that documents alone are singularly ineffective in bringing about real change; we realized that much of what we articulated with passion in regard to our life and our mission had already been said, often more eloquently, in preceding General Chapter documents. The question before us now in the Spiritan family is how to bridge the gap between our lived reality and what we profess to be in our Spiritan Rule of Life and in our Chapter documents.

As you are aware, the church has designated this year as a "Year of Faith" with a special focus on a "new evangelization" to mark the fiftieth anniversary of the opening of the Second Vatican Council. The message issued at the conclusion of the recent Synod of Bishops (*The New Evangelization for the Transmission of the Christian Faith*) offers some profound insights that can help us as we seek to live our Spiritan vocation more authentically. At the heart of our faith and our Spiritan calling is a personal encounter with Jesus and "the work of the new evangelization consists in presenting once more the beauty and perennial newness of the encounter with Christ to the often distracted and confused heart of the men and women of our time, above all to ourselves" (no. 3). We are invited "to contemplate the face of our Lord Jesus Christ" and to "enter into the mystery of his life given for us." The document points out that this new evangelization is not about the invention of new strategies but about rediscovering in the Gospels the ways in which Jesus approached and called people in their everyday lives. For us as Spiritans it is an invitation to turn once again to contemplative prayer and to a contemplative living out of the mission entrusted to us and the mysteries we celebrate throughout the liturgical year. The fact is that, as the gospel stories clearly show, every authentic encounter with Jesus is transformative; we cannot truly encounter the Lord and remain unchanged. In addition to our prayer, we encounter Jesus in a special way by "placing ourselves side by side with those who are wounded by life" because "the presence of the poor in our communities is mysteriously powerful: it changes persons more than a discourse does, it teaches fidelity, it makes us understand the fragility of life, it asks for prayer: in short it brings us to Christ" (Final Message of Synod, no. 12).

The mystery of the incarnation which we will shortly celebrate invites us to a profound reflection on the quality of our missionary engagement as Spiritans in the contemporary world. Libermann once pointed out that the fundamental role of the Spiritan is to show by his life and words "a little of what God is like" (cf. ES, Sup., 111). This is a simple but very profound insight. We are called in our lives and in our ministry to witness to a God who identified himself totally with the fragility of our human condition, who made himself truly at home with us, who found joy and fulfilment in our midst especially among the poor and marginalized of his day, who gave totally of himself in the service of others so that they in turn might rediscover their dignity and find life, love and happiness.

> What God has done in Jesus Christ 'once for all' (Heb. 7:27, 9,:26-28) in the historico-cultural terms of one particular people, the Church must do among all peoples . . . emptying herself of power, foreign riches and alien accretions, thus opening herself to modes of human existence, experience and celebration that were not hers previously . . . make herself completely at home among each people in the same authentically human way that Jesus was at home in Nazareth ("Inculturation," *New Dictionary of Theology*. Collegeville: Liturgical Press, 1991).

At a personal level, it means that each one of us is called to take on the flesh and blood of the people to whom we are sent, to be truly at home among them, to find joy and fulfilment in their service, especially the excluded and forgotten of our own day. As Spiritan Lay Associate, Maria Jesus de Souza, put it so beautifully in her presentation to the Chapter, mission is about "helping people to see, feel and understand the merciful and loving face of God." At the level of our Congregation and our different communities, the incarnation is a call to true brotherhood and equality. Brought together by Jesus from different backgrounds like the early disciples, we form a single family gathered around him where everyone should feel accepted and valued and experience a true sense of belonging.

While we may agree spontaneously with the above reflections, there were indications at the Chapter that, in practice, we often only give them notional assent. A number of our priority missionary commitments among the poor and excluded are in danger of closure simply because of the difficulty of getting personnel to go there. Mission appointments are sometimes seen more in terms of an adventure and a short-time personal experience than a joyful giving of one's life to a people among whom we are called to be completely at home and in whose service we will find true fulfilment. Personal comfort and security can so easily take precedence over self-giving for others, attachment to one's family and friends over identification with the people to whom we are sent. Inter-personal tensions and internal division in our circumscriptions and communities can militate against genuine fraternity and equality and undermine the effectiveness of our witness to the One who called us and who found a home in our midst.

May our meditation on the incredible mystery we celebrate at Christmas be an occasion for us to encounter Jesus anew and open a pathway for us in our personal lives, in our communities and in our Congregation towards true conversion.

Pentecost 2013

BROUGHT TOGETHER BY THE SPIRIT OF PENTECOST

Dear Brothers and Sisters in the Spiritan Family,

One of the fascinating aspects of the General Chapter at Bagamoyo was the cultural diversity of the participants: of the 75 delegates, 35 originated from Africa (5 of them representing circumscriptions in the Northern hemisphere), 27 from Europe, 6 from the Caribbean, 4 from North America, 2 from the Indian Ocean and 1 from South America; the four invited Spiritan Lay Associates came from four different continents. This diversity, of course, was reflected in the election of the members of the general council which now consists for the first time of seven confreres all of different nationality.

A brief analysis of the statistics of the Congregation over the years makes very interesting reading.

> In 1980, 146 (3.9%) of the total membership (3,769) were from Africa, representing 4 circumscriptions of origin, and 22 (0.6%) came from South America; by 1992 this had changed to 521 (15.8%) from Africa representing 8 circumscriptions of origin, 47 (1.4%) from the Caribbean, 32 (1%) from South America, 10 (0.3%) from the Indian Ocean, with the membership from Europe and North America at 72.9% and 8.6% respectively.
>
> The latest statistics published on December 31, 2012 show that 1,452 (52%) of the confreres now come from 24 African circumscriptions, 1,068 (38.3%) from Europe, 129 (4.6%) from North America, 63 (2.3%) from the Caribbean, 44 (1.6%) from the Indian Ocean, 29 (1%) from South America, with 4 from Asia and 1 from Oceania. Perhaps even more striking is the fact that today 478 (92.8%) of our 515 professed students in formation are from Africa, 13 (2.5%) from Europe, 12 (2.3%) from the Indian Ocean, with the remainder originating from North and South America, Asia and the Caribbean.

This remarkable evolution in the demographic composition and cultural spread of the membership of the Congregation is in itself an extraordinary testimony to the relevance of our Spiritan charism in the contemporary world. "Our Congregation is truly a gift that God has given, and continues to give, to the church and to the world. Today, and even more in the future, the church and the world have need of the charism that has been confided to us—the evangelization of the poor, in the light of the spirituality that characterizes us." (Fr. Jean-Paul Hoch, C.S.Sp., "Address to the Irish Chapter, 2006"). Our Spiritan Rule of Life rightly points out that the diversity of our membership is the work of the Spirit of Pentecost who brings us together into one large family, *"from different cultures, continents and nations"* (SRL, 37). Much more than an inevitable consequence of the geographical spread of our missionary endeavors or a testimony to the success of those who have preceded us, the cultural diversity of our membership is truly integral to our charism in the contemporary world.

> Conflict, racialism and the cult of the individual are all too prevalent in the world of today. By coming together from so many different places and cultures, we are saying to our brothers and sisters that the unity of the human race is not just an impossible dream. In this way, our community life is an integral part of our mission and a powerful witness of the Gospel (Maynooth, 117).

International community living is a "response to the call of the Holy Spirit to all of us, to witness to a new quality of human solidarity, surpassing individualism, ethnocentrism and nationalism" (Torre d'Aguilha, 2.1). This reality was brought home to me in a striking way some years ago when, on a visit to Auteuil, France, one of the lay employees said to me that the single most important contribution made by the Spiritan international community to the students they served there was the witness given by the confreres to the possibility of living together in joy and harmony.

One of the important consequences of the change in the demographic composition of the Congregation is that it is leading us to a new understanding of Spiritan mission. We have tended to conceive of the older circumscriptions as comprising principally members of the country of origin, albeit more recently with some assistance from the newer circumscriptions as internal resources age and diminish. The fact is that in a number of such circumscriptions their principal missionary commitments now depend significantly, if not uniquely, on confreres originating from other circumscriptions. We are being invited to move away from a nationalistic understanding of Province—where there are those who belong and those who have come to help—to the concept of international

Spiritan presence and mission in a particular country. Already a reality in our present international groups, this is a much more inclusive notion from the point of view of creating a true sense of ownership of the Congregation's mission. It also presents a major challenge to both the receiving circumscriptions in terms of fostering a genuine sense of belonging for those who come from "outside" and to the confreres concerned in terms of identifying fully with the mission to which they have been appointed.

If, as Torre d'Aguilha stated, our international and intercultural living is a call from the Holy Spirit to witness to a new quality of human solidarity in a global world, our circumscriptions and our communities must be "places where the truth is spoken and lived, where domination and subjugation do not occur, where differences are acknowledged and affirmed without compromising unity."[1] In his address to the Dominican General Chapter on "Preaching the Gospel in the 21st Century," Robert Schreiter stressed the vital importance of community witness:

> Your emphasis on community, too, plays a role in all of this. First of all in mirroring the kind of communion to which we are called, a communion which can encompass and value our differences, yet make them a source of challenge and enrichment rather than one of division and diminishment . . . community must find today its deepest roots theologically, in a Trinitarian God where difference and unity find their deepest communion.

This vision has a number of practical consequences for us as Spiritans who are called to live in community by the very nature of our vocation (SRL, 27, 28). In the first place, it is a call to develop a style of leadership in our circumscriptions and communities that fosters equality and inclusiveness, participation in decision-making and shared responsibility. This, in turn, means that we have a responsibility when we gather at Chapters or Assemblies to choose our leadership not merely on the basis of their organizational skills or human qualities but on their ability to embody the mission we are called to live and to preach. Our communities should be places of openness and mutual respect where diversity and difference of opinion are valued rather than seen as a potential source of division and conflict. In this regard, the Bagamoyo Chapter has invited us to reflect on the issue of "*Spiritan culture*"; this is a mutually enriching exercise in sharing and listening with a view to greater understanding of

---

1. Schreiter, "Globalization and Reconciliation."

the inspiration we hold in common but which is expressed in such a wide and ever-increasing variety of cultures. Should tensions among us arise, as inevitably will be the case, it is imperative that we work for healing and reconciliation in our own midst; otherwise our ministry is seriously undermined and our witness hollow.

Francis Libermann stressed that our most effective homily lies in the quality of our own lives (ND, XIII, 144, Letter to Mr. Lairé, 8 May 1851) and that, if there is a perceivable gap between what we preach and what we live, others will easily see through it and say that *"we are simply doing our job."*[2] His words continue to have profound implications for us in terms of the witness we are called to give as an international Congregation in an increasingly fragmented and individualistic world. May the Spirit of Pentecost who brought us together into one great family continue to fashion us so that we can truly give effective witness to the message we preach.

October 2, 2013

THE ANIMATION PLAN

Brothers and Sisters in the Spiritan Family,

You have received—and I hope you have also had the opportunity to read—the documents of the Bagamoyo Chapter. You will have seen that a strong conviction emerges from them: that of being a true religious and missionary family that moves forward in the footsteps of its Founders, of having a more authentic, more coherent lifestyle. We must live more of what we say we are. Our Chapters have followed one another and have produced wonderful texts on our spiritual heritage, on our mission in the contemporary world, on the importance of community life in a large international and intercultural family where everyone feels included and lives a true belonging . . . In reality, these beautiful documents do not seem to have brought about the transformations we desired: if we are honest with ourselves, we must recognize that we have a long way to go to bridge the gap between what we live and what we profess in the Rule of Life and in our Chapter texts. The words of Pope Paul VI, written so long ago, are still relevant: We are asked insistently: Do you really believe

---

2. *Provisional Rule*, 50.

what you proclaim? Do you live what you believe? Do you preach what you live?

The essential message of Bagamoyo is therefore a call to conversion to each of us, to you and me individually, to each community, to each constituency. This is what motivated the decision to launch a process of animation in the whole Congregation, a process that we want to inaugurate today and that must continue until our General Chapter in 2020. The general council, in accordance with the wishes of the Chapter, has drawn up a plan to respond to this call, in dialogue with the circumscription superiors and the coordinators of the Unions. This plan presents four themes that are at the heart of the call to Spiritan life: *Spiritan identity and vocation, the Holy Spirit, community life, mission.* We start today! From now until 2 February 2015, we will reflect on our Spiritan vocation and identity. We will reread together the first chapter of our Rule of Life. We will ask ourselves about the meaning of Spiritan life, in today's world, in the footsteps of Claude Poullart des Places and François Libermann. How can we be more true to our goal of "evangelizing the poor"? How can we live our "apostolic life" more deeply in a spirit of "practical union"?

In the coming months, you will receive some documents and tools to help you live this process—testimonies from confreres and lay associates, suggestions for times of reflection and sharing in community, texts for possible liturgical celebrations . . . You too can share your ideas and suggestions with others. We know that many of you have very busy lives, that you are caught up in the daily demands of your ministry, that you have many meetings with the diocese, the parish, the Congregation . . . The proposed plan is not intended to be a burden or an extra activity. It is designed to fit easily into the activities you already have planned for the community or constituency. Some people will be put off by the very idea of an animation plan as a process developed and imposed from above by the general council, without regard for local practical realities. However, what is at stake here is very important. We are all invited to a collective rediscovery of our own narrative as Spiritans, to a pilgrimage into our past so that the insights and dream of our Founders can reshape our spirituality, our life and our mission. It is an invitation to each of us to rediscover the meaning of our own call and what unites us most deeply to the brothers and sisters of the Spiritan family. The future of the Congregation depends on this pilgrimage which begins today.

May the Holy Spirit accompany us.

Christmas 2013

A NEW BEGINNING

Dear Brothers and Sisters in the Spiritan Family,

During the past year, two thought-provoking presentations were given at successive meetings of the Union of Superiors General which I attended here in Rome. They concerned the exercise of leadership in a church and in a society in crisis. Although the presentations were not intentionally connected and dealt with different subjects—"The Role of the Church in the Context of the Recent Financial Crisis," and "The Service of Leadership in Religious Life Fifty Years after Vatican II"—the conclusions of both were strikingly similar.

Professor Stefano Zamagni of the University of Bologna, speaking at length on the nature and causes of the financial collapse that began in the USA in 2007, stressed that the crisis was directional rather than technical in nature; it is therefore much more difficult to resolve. He added that while bankers and financiers are readily blamed, essentially, we were all complicit in what happened. Whether we care to admit it or not, we are all affected by the most immediate cause of the crisis, namely the passion to possess. This crisis, unlike other financial crises in the past, cannot be fixed by simply re-adjusting the system from within. It requires the discovery of a new value system, a new direction for the world. Professor Zamagni emphasized that such a new direction will ultimately be founded on the witness of individual lives to whom others can look for inspiration, for hope, and for meaning.

Similarly, political theologian, Bartolomeo Sorge, S.J., referred to a structural crisis in contemporary society. We have seen the emergence today of a new globalized and technocratic civilization marked by the separation of culture from faith, of politics and economics from ethics. This new civilization is pervaded by an exaggerated individualism, materialism, and subjectivism that again affect all of us, religious and non-religious alike. Significantly both speakers pointed out that there are few if any precedents in world history to turn to for a model of an evangelical response. It is a matter of returning to the originality and simplicity of the Gospel, to the witness of lives transformed by an encounter with Christ. Fr. Sorge noted that each time the church becomes rich and powerful, weighed down by human privilege, each time diplomacy prevails over prophecy, when the Christian community falls back on its own internal problems and loses its missionary zeal, the Holy Spirit intervenes to purify and renew the church and bring it back to the purity of its origins.

A similar conviction of the need to return to our Spiritan origins and to rebuild anew permeated our discussions at the General Chapter of Bagamoyo. There was a strong awareness that the fundamental call addressed to us at this point in our history as a religious missionary Congregation is to return to a more authentic lifestyle, a life more visibly in conformity with the intuitions of our Founders and with the Spiritan Rule of Life which gives concrete expression to those intuitions today. The question of Spiritan identity was raised several times at the Chapter. The discussions returned repeatedly to SRL 4: *The evangelization of the poor is our purpose*. Fidelity to this commitment, which is at the heart of the charism we have inherited from our Founders, is what truly identifies us rather than some external symbol or clothing.

Undoubtedly, the collective awareness of our fragilities, our mistakes, and our sins colored the fundamental orientations of the Bagamoyo Chapter. The realization that the Congregation itself has been touched by the current sexual abuse crisis in the church and by the failure of leadership in a number of cases to deal appropriately with the issue was a stark reminder of this reality. A survivor of sexual abuse contacted me shortly after my arrival in Clivo di Cinna poignantly pointing out that the suffering inflicted on him by one of our members was a sad reflection on our Spiritan commitment to "make ourselves 'the advocates, the supporters and the defenders of the weak and the little ones against all who oppress them'" (SRL, 14). While we deplore the actions of those who perpetrated such crimes, if we are honest with ourselves we will admit that there is a gap in all of our lives between the image we present and the reality we live and each one of us has subtle mechanisms for exploiting others to our own benefit. Transparency, accountability, and the willingness to humbly acknowledge our errors, are central to the process of renewal in the Congregation. Mission in the contemporary world is above all about the witness of our lives; people are looking for spiritual leadership, for men and women who have found meaning and hope in their own personal lives, men and women of prayer who have discovered God and whose lives have been deeply touched by this experience. The manner in which the simple lifestyle and message of Pope Francis has profoundly affected the lives of so many people is an eloquent testimony to the truth of this assertion.

The first phase of our Congregation-wide Animation Plan is precisely a call go back to our beginnings, to allow Poullart des Places and Libermann to reshape our spirituality, our personal and community lives and our missionary commitments today. We need to listen again to our own story, as it began in the lives of our Founders and as it unfolded in the inspirational lives of our Spiritan ancestors. We need to rediscover our own personal inspiration in re-reading the stories of the early Spiritan pioneers: Spiritans such as Fr. Allenou, a canon in Quebec who gave everything he owned for the poor and died in the "odor of sanctity"[3]; Bishop Kerhervé of Indo-China, whose episcopal wardrobe consisted of an old cassock and a worn-out pair of shoes; Fr. Maillard, whose secret of success among the Micmac Indians is ascribed to the fact that he identified totally with the lifestyle of the people he served.[4]; Bishop Pottier of China who wrote. "The fewer needs we create for ourselves, the richer we are"; Fr. Lanoë, a missionary in Guyana who stated: "I would like to see us here 'one heart and one soul' without that wretched mine and yours' which causes so many disorders."[5] Each of us can certainly add other more contemporary names of Spiritans who have provided personal inspiration to us on our Spiritan journey and who have helped us to remain faithful to our Spiritan ideals.

A pilgrimage into our past will reveal that our beginnings as a Congregation were very humble indeed but that God accomplished wonderful deeds through the lives of simple, committed Spiritans who were aware of their limitations but were open to the power of the Spirit. Reflecting on the founding of the "poor little" Society of the Missionaries of the Holy Heart of Mary, Eugene Tisserant pointed out that, unlike the Jesuits and the Franciscans, we have "no remarkable figures or men of great talent; all we have are people of good will, unsure as to how they were brought together . . . without the ability to put any project together but feeling themselves led by an invisible force who directs them and who removes from their path difficulties which seem truly insurmountable . . . "[6] (ND, I, 589-90; 13 October 1842). We are often concerned about diminishing numbers in the Congregation but Francis Libermann had great confidence in the effectiveness of a small group of people who

3. Cf. Koren, *Essays*, 19; cites J. Michel, *Poullart des Places*, 289ff.

4. Koren, *Essays*, 20. See also Koren, *Knaves or Knights*, 78-84.

5. Koren, *Essays*, 20. Cites Letter of Lanoë to Fr. Becquet, November 7, 1784 in Archives C.S.Sp. 4-B-III.

6. See Tisserant, "Memorandum."

share the same vision and are totally committed to the same aims (see, for example, LS, I, 489-490: Letter to a director of a seminary, 23 April 1838).

We will shortly celebrate the feast of Christmas, the astounding fact that the Son of God "pitched his tent among us" and shared the fragility and vulnerability of our human condition. May our meditation on this incredible mystery deepen our awareness of the need for greater simplicity and authenticity in our lives as Spiritans and of our calling to give inspirational witness to our brothers and sisters in a world desperately in search of hope and meaning.

Pentecost 2014

" IT IS WHEN I AM WEAK THAT I AM STRONG . . . " (2 COR 12:10)

"Do not be afraid of your fragility," was the simple but challenging message of Pope Francis at his Angelus address on February 9, 2014 anticipating the World Day of the Sick which followed two days later. Perhaps this is precisely the message we as Spiritans need to hear today as we prepare together for the coming Feast of Pentecost with a growing sense of our vulnerability and of our limitations as a Congregation. The term "fragile" has become commonplace in our Spiritan vocabulary of recent years. We speak readily in the Congregation today of "fragile circumscriptions," "fragile communities" and even of "fragile confreres"; it is a common topic of conversation at the general council table. As a Congregation, we have become much more conscious of our limitations and our inadequacies in different parts of the globe for a wide variety of reasons—the experience of diminishing and ageing personnel in many of our older Provinces; the lack of young people who wish to identify with our way of life in countries where Spiritan vocations once flourished; inadequate financial resources, sometimes even to meet basic needs, in several of our newer circumscriptions; disunity and division among the members of a circumscription; the realization of our mistakes and of our failures, as groups or as individuals, to live our missionary religious vocation authentically and to be true to the commitment we made publicly on the day of our profession. All of this is compounded by the fact that the church itself has lost much of its credibility of recent years as an authoritative source of hope and direction for others. Today we are being invited to embrace a sense of mission based not on strength as perhaps in former times but rooted in fragility and powerlessness.

It is important to remember that our Congregation was born in fragility and knew many fragile moments in its history. It began with a small group of seminarians gathered together on Pentecost Sunday with very simple aspirations; their young charismatic leader, Claude Poullart des Places, to whom they looked for inspiration and direction, would be dead a short few years later. Without a formal Rule or official existence for three decades, the Congregation was later suppressed and restored on two separate occasions between 1792 and 1816; subsequently deprived of essential funding and its buildings seized by the army, it only survived due to the extraordinary dedication of a handful of its members. The Society which was ultimately responsible for its revival was equally fragile. Founded again by seminarians and led by a young convert of fragile health who himself had no hope of ordination at the time, it saw its initial missionary venture to West Africa end in disaster. The challenges faced by Libermann as he tried to deal with tensions within the small community, doubts about his competence as a leader, difficulties in communication, the untimely death of several of his most committed and competent confreres[7] and extremely limited resources[8] are often forgotten today and make very interesting reading in our contemporary context. The new project in Australia, which seemed so providential at the time and which was undertaken with such enthusiasm, saw the refusal of one confrere to accept his appointment, the death of another on arrival, the departure of a third from the young society during his mission appointment, and the disregard of the terms of the initial contract with the authorities—some of these problems are still familiar to us today—and it too was to end in failure. It was no wonder that Libermann spoke readily of his "poor and weak Congregation" [cf. ND, XIII, 13]. "We are all wretched men," he wrote to M. Briot in August 10, 1843, "brought together by the will of the

---

7. See, for example, Letter to Mgr. Kobès in *Letters to Clergy and Religious*, 1, 317-322, here 318: "[God] takes away from us precisely those who seemed most capable ... *Among those whom it pleased God to call to himself over the [past] nine years ... there were eight or nine who could have become excellent community or even mission superiors*; he has left us with those who are the least gifted." 1 Nov. 1851 (ND, XIII, 351; LS, IV, 680). [text in italics were elided in the English translation. Ed].

8. See, for example, Letter to Mgr. Kobès, 26 April 1851 (ND, XIII, 112-113): "Our Gard house is on a very poor footing and I do not believe there is another establishment in France so poorly set up; we have barely what is strictly necessary to keep a house in order which has 70 people in three communities."

Master, who is our only hope. If we had powerful means at our disposal we would not accomplish much good; but now that we are nothing, have nothing, and are good for nothing, we are permitted to conceive great projects, because our hope does not rest but on him who is almighty."[9] Fr. Amable Fourdinier, then superior general, had echoed the same sentiments some years earlier when he said: *"I put my trust in God . . . The more powerless I am, the more confidence I have."* If in the eyes of many outsiders our history has been one of extraordinary success in terms of evangelization over the last three centuries, as is evident in the texts of the Novena you have received, it has been written for the most part by the lives of simple, ordinary, committed confreres who were aware of their limitations and their mistakes but were open to the transforming power of the Holy Spirit.

Interestingly, it is precisely the discovery of our fragility that enables us to see things in their proper perspective, that frees us from our compulsions and illusions. "It is in what we lack that we are most open to what we will become," wrote British author Margaret Silf. "The Samaritan woman at the well would never have met Jesus if she'd had a water supply at home."[10] The revelations of the recent child sexual abuse and financial scandals in the church, of the complicity of leadership in covering up the former to protect the institution at the expense of the victim, have shattered our illusions of a divine institution that was beyond reproach and have served to call us back to fundamental gospel values, to authenticity and integrity of life, to the need for accountability and transparency in our dealings with others, and for ongoing conversion at both institutional and personal levels. In the case of our own Congregation, the experience of our fragilities and vulnerabilities has allowed the Holy Spirit to bring us back to the simplicity of the message of our Founders, to the realization that the mission to which we are called is God's mission not ours, and that our role is simply to be docile instruments at God's service. Perhaps the rightful emphasis in Vatican II on apostolic activity as "of the very nature of religious life" [PC, 8] in Congregations such as ours seduced us into believing that we were "master-builders" rather than simple "workers," "messiahs," rather than "ministers" in the vineyard of the LORD. An over-emphasis on activity, efficacy, accomplishment, and success will ultimately bring us face to face with our own poverty. A sense

---

9. ND, IV, 303; *Letters to Clergy and Religious*, 1, 210-211.
10. Silf, *Compass Points*, 140.

of powerlessness, therefore, should not lead to paralysis but to a renewed conviction that God's power is most effective in our human frailty. In fact, as Timothy Radcliffe, O.P., pointed out, a sense of our own powerlessness is actually an essential condition for credibility as a preacher of the Word of God today:

> To be a preacher is not just to tell people about God . . . We have a word of hope only if we glimpse from within the pain and despair of those to whom we preach. We have no word of compassion unless somehow we know their failures and temptations as our own. We have no word which offers meaning to people's lives unless we have been touched by their doubts and glimpsed the abyss.[11]

Pentecost is the story of a fragile group of people united together in prayer with Mary and bound together by a personal and collective sense of powerlessness. The coming of the Spirit did nothing to change the chaos of the world around them; rather it led them to the discovery of a new strength within themselves to confront a world which up to then had frightened them, a capacity to communicate in a language that somehow all could understand despite the barriers that separated them, a power to unite and create communion in a divided world. Libermann saw clearly that God comes to us and calls us exactly in the reality of our concrete situation, not as we were in the past or as we would wish to be today or in the future. As we prepare together in prayer for our patronal feast of Pentecost, perhaps we can make our own the words he addressed to Sr. Saint Agnes less than two years before he died: "God accepted you poor and weak, he knew well what you were; abandon yourself to the goodness and mercy with which he received you" [ND, XII, 171].

"Now to him who is able to accomplish far more than all we ask or imagine by the power at work within us, to him be glory in the church and in Christ Jesus to all generations, forever and ever." (Eph 3: 20-21).

---

11. Radcliffe, *Sing a New Song*, 125.

Christmas 2014

REMEMBER THE WONDERS THE LORD HAS DONE (PS 105:5)

On September 7th this year, I had the privilege of participating in the ceremony which marked the closure of the 150th anniversary celebrations of the founding of the Spiritan community at Chevilly-Larue in France. In 1863 Fr. Ignace Schwindenhammer, with the help of his own patrimony, purchased a hunting lodge on the outskirts of Paris belonging to the nobility of the day and transformed it into a home for future Spiritan missionaries and for the superior general of a Congregation dedicated to the service of the poor. Written by the lives of ordinary, simple Spiritans, Brothers and Priests, and their collaborators, the story of Chevilly is truly a remarkable one. It is the story of successive generations of formators and professors who through their wisdom and witness shaped the lives of some 4000 missionaries who in turn founded, formed, and inspired flourishing Christian communities across the globe; more recently it is the story of the evolution of a community, once uniquely dedicated to the formation of young missionaries who left for foreign lands, into a home for them when they finally return due to old age or illness and when their mission takes on a new form, perhaps more important than when they were young and active, that of accepting their limitations with faith, dignity, and joy, and witnessing to God's healing and transforming presence in a world in need of hope and meaning.

The 150th anniversary of the founding of the community at Chevilly was but one of a series of similar events that took place in different parts of the Spiritan world in 2013 and 2014. These included the establishment of the Catholic Church on the island of Zanzibar; the opening of St. Mary's College in Port-of-Spain, Trinidad, and the beginning of Spiritan presence on the island; the founding of Rockwell College, Ireland; the arrival of Spiritan missionaries and the foundation of the local church in Sierra Leone, West Africa, where the celebrations envisaged for November 2014 have been postponed indefinitely due to the tragic outbreak of the Ebola virus; coincidentally, 2014 is also the 150th anniversary of the death of Blessed Jacques Laval in Mauritius. These various anniversaries reflect a period of extraordinary diversification and international expansion of the Congregation after the death of Francis Libermann and, consequently, the imaginative and courageous decisions taken with very limited resources by his gifted, if controversial, successor,

Fr. Schwindenhammer. His period in office (1852-1881) incredibly saw 79 new foundations, 33 of which were in Europe or the United States, 25 in the West Indies and other former colonies, and the remainder in Africa. Several of these new foundations were actually seminaries, colleges or agricultural schools, and many were dedicated to the education and training of underprivileged young people in the society of the day.

It is very important that we commemorate and celebrate these and other significant milestones in our Spiritan history, particularly in the context of our current reflection on our identity as Spiritans. In the first place, memory is essential to our identity as the people of God. "Remember the wonders that the LORD has done," the Psalmist invites us (Ps 105:5). The role of the Holy Spirit is precisely to remind us of all that the LORD has done in and through our human story, to help us discover the presence and action of God shaping his plan of love through the fabric of our human history, through the lives and actions of ordinary men and women, despite their limitations and mistakes. As so many of the gospel parables tell us, memories of our experience of God's compassion, love and, forgiveness in our own personal lives lead us in turn to be compassionate, loving, and forgiving towards our brothers and sisters. Faith and memory are very closely linked; forgetfulness is often at the root of our failures. "Do not forget all his gifts" (Ps 103:2).

Secondly, as we recall memories of the past and the stories of those who have gone before us, we get in touch once again with our own deepest motivations as missionary religious, with what unites us most profoundly with our brothers and sisters in the Spiritan family, the call and the charism we share in common. We realize how much we owe both personally and collectively to those who have preceded us, to their inspiration, their vision, and their courage. We are reminded once again that God can truly do wonderful things through the lives of ordinary men and women who are conscious of their own limitations but open to the power of the Holy Spirit. We discover that human weakness and failure are not necessarily an obstacle to God's grace or to the effectiveness of our witness. As Pope Francis pointed out in his address to Superiors General in November 2013, "a religious who recognizes himself as weak and a sinner does not negate the witness he is called to give, rather he reinforces it and this is good for everyone."[12]

---

12. Spadaro, "Wake up the World," 3.

I recently visited the Province of Canada in Quebec which has this intriguing motto: "*Je me souviens* (I remember)." "This motto has only three words," explained historian Thomas Chapais, "but these three words are worth more than the most eloquent speeches. Yes, we remember. We remember the past and its lessons, the past and its misfortunes, the past and its glories . . . [This motto] says so eloquently in three words the past as well as the present and the future," adds archivist Pierre-Georges Roy. Memory not only concerns the past. The way we remember the past determines to a large extent how we live in the present and actually shapes our future. Just as negative memories of hurt and injustice affect the way we perceive the world, our relationships with others and our capacity for enjoyment, and to a very real extent limit the possibilities for our future, so positive memories of the experience of love, of acceptance, of the inspiration and support of others, equally colour our ability to relate to our brothers and sisters and shape our future in a positive way. "Memories of love make possible all our achievements," said Mr. William Dietrich, the American philanthropist, as he gave away his vast fortune in 2011 to various educational institutions in Pittsburgh. "They give us the confidence to take risks and reach beyond ourselves."

Margaret Silf, the British writer, expresses the same conviction in a different way:

> Everything that has happened to and in (this place) has made it what it is today, which in turn is the seed of everything it has the potential to become . . . our history matters- our collective stories and personal ones. When we listen to our memories, we expose hidden layers of who we are. We have a sacred duty to share our treasure with those who follow. If we don't, we risk becoming one-dimensional beings with no depth beyond the immediate impulse, no hinterland to lend perspective, and a very diminished sense of who we are. Let us tell our stories. They are our gift to the future.[13]

In the words of Pope Francis: "Tradition and the memory of the past must help us to have the courage to open up new areas to God" (Interview with Antonio Spadaro, S.J., August 2013).

We will shortly celebrate the foundational story of our Christian faith, the coming of the Son of God among us, divesting himself of status and dignity and identifying himself totally with our human condition,

---

13. Silf, *Compass Points*, 208.

thus opening up a new future for humanity. May the commemoration of this extraordinary event deepen our awareness of our call as Spiritans to identify with and share the lives of those on the margins of contemporary society, giving them new hope and dignity; may it give us, as it gave those who preceded us, the courage to open up in our hearts, in our communities and in our Congregation "new areas to God."

Pentecost 2015

THE HOLY SPIRIT COMES TO HELP US IN OUR WEAKNESS (ROM. 8:26)

The American theologian, David Tracy, once wrote that "there is never an authentic disclosure of truth which is not also transformative." In other words, we cannot truly encounter God—whether in prayer, in the faces of the poor, or in the events of our own life—and remain unchanged. In the final analysis, it is personal transformation that is the test of the authenticity of our encounter with God.

A fascinating example is the present Pope Francis. Paul Vallely, in his intriguing book, *Pope Francis—Untying the Knots*, traces the remarkable evolution of Jorge Bergoglio from a politically and religiously conservative priest, who initially actively resisted both the radical changes sought by Vatican II to revitalize the church and the prevailing Liberation Theology in Latin America centered on the option for the poor, to the Pope that would systematically challenge the complacency of an introspective church and champion "a poor church for poor people." Vallely attributes this radical transformation to the lengthy hours of personal prayer that became an integral part of Fr. Bergoglio's day after a difficult period in his earlier life as a Jesuit. He sees in him "a man who has undergone, if not a religious conversion, then at any rate a deep inner transformation which has wrought a profound and long-lasting change in both his personal and political vision . . . a man who has become aware of his own frailties and devised, through prolonged prayer, a strategy to handle them."

Despite his busy schedule, Pope Francis continues to devote up to two hours daily to personal prayer which he speaks of in simple terms: "Prayer should be an experience of giving way, of surrendering, where our entire being enters into the presence of God . . . This is where dialogue, listening, and transformation begin. Looking at God, but above all sensing that we are being watched by him . . . Sometimes I allow myself to fall asleep while sitting there and just let him look at me. I have a sense of being in someone else's hands, as though God were taking me by the hand."

Francis Libermann shared very similar views on the simplicity of prayer, its importance and its transforming power: "You must make your method of mental prayer as simple as possible," he wrote to M. Collin on January 29, 1845, "You need not make numerous considerations. Do not seek to execute every detail of the method of Saint Sulpice; you would not succeed. What, then, ought your mental prayer to be? It should consist in a simple, calm and fully confident repose in our LORD's presence"[14] (ND, VII, 37-38). His own personal experience taught him that people cannot be fitted into a fixed system but that the Holy Spirit leads each one of us individually, according to our own personality, our temperament, our gifts and our weaknesses. God has made us as we are and we have to find our own unique path to God, our own unique way of praying. One of his key insights was that God always comes to meet us in the reality of our situation, God always finds us where we are. It is God who takes the initiative in prayer; we simply have to discover the path along which he is inviting us.

Prayer for Libermann can be described simply as loving attention to God. Love is the measure of the quality of our prayer; it is our attention to God that distinguishes our prayer from all our other daily activities. Although he was aware of the difficulties of climate and fatigue facing his early missionaries in Africa, he nevertheless insisted on an hour of personal prayer each day whatever the demands of their ministry, even if the time spent at prayer seemed of little use: "It costs us a bit to stay a long while at prayer when we are preoccupied with many things throughout the day. These things invade our prayer; the time for the end of the prayer approaches and we are inclined to say that we have wasted an hour of our morning. I could have spent it much more profitably than battling with distractions, I am tempted to say to myself . . . but if we think that we are greatly mistaken" (ND, VIII, 398: Letter to the community in Dakar, 27 December 1846).

Libermann was convinced of the value of prayer because he was convinced that prayer gradually changes us, or rather that God slowly changes us through prayer, shaping us to be the person he has called us to be. He emphasized that prayer enables us to see God's action more

---

14. *Letters to Clergy and Religious*, 3, 238.

clearly in our own lives and in the lives of others, to see ourselves and others with God's eyes; prayer helps us to overcome our faults and weaknesses, freeing us from our compulsions and from oversensitivity to misunderstanding and contradiction; prayer gradually enables us to accept ourselves and our limitations and those of others with patience, gentleness and peace. All of this Libermann learned from his own personal experience. The foundation and early development of his new Society made enormous demands on his time and energy as he battled with ill-health, with criticism and misunderstanding by others, and with his own self-belief as he had to face the reality of failure. There were times when he admitted to feeling overwhelmed by it all. It was his practice of "examining everything before God," of spending time with God on a daily basis, whatever the demands of his work, that helped him to keep things in perspective and gave him the energy to continue. It was in prayer that he found light, patience, and serenity.

"Prophetic action is the public face of mysticism," wrote Sr. Sandra Schneiders. "Only a life of ever deepening and faithful contemplation can keep the prophet attuned to the dream of a suffering God for humanity and the earth." Ultimately the encounter with God in prayer would lead both Jorge Bergoglio and Francis Libermann to a profound love for the poor, to share a worldview seen from the perspective of the marginalized and excluded, and to a deep commitment to create a more equal world where the dignity of all is respected and treasured.

> If you have an ardent zeal, full of love for God . . . you will be deeply moved seeing the wretchedness of the peoples among whom you will live. You will think of them constantly, night and day; sometimes you will feel exhausted. You will beg God to enlighten you and move them; you will seek for the means to cure them of their blindness, and without any doubt, you will find thousands of means to procure the good of those poor souls . . . [15]

Prayer then is not a peripheral activity for us as Spiritans, relegated to occasional free moments in an otherwise very busy schedule; it is at the very heart of our mission to serve the poor in the footsteps of our Founders. "Let us cultivate the contemplative dimension, even amid the whirlwind of more urgent and heavy duties. And the more mission calls

---

15. *Provisional Rule*, 324 (chap 10, Art. VIII, Gloss).

you to go out to the margins of existence, let your heart be more closely united to Christ's heart, full of mercy and love," urges Pope Francis.

May the Spirit of Pentecost come to help us in our weakness when we do not know how to pray as we ought; may the Spirit continue to shape our personal and community lives (SRL, 10), lead us along new missionary paths (SRL, 85) and enable us to hear his voice speaking to us through the church, through our environment and the world in which we live (SRL, 44.1).

Christmas 2015

"HE BECAME POOR . . . SO THAT THROUGH HIS POVERTY YOU MIGHT BECOME RICH" (2 COR 8:9)

On February 13 this year, Pope Francis and the Consistory of Cardinals gathered for the first time in the Synod Hall in the presence of a number of lay experts to review the financial situation of the Holy See with the aid of detailed power-point presentations, graphical projections and charts. On October 29, I was among the many people invited to a public presentation of the statutes of the new economic structures of the Holy See, led by the Cardinal Prefect of the recently established Secretariat for the Economy at the Vatican. These events are indicative of a completely new approach to the management of the Vatican finances, formerly shrouded in secrecy and understandingly subject to considerable criticism and suspicion. Early in his pontificate, Pope Francis set about reforming the Vatican Bank, which had long been associated with scandals and intrigue, with a view to transparency and accountability. Lay financial specialists were appointed, international accounting standards introduced, and hundreds of accounts, which did not correspond to strict criteria, were closed. A new Secretariat for the Economy was established in February 2014 and a Council with several lay experts was appointed to advise on policy. Today all Vatican Departments are required to submit annual budgets and quarterly reports and are subject to close oversight by an internal Auditor General. It would appear that Pope Francis initially considered simply closing the Vatican Bank: "*St. Peter did not have a bank account,*" he announced in June, 2013. But he quickly realized that the Vatican Bank was a very effective instrument in assisting the church to accomplish its mission, in particular in helping poor dioceses in Africa and Asia to safeguard their limited funds and in enabling charities to channel their financial resources quickly to the needy in situations of crisis and natural disaster.

Less well known is the fact that, at the specific request of Pope Francis, the general bursars of all religious Congregations and Societies of Apostolic Life were convoked by the Congregation for Religious to a symposium in March 2014 to reflect on the ethical management of their material resources. The essential message of the symposium was a strong reminder that the goods of a religious Institute are at the service of its charism and mission in the church and therefore must be cared for, managed, and used strictly with this end in mind. A circular letter sent to all Congregations by the Holy See after the symposium drew attention in some detail to the consequences of this fundamental principle: the fidelity of a Congregation to the charism of its Founders is the primary criterion for the economic decisions it makes; this, in turn, obliges us to regularly re-examine our works and the material resources we possess to ensure that they continue to express our charism in the contemporary social and cultural reality; in the light of this evaluation we must decide the works and the buildings we should retain, modify or discontinue, as well as the new missionary initiatives we should undertake, if we are to remain faithful to our charism in the contemporary world; we must therefore have in place proper financial procedures to enable us to plan effectively for the use of our resources. This includes budgeting projections, accurate accounting, internal controls and auditing, with the aid of competent lay professionals or members of other religious institutes and following national and international best practice. We should aim at the self-sustainability of our works, and those that are not cost effective need to be closely monitored and the deficits addressed to avoid an attitude of dependency and the wastage of resources that could be used more effectively elsewhere; all members of the community should be involved in the budgeting process so that they are not divorced from the lived reality around them and in order that they can reflect together on the genuineness of their community and personal witness to poverty; the management of our financial affairs should never be seen to be a matter for the bursar alone and he in turn must exercise his responsibility in a spirit of service rather than of domination or power; vigilance and transparency in the use of our resources are integral to our evangelical witness.

This letter from the Congregation for Religious (available in Italian on the Vatican website) calls us as Spiritans to a profound reflection on the use and management of our material resources in the service of our mission, namely the evangelization of the poor (SRL, 4, 229; Bagamoyo 5.3ff). More fundamentally it challenges us as religious vowed to poverty to examine our attitude towards money and material possessions and the witness we give in this regard at the community and personal levels. In a very real sense we do not own the material resources we possess in that we are not free to do with them as we wish; they are given to us in trust for the accomplishment of our mission in the church. Interestingly, in a number of countries in Europe and North America, it is the secular laws regulating charitable organizations that remind us of this basic principle and compel us to respect it. Our vow of poverty is intended to challenge forcefully the idolatry of money (cf. *Vita consecrata*, 90) in a consumerist world where greed and the accumulation of riches on the part of some are responsible to a significant degree for the dehumanizing poverty of countless millions of people. The simplicity and hospitality of religious communities who are content with basic necessities is meant to offer an alternative lifestyle and to serve as a model for those who are indifferent to the needs of their brothers and sisters: "Today, more than in other ages, the call to evangelical poverty is also being felt among those who are aware of the scarcity of the planet's resources and who invoke respect for and conservation of creation by reducing consumption, by living more simply and by placing a necessary brake on their own desires." (*Vita consecrata*, 90).

If we are honest with ourselves, however, we too are often deeply affected by the individualistic and consumerist attitudes we are called to challenge. We carefully distinguish and protect what we consider to belong to ourselves rather than to the community or to the Congregation; we tend to see salaries, stipends and gifts, as intended primarily for personal use and have difficulty in sharing these with the community to which we belong (cf. SRL, 65); we are attracted by the latest gadgets and luxury items and often justify their purchase by some possible advantage for our ministry; we see community resources as there to be exploited rather than cared for, sometimes offering us a lifestyle that is significantly superior to that of the people among whom we live and minister (cf. SRL, 71); we are at times indifferent to the needs of our Spiritan brothers and fail to share our collective resources within our circumscription; some of us are even tempted to use for our own personal ends funds entrusted to us for other purposes.

May our contemplation of the mystery of the incarnation, of the simple lifestyle chosen by him who made himself poor so that through his poverty we might become rich, enable us to see that "less is more," help us rediscover our call to a prophetic way of life beyond the obsessive consumerism and rampant individualism of our day,[16] so that we like Jesus can be truly present to each other and to our brothers and sisters, especially to the poor whom we are privileged to serve (see no. 226).

Pentecost 2016

SEND FORTH YOUR SPIRIT, O LORD . . . (PS 104:30)

One of the characteristics of the times in which we live is that we are called on to attend seemingly endless meetings. Whatever the nature of our ministry—and even in retirement—there are so many issues that call for our participation in group discussion and community discernment whether at level of the diocese, the particular institution or organization we serve, the Congregation, the circumscription, or the local community. Often these meetings compete with each other for our limited time, interfere with our already busy schedules, and appear to be an unwarranted waste of time and energy. We wonder whether, in fact, such meetings are effectively changing anything, and if life would be any different—other than more relaxed and pleasant—should all these meetings cease and we simply gave ourselves wholeheartedly to the work with which we have been entrusted. When we are tempted to grow tired, discouraged and cynical about the various meetings we are asked to attend, however, it is important to remind ourselves that Pentecost, one of the central events that shaped Christian history and indeed history in general, happened not to an individual praying alone but to a group gathered together in a common room:

> Pentecost happened at a meeting and it happened to a community, to a church congregation assembled for prayer, to a family of faith gathered to wait for God's guidance . . . In Christian and Jewish spirituality there are two non-negotiable places where we meet God, alone and in the family. These are not in opposition but complementary . . . We need to spend time together waiting for God, waiting for a new outflow of heavenly fire that will give us the courage, language, and power we need to make happen in the world what our faith and love envision.[17]

16. Cf. *Laudato Si*, no. 222.
17. Rolheiser, "Pentecost Happened at a Meeting."

From June 19 to July 2, 2016 a meeting vital to the life and mission of the Congregation—the Enlarged General Council—will take place at the Passionist Retreat House in Rome. This gathering will bring together the general council with 23 representatives and 2 Lay Spiritan Associates from the different Unions and circumscriptions that comprise the Spiritan world for essentially a threefold purpose: To evaluate the implementation of the Bagamoyo General Chapter, to look at new means of strengthening and bringing about the Congregation's objectives, and to reinforce collaboration between the circumscriptions, the Unions, and the general council. Interestingly, the meeting will take place in the context of the 50th anniversary of the transfer of the general administration from rue des Pyrénées, Paris to Clivo di Cinna, Rome in 1966. Monsignor Marcel Lefebvre, the superior general at the time, saw this geographical transfer as symbolic of the need for an increasingly international Congregation to reposition itself in the contemporary world, a perennial challenge if we are to be true to our charism and to respond creatively to the needs of evangelization of our times. The event will be marked by a special liturgy on Sunday, June 26 attended by the members of the EGC, several of the members of former general councils, 31 of whom are still alive, including three superiors general, and present and former lay personnel. We will also be united in spirit and in prayer with the other 45 surviving confreres who served in various capacities at the generalate during the past 50 years and in so doing made an invaluable contribution to the life and mission of the Congregation.

Inter alia, four important documents requested by the Bagamoyo Chapter will be presented for discussion at the Enlarged General Council: a *Guide for Spiritan Education*, a *Guide for Lay Spiritan Associates*, a *Guide for Financial Management* and a revised *Directory for the Organization of the Congregation*. In many ways these documents encapsulate our collective efforts to "reposition ourselves in the contemporary world," to respond creatively in the light of our charism to the evolving reality of the Congregation throughout the world and the changing circumstances in which we exercise our ministry at the service of the contemporary poor. We will also revisit the vital issues of safeguarding policies for children and vulnerable adults, the coordination of second cycle formation throughout the Congregation, funding for contemporary mission, and the strengths, weaknesses, and challenges of the Unions of Circumscriptions.

However, at the heart of all our discussions and deliberations will be an evaluation of our progress in regard to the two central challenges of the Bagamoyo General Chapter: a greater authenticity in our Spiritan life and mission in fidelity to the charism of our Founders and a more inclusive Spiritan family marked by a true sense of belonging and a collective ownership of our missionary commitments and our common future. Conscious of the perceptible gap between the vision expressed in our documents and our lived reality, the Bagamoyo Chapter requested the general council to initiate an eight-year animation plan to address this deficiency and to build and strengthen our Spiritan identity. A focal point of our EGC reflections will be an assessment of the impact of this animation plan to date and the identification of possible ways in which its effectiveness can be improved between now and the next General Chapter.

At this point in our mandate, the abiding question with which we grapple as a council is how change can truly be effected in an institution. There has been an increasing call at recent General Chapters for a more centralized authority at the level of the general council. Libermann was opposed to excessive centralization in the church; he saw it as a dangerous tendency, contrary to the spirit of the gospel and an obstacle to the action of the Holy Spirit [Letter to Schwindenhammer, ND, XI, 97-98]. Genuine and lasting change cannot be imposed from outside; it begins in the heart of each individual member. Richard Holloway writes:

> Transformation begins in our hearts, in our attitudes ... My belief in the Resurrection means that I must commit myself to the possibility of transformation and, however I feel, take the first faltering step towards personal change. Resurrection is refusing to be gripped forever by the fingers of winter, whatever our winter may be. If we say we believe in the Resurrection, the claim only has meaning if we believe in the possibility of transformed lives, transformed attitudes and transformed societies ... (if we see) stones rolled away and new possibilities rising from old attitudes.[18]

Perhaps the problem with adults is that, unlike children, we let go of our hopes and our dreams; our experience of the harsh reality of life erodes our capacity to believe in a better future. Louis Evely, the well-known American writer, saw the refusal to believe in the possibility of change as the fundamental sin against the Holy Spirit:

> Sinning against the Holy Spirit means no longer believing he can change the world because we no longer believe he can change us.

---

18. Holloway, *The Observer*, 15th April 2001.

The genuine atheist isn't the person who declares, "God doesn't exist," but the one who maintains that God can't remold him or her and denies the Spirit's infinite power to create, transform, and raise him from the dead. This is the type of person who, whether sixty years old or just fifteen, goes around announcing, "At my age, I can't change any more: I'm too old, too weak, too far gone. I've tried everything, and it hasn't worked. No, there's nothing to be done for me!"[19]

As we approach the feast of Pentecost let us make our own the words of the Psalmist for our forthcoming Enlarged General Council and for our Congregation:

"Send forth your Spirit, they are created and You renew the face of the earth!" (Ps 104: 30).

Pakistan-Bakti

Christmas 2016

THAT ALL MAY BE ONE (JOHN 17:21)

When Pope Francis met with the Union of Superiors General in November 2013, he was asked what he, as the first Pope from a religious order in over 180 years, expected of religious in today's church. His reply was both spontaneous and emphatic: "What I expect of you is to give witness. Be witnesses of a different way of doing things, of acting, of living! It is possible to live differently in this world."

---

19. Evely, *That Man is You*, 195-196.

We are only too aware that the world we live in is a fractured world, divided by ideological conflicts, inter-religious and inter-ethnic tensions, where discrimination and violence are everyday realities for countless communities and individuals across the globe. At a time of unprecedented global migration, the stranger, forced to leave his or her homeland for reasons of personal safety or economic survival, is often treated with fear, mistrust and hostility, a situation compounded by the spread of international terrorism and the threat of ongoing sporadic attacks on innocent people across the world.

In line with our Spiritan charism to be *"advocates, supporters and defenders of the weak and the little ones against all who oppress them"* (SRL, 14), many of us are actively and passionately involved in a variety of ways in denouncing violence and injustice and in initiatives to reach out in hospitality to the stranger in our society. If we are honest with ourselves, however, as a Congregation with a tremendous richness of cultural diversity among our own membership, we are often much less successful in witnessing to the "new quality of human solidarity, surpassing individualism, ethnocentrism and nationalism" to which we are called by the Holy Spirit (Torre d'Aguilha, 2.1). The concerns shared at successive meetings of new superiors and at the recent Enlarged General Council indicate the presence in our own midst of mistrust and prejudice, often based on national, racial, or ethnic grounds. Such considerations can affect *inter alia* the process of election of superiors, the inclusion of confreres in decision-making processes in the circumscription, the sharing of responsibilities in community, equity in access to financial resources, and the transition from one leadership team to another, with serious negative consequences for our internal life and for our community witness. To cite but one example, an African Bishop who has strongly supported our Spiritan mission since he first welcomed us into his diocese several years ago, recently confided in me a deep concern: although Spiritans are greatly admired in his country for their apostolic zeal and availability, he said, they seem "unable to live with each other" to the detriment of the effectiveness of their ministry.

As Pope Francis pointed out when we met him, conflicts are inevitable in every human family; in a sense they need to happen if the community is truly to live sincere and honest relationships. However, it is vitally important to acknowledge the conflicts that do exist in the community, to face them directly and to accompany them with "Eucharistic tenderness," involving where necessary outside professional assistance. If we have the humility to admit the tensions and conflicts among us and the courage to face them we, as religious missionaries, can be effective witnesses to the humanizing power of the Gospel. We need to continually remind ourselves that *"fraternity is the first and most credible Gospel that we preach"*; it is therefore intimately connected with both our mission in the world and the hope of attracting new vocations, both lay and professed, to the Spiritan way of life.

A family of 2615 members from 46 circumscriptions of origin, we carry out our Spiritan mission today in over 60 countries throughout the world. The vast majority of our circumscriptions bring together confreres from widely different cultural backgrounds called by the same Spirit to the same mission; the generalate community itself comprises 17 confreres from 9 different nationalities. If we are to be credible witnesses to the Gospel in a divided world, we are called to build truly intercultural communities, places where we are genuinely at home together, where there are no "insiders" and "outsiders," where no single culture dominates, but where each one's cultural identity finds expression and affirmation, where the dignity of difference is cherished and enriches our common vision.

In his recent book, *Living Mission Interculturally,* Spiritan anthropologist and theologian, Fr. Anthony Gittins, points out that simple goodwill is not sufficient to achieve this end; it requires commitment and conversion on the part of every member in the community, together with the willingness to acquire the appropriate skills.[20] Although we often use the terms multicultural and intercultural interchangeably, the terms refer to quite distinct realities. Multiculturalism describes a situation in which people of different cultures simply coexist in the same physical space. They may do so in mutual respect and tolerance—or in mutual hostility—but each of the respective cultures is only minimally affected by the others; it has been described as "living together separately." Obviously, members of a religious community, brought together by a common faith, sharing a common call to mission and a common vision, are called to go beyond simple multicultural coexistence. They are called to live interculturally, to share a common commitment to building a new reality out of the cultural diversity that comprises the community, a "home" where everyone, without losing his own core cultural identity, is prepared to leave his comfort zone and be changed by the presence of the other.

---

20. Gittins, *Living Mission Interculturally,* 100ff.

As Fr. Gittins shows in considerable detail, our individual culture is an intrinsic component of our social persona and a major factor in the shaping of our faith. In a community comprising people of different cultural backgrounds, there are very different understandings of family, authority, appropriate interpersonal interactions, privacy, hospitality, time, the role of ritual and so on. Similarly, in the Spiritan context, we bring with us different understandings of some of the basic elements of our lifestyle—poverty, community, leadership, etc. Many of our misunderstandings and tensions originate in our different cultural perspectives. If a truly intercultural community is to be gradually constructed, its members must be committed to a journey of mutual discovery of the each other's culture, through dialogue and personal study, and to making appropriate adjustments in order to create what is effectively a new culture—in our case, a new Spiritan culture (Bagamoyo 4.1)—where everyone is at home. Mutual trust and respect are essential from the outset, as is each individual's openness to conversion and transformation, particularly in regard to any unredeemed elements in his worldview, which are present in all cultures.

One specialist in the area of intercultural sensitivity, Milton J. Bennett, has described this journey as effectively from ethnocentrism to ethnorelativism, from the tendency to see and interpret the world purely from the perspective of my own culture to the realization that my beliefs constitute simply one perspective among many viable others and that we are profoundly enriched by openness to each other's culture. There are several steps on this continuum: it begins with an uncritical approach to my own culture perceived as the best and most evolved; gradually I come to accept another's worldview as valid and meaningful, but I judge it solely from the standpoint of my culture; finally I can see the world through different eyes and integrate my experiences of other cultures and my personal cultural identity into a new reality. On this journey, those entrusted with leadership have an essential role to play in promoting mutual trust and respect, unveiling unacceptable attitudes and behaviors, and facilitating possibilities for meaningful dialogue and for the acquisition of the appropriate skills for intercultural living. In a very real sense the future of our mission and the credibility of our witness depend on our willingness to commit ourselves as individuals and as communities to this challenging venture.

As we reflect together on the theme of community, may the LORD who came among us at Christmas to create one human family bound together in love, beyond the ties of natural family or ethnic bonds, accompany and inspire us on our journey.

Pentecost 2017

THE SPIRIT BLOWS WHERE IT WILLS (JOHN 3:8)

In order to understand the spiritual tradition of a religious Congregation, Paul Murray, O.P., suggests that it is sufficient at times to identify some of the key words common to that tradition and follow them back in time "as you would hold on to a piece of string to see how far it leads."[21] In the case of his own Dominican tradition, he singles out "happiness" as one such word tracing it back to the very origins of his Order. As we reflect together on our common Spiritan culture, this is an exercise which we could very profitably undertake both as individuals and as communities. What are the key words in our Spiritan spiritual tradition and how do we understand them today from our different cultural perspectives? Such words would undoubtedly include: mission, community, the poor . . .

Our own historian, Henry Koren, identified the word "availability" as central to our Spiritan charism: "It seems to me that our lived spirituality can best be described as an *evangelical availability, which remains attentive to the Holy Spirit manifesting himself in the concrete situation of life.*"[22] This evangelical availability has two aspects, availability before God, and availability before our brothers and sisters. It implies "a constant opening to the experience of life in its ever changing evolution" and a willingness to let go of the past when it no longer speaks meaningfully to our times. An 18th century testimony by Charles Besnard, superior general of the Montfortists, clearly indicates that evangelical availability was perceived to be a hallmark of the Congregation founded by Poullart des Places. He wrote that Spiritans are:

> ready to go anywhere there is work to be done for the salvation of souls. They consecrate themselves preferably to missionary activity both foreign or domestic, offering to go and stay in the poorest and most abandoned places for which it is especially difficult to find candidates. Whether it is a question of being exiled into the remote countryside or buried in the caverns of a hospital, teaching in a college, lecturing in a seminary . . . or

21. *New Wine of Dominican Spirituality*, 45.
22. Koren, *Essays*, 15.

even crossing the seas and going to the very ends of the earth
. . . , their motto is: 'Behold we are ready to do thy will.[23]

Likewise, for Francis Libermann, total availability in the hands of the LORD for the service of the despised and excluded was central to the missionary spirituality of the Society he founded. This was enshrined in the *Act of Consecration to Our* LORD *Jesus Christ* which was obligatory for every member prior to his departure on mission: "I offer and give myself to you entirely to be used for my whole life for the salvation and sanctification of souls . . . I devote and consecrate myself particularly to those who are most despised and forgotten . . . " (ND, II, 361). In our personal lives and in our ministry, this availability is lived out through openness to and peaceful compliance with the action of the Holy Spirit: "Your soul is the ship, your heart represents the sail, the Holy Spirit is the wind; he blows into your will and your soul goes forward, proceeding towards the goal God proposes for it" (ND, VII, 148). The fundamental prayer of the Spiritan, therefore, is that of our co-founder himself: "O divine Spirit, let me hear your gentle voice . . . I wish to be before you like a light feather, so that your breath may carry me off where it wishes and that I may never offer it the least resistance."[24]

The term "availability" actually appears five times in our Spiritan Rule of Life: it is a basic characteristic of our Spiritan calling, a readiness to go wherever we are sent by the Congregation (SRL, 25); like Mary we live out our mission in willing obedience to the Holy Spirit, making a complete gift of ourselves in total availability for the mission of Jesus (SRL, 5, 75); the purpose of our religious profession is to allow the Holy Spirit to take possession of us, so that we may become instruments completely at the service of the Good News (SRL, 60, 74). The inspiration of the Holy Spirit, however, is not merely a matter of personal interpretation, but it is the result of a process of community discernment and is ultimately mediated to us through the decision of those whom we have entrusted with the service of leadership (SRL, 77, 77.1 and 77.2).

At the 2016 Enlarged General Council, concerns were expressed that we were losing a sense of this fundamental aspect of our Spiritan charism. Several examples can be cited:

---

23. Koren, *Spiritual Writings*, 289.
24. *Jesus Through Jewish Eyes*, Part 1, 73.

* Despite the fact that our stated congregational priorities include primary evangelization, work with indigenous people and inter-religious dialogue, the commitments which best express these ministries continue to be among the most fragile in the Congregation: there are only 5 confreres at present in Algeria, 2 in Mauritania, 5 in Pakistan, 3 in Papua New Guinea, 3 in Aboriginal ministry in Australia, 9 in Amazonia. In a number of cases, the survival of these missions depends on elderly confreres who have already spent much of their missionary lives there.

* The present level of mobility of personnel within the Congregation is undermining the stability of a number of our missionary undertakings. While several confreres have been appointed to these and other groups over the years, many have only remained for a relatively short term before moving on to another ministry elsewhere.

* Of the 57 confreres who received their mission appointment in 2016, 19 presented their circumscription of origin as their first preference in their letter to the generalate and 32 included their circumscription of origin among their three stated preferences. The circumscription superiors involved requested to retain 23 of the 57 at home.

* Although we are called where appropriate to free ourselves from existing engagements in order to respond to the needs of our times (SRL, 25), many circumscriptions are reluctant to face the challenge of disengaging from historical commitments and seeking new peripheries for Spiritan mission more in line with our charism in the local church.

While I realize that there are complex issues involved and that statistics do not tell the whole story, nevertheless, as we try to become more authentic followers of Claude Poullart des Places and Francis Libermann, it is important that we ask ourselves a number of questions. Does maintaining existing commitments in the circumscription take precedence over our duty as Spiritans to respond creatively to the needs of evangelization of our times (SRL, 2, 25)? To what extent am I truly open to an appointment from the Congregation that is not among my immediate preferences and threatens the security of my comfort zone? Have I become so identified with a particular ministry or community that effectively I am unavailable to answer a new call of the Spirit?

As the inspirational example of many Spiritans who have gone before us reminds us, "Life grows by being given away, and it weakens in isolation and comfort. Indeed, those who enjoy life most are those who leave security on the shore and become excited by the mission of communicating life to others . . . This is certainly what mission means" (*Evangelii gaudium*, 10).

In preparing for the coming feast of Pentecost let us pray that the Holy Spirit may renew our minds and hearts as Spiritans so that we, in turn, can truly be his instruments in renewing the face of the earth.

Christmas 2017

REVITALIZING SPIRITAN COMMUNITY LIFE

I recently received a letter from a 93 year-old retired confrere stressing the need for me to address the issue of community life once again in my Christmas letter. "More and more I am conscious of how much is lost," he wrote, "if we are not aware that community life is essential to the way we live." I suspect that he is voicing a frustration felt by many Spiritans, namely that, while community living has been addressed in considerable detail in the past three General Chapters and inspiring texts have been produced, there is little evidence of effective change in many communities or circumscriptions. Interestingly, Diarmuid O'Murchu MSC, in his latest book notes that this has been a common experience of many religious Congregations in recent years:

> "(In assemblies and Chapters) we have often drawn up strategies to improve the quality of community life. The outcomes rarely prove to be satisfying, so we return to the drawing board and create yet another set of aspirations. Some groups have done that many times without a satisfying outcome. Something seems to be blocking us from reaching our goals."[25]

O'Murchu suggests that our discussions around authentic community are often too pragmatic and we fail to face "the onerous task of discerning the deep aspirations within and behind our desire for meaningful community." As the third phase of our animation plan, dedicated to Spiritan community living, enters its last months perhaps this is precisely the task that should form the framework for our remaining reflections

---

25. *Religious Life in the 21st Century*, 183.

together. Called together in Christ's name (Matt 18:20), community is meant to be life-giving for us personally, for our prayer and for our ministry. It is intended to be the context from which arise all our lifelong discernments—personal, ministerial, and congregational; it is neither an end in itself nor simply a base where we find security and comfort but a resource that empowers us for mission. In the words of American Sister of St. Joseph, Amy Hereford, "Jesus is the foundation, the gospel is the task, and community is the process."[26] This is precisely the vision of Libermann: "The apostolate is the end and purpose of our Congregation. Community life is the means by which we strive for that end."[27]

I find particularly helpful O'Murchu's analysis of the different stages of decline in the life of a group or community which originally began with admirable zeal and enthusiastic commitment to live out its founding charism. Authenticity begins to erode when tensions and agreements about external issues set in—such as the times for prayer, meals, community meetings etc. –and take precedence over the more substantive issues of mission and lifestyle. Later the financial security and comfort of the group become the primary concern with the gradual erosion of a simple lifestyle and the accumulation of wealth and unnecessary appliances. As long as the group attends to the daily Eucharist and prayer times, as well as the annual retreat, it is assumed that there is nothing to worry about. However, there is an unacknowledged spiritual crisis developing in the group and unhealthy individualism is beginning to dominate the life of the community. At this point, a few members begin to raise questions about the lifestyle and mission of the group and its fidelity to the founding charism; an in-depth evaluation of the missionary project of the community is called for in the light of the signs of the times. These confreres, however, are dismissed by the majority of the community and there is a resistance to serious dialogue. The community stresses its usefulness and good work in the service of the church and the world. Survival rather than reform then becomes the main concern of the group; confreres are pleasant to each other and avoid disturbing the peace. O'Murchu sees these successive stages as essentially the gradual path of decline and disintegration that ultimately led to the extinction of some seventy-five per cent of all religious Orders and Congregations ever founded. Can we

---

26. Hereford, *Religious Life at the Crossroads*, 194-195.
27. *Provisional Rule*, 119.

recognize our own community at some point on this so-called vitality curve?

It is clear that the revitalization of our community life in the Congregation depends on our willingness to engage together key questions around our lifestyle and mission, with specific reference to the signs of the times in which we live. At first sight this might seem a challenge simply for those of us who are engaged in active ministry rather than for the many who are now retired after several years of dedicated service to the church and to the Congregation. This would be to underestimate the importance of the ongoing mission of the elderly and retired. I have seen a number of creative initiatives in our retirement communities to reach out to the poor and excluded around them and, in simple but effective ways, to actively promote issues pertaining to justice, peace and the integrity of creation.

A particular touchstone of the vitality of a community is its ability to welcome the stranger: "Communities that have trouble making room for strangers because they have grown so insulated, or so preoccupied with their own needs and struggles, are communities that are dying,"[28] wrote Jean Vanier. In the contemporary world where there is so much dislocation and migration as people search for safety, security and economic survival, "the hunger for genuine hospitality ranks as one of the most urgent needs of our time"[29] (O'Murchu). Again, several of our communities have offered welcome and shelter to the increasing number of refugees and asylum seekers that have crossed borders of recent times. It is important that all of us honestly engage this challenge whatever the limitations of our resources and facilities.

Equally essential to authentic community living is mutual interest in and support for each other in our life and ministry. "We ourselves are in need of the very things that we strive to bring to others—friendship, respect, mutual help, a readiness to challenge and be challenged when necessary, encouragement, love and joy" (Maynooth, 110-111). This support takes on a particular importance in the case of confreres who explore new ways of living the Spiritan charism today by engaging issues of structural injustice, empowerment of the excluded, ecology, new forms of community living etc. Although many of us may have difficulty in understanding the significance of these creative initiatives or their

---

28. Vanier, *Community and Growth*, 267.
29. O'Murchu, Religious Life in the 21st Century, 194.

compatibility with our founding charism, it is essential for the future of our Congregation that we accompany them with our prayers and effective support.

It is evident that the authenticity of our community living is intimately linked with the question of vocations to our way of life, which is such a preoccupation for many circumscriptions. Suffice it to quote the conclusion of American journalist, John Allen, to the findings of a comprehensive 2009 study in the US of the reasons that motivated young people to enter religious life: they were clearly attracted to "a church of passionate members; a community of people deeply involved in one another's lives and more willing than most to come to one another's aid; a peer group of knowledgeable souls who speak the same language (or languages) are moved by the same texts, and share the same dreams."[30]

May the coming of the LORD who identified totally with our human condition give us the courage to engage new ways of bringing his Good News to the people of our times and of revitalizing our communities at the service of our mission.

Pentecost 2018

FAN INTO A FLAME THE GIFT THAT GOD HAS GIVEN YOU (2 TIM 1:6)

Five years ago, we began together a Congregation-wide journey of conversion and renewal in response to the call of the Bagamoyo General Chapter for greater authenticity in our Spiritan life and witness. With the aid of inspirational texts, videos and liturgical celebrations, we have reflected successively on our Spiritan vocation and identity, the role of the Holy Spirit in our life and ministry, and our community living, which continues to become more international and intercultural.

We now embark on the final phase on that journey focused on our Spiritan mission, which is effectively the touchstone of our authenticity in every age as true followers of Claude Poullart des Places and Francis Libermann. "The evangelization of the 'poor' is our purpose," states our Spiritan Rule of Life, no. 4, echoing the founding intuition of Poullart des Places to educate poor students who in turn would announce the Gospel to the poor of their day, taking on by preference the tasks for which the

---

30. Allen, "*'High tension' and 'low tension' Religious Life.*"

church had most difficulty in finding laborers. Libermann, equally drawn to serve the poorest and abandoned of his own time (ND, XIII, 170), saw mission as the essential aim of the Society he founded, with religious life, community living and the Society's internal organization at the service of this aim. "For the perfection of the apostolic life which is its purpose ... the Congregation has taken the common life as its fundamental rule,"[31] he stated in the revised Rule after the fusion with the Congregation of the Holy Spirit [*Règlements* of 1849; ND, X, 454]. "The mission is the end," he wrote to Mgr. Kobès in 1851, "but religious life is the essential means" [ND, XIII, 354-355]. "The aim of our vocation is not to practice poverty; poverty for us must be a means of practicing the apostolic life and its virtues ... if we have to dress in fine clothes to save souls, let us do so,"[32] notes his commentary on the original Provisional Rule [ND, XIII, 678].

Our charism, like that of every religious Congregation, is a unique gift to the Church and to the people of God. We cannot simply content ourselves with maintaining the works we have traditionally held for several years in the conviction that we are providing a useful pastoral service. We have a sacred responsibility to ensure that our charism is placed at the service of the local and universal church in the particular circumstances of every era, a responsibility that necessitates ongoing prayerful discernment in the light of the changing reality in which we carry out our mission. It is precisely for this reason that our Rule of Life requires that "attentive to the signs of the times, we re-examine periodically the reasons that underlie our present commitment and our present apostolate" and "accept to free ourselves from an engagement in order to respond to new and different calls from a local church or from the universal church" (SRL, 25). If we are to be truly faithful to the charism of our Founders and to our Spiritan tradition, we must regularly review our existing commitments, our missionary methodologies, our organizational structures and our formation programs, in order "to respond creatively to the needs of evangelization of our time" (SRL, 2). In the words of Pope Francis, we are continually called to "leave security on the shore"[33] and to reach out to new peripheries of poverty and exclusion in the contemporary world.

---

31. English translation in Daly, *Spiritan Wellsprings*, 71.

32. Translation in *Provisional Rule*, 129: "our end and purpose is the salvation of souls and our reason for practicing poverty must be that the practice of it will serve as a surer means to attain that end; it is not principally in order to practice the virtue of mortification ... "

33. *Evangelii gaudium*, no 10, citing *Aparecida Document*, 360.

The Bagamoyo Chapter requested every circumscription to elaborate a strategic mission plan in keeping with our charism and taking into account local social and ecclesial contexts (1.9). Only a very small number of circumscriptions have addressed this challenge to date and yet it is at the heart of our journey towards greater authenticity. The tendency towards the gradual "diocesization" of our mission in several circumscriptions was noted with considerable concern at the 2016 Enlarged General Council, with confreres often living alone, more committed to the diocese they serve than the Congregation to which they belong, their life and ministry virtually indistinguishable from their diocesan counterparts. An unrealistic number of commitments in the local church, often for reasons of tradition, is regularly to the detriment of our community life and is a contributing factor in the worrying tendency of young confreres to present their home circumscription as their primary preference for their mission appointment. The diocesan and Spiritan vocations have different and complementary services to offer to the local church; the confusion of both, in addition to undermining our specific mission, clearly impacts negatively on the witness we seek to give to young people who may be called to the Spiritan way of life. It is important to realize that we cannot meet every need addressed to us by the local church. Our resources both in personnel and in finance must be truly at the service of our Spiritan charism and our present and future commitments must be examined honestly and courageously in this light.

As we enter into the final phase of our animation plan we are effectively beginning the preparation for the next General Chapter in 2020. The primary role of a General Chapter is to verify and ensure fidelity to our spiritual patrimony (Canon 631), namely to the fundamental purpose of the Congregation, "the evangelization of the 'poor.'" With this in mind the general council is requesting that *every circumscription* address the following questions:

1. What are the new forms of poverty in the local circumstances of our circumscription today? Who are today's marginalized and excluded?
2. Are our existing commitments truly in line with our Spiritan charism?
3. Are there existing commitments that we should leave in favor of others more in line with our Spiritan charism?
4. Is our approach to/style of mission relevant for today's world?

5. Are our resources being overstretched to the detriment of our Spiritan life?
6. If Spiritans were coming to our country for the first time, what works would they undertake?
7. Are there aspects of our formation programs that need to be changed if we are truly to prepare our younger confreres for Spiritan mission in the future?

In addition, in preparation for the General Chapter, we request *every Union of Circumscriptions* to convene a seminar or symposium between now and August 1st, 2019 to reflect on *the future of Spiritan presence and mission over the next ten to fifteen years* within the geographical area it serves. This gathering should include competent resource personnel, Spiritan or non-Spiritan, as well as an experienced facilitator and a number of confreres from each member circumscription who could make a valuable contribution to its deliberations. The general council has already constituted a Mission Committee, comprising Frs. Eugene Elochukwu, John O'Brien, and Marc Botzung, to assist it in its own reflections on the subject; a member of this committee may be available on request to assist also in these local symposia.

The effectiveness of this final phase will largely determine the success or otherwise of the journey of renewal we began together in the wake of the Bagamoyo Chapter. We have purposely chosen to initiate it on the feast of Pentecost which brings us back to the original inspiration of our Founder, reminding us that the Spirit is the protagonist of mission in the church in every age and that it is only in listening and faithfully responding to the Spirit's whisperings that we can authentically live our Spiritan charism in the world.

Christmas 2018

BEHOLD I AM DOING A NEW THING (ISA. 43:19)

In January 2017, the Congregation for Institutes of Consecrated Life and Societies of Apostolic Life published a set of guidelines entitled *New Wine in New Wineskins* resulting from its plenary session some three years previously to mark the 50th anniversary of the publication of *Lumen gentium* and *Perfectae caritatis*. Emphasizing the role of consecrated men and women to "undergo new changes so that ideals and doctrine become real in our lives: systems, structures, *Diaconia*, styles, relationships, and language" (Introduction). These Guidelines offer a frank assessment of the extent to which the adaptation and renewal of religious life desired by the Vatican Council has truly taken place. They identify "inadequate practices and gridlocked processes" and propose ways forward for greater authenticity of religious Congregations in the contemporary world. In the context of our own preparation for the next General Chapter in 2020, as we discern together the manner in which the Spirit is calling us as Spiritans to respond creatively to the needs of evangelization of our times, the document raises a number of serious questions and challenges that we need to address. It is worth noting that several of these issues have already emerged in the feedback to the initial Congregation-wide consultation for the Chapter agenda.

While stressing that the necessary changes can only result from a process of collective discernment, the document points out that "allowing ourselves to be destabilized by the life-giving provocations of the Spirit is never painless." It is normal, in other words, for an Institute to be resistant to change. "Sometimes this is done by concealing inconsistencies; other times, by accepting to tarnish old and new, by denying realities and frictions in the name of fictitious harmony, or even by concealing its own objectives through superficial adjustments."[34] New poverties have emerged in our world calling us as religious to new and creative responses in fidelity to our charism but we often tend to be "completely wrapped up in day-to-day management or in actually surviving," and leadership is unable to pass from ordinary administration to the risk-taking that is necessary in order to embrace these new challenges.

A significant number of religious, male and female, young and old, continue to leave religious life every year. Interestingly, the document points out that this is not always due to an affective relationship that has developed, as we might easily assume. It is often the result of a personal crisis that has arisen from living an inauthentic common life, a perceptible gap between proposed values and the lived reality in the community, or an excessive number of activities that do not allow for a solid spiritual life or sustain the desire to remain faithful to one's calling.

Our younger members are often criticized for lacking the dedication and commitment of those who have preceded them, but sociological research has shown that that they do not lack aspirations towards

---

34. *New Wine in new Wineskins*, no. 11.

genuine values to which they are willing to commit themselves; they are capable of being passionate about causes of solidarity, justice, and freedom. While there are many potential contributory factors that might influence a young confrere to leave his mission or indeed the Congregation—including difficulties arising from different generational or cultural perspectives, different ecclesiastical models or ways of praying, a negative experience of authority, conflicts in the community, a lack of true fraternity—fundamentally the formation process is called into question. The Guidelines note that formation today often seems more informative than performative, failing to integrate sufficiently the spiritual and human dimensions of the person's growth process and, consequently, to touch and transform the heart. "The result is that people maintain a certain fragility, both in their existential convictions and in their journey of faith. This leads to minimal psychological and spiritual endurance and the subsequent inability to live one's own mission with openness and courage when it comes to dialogue with culture and social and ecclesial integration" (no. 12). The choice of suitable formation personnel is obviously therefore crucial, formators who are "familiar with the path of seeking God," capable of transmitting "the beauty of following Christ" and the depth of the charism of the Founder; capable of following an initiation style model adapted to each individual where "the master and disciple walk side by side in trust and hope." In the words of Pope Francis, "We must not form administrators, managers, but fathers, brothers, travelling companions."[35] It is about forming "a free heart to learn from the story of each day throughout life in the style of Christ to be of service to all" (no. 35d)

Formation, of course, is a life-long process, if we are to remain authentic followers of our Founders in the times in which we live and at the various stages of our lives. It involves not only a theoretical updating in theology and spirituality, but more importantly the evaluation and verification of our lived experience; it is a journey of growth in creative fidelity that has significant and lasting effects in our actual lives. In our own Congregation, ongoing formation is often reduced to specialized studies or a period of sabbatical ministry away from one's circumscription of appointment. True ongoing formation involves a continual attitude of listening at the level of the heart in our daily lives and ministry: "each individual is called to let himself or herself be touched, educated, provoked,

---

35. *New Wine in New Wineskins*, no 34, citing Pope Francis, "Wake up the World!" 11.

and enlightened by life and by history, by what he or she proclaims and celebrates, by the poor and excluded, by those near and far" (no. 35c).

The Guidelines emphasize in a particular way our prophetic role as religious in the contemporary world: a true respect for the "feminine genius" in a chauvinistic society and a clerical church through the promotion of brotherly and sisterly relationships between consecrated men and women that witness to genuine complementarity, and reciprocity; true intercultural fraternal communion where diversity is received as a gift, where everyone is involved in the community project "in such a way that it becomes a mutual support for all in fulfilling the vocation of each"; a style of leadership that is truly at the service of communion, fostering individual growth and responsible fidelity rather than focused on the personal authority and privilege of the superior; a community where material resources are shared in a spirit of solidarity that ensures justice and equity among all, reaches out to the poor, and witnesses to economic and financial transparency.

The document concludes by stressing that the search for new wineskins requires commitment, skill and the willingness to change on the part of all. In this ongoing task of discernment and renewal, General Chapters have a particularly important role as a forum of personal and collective prayerful listening to the Holy Spirit. This process, which involves every member of the Congregation, "does not stop at describing the various situations . . . but which always goes a step further and is able to see an opportunity, a possibility, behind every face, every story, every situation" (no. 50) in ensuring fidelity to our spiritual patrimony in the contemporary world.

May our reflection on the mystery of Christ among us at Christmas open our minds and hearts to the signs of his action in the world today and give us the courage to move beyond outdated structures and models of ministry so that we may truly bring his Good News to the people of our day.

Pentecost 2019

THE SPIRIT COMES TO HELP US IN OUR WEAKNESS (ROM 8:26)

In this final phase of our Congregation-wide Animation Plan, and in preparation for our forthcoming General Chapter, we have embarked on an in-depth reflection on our Spiritan mission in the contemporary world. Are we truly faithful today to the intuitions of Claude Poullart des Places and Francis Libermann who saw the fundamental purpose of the Congregation as the "evangelization of the poor"? How best can we place our missionary charism, a precious gift of the Holy Spirit, at the service of the different local churches in which we serve, taking into account our actual and often limited resources and in such a way as to ensure genuine community living which is integral to our Spiritan way of life?

In addition to seeking to clarify a vision and a strategy for Spiritan mission in response to the signs of the times in which we live, however, it is equally important that we rediscover the missionary spirituality that sustains and gives life and meaning to all that we do. Many of us carry out our mission today in very difficult and personally challenging circumstances: the reality of conflict, insecurity, and the daily threat of violence; crippling poverty, corruption and injustice; pervasive secularism where our faith is eroded and undermined; a church whose credibility has been seriously damaged by the revelation of successive scandals and the failures of leadership; circumscriptions and communities that are divided by internal tensions and interpersonal mistrust. We need deep inner resources to sustain and support us in these situations and to enable us to avoid falling prey to pessimism, discouragement and disillusion.

Francis Libermann had to face the limitations of his own nervous temperament and debilitating illness, the pain of rejection by his father and hurtful criticism from others, among them church leaders and close associates (cf. ND, VI, 38 to M. Desgenettes; LS, IV, 273ff to Levavasseur) and the devastating failure of his first missionary venture. He felt inadequate as a leader of a new missionary Society and at times was overwhelmed by the tasks with which he was confronted (cf. LS, IV, 275 to Levavasseur; ND, VII, 5 to Samson Libermann). Yet his profound inner spiritual resources enabled him to hear the voice of the Holy Spirit in the midst of it all and to continue unwaveringly on the path to which he believed the LORD had called him. At the heart of his spirituality was the conviction that God is present, not primarily in miraculous signs or events, but in the midst of the reality that we live—even when at times he appears painfully absent—and that it is precisely in this situation that we must hear his voice and discern his call. Martin Buber points out that finding God in the reality of the human situation is rooted in biblical spirituality: "The believing Jew," he says, "lives in the consciousness that the proper place for his encounter with God lies in the ever-changing situation of life . . . Again and again he hears God's voice in a different way in the language spoken by unforeseen and changed situations."[36] In a similar vein, Orthodox Archbishop Timothy Ware, reflecting on the role of the Holy Spirit in the life of the Christian, writes:

> We do not find the Holy Spirit merely on some rarefied level . . . but he is present in all the events of our daily life. True 'mysticism' is to find the extraordinary in the ordinary. My 'spiritual life' is the same as my daily life lived out in its fullness . . . *This* moment through which I am now passing, *this* familiar task which I perform each day, *this* person with whom I am at present talking—each is of infinite value . . . Sacred space and sacred time are nothing else than this place and this moment, seen for what they are—as filled with the Holy Spirit.[37]

The perennial temptation for all of us is that of the two disciples in the Gospel who, after the death of Jesus, departed Jerusalem for Emmaus—the temptation to leave behind the place of our hurt and disenchantment in search of an alternative and illusory future. Together with St. Luke, Libermann reminds us that the true place of encounter with the Risen LORD is in Jerusalem, in the midst of the suffering to which our discipleship has brought us and which we would probably prefer to avoid. It is precisely into this situation that the Spirit comes bringing renewed meaning and hope and empowers us anew for our mission.

As in the case of Mary and the disciples in the upper room, the experience of our limitations and powerlessness is paradoxically the necessary condition for the rediscovery of the presence and power of the Spirit in the most unlikely situations. Libermann, based on his own experience, spoke often about the need for the serene acceptance of our limitations, weaknesses, and mistakes (e.g., ND, XII, 171 to Sr. Agnes). In a similar way, he recognized that there are situations and circumstances that are beyond our control; we need to know how to accept patiently obstacles that cannot be overcome, at least in the present circumstances, and wait for "the moment of God" (cf. ND, IX, 328-9 to the Community in Dakar and Gabon). In words which could well have been spoken by Libermann himself, Yves Congar writes:

> "If my God is the God of the Bible, the living God . . . My action, then, consists in handing myself over to God, who allows me to

---

36. Buber, *Der Glaube der Profeten*, 104ff, cited in Koren, *Essays*, 26.
37. Ware, "The Holy Spirit in the Personal life of the Christian," 153.

be the link between his divine activity regarding the world and other people . . . I can only place myself faithfully before God, and offer the fullness of my being and my resources, so that I can be there where God awaits me, the link between this action of God and the world."[38]

Essentially, Libermann calls us to a contemplative view of the world in which we live and of the mission with which we are entrusted. It is an invitation to see ourselves, our brothers and sisters, our mission and the world from God's perspective rather than from our own; it involves letting go of our preoccupations with ourselves and our compulsions, of our desires for success and recognition, in the serene knowledge that we are simply limited participants in a mission that is ultimately God's, not ours. This is precisely the purpose of the "practical union" or "union of operation" on which he insisted for his missionaries (cf. ND, XIII, 699) : it is an ongoing disposition throughout all our activities to "let that mind be in us which was in Jesus Christ" (Phil 2:5), an acknowledgement of our dependence and the expression of trust in the most difficult situations, whether personal or in my ministry, a persistent desire to align my activity with that of the Holy Spirit or, more simply, to allow the Spirit to accomplish his mission through my actions.

May the coming of the Spirit this Pentecost renew our hope, our confidence and our courage in the midst of the difficulties and challenges our mission entails and empower us anew in his service.

Christmas 2019

JESUS CHRIST IS ETERNAL NEWNESS (*EVANGELII GAUDIUM*, 11)

Of more recent times it has been customary to adopt a motto or theme for the General Chapter, which in some way tries to encapsulate the essential challenge we face as a missionary religious Congregation at this point in our history.

After considerable reflection, and having taken into account the many different themes suggested from the various circumscriptions around the globe, the general council chose the short quotation from

---

38. "Action et contemplation," 204, cited in Murray, *The New Wine of Dominican Spirituality*, 22-23.

the Prophet Isaiah: "Behold I am doing something new" (Isa 43:19) as the motto for the Lichen Chapter. Written in a time of great confusion, turmoil, and radical change, this fundamental insight from Isaiah was ultimately the source of a completely new departure in the history of Israel. The Babylonian captivity had deeply affected the sense of identity of the people of God; they had lost the traditional symbols that supported their faith and the found themselves without power or privilege in an unknown land; the traditional religious paradigms had broken down and no longer helped to give meaning to their new experience; secular forces rather than God appeared to be in control of the world and prospects for the future seemed very bleak.[39]

While many distanced themselves from their inherited faith, a small anonymous group of people, young and old, remained convinced that God's liberating power was not only active in the past but that it was still alive in their own day, if only they had eyes to see it. So they set about, through listening, dialogue, reflection and prayer, looking for the signs of God's presence in a new and unfamiliar world. It was a process that would lead them to exciting new discoveries; they began to see that some of their most precious symbols were imprisoned by the ideologies of the time and that it was necessary to reinterpret the central values of their faith in a way that was life-giving for a different and unprecedented situation; ultimately and most importantly, they began to understand their mission in the world in an entirely new way: they were called to be a light to the nations, to be a suffering servant carrying the sins of others, to be a source of blessing for all peoples.

These texts are conspicuous for their courage and openness to rethink everything," wrote Carlos Mesters. "They knew how to be creative. They went beyond the frontiers of the traditional and, faithful to the true tradition, dreamed of a new world. Instead of lamenting the past which they had lost, they greeted the future which had just been born with much pain. They accepted the situation as a new mission for the people of the world."

The Chapter motto, chosen in the light of the preparatory consultation of the wider Congregation and the lived experience of the general council, is intended to serve as a fundamental reference point during the Chapter discussions and ultimately to help to shape its eventual orientations and decisions. In a sense, it may be seen as an attempt to crystallize

---

39. See Mesters, "Religious Life and its Mission."

in an inspirational formula the perennial call of Francis Libermann to the Congregation: "The world has changed . . . So let us welcome the new ways with openness and simplicity, bringing to them the spirit of the Gospel" (ND X, 151). Similar thoughts are echoed by Pope Francis in the recent *Christus Vivit* (200): "We are sent today to proclaim the Good News of Jesus to a new age. We need to love this time with all its opportunities and risks, its joys and sorrows, its riches and its limits, its successes and failures."[40]

As Pope Francis reminds us, we live today in an age of extraordinary change: "Today's vast and rapid cultural changes demand that we constantly seek ways of expressing unchanging truths in a language which brings out their abiding newness" (EG, 41). As a church and as a Congregation, we have been humbled and shamed by the continuing revelations of sexual and financial abuse on the part of some our members and the failure of leadership to respond appropriately. We are called to profound personal and institutional conversion, to distance ourselves from a clericalized understanding of ministry, and to return to the original freshness of the Gospel, where "new avenues arise, new paths of creativity open up, with different forms of expression, more eloquent signs and words with new meaning for today's world" (EG, 11). Digitization has had a profound impact on our ideas of time and space, on our self-understanding and our understanding of the world in which we live, as well as on our ability to communicate and to enter into relationship with others; secularization in several traditionally Christian countries invites us to fundamentally rethink and reimagine our presence in societies where people still continue to search for purpose and meaning; the impact of climate change, particularly on the poorest and most vulnerable, calls us to personal and community changes in lifestyle, to the cultivation of an appropriate spirituality, if we are to contribute to the creation of a more sustainable planet and ensure its future for the generations that will follow us; new faces of poverty—the hungry, the homeless, drug-addicts, migrants, political and environmental refugees, indigenous peoples — call us to new and creative responses in the light of our charism.

Mission in the twenty-first century has also significantly changed from the traditional model which we have inherited from previous generations and calls for a new understanding, a new approach, and a new methodology. Many of the local churches in which we serve today have

---

40. *Christus Vivit*, no. 200, citing Pironio, *Message to Young Argentinians*, 2.

developed considerably over the years and, thanks to an increasing influx of local vocations, have sufficient diocesan personnel today to take responsibility for the majority of their pastoral and administrative needs. In countries where Spiritans founded the local church or have been present for many decades, we sometimes find ourselves limited by our own history, in the sense that we expect or are expected to continue to maintain parish commitments we have held for several years, not infrequently at the expense of genuine community life. The result is an impoverishment of our role in the local church where we, as religious, are called to reach out to new peripheries in fidelity to our charism, and where necessary, freeing ourselves from existing engagements to respond to new and different calls of the Spirit.

The challenging letter of the Holy See for the year of Consecrated Life, *Keep Watch!*, points out that "consecrated life is at a crossroads, but it cannot stay there forever. We are invited to make the transition . . . into an opportune moment . . . This is not a matter of answering the question of whether what we are doing is good: discernment looks to the horizons that the Spirit suggests to the church" (no. 11). Pope Francis (Pentecost Homily, 2013) adds that "newness always makes us a bit fearful, because we feel more secure if we have everything under control, if we are the ones who build, program, and plan our lives in accordance with our own ideas, our own comfort, our own preferences . . . We fear that God may force us to strike out on new paths and leave behind our all too narrow, closed, and selfish horizons in order to become open to his own."

We have begun a journey together that will culminate in Lichen, Poland, next summer. "The goal of this journey is marked out by the rhythm of the Spirit; it is not a known land. In front of us appear new frontiers, new realities, other cultures, different necessities, *peripheries*" (*Keep Watch!*, no. 11). As we welcome the eternal newness that Christ brings at Christmas, let us pray that we will have the humility and the wisdom to discern these new peripheries for our Spiritan life and mission and the courage to embrace them wholeheartedly.

Venerable Francis Mary Paul Libermann

BIBLIOGRAPHY

Allen, John L. Jr. "'High tension' and 'low tension' Religious Life." NCR, August 14, 2009.
Aparecida Document. Fifth General Conference of the Latin American and Caribbean Bishops, 29 June 2007.
Benedict XVI. Encyclical *Deus Caritas Est*. On Christian Love. 25 December, 2005.
Bevans, Stephen B. and Roger P. Schroeder. *Constants in Context: A Theology of Mission for Today*. Maryknoll, NY: Orbis, 2004.
Blanchard, Pierre. *Le Vénérable Libermann*. 2 vols. Lyon: Descléee de Brouwer, 1960.
Bonhoeffer, Dietrich. *Letters and Papers from Prison*. The Enlarged Edition Paperback. Macmillan, January 1, 1978. Letter of April 30, 1944.
Buber, Martin, *Der Glaube der Profeten*, 1950.
Congar, Yves. "Action et contemplation: D'une lettre du père Congar au père Régamey' (1959)," *La Vie Spirituelle*, 152, 727 (1998).
Congregation for Institutes of Consecrated Life and Societies of Apostolic Life. *Keep Watch!* Year of Consecrated Life. 2014.
———. *New Wine in New Wineskins: The Consecrated Life and its Ongoing Challenges since Vatican II*. Libreria Editrice Vaticana, 2017.
Daly, John, C.S.Sp. *Spiritan Wellsprings. The Original Rules with Commentaries, of the Holy Ghost Congregation*. Dublin: Paraclete Press, 1986.
Evely, Louis. *That Man is You*. NY: Paulist, 1964.
Farragher, Sean. *Edward Barron, unsung Hero of the Mission to Africa*. Dublin: Paraclete, 2004.
Fitzsimmons, J. *Father Laval*. London: Print Origination, January 1, 1973.
Gay, Most Rev. Jean. *François Libermann: Les chemins de la paix* (Collection Pionniers de la charité). Paperback. January 1, 1974. Consult also, idem, *The Spirit of Venerable Libermann*. Society of St. Paul, 1954.
Gittins, Anthony J. *Living Mission Interculturally: Faith, Culture, and the Renewal of Praxis*. Glazier, 2015.
Hereford, Amy. *Religious Life at the Crossroads*. NY: Orbis, 2013.
Hollande, J. Kirkels. "Méthodologie missionnaire de Libermann: l'intégration de l'église dans le milieu africain," *Spiritus* 65 (1976) 411-419.
Holloway, Richard. *The Observer*. 15th April 2001.
John Paul II, Post-Synodal Apostolic Exhortation *Vita consecrata* on the Consecrated Life and its Mission in the Church and in the World. March 25, 1996.
———. *Redemptoris mater* On the Blessed Virgin Mary in the Life of the Pilgrim Church. March 25, 1987.
———. Encyclical Letter *Redemptoris missio*. http://www.vatican.va/content/john-paul-ii/en/encyclicals/documents/hf_jp-ii_enc_07121990_redemptoris-missio.html. 1990.
———. Apostolic Exhortation *Ecclesia in Africa*, On the Church in Africa and its Evangelizing Mission Towards the Year 2000, 1995.
———. Apostolic Letter, *Novo millennio ineunte* To the Bishops Clergy and Lay Faithful at the Close of the Great Jubilee of the Year 2000, Jan 6, 2001.

———. Encyclical Letter *Ecclesia de Eucharistia*, On the Eucharist in its Relationship to the Church, 2003.

Paul VI. Apostolic Exhortation *Evangelii nuntiandi*. http://www.vatican.va/content/paul-vi/en/apost_exhortations/documents/hf_p-vi_exh_19751208_evangelii-nuntiandi.html. 1975.

Koren, Henry J. *The Spiritual Writings of Father Claude François Poullart des Places*. Duquesne University, 1959.

———. *Knaves or Knights? A History of the Spiritan Missionaries in Acadia and North America, 1732-1839*. Pittsburgh : Duquesne University, 1962.

———. *Essays on the Spiritan Charism and on Spiritan History*. Bethel Park, Spiritus, 1990.

Le Floch, Henri. *Claude François Poullart des Places. Fondateur du Seminaire et de la Congrégation du Saint-Esprit (1679-1709)*. Nouvelle edition, Paris, 1915.

Libermann, Francis Mary Paul, C.S.Sp. *Jesus through Jewish Eyes, A Spiritual Commentary on the Gospel of St. John*. 3 Parts. Translated by Myles L. Fay, C.S.Sp. Dublin: Paraclete, 1999.

Mesters, Carlos. "Religious Life and its Mission among the poor, in the Light of the Word of God." *SEDOS Bulletin* 28 (1996) 171-179. Keynote Address to SEDOS, May 1996.

Michel, Joseph. *Le Père Jacques Laval (1803-1864)*. Paperback. Beauchesne, April 1, 1997.

———. *Claude-François Poullart des Places, Founder of the Congregation of the Holy Spirit 1679–1709*. Translated from the French by Vincent O'Toole, C.S.Sp. Pittsburgh: Center for Spiritan Studies, 2020.

Morel, Gerard. "Mgr Edward Barron (1801-1854) ou le vent d'Amérique et la reprise de la mission a la côte d'Afrique," *Memoire Spiritaine*, no. 15 (2002) 53-80.

Murray, Paul, O.P. *The New Wine of Dominican Spirituality*. Burns and Oates, 2006.

O'Murchu, Diarmuid. *Religious Life in the 21st Century: The Prospect of Refounding*. Orbis, 2016.

Pironio, Eduardo. *Message to Young Argentinians at the National Youth Meeting in Cordoba*, (12-15 September 1985).

Pope Francis. 2013. Apostolic Exhortation *Evangelii gaudium*. https://www.vatican.va/content/francesco/en/apost_exhortations/documents/papa-francesco_esortazione-ap_20131124_evangelii-gaudium.html.

———. "Wake up the World! Conversation with Pope Francis about the Religious Life," *La Civiltà Cattolica*, 165/1 (2014).

———. Encyclical Letter *Laudato Sí* On Care for our Common Home, 2015.

———. *Christus Vivit*, Post-Synodal Apostolic Exhortation to the Young People and the Entire People of God, 25th March 2019.

Radcliffe, Timothy. O.P. *Sing a New Song The Christian Vocation*. Templegate, June 1, 1999.

Rath, Joseph Theodore. C.S.Sp. *Geschichte der Kongregation vom Heiligen Geist*. Missionsverlag, Jan 1, 1972.

Rolheiser, Ron, O.M.I. "Pentecost Happened at a Meeting." January 26, 2003. https://ronrolheiser.com/pentecost-happened-at-a-meeting/#.YIlpoKySmUk accessed April 27, 2021.

Scherer, James A. *Missionary go Home: A Reappraisal of the Christian World Mission*. Englewood Cliffs, NJ: Prentice Hall, 1964.

Schreiter, Robert J. "Changes in Roman Catholic Attitudes toward Proselytism and Mission." In James A. Scherer and Stephen B. Bevans. *New Directions in Mission and Evangelization*. Maryknoll, NY: Orbis, 1994, 113-25.

Schreiter, Robert J. "Globalization and Reconciliation – Challenges to Mission." Presentation given at SEDOS, April 8, 2000.

Silf, Margaret. *Compass Points: Meeting God Every Day at Every Turn*. Loyola, April 1, 2009.

Spadaro, Antonio, S.J. " 'Wake up the World': Conversation with Pope Francis about the Religious Life." *La Civiltá Cattolica* 1 (2014) 3-17 (original is Italian)

A Spiritan Anthology. Writings of Claude-François Poullart des Places (1679-1709) and François Marie-Paul Libermann (1802-1852). Chosen and presented by Christian de Mare, C.S.Sp. Rome: Clivo di Cinna, 2011.

Tisserant, Eugene. « Memorandum on the Work for the Black People. » *Spiritan Anthology*, 1, 83-96.

Vallely, Paul. *Pope Francis – Untying the Knots*. Bloomsbury Academic, 2013.

Vanier, Jean. *Community and Growth*. NJ, Paulist, 1989.

Vatican Council II. Decree on the Missionary Activity of the Church, *Ad gentes*. http://www.vatican.va/archive/hist_councils/ii_vatican_council/documents/vat-ii_decree_19651207_ad-gentes_en.html.

Vatican Council II. Declaration on the Relation of the Church of Non-Christian Religions, *Nostra aetate* . http://www.vatican.va/archive/hist_councils/ii_vatican_council/documents/vat-ii_decl_19651028_nostra-aetate_en.html.

Ware, Kallistos. "The Holy Spirit in the Personal life of the Christian." *Unity of the Spirit – Diversity of the Churches*, the Report of the Conference of European Churches' Assembly VIII. Crete, 18-25 October 1979.

www.ingramcontent.com/pod-product-compliance
Lightning Source LLC
Chambersburg PA
CBHW070009010526
44117CB00011B/1479